HER MAJESTY'S ARMY

VOL. II.

The Naval & Military Press Ltd

Published by

The Naval & Military Press Ltd
Unit 5 Riverside, Brambleside
Bellbrook Industrial Estate
Uckfield, East Sussex
TN22 1QQ England

Tel: +44 (0)1825 749494

www.naval-military-press.com
www.nmarchive.com

In reprinting in facsimile from the original, any imperfections are inevitably reproduced and the quality may fall short of modern type and cartographic standards.

THE HONOURABLE ARTILLERY COMPANY.

(CAVALRY.)

Her Majesty's Army

THE 24th SOUTH WALES BORDERERS.

VOL. II.

HER MAJESTY'S ARMY

A DESCRIPTIVE ACCOUNT

OF THE

VARIOUS REGIMENTS NOW COMPRISING THE QUEEN'S FORCES, FROM
THEIR FIRST ESTABLISHMENT TO THE PRESENT TIME

BY

WALTER RICHARDS

With Coloured Illustrations

VOL. II.

CONTENTS.

VOL. II.

	PAGE
Duke of Cambridge's Own Middlesex Regiment	1
Royal Munster Fusiliers	11
Norfolk Regiment	27
Northamptonshire Regiment	34
Northumberland Fusiliers	38
Oxfordshire Light Infantry	42
Rifle Brigade (Prince Consort's Own)	53
Royal Fusiliers (City of London Regiment)	62
Black Watch (Royal Highlanders)	66
Royal Scots Fusiliers	73
Cameronians (Scottish Rifles)	77
Seaforth Highlanders (Ross-shire Buffs)	81
King's (Shropshire) Light Infantry	88
Prince Albert's (Somersetshire) Light Infantry	94
Prince of Wales's (North Staffordshire) Regiment	97
South Staffordshire Regiment	100
Suffolk Regiment	105
East Surrey Regiment	110
The Queen's (Royal West Surrey) Regiment	112
Royal Sussex Regiment	117
South Wales Borderers	119
Royal Warwickshire Regiment	124
Royal Welsh Fusiliers	127
Welsh Regiment	134
Duke of Wellington's (West Riding) Regiment	139
The Duke of Edinburgh's (Wiltshire) Regiment	146
Worcestershire Regiment	150
York and Lancaster Regiment	155
King's Own (Yorkshire Light Infantry)	161
Princess of Wales's Own (Yorkshire) Regiment	168
East Yorkshire Regiment	172
Prince of Wales's Own (West Yorkshire) Regiment	176
Royal Marines	180

CONTENTS.

	PAGE
ARMY CHAPLAINS	199
MEDICAL DEPARTMENT	203
ARMY SERVICE CORPS	206
HONOURABLE ARTILLERY COMPANY	207
MILITIA	224
YEOMANRY	262
VOLUNTEER CAVALRY	275

    Fifeshire Light Horse Volunteers.   Roxburgh Mounted Rifles.
    Forfarshire Light Horse Volunteers.

VOLUNTEER ARTILLERY 275

    Tynemouth Artillery.
    1st and 2nd Northumberland Artillery.
    Berwick-on-Tweed Artillery.
    1st and 2nd East Riding of Yorkshire Artillery.
    1st North Riding of Yorkshire Artillery.
    1st Cumberland Artillery.
    1st, 2nd, 3rd, and 4th Durham Artillery.
    1st, 2nd, and 4th West Riding Artillery.
    Newcastle-on-Tyne Artillery.
    Lancashire Artillery.
    1st Cheshire and Carnarvonshire Artillery.
    1st Shropshire and Staffordshire.
    Norfolk Brigade.
    Essex Brigade.
    Harwich Cadet Corps.
    Lincolnshire Brigade.
    1st Sussex Brigade.
    2nd Sussex Brigade.
    1st Kent Artillery.
    Cinque Ports Brigade.
    Woolwich Arsenal Brigade (3rd Kent).
    2nd and 3rd Middlesex Artillery.

    1st City of London Artillery.
    1st and 3rd Hampshire Artillery.
    Dorsetshire Artillery.
    1st and 2nd Devonshire Artillery.
    1st Cornwall (Duke of Cornwall's).
    City of Edinburgh Artillery.
    Berwickshire Artillery.
    1st Midlothian Artillery.
    Banff Artillery.
    Forfarshire Artillery.
    Renfrew and Dumbarton Artillery.
    Fifeshire Artillery.
    1st Lanarkshire Artillery.
    Ayrshire and Galloway Artillery.
    Argyll and Bute Artillery.
    Caithness Artillery.
    Aberdeenshire Artillery.
    Inverness-shire (Highland) Artillery.
    Orkney Artillery.
    1st Glamorganshire Artillery.
    1st Gloucestershire Artillery.
    Worcester and Monmouth Artillery.

VOLUNTEER ENGINEERS 287

    1st Newcastle-on-Tyne Engineers.   1st Durham Engineers.

ROYAL SCOTS, VOLUNTEER BATTALIONS 291

    Queen's City of Edinburgh R.V. Brigade.   2nd Midlothian R.V.
    2nd Edinburgh R.V.   1st Haddington R.V.
    1st Midlothian R.V.   1st Linlithgowshire R.V.

QUEEN'S (WEST SURREY) VOLUNTEER BATTALIONS 295

    2nd Surrey R.V.   6th Surrey R.V.
    4th Surrey R.V.   8th Surrey R.V.

BUFFS, VOLUNTEER BATTALIONS 296

    2nd Kent R.V.   5th Kent R.V.

KING'S OWN (ROYAL LANCASTER), VOLUNTEER BATTALION . . 296

    10th Lancashire.   Rossall Cadet Corps.

NORTHUMBERLAND FUSILIERS, VOLUNTEER BATTALIONS 297

    1st Northumberland and Berwick-on-Tweed.   1st Newcastle-on-Tyne.
    2nd Northumberland.

ROYAL WARWICKSHIRE, VOLUNTEER BATTALIONS 298

    1st and 2nd Warwickshire.   King's Grammar School Cadet Corps.
    Rugby School Cadet Corps.

ROYAL FUSILIERS (CITY OF LONDON), VOLUNTEER BATTALIONS . 299

    10th Middlesex.   23rd Middlesex.

KING'S LIVERPOOL REGIMENT, VOLUNTEER BATTALIONS 300

    1st Lancashire.   18th Lancashire (Liverpool Irish).
    5th Lancashire.   19th Lancashire (Liverpool Press Guard).
    13th Lancashire.   Isle of Man.
    15th Lancashire.

CONTENTS.

	PAGE
NORFOLK REGIMENT, VOLUNTEER BATTALIONS	301

    1st, 2nd, 3rd, and 4th Norfolk.

LINCOLNSHIRE REGIMENT, VOLUNTEER BATTALIONS 301

    1st and 2nd Lincoln.

DEVONSHIRE REGIMENT, VOLUNTEER BATTALIONS 302

    1st Devonshire (Exeter and South Devon).   4th Devonshire.
    2nd Devonshire (Prince of Wales's).   5th Devonshire (The Hay Tor).
    3rd Devonshire.

SUFFOLK REGIMENT, VOLUNTEER BATTALIONS 303

    1st Suffolk.   1st Cambridgeshire.
    6th Suffolk.   2nd Cambridgeshire (Cambridge University).

SOMERSETSHIRE REGIMENT, VOLUNTEER BATTALIONS 303

    1st, 2nd, and 3rd Somerset.

PRINCE OF WALES'S (WEST YORKSHIRE) REGIMENT, VOLUNTEER BATTALIONS . . 304

    1st, 3rd, and 7th West Riding.

EAST YORKSHIRE REGIMENT, VOLUNTEER BATTALIONS 304

    1st and 2nd East Riding.

BEDFORDSHIRE REGIMENT, VOLUNTEER BATTALIONS 305

    1st and 2nd Hertfordshire.   1st Bedfordshire.

LEICESTERSHIRE REGIMENT, VOLUNTEER BATTALION 305

    1st Leicestershire.

PRINCESS OF WALES'S OWN (YORKSHIRE) REGIMENT, VOLUNTEER BATTALIONS . 305

    1st and 2nd North Riding.

LANCASHIRE FUSILIERS, VOLUNTEER BATTALIONS 306

    8th Lancashire (Bury).   17th Lancashire.
    12th Lancashire.

ROYAL SCOTS FUSILIERS, VOLUNTEER BATTALIONS 308

    1st and 2nd Ayrshire.   Galloway (Kirkcudbright and Wigtown).

CHESHIRE REGIMENT, VOLUNTEER BATTALIONS 309

    1st Cheshire.   3rd, 4th, and 5th Cheshire.
    2nd Cheshire (Earl of Chester's).

WELSH FUSILIERS, VOLUNTEER BATTALIONS 310

    1st Denbigh.   1st Flintshire and Carnarvon.

SOUTH WALES BORDERERS, VOLUNTEER BATTALIONS 310

    1st Brecknockshire.   1st, 2nd, and 3rd Monmouthshire.

KING'S OWN (SCOTTISH) BORDERERS, VOLUNTEER BATTALIONS 310

    Roxburgh and Selkirk (The Border).   1st Dumfries.
    1st Berwickshire.

CAMERONIANS, VOLUNTEER BATTALIONS 311

    1st, 2nd, 3rd, 4th, and 7th Lanarkshire.

GLOUCESTERSHIRE REGIMENT, VOLUNTEER BATTALIONS 313

    1st Gloucestershire (City of Bristol).   Cheltenham College Cadet Corps.
    2nd Gloucestershire.

WORCESTERSHIRE REGIMENT, VOLUNTEER BATTALIONS 314

    1st and 2nd Worcestershire.

EAST LANCASHIRE REGIMENT, VOLUNTEER BATTALIONS 315

    2nd and 3rd Lancashire.

EAST SURREY REGIMENT, VOLUNTEER BATTALIONS 316

    1st Surrey (South London).   3rd, 5th, and 7th Surrey.
    Dulwich College Cadet Corps.

DUKE OF CORNWALL'S LIGHT INFANTRY, VOLUNTEER BATTALIONS . . . 318

    1st and 2nd Cornwall.

CONTENTS.

                                                      PAGE

DUKE OF WELLINGTON'S (WEST RIDING) REGIMENT, VOLUNTEER BATTALIONS . . 318
    4th, 6th, and 9th West Riding.

BORDER REGIMENT, VOLUNTEER BATTALIONS 319
    1st Cumberland.   1st Westmoreland.

ROYAL SUSSEX, VOLUNTEER BATTALIONS 320
    1st and 2nd Sussex.   1st Cinque Ports.

HAMPSHIRE REGIMENT, VOLUNTEER BATTALIONS 321
    1st, 2nd, 3rd, and 4th Hants.   Winchester College Cadet Corps.
    1st Isle of Wight (Princess Beatrice's).

SOUTH STAFFORDSHIRE REGIMENT, VOLUNTEER BATTALIONS . . . 322
    1st, 3rd, and 4th Stafford.

DORSETSHIRE REGIMENT, VOLUNTEER BATTALION 323
    1st Dorsetshire.

PRINCE OF WALES'S VOLUNTEERS (SOUTH LANCASHIRE), VOLUNTEER BATTALIONS . . 323
    9th Lancashire.   21st Lancashire.

WELSH REGIMENT, VOLUNTEER BATTALIONS 324
    1st Pembrokeshire.   1st, 2nd, and 3rd Glamorganshire.

BLACK WATCH (ROYAL HIGHLANDERS), VOLUNTEER BATTALIONS . . . 325
    1st Forfarshire (Dundee).   1st Perthshire.
    2nd Forfarshire (Angus).   2nd Perthshire (Perthshire Highlanders).
    3rd Forfarshire (Dundee Highlanders).   1st Fifeshire.
    Dundee Cadet Corps.   Glenalmond College Cadet Corps.

OXFORDSHIRE LIGHT INFANTRY, VOLUNTEER BATTALIONS 326
    1st Oxfordshire (Oxford University).   2nd Bucks (Eton College).
    2nd Oxfordshire (Oxford City).   Oxford Military College Cadet Corps.
    1st Bucks.

ESSEX REGIMENT, VOLUNTEER BATTALIONS 326
    1st, 2nd, 3rd, and 4th Essex.   Forest School Cadet Corps.
    Ongar School Cadet Corps.

SHERWOOD FORESTERS (DERBYSHIRE REGIMENT), VOLUNTEER BATTALIONS . . 327
    1st and 2nd Derbyshire.   1st Nottinghamshire (Robin Hood).
    Derby Cadet Corps.   2nd Nottinghamshire.
    Trent College Cadet Corps.

LOYAL NORTH LANCASHIRE, VOLUNTEER BATTALIONS . . . 328
    11th Lancashire.   14th Lancashire.

NORTHAMPTONSHIRE REGIMENT, VOLUNTEER BATTALION . . . 329
    1st Northamptonshire.

PRINCESS CHARLOTTE OF WALES'S (ROYAL BERKS) REGIMENT, VOLUNTEER BATTALION . 329
    1st Berkshire.   Bradfield College Cadet Corps.
    Wellington College Cadet Corps.

QUEEN'S OWN (ROYAL WEST KENT), VOLUNTEER BATTALIONS . . . 329
    1st and 3rd Kent.   4th Kent (Woolwich Arsenal).

KING'S OWN (YORKSHIRE LIGHT INFANTRY), VOLUNTEER BATTALION . . 330
    5th West Riding.

KING'S (SHROPSHIRE) LIGHT INFANTRY, VOLUNTEER BATTALIONS . . 330
    1st and 2nd Shropshire.   Hereford and Radnor.

DUKE OF CAMBRIDGE'S OWN (MIDDLESEX) REGIMENT, VOLUNTEER BATTALIONS . . 330
    3rd Middlesex.   11th Middlesex (Railway).
    8th Middlesex.   17th Middlesex (North Middlesex).

KING'S ROYAL RIFLE CORPS, VOLUNTEER BATTALIONS 334
    1st Middlesex (Victorias).   6th Middlesex (St. George's).
    South Middlesex.   9th Middlesex (Harrow).
    4th Middlesex (West London).   12th Middlesex (Civil Service).
    5th West Middlesex.   13th Middlesex (Queen's Westminster).

CONTENTS.

	PAGE

KING'S ROYAL RIFLE CORPS, VOLUNTEER BATTALIONS—*Continued.*

21st Middlesex (Finsbury Rifles).
22nd Middlesex (Central London Rangers).
25th Middlesex (Bank of England).
Harrow School Cadet Corps.
Marlborough Place Cadet Corps.
1st London (City of London Rifle Brigade).
2nd London.
3rd London.

DUKE OF EDINBURGH'S (WILTSHIRE) REGIMENT, VOLUNTEER BATTALIONS 338

1st and 2nd Wiltshire.
Marlborough College Cadet Corps.

MANCHESTER REGIMENT, VOLUNTEER BATTALIONS 338

4th Lancashire.
6th Lancashire (1st Manchester).
7th Lancashire.
16th Lancashire (3rd Manchester).
20th Lancashire (2nd Manchester).
22nd Lancashire.

PRINCE OF WALES'S (NORTH STAFFORDSHIRE) REGIMENT, VOLUNTEER BATTALIONS . . 339

2nd and 5th Staffordshire.

YORK AND LANCASTER REGIMENT, VOLUNTEER BATTALIONS. . 339

2nd West Riding (Hallamshire).
8th West Riding

DURHAM LIGHT INFANTRY, VOLUNTEER BATTALIONS 339

1st and 2nd Durham.
3rd Durham (Sunderland).
4th and 5th Durham.

HIGHLAND LIGHT INFANTRY, VOLUNTEER BATTALIONS . . 340

5th Lanarkshire.
6th Lanarkshire.
8th Lanarkshire (The Blythswood).
9th Lanarkshire.
10th Lanarkshire (Glasgow Highland).

SEAFORTH HIGHLANDERS (ROSS-SHIRE BUFFS), VOLUNTEER BATTALIONS . 342

1st Ross-shire (Ross Highland).
1st Sutherland (Sutherland Highland).
1st Elgin.

GORDON HIGHLANDERS, VOLUNTEER BATTALIONS 343

1st Aberdeenshire.
2nd Aberdeenshire.
3rd Aberdeenshire (The Buchan).
4th Aberdeenshire.
1st Kincardine and Aberdeen (Deeside Highland).
1st Banffshire.

QUEEN'S OWN (CAMERON) HIGHLANDERS, VOLUNTEER BATTALION . . 343

1st Inverness-shire.

PRINCESS LOUISE'S (ARGYLL AND SUTHERLAND) HIGHLANDERS, VOLUNTEER BATTALIONS . . 343

1st, 2nd, and 3rd Renfrewshire.
1st Stirlingshire.
1st Argyll.
1st Dumbartonshire.
1st Clackmannan and Kinross.

RIFLE BRIGADE (PRINCE CONSORT'S OWN), VOLUNTEER BATTALIONS 344

7th Middlesex (London Scottish).
14th Middlesex (Inns of Court).
15th Middlesex (Customs and Docks).
16th Middlesex (London Irish).
18th Middlesex.
19th Middlesex (St. Giles's and St George's, Bloomsbury).
20th Middlesex (Artists').
24th Middlesex (Post Office).
Tower Hamlets Rifle Brigade.
2nd Tower Hamlets.

LIST OF ILLUSTRATIONS.

VOL. II.

	PAGE
THE HONOURABLE ARTILLERY COMPANY (CAVALRY)	*Frontispiece*
THE 24TH—SOUTH WALES BORDERERS	*Vignette*
THE 57TH—DUKE OF CAMBRIDGE'S OWN (MIDDLESEX)	*Facing Page* 1
THE 43RD—OXFORDSHIRE LIGHT INFANTRY	42
THE 42ND—THE BLACK WATCH (ROYAL HIGHLANDERS)	66
THE 21ST—ROYAL SCOTS FUSILIERS	73
THE 72ND—SEAFORTH HIGHLANDERS	81
THE 2ND—QUEEN'S (ROYAL WEST SURREY)	112
THE 35TH—ROYAL SUSSEX	117
THE 23RD—ROYAL WELSH FUSILIERS	127
THE 15TH—EAST YORKSHIRE	172
THE QUEEN'S OWN ROYAL (STAFFORDSHIRE YEOMANRY)	267
THE 1ST MIDDLESEX (VICTORIA RIFLES)	334
THE 7TH MIDDLESEX (THE LONDON SCOTTISH)	344
THE 20TH MIDDLESEX (ARTISTS')	348

THE 57th—DUKE OF CAMBRIDGE'S OWN (MIDDLESEX).

HER MAJESTY'S ARMY.

THE DUKE OF CAMBRIDGE'S OWN * (MIDDLESEX REGIMENT)—Regimental District No. 57—consists of two very famous regiments, of which the former, at any rate, is familiar by its sobriquet, "The Die-hards," to the most superficial student of the career of Her Majesty's Army. The 1st battalion—the 57th—was raised in 1755 by Colonel John Arabin, chiefly in the counties of Gloucester and Somerset, and the first service of the new regiment was as marines with the fleet in the Mediterranean. The following twenty years were passed chiefly in Gibraltar, Minorca, and Ireland. The 57th joined the force under Lord Cornwallis, and the following year took part in the battle of Brooklyn on August 26th, 1776. Afterwards they shared in the storming of Redbank, the capture of York Island, the attack on Powell's Hook, and the storming of Port Montgomery, at which place they sustained heavy losses. In 1778 the flank companies were formed into separate battalions, and were busily engaged throughout the troublous times that followed, the light company being among the garrison at Fort York under Lord Cornwallis, who were taken prisoners in October, 1781. Even on the disaster at York Town we are able to look back without any feeling of humiliation. In September Lord Cornwallis was directed to make as good a defence as possible, receiving assurance of speedy and effective succour. "On the 28th of September," writes an author whose works of fiction contain historical sketches of which the accuracy is only equalled by the fascination of their style,† "the combined army of French and Americans, consisting

---

* The Duke of Cambridge's Own (Middlesex Regiment) bears as badges the coronet and cypher of the Duke of Cambridge, with the Prince of Wales's Plume and the word "Albuera" on cap and collar; the motto is that of the Prince of Wales. On the colours are: "Seringapatam," "Albuera," "Ciudad Rodrigo," "Badajoz," "Vittoria," "Pyrenees," "Nivelle," "Nive," "Peninsula," "Alma," "Inkerman," "Sevastopol," "New Zealand," "South Africa, 1879." The uniform is scarlet, with facings of white.

† G. A. Henty, "True to the Old Flag." Blackie and Son.

of 7,000 of the former and 12,000 of the latter, appeared before York Town and the post at Gloucester. Lord Cornwallis had 5,960 men, but so great had been the effects of the deadly climate in the autumn months, that only 4,017 men were reported fit for duty. The enemy at once invested the town and opened their trenches against it. From their fleet they had drawn an abundance of heavy artillery, and on the 9th of October their batteries opened a tremendous fire upon the works. Each day they pushed their trenches closer, and the British force was too weak in comparison with the number of its assailants to venture upon sorties. The fire from the works was completely overpowered by that of the enemy, and the ammunition was nearly exhausted. Day after day passed and still the promised reinforcements did not arrive. On the 16th, finding that he must either surrender or break through, Lord Cornwallis determined to cross the river and fall on the French rear with his whole force. In the night the light infantry (including the company of the 57th) and other regiments were embarked in boats, and crossed to the Gloucester side of the river before midnight. At this critical moment a violent storm arose which prevented the boats returning. The enemy's fire re-opened at daybreak, and the engineer and principal officers of the army gave it as their opinion that it was impossible to resist longer. Only one eight-inch shell and a hundred small ones remained. The defences had in many places tumbled to ruins, and no effectual resistance could be opposed to an assault." Accordingly, on the 19th, Lord Cornwallis surrendered, and five days later the long-promised reinforcements arrived —too late!

From 1783 to 1790 the 57th served in Nova Scotia, and in the latter year returned to England. In 1794 they joined the Duke of York's forces at Malines, and served in Flanders until the close of the year. In 1796 the regiment was ordered to Barbadoes, where they assisted in the capture of St. Lucia, returning, after a sojourn of a few years in Trinidad, to England in 1803.

Six years later, in 1809, commenced the era, glorious in the making of splendid names, amongst which none gleams with a clearer and more enduring brilliancy through the intervening years, than does that of the gallant 57th, the Die-hards of Peninsular fame.

The first scene of the war tragedy which was enacted after the 57th had joined Wellington's army was the battle of Busaco. "Nothing," writes Colonel Leith Hay, "could be conceived more enlivening, more interesting, or more varied than the scene from the heights. Commanding a very extensive prospect to the eastward, the movements of the French army were distinctly perceptible; it was impossible to conceal them. Rising grounds were covered with troops, cannon, or equipages; the widely extended country seemed to contain a host moving forward, or gradually condensing into numerous masses, checked in their progress by the grand natural barrier. In imposing appearance as to numerical strength, there has been rarely seen anything comparable to that of the enemy's army from Busaco; it was not an army alone encamped before us, but a multitude, cavalry, infantry, cars of the country, horses, tribes of mules with their attendants, sutlers, followers of every description crowded the moving scene." Yet ere many hours had passed this mighty host was in full retreat, beaten by the army whose honours the 57th had to share and increase.

The following year, the 57th joined in the pursuit of Massena, and at Albuera earned for themselves immortal fame by their conduct, the record of which is, so to speak, *crystallized* in their before-mentioned sobriquet of the "Die-hards." The fortunes of the day were wavering; everywhere the Spaniards were falling back, despite the dauntless courage and personal exertions of Beresford, who actually seized a Spanish officer and by main force carried him to the front, only for the dastard to run back again when the iron grasp was released. Then Stewart brought up Houghton's Brigade, with which were the 57th. Fierce, indeed, was the conflict! Cannon and musketry at *pistol range* belched forth death against the indomitable British regiments. Stewart was twice wounded, the gallant Houghton fell dead even as he called to the heroic 57th, "Die hard, my men, die hard!" And undismayed, with grim valour *dying hard* before the hurtling shower of grape and shot and shell, the 57th stood, giving back death for death and defiance for defiance, while officers and men were stricken down with awful quickness. Then came Coles's splendid charge, before which the erst triumphing legions of France quailed and fled, and "like a loosened cliff went headlong down the steep; the rain flowed after in streams discoloured with blood, and one thousand eight hundred unwounded men, the remnant of six thousand unconquerable British soldiers, stood triumphant on the fatal hill." Of the five hundred and seventy of all ranks with which the 57th went into action that day, only a hundred and thirty remained to be marched off the field by the adjutant, while amongst the heaps of dead and wounded were Colonel Inglis, twenty-two officers, and over four hundred men of the regiment which had fought and died so hard. "It was observed that our dead, particularly the 57th Regiment, were lying as they had fought in the ranks, and that every wound was in front." The King's colour received seventeen shots, while the regimental colour was pierced by twenty-one. "Here was won the laurel wreath, of which any corps might well be proud."

It is impossible to dwell at length upon the prowess of the 57th throughout the Peninsular War; though not all of the battles are inscribed on their colours, there were but few places made famous by the gallantry of British troops where the 57th did not participate in that gallantry. Vittoria, the Pyrenees, Nivelle, the Nive—these are the triumphs recorded on the colours; but it must not be forgotten that "Peninsula" covers the countless smaller actions and operations performed by the Army, and in these the 57th ever gave evidence of the accuracy of the popular and professional judgment which then, as now, assigned them one of the foremost places amongst British regiments. At St. Pierre—the remarkable omission of which from the list of distinctions has been before noticed—the 57th were in the right wing under General Byng, which found itself opposed by the strong force led by d'Armagnac. During the action they were taken to strengthen Barnes's position in the centre, and materially aided in the repulse of Soult, which was practically the crisis of the battle which made "Hill's day of glory complete."

During 1814 the regiment was in Quebec, returning to England in August, 1815, immediately after which they joined the army of occupation in France, with which they served until November, 1818. From that date till the Crimea no particular fighting of note fell to their share, though they rendered good service at Mangalore in 1837. The entire regiment was garrisoned at Madras from 1840 to 1845, when they removed to Poonamalee; returned home in 1846, and during the disturbed period in Ireland in 1848. In September, 1854, the regiment joined General Cathcart's Division in the Crimea, and took up their position before Sevastopol. At Balaklava they acted as support to the Artillery. At Inkerman, when the Guards were maintaining their splendid resistance to the masses that threatened to overwhelm them, Sir George Cathcart led on his Division in the hope to relieve the Guards from the assault they were sustaining with such high valour; and despite the vast disparity of force—the Russians opposed to him numbered 9,000 men—he gave the order to charge, falling dead as he led on his men sword in hand. The 57th lost heavily; amongst the killed being their former colonel, Brigadier Goldie.

On the occasion of the assault on the Redan, the 57th led the assault on the right flank of the fort, and lost no fewer than six officers and a hundred and ten men. Amongst the numerous acts of individual heroism which redeemed the comparative failure of the attack must be mentioned that of which Colour-Sergeant Gardiner of the regiment was the hero.* When retreat became inevitable, Sergeant Gardiner persuaded some of the men of the regiment to delay returning to our lines and try the effect of a little more firing. The little band made such shelter as they could for themselves by taking advantage of the deep holes torn by the shells, by the side of which they improvised a somewhat ghastly breastwork with the bodies of their dead comrades; and here they remained, inflicting no little annoyance on the enemy till their ammunition was exhausted. This was done under a fire in which nearly half the officers and a third of the rank and file of the storming parties were put *hors de combat*. For this achievement, coupled with his gallant conduct on the 22nd of March, Sergeant Gardiner was rewarded with the Victoria Cross. During the siege, another soldier of the " Die-hards," Private M'Corrie, gained the same coveted honour for his coolness and courage in picking up a live shell which had fallen into the trenches and throwing it over the parapet—fortunately without injury to himself, though he subsequently died before receiving the coveted decoration.

The 57th took part, in the following September, in the expedition against Odessa, and were in the first brigade of the force which was despatched to effect the reduction of Kinburn, on which occasion, despite the small loss which our troops actually suffered, a rumour reached the camp that the 57th had been cut to pieces. From Kinburn, after a skirmish with some Cossacks near Shadoffka, they returned to Sevastopol, after the surrender of which they proceeded to Malta, and later on to India. Here they remained for three years, when they were ordered to New Zealand on the outbreak of the Maori war, where they performed some sterling service. But this service was not rendered without loss.

In 1863 Lieutenant Targett and a party of six men of the regiment, who were acting as escort in charge of a prisoner to be tried by court-martial, were all slain by Maories in ambush, one man only escaping to tell the tale and evoke a determination in the breasts of the gallant 57th to avenge the death of their comrades. General Warre, the historian of the regiment, thus describes the incident:—" On reaching the Wairan (the name of a small stream) the escort was suddenly fired upon by an ambuscade of thirty or forty rebel natives, and the whole party were killed or wounded.

* Sergeant Gardiner had before this greatly distinguished himself on the occasion of the sortie of the 22nd of March, when, seeing that the covering parties had been driven in and were in some confusion, he rallied them, and at their head attacked the Russians, who were speedily driven out of the trenches again.—*Knollys*.

Private Florence Kelly, although wounded, escaped into the fern, subsequently joining a party under Lieutenant Brutton, which had been sent on the report of the murders being conveyed by a mounted orderly." An opportunity for revenge occurred on June 4th, in the attack and capture of the rebels' pah, when the regiment fought with marked courage and dash. Later in the same year occurred a severe encounter with the natives at Pontoko, where the British gained a complete victory over much superior numbers, though the 57th suffered some loss. "Ensign Down and Drummer D. Stagpool were recommended for, and eventually received, the Victoria Cross, for their gallant conduct in rescuing a wounded comrade from the clutches of the rebel natives." On the occasion of the storming of the Otapawa Pah, the 57th, numbering one hundred and thirty rank and file under Colonel Butler, again distinguished themselves, though they had to mourn the death of Lieutenant-Colonel Hassard, who fell inside the pah, while leading on his men. It would seem on this occasion as though the natives had been studying the "*fas est ab hoste doceri*" doctrine, for they kept perfectly quiet till our men were within about thirty or forty yards, when they commenced a most severe and unusually well-directed fire. Lieutenant-Colonel Hassard, with a party of the regiment, drove out the enemy on the left, and then proceeded against those on the right. "At the same moment the remainder of the 55th, gallantly led by Lieutenant-Colonel Butler, reached the left angle of the work. The Maories fought desperately for a time, but in vain; a portion of the palisading being cut down by Private Doakes, 57th Regiment, the troops entered the works and carried all before them." In addition to Lieutenant-Colonel Hassard* the regiment lost two sergeants and five privates killed and many wounded. Amongst those killed was Private Doakes, whose gallantry had been such as to have decided the commander to recommend him for the Victoria Cross.

The regiment returned to England in 1866, remaining at home till the Zulu war. They arrived in South Africa from Ceylon shortly before the battle of Ghinglovo, and suffered somewhat more than the other troops from the wet and cold, in consequence of the greater change of climate. The 57th and 91st were stationed on that face of the lager on which the Zulus, after their repulse by the Rifles, hurled the whole force of their attack. How well that attack was repulsed is matter of common know-

---

* Colonel Hassard is thus referred to in the official despatch: "In Lieutenant-Colonel Hassard the service has lost one of its bravest officers: he led his men with the greatest gallantry, and fell inside the Pah, nobly performing his duty."

ledge now. From Ghinglovo they proceeded with Lord Chelmsford to the relief of Colonel Pearson at Etschowe. When Sir Garnet Wolseley took the direction of affairs, the command of one of the columns was given to Colonel Clarke of the 57th, and that of the regiment devolved upon Major Tredennick. Later on the regiment was actively employed in the pursuit of Cetewayo, and in September returned to England. The following year—to quote from Colonel Archer—"many deserved honours were bestowed on officers of the corps, including Lord Gifford, the pursuer of Ketchewayo, for services in the Zulu war; and the gallantry of Private Howard, who, with Lieutenant Torrens of the Scots Greys, assisted in rescuing the crew of the brig *Robert Brown*, wrecked off the Pigeon House Fort, was publicly commended by the commander-in-chief." Since the Zulu war the 57th have not been engaged in any active service.*

The 2nd battalion of the Middlesex Regiment is the 77th Foot, which was raised in 1787 for service in the East Indies. The regiment arrived in India in August, 1788, and joined the force under Abercromby. They were at the siege and surrender of Canonore, December 18th, 1790, and then advanced upon Periapatam; but, on Lord Cornwallis suspending operations returned to cantonments. In December, 1791, under Abercromby they entered Mysore and joined Lord Cornwallis before Seringapatam in February of the following year. Throughout the campaign against Tippoo, in which they lost over two hundred men, the 77th acquitted themselves with great credit, and on the conclusion of the campaign proceeded to Canonore, and thence to Bombay, a few

---

* On the occasion of fresh colours being presented to this splendid regiment, the old ones were deposited in St. Paul's Cathedral, under circumstances which provoked some remark. The following letter which appeared in the *Times* correctly represents the general feeling.—"Sir—Between one and two o'clock to-day was seen a small military detachment in uniform, marching from Cannon Street to the Mansion House. A field officer, three other officers, and about eight non-commissioned officers and men, were taking to their final resting place in St. Paul's Cathedral, the old colours of the 57th Regiment—the West Middlesex—the 'Die-hards.' They were cordially received by the Lord Mayor, and with equal cordiality at the Cathedral, where, after a short, impressive ceremony the colours were placed on its walls. They were the colours of the Crimea, and especially of Inkerman. They were accompanied on this their last march by the condition that 'no expense was thereby to be entailed on the public.' As this detachment of honour passed from the Mansion House and along Cheapside little did the rich and busy crowd think that the officers' private purses had saved to the country the railway fare from Woolwich, and thus added to our economical, if not quite to our military, credit." An influential paper of the time thus comments on the foregoing letter:—"It cannot fail to infuse into the breast of every Englishman who reads it a glow of pleasure. There is nothing like maintaining amongst our soldiery a sober enthusiasm for Queen and country; and by our own feelings as we read of this apparently trifling but truly significant little incident, we may judge of the sentiments which animated that small company of soldiers as they marched to the Cathedral—without parade, without ostentation; indeed, rather sneaking than marching—to place the colours that waved at Inkerman in their final resting place. Every heart beat high with the thought that although the dear flag was being carried through the streets as a pauper corpse is trotted to the grave, the noblest principles of government were vindicated in an almost pathetic manner, 'no expense was thereby entailed on the public.'"

months later taking part in the reduction of the Dutch settlements at Cochin. They took part in the operations under Colonel Stewart against the Dutch Settlements, and later on in the expedition against the Rajah of Cotiote. In January, 1799, the 77th joined the Bombay army and occupied the signalling station of Sudapore, between Stewart and Harris's forces. Here the enemy, headed by the Sultan in person, appeared suddenly in order of battle, and, being greatly superior in numbers, turned the position, and cut off its communications with the Bombay force. But the 77th, with whom were the 75th, by a brilliant effort recovered the advantage before General Stewart had reached them with his support. In 1799 they again found themselves before the walls of Seringapatam. The 77th furnished their flank companies for the storming party. The troops moved to the attack on the left under Lieutenant-Colonel Dunlop, of the 77th. Under a terrible fire from cannon, jingalls, and musketry the glacis and ditch were passed, and the storming party swarmed up the breach. "Lieutenant-Colonel Dunlop was here wounded by a Sidar of Mysore who met him scimitar in hand. Parrying a cut with his sabre the Colonel slashed open his antagonist's breast and mortally wounded him. The Sidar made another cut that nearly hewed off the head of the Colonel, and falling back into the breach was instantly bayonetted. Dunlop reached the summit and then fell from loss of blood."

In 1799 the regiment was quartered at Mangalore; "and in 1800, at Cochin and Calicut. In June, 1800, they captured Arrakerry; served under Wellesley at Dhoondra, and took part in the capture of Bednore, Coongull, Subtitee, and Ilumaul (at the assault of which latter Captain McPherson distinguished himself); and at the final defeat of Dhoondra." In 1801 they were engaged in operations against Coliote and Wynand, and in the attack of Panjalamcourchy, which was captured with a loss of two officers and fifty-one men. Subsequently the regiment operated against the Polygars, took part in the attack on Bollaum Rajah; and, in 1802, in the second capture of Arrakerry, and subsequently in the operations against the Mairs.

The 77th returned to England in 1807 after an absence of nineteen and a half years, during by far the greater part of which they had been actively engaged. Under the Earl of Chatham, they shared in the operations in Flanders in 1809, and were present at the capitulation of Ramakins and Flushing. After a few months in England the regiment went to Portugal in July, 1810, and very shortly after landing commenced war in earnest. At El Bodon in September, 1811, where "the action began disadvantageously for the allies," the 77th, under Lieutenant-Colonel Bromhead, evinced splendid valour. In conjunction with the 5th they several times *charged* the French Cavalry, on whose numbers neither artillery nor musketry volleys seemed to make any impression. At one time by a movement of the Portuguese, "the 5th and 77th, two weak battalions formed in one square, were quite exposed, and in an instant the whole of the French horsemen came thundering down upon them." Perhaps in all Napier's brilliant pages there is no passage which eclipses in beauty his description of the deeds of the 77th and their comrades on that day. "But how vain, how fruitless," he continues, "to match the sword with the musket, to send the charging horsemen against the steadfast veteran! The multitudinous squadrons, rending the skies with their shouts, closed upon the glowing squares like the falling edges of a burning crater and were as instantly rejected, scorched, and scattered abroad; then a rolling peal of musketry echoed through the hills, bayonets glittered at the edge of the smoke, and with firm and even step the British regiments came forth like the holy men from the Assyrian's furnace." At Ciudad Rodrigo, under Colonel Dunkin, the 77th with two other regiments pushed up the great breach amidst a whirlwind of death and horror and confusion, such as might have swept through a hell of warring demons. Curses and yells of anguish strove for the mastery over the crash of shell and shot; stones and pieces of masonry fell thick around, and gleaming amongst them through the heavy cloud of smoke came thick and fast the glint of gory bayonets, like the red lightning playing across the track of an avalanche. After Badajoz—the name of which they bear on their colours—the 77th returned to Lisbon, rejoining the army in the field in October, 1813, and being actively employed in the investment of Bayonne, where they assisted in carrying the entrenched works.

At the close of the war the 77th embarked for home, where they stayed until 1824, in which year they went to Jamaica, remaining there for ten years, losing during this period twelve officers, eleven sergeants, and two hundred and thirty of other ranks, and finding their only active employment in the operations which became necessary in 1831 against the insurgent slaves. On returning to England they were engaged on peace duties for twenty years, during which time they were stationed at Malta, Canada, Jamaica, the Ionian Islands and Nova Scotia. On the outbreak of the Crimean War they proceeded to the front, and were with the Light Division under Sir George Brown. At the Alma the advance of the Light Division was acknowledged to be one of the finest performances of the campaign, and right well did the 77th carry out their part in it. Again at Inkerman they distinguished themselves, some forty of the regiment following the heroic charge of Lieutenant Clifford of the Rifle Brigade against a strong force of Russians, who, unperceived, had approached dangerously near the camp of the Second Division. The right wing of the regiment received deserved commendation for the three brilliant charges it made against the enemy. On the occurrence of the sortie of the 22nd of March, 1855, the 77th again won deserved honour in the fierce fighting which ensued before the enemy were repulsed.

It was on the occasion of the above-mentioned sortie that Private Alexander Wright, 77th Regiment, performed one of the acts of valour which earned him the Victoria Cross. As mentioned in the account of the 97th Regiment—who with the 77th were guarding the trenches—our men were surprised by the Russians, who rushed in upon them before they had "barely time to snatch their arms and defend themselves." It was a time to try the mettle of the most seasoned soldier, and Alexander Wright proved himself to be, like William of Deloraine "good at need." At the affair of the rifle pits of the 19th April, the 77th were again to the fore. With a wing of the 33rd Regiment they carried the rifle pits at a rush, despite a fierce fire which the enemy directed on them. Colonel Egerton and Captain Lempriere were wounded,* as were other officers, including Sergeant Park of the regiment, who was awarded a Victoria Cross. Private Wright again distinguished himself on this occasion. At the assault of the Redan, a hundred and sixty of the regiment, under the gallant Major Welsford, formed part of the party in charge of the scaling ladders. Alas! scarcely had the order been given "Ladders to the front!" than their gallant bearers fell thick and fast. Major Welsford had his head blown off by a cannon ball fired by a Russian officer, who afterwards surrendered himself to a sergeant of the 97th. The stormers struggled on and gained the Redan, only, as is well known, to be driven out by overwhelming numbers after an hour and a half of such fighting as rarely falls to the lot of any soldiers. There was no need to carry out the intended re-assault on the morrow; the Russians had evacuated their city, and so closed a war which had gained for the 77th much glory, and had cost them the loss of fifteen officers and nearly nine hundred men.

Since the Crimea no war service has been demanded of the 77th, who have been stationed in various quarters of the globe, including India and New South Wales. "Peace hath its victories," however, and amongst these may be instanced that of the 77th in gaining for two successive years the honour due to the "best shooting regiment of the army."†

* These officers subsequently died.
† The nickname of the 77th is "The Pothooks," from a supposed resemblance of the figure 7 to a pothook.

THE ROYAL MUNSTER FUSILIERS*—Regimental District No. 101—consist of the 101st and 104th Regiments, both old regiments of the old East India Company.

The 1st battalion of the Royal Munster Fusiliers, the 101st Regiment, date their origin from December, 1756, when, amid the chaos of doubt and terror, of incapacity and impending ruin, the Man arrived with the Hour. As one of his first steps towards the salvation of British India, Clive organized the Bengal European Battalion, and placed in command Major Kilpatrick. Like another famous regiment whose career we have sketched,† though a date can be given with exact or approximate accuracy for its origination, yet that process in the case of the Bengal European Regiment partook rather of the nature of crystallisation. For many years prior to 1756 there had existed scattered, more or less independent, companies of Europeans in the military service of the Company; as in the days of the "blameless king"

> "here and there a deed
> Of prowess done redressed a random wrong,"

and Clive was the first who drew together this knighthood errant into the "glorious company" of the 101st Fusiliers. From its very commencement the 101st has been eminently a fighting regiment. From the interesting account which appeared of it a few years ago,‡ the Bengal European Regiment has fought in no fewer than eighty-three known engagements, omitting the less important items which swell the total list of a campaign. It is obvious therefore that in such a sketch as the present it will be impossible to do more than mention—and even that but shortly—the more important of the battles in which the famous regiment has been engaged. While yet only a few days old, the Bengal European Regiment fought at the battle of Baj-Baj, which was won by the British, not without some slight loss to the newly-formed corps. In this connection it may not be without interest to recall an incident referred to by Colonel Innes. After the battle had been fought and won, it became necessary to take the Fort of Baj-Baj, and the troops—amongst which was the Grenadier Company of the 101st§—were

---

* The Royal Munster Fusiliers bear as badges the Royal Tiger on a grenade on cap and collar and on helmet plate and glengarry three golden crowns on a blue shield (the ancient arms of Ireland). The motto is that of the Garter. On the colours, in addition to the Royal Tiger, is the Shamrock, with the names of the following battles: "Plassey," "Buxar," "Guzerat," "Deig," "Bhurtpore," "Afghanistan," "Ghuznee," "Ferozeshah," "Sobraon," "Punjaub," "Chillianwallah," "Goojerat," "Pegu," "Delhi," "Lucknow." The uniform is scarlet, with facings of blue.

† The 3rd Buffs.

‡ "History of the Bengal European Regiment." Lieutenant-Colonel P. R. Innes. Simpkin, Marshall & Co.

§ Here and elsewhere the modern denomination of the regiment has been for brevity's sake adopted. It will be of course borne in mind that the numerical title was not given till 1861, prior to which date the regiment was—first the

mustered early the following morning for the purpose. It appeared, however, that the fort had already been taken! A certain "sailor named Strahan, who with a few of his comrades had been drinking freely in anticipation of hard work, conceived the idea of seeing what was going on inside the Fort. Clambering through the breach, Strahan found the walls deserted, and shouting to his companions, proclaimed with cheers that he had captured the fort. His companions quickly followed, but soon found themselves hotly engaged with the enemy's rearguard, who were smoking over the fire before joining their comrades, who had evacuated the Fort during the night. More of our sailors soon followed, and after a short skirmish it was proved that the drunken sailor, Strahan, was right when he proclaimed that he had taken the Fort." Strahan is not the only warrior of ancient or modern times who has proved that '*in Vino Victoria*' can be as true as the kindred saying with regard to *Veritas*.

The 101st fought at the battle of Chitpore, which in its results must be considered as one of the most important of that eventful period; at the famous Council of War which preceded Plassey, the majority of the regiment present voted for immediate action; they assisted in the winning of that memorable battle itself. Not long afterwards, the regiment received a welcome addition to its strength by the acquisition of volunteers from H.M. 39th Regiment, and from the Bombay and Madras European Regiments, the detachments of which Clive "annexed"—"finding it inadvisable to send them back." At Condore, the 101st were, with the exception of one company of Artillery, the only British soldiers present at the battle, "justly ranked amongst the decisive Battles of India," for it was one between the English and French for supremacy. Undoubtedly, the skilful change of front which the regiment made, and the daring courage with which they pressed on the bewildered French, were the chief factors in obtaining the victory. The loss of the regiment in the action was forty-five men killed and wounded. At the storming of Mussulipatam, the regiment acquitted themselves with signal heroism, the gallantry of Yorke, Fischer, and Moran being specially conspicuous. The siege of Mussulipatam was under the direction of Colonel Forde, the French Commander being Conflans. The following description of this important stronghold will serve to emphasize the gallantry of the besiegers. "The fort of Mussulipatam stood in an extremely defensible position. It was surrounded by a swamp on three sides, the other face rested on the river. From the land side it was only approachable by a causeway

Bengal European Regiment, then the 1st Bengal European Light Infantry, and lastly the 1st European Bengal Fusiliers.

across the swamp, and this was guarded by a strong cavalier, which is the military name for an outwork erected beyond the ditch of a fortress. It was in all respects capable of a prolonged defence. In form it was an irregular parallelogram about eight hundred yards in length and six hundred yards wide, and on the walls were eleven strong bastions. The morass which surrounded it was of from three to eighteen feet in depth."

There were only about three hundred and eighty Europeans and seven hundred natives composing the attacking party, which was under the command of Captain Callender, an officer of the Madras Army. One of the most remarkable occurrences connected with the siege was the disappearance of this officer just when the attack was ordered to begin. Where he was, what was the reason of his failing to appear at such a critical moment, was never known. From the following account of the capture of the fort, which we have condensed from histories of the time, it will be seen that when the fighting was at its height he reappeared, but gave no explanation, and before many minutes was shot dead. "The hour of midnight was fixed for the attack, as at that time the tide was at its lowest, and the water in the ditches round the ramparts not more than three feet deep. The French, in their belief in the absolute security of the place, had taken but few precautions against an attack, and it was not until the leading party had waded nearly breast-high through the ditch, and begun to break down the palisade beyond it, that they were discovered. Then a heavy artillery and musketry fire from the bastions on the right and left was opened upon the assailants." Fischer's party soon gained the breach, and were speedily joined by that under Yorke; the two parties then charged together, and captured an important bastion. Then Yorke and Fischer separated. As the former was moving forward, he saw a strong body of French Sepoys advancing towards the foot of the ramparts and the buildings of the town. These had been sent to reinforce the bastion just carried. Without a moment's hesitation Yorke ran down the ramparts, seized the French officer who commanded, and ordered him to surrender at once, as the place was already taken. Confused and bewildered, the officer gave up his sword, and ordered the Sepoys to lay down their arms. They were then sent as prisoners into the bastion. Then followed an incident almost identical with that related in the account of the 4th Regiment and their heroism at Badajoz. Some one called out "A mine! A mine!" and the soldiers of Yorke at Mussulipatam behaved just as, more than sixty years after, Walker's splendid troops behaved at Badajoz. Literally "frighted with false fire" they fell back in hopeless confusion, these men who unmoved had faced sweeping volleys, to whom morass and rampart had proved no obstacles, fled in unreasoning terror, scared—as Napier puts it—" by a chimera of their own raising." Yorke was left alone save for two plucky native drummer boys who stood by him. Threats and remonstrances soon brought the stormers back to a sense of their duty, and " they charged the bastion, Yorke leading with a drummer on each side playing the Grenadiers' March." The brave Yorke fell desperately wounded, shot through both thighs; with him fell dead the two brave drummer boys and many others, but it was in the moment of victory, for with loud hurrahs of triumph, and with a rush that none could withstand, the 101st and their comrades carried the formidable bastion. Meanwhile Captain Fischer had not been idle. He pressed on towards the works where was the great gate of the town. The French made strenuous efforts to resist his progress, but in vain. Reserving their fire till within a few yards of the enemy, his men threw in a staggering volley, and with a sudden charge cleared the bastion. Then Fischer at once closed the great gates and thus isolated and completely imprisoned the troops within. " Just as the division was again advancing, Captain Callender, to the astonishment of every one, appeared and took his place at its head." He offered no explanation of his absence, doubtless postponing it to a more convenient season. But such season never came; only a few shots more were fired by the already defeated garrison, and by one of these Captain Callender was killed. So ended the siege of Mussulipatam, one of the most memorable sieges and brilliant achievements in the long catalogue of British triumphs in India. The town taken by our troops had ten times as many guns and nearly twice as many men; save at certain times it was unassailable otherwise than by boats; not far distant was another large hostile force, our provisions were scanty, the fidelity of our allies more than doubtful, and some of our own force were beginning to murmur at the withholding of the long arrears of pay. Yet we took the town, and with it more than three thousand prisoners (five hundred being French), with a loss to our own men—exclusive of Sepoys and allies—of only twenty-two killed and sixty wounded. Well may it be said that " the capture of Mussulipatam may claim to rank among the very highest deeds ever performed by British arms." And in this capture none played a more prominent part than the splendid regiment now known as the 101st.* In dealing with a regiment such as that now under consideration, one feels a sort of Aladdin-like bewilderment at the amount and variety of the dazzling treasures gathered for our choice. At Biderra, near Chandernagore, they completely worsted the Dutch; at the

---

* More strictly as the " 1st Battalion of the Royal Munster Fusiliers." Chroniclers of regimental histories may, however, be pardoned for sometimes ignoring the rather cumbrous and not very comprehensible modern titles.

siege of Patna they gloriously distinguished themselves. Captain Cochrane was in command of a portion of the regiment forming part of the garrison, the remainder of which consisted of the troops of our ally, the Rajah Ram Narian. Strict orders had been given that for the present no engagement with the besieging force was to be attempted. The over-confident Rajah, however, thought he saw an opportunity, and sallied out, soon to find himself utterly overmatched by the Emperor's troops. He himself was soon surrounded and in grievous straits, and thereupon sent back to Captain Cochrane, who, conceiving that the prohibition did not extend to a case in which the Rajah's life was imperilled, went out with his companies. The Rajah's disregard of orders was to be productive of sad results for the 101st. Fighting his way gallantly to the rescue of his ally, the brave Cochrane fell dead, and with him fell his three subalterns. A sergeant of the regiment at the head of twenty-five Sepoys charged through the surrounding foes, and, rescuing the Rajah, brought him back in safety to the English lines, now commanded by a non-combatant officer, Dr. Fullerton, of the Company's medical service.

"Dr. Fullerton's name," writes the historian of the regiment, "is known to history as a brave, gallant soldier, and his military prowess never shone with greater lustre than when he brought the remnant of the Ram Narian's defeated force into the city of Patna, not, however, without leaving one of his disabled guns in the hands of the enemy; but before abandoning it, he had spiked it with his own hands. There is something most touching in the record of this great sacrifice of life of the Bengal European Regiment. Four officers gave their lives in attempting to perform a simple act of duty; the officer commanding the Sepoy regiment was also killed, as well as the only artillery officer with the force; none were left but that brave man Fullerton, who, when he saw all his comrades dead, manfully fufilled the duty to perform which these six officers had given their lives." The command of the garrison at Patna then devolved upon Dr. Fullerton, and most ably did he acquit himself in the well-nigh desperate position. The besiegers, elated with their victory outside the walls, attacked with redoubled ardour. So fierce was the assault that the Emperor's colours were once planted on the ramparts, when Fullerton rushed to the spot, and after a fierce hand-to-hand conflict captured them and drove back the assailants. Affairs began to look hopeless; it seemed impossible for the weak garrison much longer to resist, but, as often happens, "just when help was so much needed a joyful cry was raised that relief was at hand. A cloud of dust and the glitter of the sun on bayonets was seen on the other side of the river; the shouts of the Europeans and the inspiring sound of the fife and drum were distinctly heard, reviving the spirits and hopes of the besieged, who, rushing to their deserted posts, defended them with renewed vigour." Relief was not long delayed now. The sound of the familiar British cheer grew clearer and stronger, and Knox with the rest of the 101st, their colours flying, broke through the beleaguering lines, and clasped hands with their gallant comrades of long-enduring Patna. Next day French and Imperial troops gave way before the strengthened British force, and abandoned their position. At Beerpur, after six hours of tremendous and doubtful fighting, a charge of the grenadiers of the 101st obtained the victory for the British. At Bhirboom, Yorke, happily recovered from his severe wound at Mussulipatam, and White, though their forces only consisted of the 101st and a few Sepoys, routed the Rajah's army of twenty thousand foot and five thousand horse. At Suan, in January, 1761, they formed an all-important part of the force which utterly defeated the forces of the Emperor, thanks, however, in great measure to the cannon shot which killed the mahout of his Majesty's elephant, and impressed upon the sensible beast itself the advisability of executing a well-defined, even ostentatious, strategic movement to the rear. Under Law, the band of French, fighting in the Imperial army, gathered on an eminence, and from thence kept up a brisk fire at the advancing columns of English.

The 101st charged up the hill and captured the French guns. And now occurred an incident worthy of the palmiest days of knightly chivalry. The French, be it remembered, were the most formidable of our opponents; they had done their best to check the flight of the Emperor's troops, and for the last half-hour had been pouring grape and musketry into our ranks. Yet—"the Bengal Europeans now advanced with *shouldered* arms towards the French officers, thirteen or fourteen of whom stood by their commander and colours on the rising ground, with some fifty French soldiers in their rear. The Frenchmen, wearied with the vagrant, profitless life they had been leading since we had captured their possessions at Chundernagore, seemed determined to sell their lives as dearly as possible; but when they saw the English soldiers advancing with shouldered arms they were amazed at the generosity of their conquerors. Major Carnac, now ordering his soldiers to halt, advanced towards the French officers, and saluting, told them he did not wish to take their lives if they would surrender. M. Law replied that he and his comrades would submit only on the condition that they might retain their swords; but this stipulation not agreed to, they would resist to the last. The terms were accepted; and M. Law and his officers giving themselves up as prisoners of war were placed on their parole. All our officers now advanced, cordially shaking hands with their prisoners, and the British troops were marched back to their camp, where the French officers were hospitably entertained by those of the English army."

At Patna, when Major Adams had rightly and contemptuously refused the terms begged by Mir Kassim, the latter carried out the terrible massacre he had threatened on the prisoners, most of whom were men of the 101st Regiment. The Alsatian Sumru, the only man whom Mir Kassim had found willing to carry out his fiendish mandate, proceeded, in October, to the prison where the captives were confined. He told them he had "planned an entertainment to enliven their captivity, and that knives and forks were essential to the feast in order to entertain them in the English manner." The ruse was only to disarm suspicion, and render the victims an easier prey. Then the massacre began, the bodies being hacked to pieces and thrown into a well, women and children finding sex nor youth protection. "When one of the prisoners, named Gulston, was found still alive, the men employed in clearing away the bodies would have saved him, but he declined their proffer of assistance and was thrown into the well alive." Amidst the horror inspired by this sickening tale comes, like a gleam of pure, unearthly light in some devil's Sabbath, the pride and thankfulness inspired by the description given by a native of the way the men of the 101st and their comrades met their death. "Without losing courage," says the account, "they marched up to the murderers, and with empty bottles, stones, and brickbats fought them to the last man, until they were all killed."

It was obviously necessary to take Patna and to signally punish Mir Kassim and the "infamous Sumru,"* and though Adams's health was terribly shattered he felt that till this had been done his task was yet uncompleted. In the following November, by splendid fighting and magnificent heroism, the 101st (with whom were H.M.'s 84th and some Sepoys) took Patna, though with heavy loss.

Passing over, as we are compelled to do, the many and interesting incidents of the war then raging, we come to the battle of Buxar, the second distinction on the heavily blazoned colours of the regiment. At the first glance at the picture of this battle, handed down by past and present writers, we notice the features common to all the "battle-pieces" of the time—of overwhelming odds against the British. On this occasion the numbers were between 40,000 and 50,000 as against 7,080! The splendid cavalry of the enemy charged again and again, striving fruitlessly to break by sheer

* It is interesting to note that a descendant of Sumru became a colonel in the army, and married the daughter of an English Peer.

weight of men and horses—exceeding in number our whole army—the stubborn British phalanx. "A desperate struggle ensued,"—after a temporary success over our native allies emboldened the foe with the fancy of victory—"several of the men of the Bengal European Regiment being sabred in the ranks; but the British line remained firm and unbroken. The charge was again renewed with increased vigour, but the leader, in making a vigorous dash at the English line was received on the bayonet of one of our Europeans, who at the same moment discharging his musket, the chief fell a lifeless corpse amongst his gallant followers." A brilliant charge by Major Champion, with whom were two companies of the 101st, gave a favourable turn, at a critical moment, to the wavering battle. The enemy were soon in retreat, which rapidly degenerated into flight, and then followed a scene which can hardly be matched for its sickening horror. "The Nawab, accompanied by a strong party of chosen horsemen, crossed the Torah River with some of his most portable treasures, and as soon as he had ascertained that his trained brigades had followed him, *ordered the bridge of boats to be destroyed, thus completely cutting off the retreat of his infantry and camp-followers*. A fearful scene of carnage ensued: elephants, camels, bullocks, horses, men, women, and children, all pressing forward to gain the opposite bank of the river, were precipitated into the stream; indeed, so great was the indiscriminate rush that the weaker fell under the strong, so that, at last, a *mole three hundred yards long was formed by the dead and dying, across which the remnants of the fugitives made their escape*."

The British captured on this occasion a hundred and seventy-two guns; the loss to the 101st was thirty-seven men killed, and one officer and fifty-eight men wounded.

At the battle of Deeg Colonel Macrae and Captain Kelley won high fame by desperate fighting. During the prolonged siege of Bhurtpore with its renewed assaults, many were the acts of bravery chronicled of the 101st, and the names of Colonel Ryan and Lieutenants Morris, Brown, and Moore were mentioned again and again in despatches. There was yet another name—that of Sergeant Allen, of whom the historian of the regiment writes: "The gallantry of Sergeant Allen of the grenadier company should ever be remembered by the regiment with pride." It was during this siege that the 101st won their cherished sobriquet of "Dirty Shirts." The similarity of the circumstances under which they fought and worked at Delhi during the Mutiny has caused the latter occasion to be given as the date of its origin. Colonel Innes' account, however, seems definitely to fix the earlier date. The work in the trenches was intense and prolonged, and the labours of the soldiers knew scarcely an hour's intermission. On one occasion the Commander-in-Chief, visiting the trenches as was his wont, was addressed by some of the men of the 101st, who "apologised for their dirty appearance, urging as an excuse that they had not found time to change their shirts for several weeks. General Lake remarked approvingly that they were an honour to the wearers, showing that they had willingly sacrificed comfort to their duty in dirty shirts.

It was indeed a terrible undertaking, that storming of the maiden fortress of Bhurtpore. Lord Lisle writes in his despatches: "The troops, most confident of success, commenced the attack, and persevered in it for a considerable length of time with the most determined bravery; but their utmost exertions were not sufficient to enable them to gain the top of the breach. The bastion, which was the point of attack, was extremely strong; the resistance opposed to them was vigorous; and as our men could only mount by small parties at a time, the advantages were very great on the side of the enemy. Discharges of grape, logs of wood, and pots filled with combustible materials, immediately knocked down those who were ascending, and the whole party, after being engaged in an obstinate contest for two hours and suffering very severe loss, were obliged to relinquish the attempt, and retire to our trenches."

The siege was turned into a blockade, and terms subsequently agreed upon. The next of this famous regiment's many distinctions is "Afghanistan," and closely to follow their career throughout the campaign would be to write afresh, and in laudatory terms, the history of the war. At Ghuznee they fought; at Ferozeshah they again—the phrase becomes gloriously monotonous—greatly distinguished themselves. They supported the memorable charge of the 80th, which elicited such high praise from the Governor-General, and, throughout, manfully played their part in the fierce game at which our troops "within thirty hours stormed an entrenched camp, fought a general action, and sustained two considerable combats with the enemy; within four days dislodged from their position 60,000 Sikh soldiers, supported by 150 pieces of cannon, 108 of which the enemy acknowledge to have lost, and 91 of which are in our possession" (Sir Hugh Gough: Despatches). They fought at Sobraon, where the heaviest brunt of the battle seems to have fallen on them and on the 29th Regiment. Under General Gilbert they were ordered to advance, and came in front of the centre and strongest portion of the Sikh encampment, unsupported either by artillery or cavalry. Rushing forward with incredible bravery they crossed a dry nullah, and found themselves opposed to one of the hottest fires of musketry that can possibly be imagined. Retreat became inevitable; the enemy were safely ensconced behind high walls; "to remain under such a fire without the power of returning it would have been madness." In retreating, the 101st had "their ranks thinned by musketry, and their wounded men and officers cut off by the savage Sikhs." It is not remarkable after reading this to hear that the losses of the regiment were nearly the heaviest on the field.

At Chillianwallah they were surrounded on all sides, and "were compelled to have recourse to so many formations to repel the enemy that they were obliged to charge with the rear rank in front." At Goojerat, perhaps one of the most important battles ever fought in India, they were with Penny's Brigade, and had some terrible fighting in the village of Barra Kabra, which they carried at the point of the bayonet, taking three colours, and losing 149 of all ranks killed.

In the Burmese War, which is commemorated by "Pegu" on the colours, the 101st were at first in garrison at Rangoon under Colonel Tudor. In November of the same year the expedition against Pegu was decided on, and three hundred of the regiment joined the force to which this duty was confided. The Bengal and Madras detachments pushed forward, beneath the most intense heat, and exposed to the fire of a concealed enemy, till they reached the gateway of the town; here, however, they were so exhausted that a rest was absolutely necessary. Then General Godwin rode up, and after some words of deserved praise for the "superhuman exertions" they had gone through, addressed the fusiliers. "*You*," said he, "are Bengalies, and *you* are Madrassies, let's see who are the best men." The regiments addressed responded by that most eloquent and characteristic of all replies—a hearty cheer, "and the Bengal and Madras Fusiliers led the assault towards the city gate, which was after a short struggle captured; the Burmese soldiers being forced back, and seeking shelter under the walls of the Pagoda on the platform above. About noon the whole of the town and Fort of Pegu was in our possession." Sergeant-Major Hopkins of the 101st gained his commission this day, and died, thirty years later, a lieutenant-colonel in Her Majesty's army. Subsequently a detachment of the regiment under Major Gerrard relieved the garrison which had been left in Pegu, and in its turn besieged by the enemy. Early in the following year Major Seaton of the regiment led the storming party which captured Gongoh, penetrated into the very heart of the country, reducing scattered towns and villages to a peaceful recognition of our supremacy, though not without many severe skirmishes and much arduous labour. Majors Seaton and Gerrard, Captain Lambert, and Lieutenant Dairson earned the special recognition of the authorities.

We now come to the crowning epoch of the regiment's splendid service—that of the

Mutiny. When the outbreak at Meerut gave unmistakable evidence at once of the fact and extent of the Mutiny, the 101st were at Dugshai and received orders to march to Umballah. Within a few hours of receiving the order they started, eight hundred strong, under Major Jacob, and reached their destination early on the next day but one after their start. From thence they were moved on to Kurnaul, and "it was from this place that Lieutenant W. S. Hodson, of the 1st Bengal Fusiliers, performed the daring feat of riding by himself with despatches through a hostile country to Meerut and back, 150 miles."

Later on Lieutenant Butler arrived at the head-quarters from leave of absence, having in his anxiety to be at his post ridden across country on one horse, 110 miles in forty hours. The 1st Bengal Fusiliers were with the 1st brigade under Brigadier Showers, Colonel Welchman being in command of the regiment, and both they and their comrades of the 2nd Bengal Fusiliers experienced some severe fighting at Budlee-Ka-Serai, from which they completely routed the enemy. While before Delhi the regiment was engaged in daily skirmishes with the enemy, in which countless acts of valour were performed, and more than one Victoria Cross was awarded to the gallant Fusiliers. One notable feat was the capture of the works called Ludlow Castle. The official report speaks of the "steadiness, silence, and order with which the 1st Bengal Fusiliers advanced to the attack on the enemy's guns, which was well conceived and gallantly executed by Major Jacob and the officers and men of the regiment under his command, and Captain S. Greville of the regiment, commanding the skirmishers who made the first attack upon the guns." Of these latter Private Reagan was, perhaps, the most distinguished. "Rushing," writes Colonel Innes, "upon a 24-pounder howitzer, which was charged with grape, he attacked the gunners single-handed, and bayoneted one of them just as he was applying the portfire." At the battle of Nujjufghur, on the 24th of August, the 101st were again conspicuous by their valour. Previous to the engagement General Nicholson addressed the troops, and turning to the regiment he said, "I have nothing to say to the 1st Fusiliers, they will do as they always do." The result of the "doing" on this occasion was that the enemy fled "leaving the whole of their camp equipage, baggage, and 13 guns in our possession." An officer of the regiment who was present adds that we "reached our camp after an absence of 41 hours, during which time our men had only partaken of one meal." At the assault of Delhi the 1st Bengal Fusiliers were divided between the first and fourth columns, of which the former, under General Nicholson, was to "storm the breach by the Cashmere Bastion," and the latter under Major Reid "to enter the city by the Lahore Gate." The 2nd Bengal Fusiliers were with the second column under Brigadier Jones, to whom was committed the charge of storming the "Water Bastion."

The story of the capture of Delhi is too familiar to allow us to dwell upon it, identified though it so greatly is with the gallant Munster Fusiliers. At the assault the brave Speke, Nicholson, and Jacob fell, mortally wounded; Greville was shot through the shoulder; Captain Caulfield, Lieutenants Wemyss, Butler, and Woodcock all fell at this time, as well as a large proportion of rank and file. The second column, in which were the 2nd Fusiliers under Boyd, pressed forward as far as the Kabul Gate, and had somewhat less desperate fighting; the fourth column, in which were the remainder of the 1st Fusiliers under Captain Wriford, had a terrible struggle. So fierce was the fire of the enemy that the road became well-nigh impassable from the number of the dead bodies. "Reid now gave the order, 'Fusiliers to the front!' and with a wild rush they charged across the bridge, unavoidably treading under foot the wounded men who lay on the road. . . . Captain Wriford and many of the officers in advance were engaged in single combat with the mutineers, who pelted our troops from behind their breastworks with brickbats and other missiles, whilst our ranks were being rapidly thinned by the musketry fire poured upon us by the thousands of the enemy behind their barricades. Here Lieutenant Owen was severely wounded in the head, but was saved from falling under the tulwars of the enemy by Lieutenant Lambert's protection. . . . Here also fell Sergeant Dunleary of the 1st Bengal Fusiliers, whose distinguished bravery was formally mentioned in the despatches of the commander of the column." There is, however, one incident of the capture of Delhi that, associated as it is with the 101st Fusiliers—the prime mover and instigator in this incident, which materially affected the future, being an officer in the regiment—it is not out of place to relate somewhat at length; the more so as, strange though it might seem, considerable controversy has arisen concerning it. We refer to the execution of the Delhi princes by Lieutenant Hodson of the 101st, the famous organizer and commander of "Hodson's Horse."

Hodson seems to have entertained from the first a sort of prescience that some crisis would arise which would call for the exercise of *one* controlling will. Accordingly he was immeasurably relieved and delighted when he obtained full discretion to deal as he thought best with the fugitive king and princes of Delhi, the only condition being that the former's life was spared. The king came forth from his hiding-place towards the glorious gateway of his captured city, still in all seeming a king in verity, surrounded by attendants and populace far outnumbering the small band of resolute British. But Hodson was a born king of men; numbers were of comparatively small account to him; his was the dominant will in that vast assembly, and he knew it. Sitting calm and unconcerned upon his horse, he had just before turned to one of the scowling crowd—a sentry of the Royal Guard—and ordered him to fetch a light for his cigar. At the right moment he demanded the king's arms, promising that his life should be spared. Then, having intimated that this promise was conditional on absolute and effective surrender, and that if any attempt at rescue was made, the royal captive would be shot like a dog, he rode back to the gates of Delhi and handed the king to the representative of the civil power. But, though the king was secured, the three princes, the prime instigators of the rebellion, had escaped. Tidings were brought to Hodson of their whereabouts. He took with him one subaltern and a hundred men, and rode straight for the tombs where the miscreants had taken shelter. At least six thousand adherents remained with the princes—odds of sixty to one! Yet Hodson sent in word demanding unconditional surrender. This was agreed to, and Hodson started back with his prisoners to Delhi. But on the way the crowd of rebels increased, and the escort was stopped. It was the moment for action, and Hodson was the man of all others fitted for the emergency. Another minute's delay and the princes would have been rescued and their captors not improbably annihilated. Riding up, with only Lieutenant Macdowel and four troopers, he turned to the crowd with the words: "These are the men who have not only rebelled against the Government, but ordered and witnessed the massacre and shameful exposure of innocent women and children, and thus therefore the Government punishes such traitors taken in open resistance." He ordered them to strip, so as still further to degrade them, and then, with his own hand, regardless of appeals, regardless, too, of the sanctimonious horror of fireside sentimentalists or jealous compeers, he shot them dead. The effect is said to have been instantaneous. The Mohammedans of the troop and some influential moulvies among the bystanders exclaimed, "Well and rightly done! their crime has met with its just penalty. These were they who gave the signal for the death of helpless women and children, and now a righteous judgment has fallen upon them." Such was the execution of the princes of Delhi, monsters to whose hideous cruelty and more hideous lust numbers of gentle English women had been sacrificed with tortures to them worse than death. Such was their execution, executed by the dauntless courage of an officer of the 101st, and applauded by all whom a spurious sentiment has not induced to consider other nationalities first and their own—nowhere.

In all the subsequent operations up to the siege of Lucknow, Hodson was preeminent for valour and capability. With the fall of Lucknow came the end of a glorious career. "He entered the breach with General Napier and several others, just as a party was starting to attack the Begum's palace; he fell in with them. The place was quickly taken, and as he was searching for concealed rebels, he looked into a dark passage full of them. A shot was fired from the inside; he staggered back some paces and fell. He was carried by his faithful orderly out of danger. At first hopes were entertained that he might recover, but he rapidly sank from internal bleeding. His last words were: 'My love to my wife. Tell her my last thoughts were of her. Lord, receive my soul!' Thus, on the 12th of March, 1858, in his thirty-seventh year, closed the earthly career of one of the best and bravest of England's sons—one of her truest heroes," * one of the ablest and bravest officers that even the 101st Fusiliers have ever possessed.

After Delhi the 101st had some severe fighting at Namoul, where the brigade was under the command of Colonel Gerrard of the regiment. This brave officer was killed, and the command of the regiment devolved upon "Lieutenant McFarlane, an officer of only six years' standing." Many were the brave deeds done at Namoul by officers and men of the 101st. Lieutenant F. D. M. Brown won the Victoria Cross for rescuing a wounded soldier under a heavy fire; Private McGovern—who had already won the same distinction—volunteered to dislodge three of the enemy who had retired to a small turret. Avoiding by sheer quickness and presence of mind the fire of their three rifles, he dashed forward before they could reload, "shot the man in front, and, rushing on the other two, bayoneted them without giving them time to recover." Some of the regiment were with Havelock when he effected the first relief of Lucknow; subsequently the 101st formed part of Colonel Seaton's column, and at Allyghur and Puttialee earned great credit. On the occasion of the final assault on Lucknow, they were attached to the 5th brigade. On the 9th of March they were hotly engaged, and it was on this occasion that Lieutenant Adair Butler won the Victoria Cross. It was necessary to ascertain the state of defence in which a strong battery of the enemy's was. Captain Salisbury of the 101st expressed the opinion that it was deserted, and Butler volunteered to test the accuracy of this surmise. He swam a rapid stream sixty yards wide, clambered up the

* Sketches from the "Life of the late Major W. S. R. Hodson."

works regardless of the extreme probability that every corner might conceal an ambushed enemy, and finding Captain Salisbury's views correct waved his *cummerbund* as a signal. To insure its being seen he remained in a most conspicuous position under a heavy fire of musketry. The city was finally captured with but small loss, three officers and twenty rank and file of the 101st being wounded, and eight rank and file killed. Lieutenant MacGregor "greatly distinguished himself by engaging in single combat with one of the bravest of the rebels, whom he reduced to eternal submission by sending his sword through his body up to its hilt, returning to his comrades looking 'very warm and exceedingly wild and happy.'" During the following months the regiment was engaged in various skirmishes with vagrant bands of mutineers, in which Captains Cunliffe and Trevor, and Lieutenants Brown and Warner earned great distinction. When it was found that the terrible Sepoy Mutiny had been completely crushed, and men had leisure to take stock of their credit account in the lists of worthful and memorable deeds, it was found that no fewer than five individuals of the 101st had gained the envied Victoria Cross. These men—their names, even if space forbids the enumeration of their triumphs, must be recorded—were Lieutenant Adair Butler, Lieutenant F. Brown, Sergeant J. M. Guire, Private J. McGovern, Drummer M. Ryan. After the rebellion had been crushed came the Royal Proclamation by which the Majesty of England announced that, "We have resolved to take upon ourselves the government of India," and simultaneously, so to speak, therewith came the transformation of the Bengal Fusiliers into H.M.'s 101st and 104th Regiments. For a few years no serious warfare engaged the services of the regiment, for we will still look on it as a whole, but in 1863 the 101st were engaged in the Umbeyla Campaign. "An account of the campaign," quoted by Colonel Innes, has the following remarks, which throw a descriptive light on the then composition and *morale* of the regiment. "It was well known that, whatever service was to be performed, the 101st would share in it, and the young soldiers—for with very few exceptions the whole of the regiment was composed of very young soldiers who had never seen service—burned with ardour for their maiden fight, and, remembering the gallant deeds of the old regiment, were eager to have their first brush with the enemy under the new colours of the 101st." The same account gives a graphic account of the difficulties that beset our troops. The jungle was so thick that the men could only go in single file—the duties "were far harder than usually fall to the lot of soldiers"—for nearly a month accoutrements were uncharged. In November of that year, the 101st carried the "Craig Piquet" with conspicuous dash, losing in the enterprise five killed and twenty-six wounded. In a subsequent engagement, Lieutenant Chapman lost his life. He was mortally wounded, and he knew it. Beside him fell another officer, Captain Smith of the 101st, whose hurt was not necessarily fatal. Even while the cold, unrelaxing hand of death was clutching closer and closer about his own throat, Chapman knelt by his wounded comrade and began to dress his wounds, declining to be moved as " it was useless," but begging for the removal of Captain Smith. A sudden rush of the enemy frustrated this intention; "both officers fell into their hands and were hacked to pieces, their heads being cut off and their bodies shockingly mangled." Well may the writer conclude his account of this incident with the words: "In Lieutenant Chapman the 101st lost an officer of rare ability, of untiring energy, the perfect type of an English gentleman and a British officer." Before this troublesome "little war" was ended, two more officers, Ensign Sanderson and Surgeon Pitt, were killed, with many of the rank and file; the total loss in killed and wounded being eighty-seven officers and men.

So ends the military record of the 101st Regiment, which in 1871, for the first time, visited England. Since that date only the ordinary services of a regiment in peace time have fallen to their lot.

The 104th Regiment, the 2nd battalion of the Royal Munster Fusiliers, boast a record which may almost claim to vie in brilliancy, though not quite in age, with their brethren of the 1st battalion. The present 2nd battalion is the successor of previous 2nd battalions of the Bengal Fusiliers, which from time to time have become absorbed in the first. The 104th dates from 1859, and at the time of their consolidation into the Imperial Army bore on their colours "Punjaub," "Chillianwallah," "Goojerat," "Pegu," "Delhi." For their gallant services during the campaign commemorated by "Punjaub," the 2nd Bengal European Regiment were created Fusiliers, at their own request, and to mark the approbation of the Government "of their gallant, exemplary, and praiseworthy conduct." So much of the career of the gallant 104th has been noticed in dealing with the 101st that further notice is unnecessary. Together the two regiments preserve and uphold the splendid traditions of the Bengal Fusiliers of glorious memory.

We have dealt with the Royal Munster Fusiliers somewhat at length, but it must be remembered that in a sense, and that sense a military one, their history is the history, executed in relief, of the acquisition of British India; they are the representatives of the regiments which upheld, however irregularly and spasmodically, British power against French and natives, and thus, before ever a Royal regiment appeared upon the scene, laid firm hold on the glorious heritage which we of to-day enjoy, thanks to the stubborn valour of the East Indian Regiments.

THE NORFOLK REGIMENT*—Regimental District No. 9—consists of the 9th Foot, which dates from 1685, when it was raised—chiefly in Gloucestershire. On the occasion of the abdication of James II., Colonel Nicholas, of the 9th, was one of the officers who could not reconcile it with their oath to the absent King to renew it to his successor, and the colonelcy of the regiment consequently devolved upon Colonel Cunningham. It would almost seem, however, that Colonel Cunningham's view of duty was somewhat too unaccommodating for William III. The 9th were sent to subdue Londonderry, whose governor, being attached to King James, had incurred the resentment of the inhabitants. The latter accordingly determined to take the law into their own hands and to depose him, and they then offered the government to Colonel Cunningham of the 9th. He replied that, "being himself commanded by the King to obey the governor, he could not receive any application from persons who opposed that authority." The 9th thereupon returned to England. King William was so displeased that Colonel Cunningham, together with the Colonel of another regiment, the 17th, was deprived of his commission.

After some further service in Ireland, whither the regiment was again sent under a less punctilious commander, during which they fought at the Boyne, Morhill, Balleymore, Athlone, Galway, and Limerick, the 9th went in 1701 to Holland, where they shared in the siege of Kaiserswerth, and afterwards formed part of the covering army during the sieges of Venloo, Ruremonde, Stevenswart, and Liege, at the last named of which places the grenadier company of the regiment highly distinguished itself.

In 1703 they served at the siege and subsequently in the campaign under the Archduke Charles of Austria in Portugal, during which they experienced one of the more unpleasant "fortunes of war," by being made prisoners—through an act of treachery—at Castel de Vide. After being exchanged they took part in all the actions and sieges of that campaign, fighting over a district which the wars of a hundred years

* The Norfolk Regiment bears as a badge the figure of Britannia on cap and collar, and on the waistplate the Castle of Norwich. The motto is that of the Garter. On the colours are "Rolcia," "Vimiera," "Corunna," "Busaco," "Salamanca," "Vittoria," "St. Sebastian," "Nive," "Peninsula," "Kabul, 1842," "Moodkee," "Ferozeshah," "Sobraon," "Sevastopol," "Kabul, 1879," "Afghanistan, 1879—80." The tunic is scarlet with facings of white, and the officers wear a black line on the gold lace of the tunics.

later were to make familiar to all, and where we find records of the gallantry of the regiment at Valencia, Badajoz,* Albuquerque, and Ciudad Rodrigo. In 1707 was fought, on Easter Day, the battle of Almanza, the peculiarity of which was that the English commander, Lord Galway, was by extraction a Frenchman named Rouvigny, whom the anti-Protestant policy of Louis Quatorze had driven to England, while the leader of the French army was the Duke of Berwick, an Englishman, and a Royal Stuart to boot, though with the bar sinister across his escutcheon. To the 9th Regiment, however, the defeat of Almanza only brought honour and fame. They went into action 467 strong; only one hundred were left to retreat with their commander, Colonel Stewart, to Tarragona. It was necessary for the regiment to recruit, and they accordingly returned home, and for many years no fighting fell to their lot. In 1761 the 9th, then known as Whitmore's Regiment, joined the expedition under General Studholm Hodgson, against Belle Isle, and fought gallantly in the fierce engagement which preceded the capitulation. The following year they joined the army under the Earl of Albemarle against the Havannah, where, in common with the rest of our forces, they endured great hardships, and where Lieutenant Nugent particularly distinguished himself in the capture of the Morro. The regiment was stationed in Florida from 1763 to 1769, when they returned to Ireland, and in 1776 embarked for Canada. Here they took part in the engagements at Fort Ticonderago, Skenesborough, Castletown, and Fort Anne, Wood Creek; at the last-named place greatly distinguishing themselves by "standing and repulsing an attack six times their number. In the height of action Lieutenant-Colonel Hill found it necessary to change his position. So critical an order was executed by the regiment with the utmost steadiness and bravery. They also captured the colours of the 2nd Hampshire (American) Regiment," and despite the arduous nature of the struggle lost only one officer and twelve rank and file. The 9th returned to England in 1781, where they remained till 1788, in which year they embarked for the West Indies. The grenadier and light companies took part in the expedition against Tobago, under Admiral Sir John Cafney and Major-General Cuyler and received high praise in the Commander-in-Chief's despatches. In 1794 the 9th were with Sir Charles Grey's army in the attack on Martinique. In the sharp fighting which followed an unexpected onslaught of the enemy Lieutenant-Colonel Campbell of the regiment was killed. After the conquest of Guadeloupe, General Sir Charles Grey said in his despatch that he " could not find words adequate to convey an idea, or to

* Where their colonel, the Earl of Galway, lost his right hand from a cannon ball.

express the high sense he entertained of the extraordinary merit evinced by the officers and soldiers in this service."

The 9th were subsequently stationed at Grenada, not returning to England till 1796, having suffered severely from the climate. In July, 1799, the regiment was formed into three battalions. The 1st and 2nd battalions embarked for Holland in the autumn and advanced with the force under the Duke of York to attack the French and Dutch forces at Bergen, taking part the following month in the capture of Egmont-op-Zee. After this no important fighting fell to their share till 1808, when the 1st battalion embarked for Portugal. At Roleia, the first battle whose name is on their colours, the 9th formed part of the centre column under Brigadier Nightingale, and with the 29th greatly distinguished themselves. It soon became evident that the battle would be fought in the rocky passes of the hills overlooking the town. Here the two regiments were, by what Napier characterizes as a "false movement,"* suddenly exposed to the full brunt of Laborde's attack. Many fell, including the colonel of the 29th; then "the oppressed troops rallied on their left wing and on the 9th Regiment, and all rushing up the hill together regained the tableland, presenting a confused front, which Laborde vainly endeavoured to destroy; yet many brave men he struck down, and mortally wounded Colonel Stewart of the 9th, fighting with great vehemence." The loss of the regiment in this engagement was five men, including Colonel Stewart, killed, and fifty-two, of whom three were officers, wounded.

The 2nd battalion arrived in Portugal in August, 1808, and on joining the army took up a position at Vimiera, the 1st battalion being posted on the mountain on the right of the village. On the morning of August 21st, the soldiers were under arms before daybreak, and at seven o'clock the French army was seen advancing "in two great columns, supported and flanked by a cloud of skirmishers, and dressed in long white linen coats and trousers." The hill, on which the 2nd battalion of the 9th was posted, was attacked by the enemy, who were repulsed with severe loss.

"The 1st battalion proceeded to Spain, and, though stationed at Corunna, were not engaged in the battle on January 16th, but their conduct during the expedition procured for them the honour of bearing the word 'Corunna' on their colours" (*Official Record*). It was a party of the 9th that dug the grave of Sir John Moore—literally "the sod with their bayonets turning"—and attended to his obsequies. After this they returned to

---

* The nature of this false movement is finely described in the historian's inimitable style as a "fierce neglect of orders in taking a path leading immediately to the enemy."

England, embarking six months later, with the expedition against Holland, where, however, they only remained three weeks.

In April, 1810, the light company of the 2nd battalion, which had been stationed at Gibraltar, was withdrawn from there to take part in the defence of Tarifa. The 1st battalion meanwhile landed at Lisbon in March of the same year to join Wellington's army.

On the 26th of September, the eve of the battle of Busaco, "the armies lay down for the night on the ground under the open sky. In the balmy autumn night none complained of nature's couch, and before dawn 100,000 men stood quietly to arms. While the grey mist of early morning still shrouded the ridge the French lines were formed for the attack, and their forward movement began. Ney was to make an assault on the allies' left, and, at a distance of three miles from him, Reynier on the allies' right, while Junot was kept in reserve."

The distinguished conduct of the regiment on this occasion is thus described in the official record of its career: "Major-General Leith led the 9th Regiment to attack the enemy on the rocky ridge, which they did without firing a shot. That part which looks behind the sierra was inaccessible, and afforded the enemy the advantage of out-flanking the 9th on the left as they advanced, but the order, celerity, and coolness with which they attacked panic-struck the enemy, who immediately gave way on being charged with the bayonet, and the whole were driven down the face of the sierra, in confusion and with immense loss from the destructive fire which the 9th opened upon them as they fled with precipitation after the charge. The steadiness and accuracy with which the 9th attended to the direction of the march which, before they were engaged, was continually changing, in order to form in the most advantageous manner for the attack of the enemy; the quickness and precision with which they formed line under a heavy fire; their instantaneous and orderly charge, by which they drove the enemy, so much superior in number, from a formidable position, and the promptitude with which they obeyed orders to cease firing, was, altogether, conduct as distinguished as any regiment could have shown." Afterwards the 9th were posted at Alcantara, and in December went into quarters at Torres Vedras, where they remained three months.

The 2nd battalion meanwhile embarked from Gibraltar early in 1811 to take part in an attack on the rear of the enemy's lines before Cadiz. At Barossa the flank companies of the 9th were with the force under General Browne, which "Graham's Spartan order had sent headlong" against the French, and of which nearly one-half went down under the first fire. Then when the 87th under General Dilkes forced their way to the rescue, the whole British force rushed up to the summit of the slope, where 'a dreadful, and for some time doubtful, combat raged, but the English bore strongly onward, and their incessant slaughtering fire forced the French from the hill with the loss of three guns and many brave soldiers.' Subsequently they embarked for Tarifa, and, after a short stay, returned to Gibraltar. The 1st battalion remained at Torres Vedras until the French army began to retreat towards Spain, when it followed with the army in pursuit, and on April 3rd, 1811, came up with a body of French at Sabugal. In the fierce combat that ensued, described by Wellington himself as "one of the most glorious actions British troops were ever engaged in," the 9th did their service gallantly, driving their opponents over the bridge at the point of the bayonet. After taking part in the battle of Fuentes d'Onor they went into cantonments, their next piece of important fighting being at the storming of Ciudad Rodrigo and Badajoz. In neither of these exploits, however, do they seem to have taken any prominent part. Very different, however, was the case at Salamanca. Here the 9th were a quarter of a mile in front of the other regiments, when a forward movement became of vital importance. One of Wellington's aides-de-camp rode up and said, "The 9th is the only regiment formed, advance!" And advance they did, though for a time comparatively unsupported, and throughout the engagement fought most gallantly, moving forward in pursuit of the enemy on the day following. They were with the force which compelled Clausel to abandon Valladolid, and then joined in the advance on Madrid. In October, the 9th, "not mustering 300 men, with scarcely an officer to a company," were ordered to take an active part in defending the bridge of Muriel and the fords. The contest was so obstinate that the men were twice supplied with ammunition. The regiment lost 1 sergeant and 16 rank and file killed; 8 officers, 4 sergeants, and 50 rank and filed wounded. During the retreat from Burgos the 9th were distinguished for the order and discipline they observed, and in consequence did not consider themselves implicated in the severe censure published in general orders.

In the spring of 1813, 10 sergeants and 400 rank and file from the 2nd battalion joined the regiment in Portugal in time to share in the memorable battle of Vittoria, where they behaved with their customary courage. At the siege of San Sebastian one of the first objects was the reduction of San Bartolomeo, and here the 9th gained conspicuous honour. Colonel Cameron led the grenadier company down the face of the hill, exposed to a heavy cannonade from the horn work. His spirited advance occasioned the French to abandon the redoubt, and the grenadiers of the 9th jumped over the wall and assaulted both the convent and the houses of the suburb with the most heroic gallantry. A fierce struggle took place in the suburb. Capt. John Woodham of the 9th fought his way into the upper room of a house and was there killed; Lieutenant and Adjutant Thornhill was also killed: in the meantime the grenadiers carried the convent with such rapidity that the French had not time to explode some mines they had prepared. The companies of the regiment with the right attack were no whit behind their brethren in gallantry and dash, and the severity of the fight may be judged from the fact that in this encounter the regiment had upwards of seventy officers and men killed and wounded.

On the renewal of the siege the following month a determined sortie of the French was repulsed by the bayonets of the 9th. The terrible and dramatic features of this siege are familiar to all from the pages of Napier. The singular distinction gained during its progress by the 9th Regiment will be most effectively shown by an unvarnished extract from the official record, the stern simplicity of which has an eloquence all its own. At the storming there was in command of a forlorn hope a Lieutenant Colin Campbell,* known to after days as Field-Marshal Lord Clyde. His position was in the centre of the Royals, for the purpose of carrying the high curtain work after the breach should be won. Lieutenant-Colonel Cameron and Lieutenant Campbell distinguished themselves on this occasion, the latter receiving a cut from a sabre and a stab from a bayonet. On the morning of August 27th, 1813, a hundred soldiers of the 9th, commanded by Captain Hector Cameron, proceeded to attack the island of Santa Clara in the bay of San Sebastian. As the boats approached the shore a heavy fire was opened upon them. The island was, however, captured and the French garrison made prisoners, and the conduct of Captain Cameron on this occasion was commended by Wellington in his despatches. San Sebastian was again attacked by storm on August 31st, when the 9th lost 4 officers, 5 sergeants, and 42 rank and file. Lieutenant-Colonel Campbell and five other officers were wounded, and over a hundred men.

At the passage of the Bidassoa on October 7th, the 9th took post in the left wing of the allied army. The German light troops had driven the French back to the important post of the Croix des Bouquets; this, however, was the very key of the position and the

* It has been asserted of the East Norfolk Regiment that it "may be said to have commenced its military career with his arrival, as its colours, then virgin, were only about to be decorated with the names of the battles in which he first saw fire." This is somewhat hard on a regiment which has a previous history of over a hundred years, but the *distinctions* certainly synchronise with the joining of the future hero of the Crimea and Lucknow.

enemy made a stubborn and effective resistance. Led by the gallant Colonel Cameron the 9th rushed up the height "with a furious charge" and cleared it, when the French infantry fled to a second ridge, where they could only be approached by a narrow front. Colonel Cameron then formed the regiment into one column and advanced under a concentrated fire. The 9th moved steadily forward until they arrived within a dozen yards of their antagonists, when, "raising a loud shout, they rushed on the opposing foe. The enemy fled and the ridges were won. The conduct of the 9th elicited the commendations of the general officers who witnessed their intrepid bearing, and the regiment was thanked in the field by Wellington." They subsequently took part in the battle of the Nive, and at Biaritz captured no fewer than one hundred and sixty prisoners.

Immediately after the termination of the war in the Peninsula, in which they had won so fair a renown, the 9th were ordered to Canada, returning the following year, though too late to take part in the battle of Waterloo. They served, however, with the army of occupation, and were stationed at Paris, Compiegne, and St. Armand successively, returning to England in October, 1818.* Three months later they proceeded to the West Indies, where they remained for eight years, being stationed at St. Vincent, Dominica, and St. Lucia, Grenada, and Trinidad. After a short stay in the United Kingdom, in 1833 the regiment went to the Mauritius, leaving there two years later for Bengal. Some six years passed before an opportunity occurred for them to share in any fighting. In December, 1841, however, they proceeded from Meerut *en route* to Ferozepore, for the purpose of being employed on active service beyond the Indus, and were engaged at the Khyber Pass, and in the actions in the Valley and Pass of Tezeen. The regiment then proceeded to Kabul, where they arrived on September 15th, and the following month assisted at the assault and capture of Istalif. In 1845, after being stationed in and about Kabul since its capture, the 9th joined the army of the Sutlej, and took part in the battles of Moodkee, Ferozeshah, and Sobraon.

The particulars of these battles are elsewhere given, and it need only be here observed that the 9th acquitted themselves as they have ever done. They returned to England in 1847, and found their next warlike service in the Crimea, where they arrived in November, 1854, and from the time of their arrival to the evacuation of Sevastopol, took part in all the arduous and dangerous duties which devolved upon our gallant army. In 1858 a second battalion was raised chiefly in Yarmouth, and has

* The 2nd battalion was disbanded at Chatham at the end of 1815.

added to the distinctions the two last names on the colours of the regiment; previously to which it had served in China and Japan, and in the Jowaki expedition of 1877—78. In the Afghan war of 1879—80, the 9th were with General Gough's column, which arrived at Kabul on Christmas Day, "sorely disappointed at being too late to share in the recent action," when the British reoccupied the city. Later on they formed part of the force under General Ross, which two days before the battle of Ghazni marched to join the force under Sir Donald Stewart. The junction, however, was prevented by the unexpectedly hostile attitude of the chiefs of the intervening territory. After the order to evacuate Kabul had arrived the 9th had a fierce skirmish with the Ghilzies at a place called Syazabad. It was after this encounter that Lieutenant Lorne Govan attacked a couple of Ghazis who had just murdered a man of one of our Ghoorka regiments. One he killed and the other was shot by the infuriated comrades of the murdered man. The Afghan war terminates the active service record of the gallant Norfolk Regiment, as it is beyond the scope of this work to treat of hostilities which—at the time of publishing—are still in operation.

The Northamptonshire Regiment *—Regimental District No. 48— consists of the 48th and 58th Regiments of Foot. The former dates from 1740, and a year after its formation, received its numerical distinction. There seems, according to Archer, whose sketch is the most readily available, to be some doubt whether they actually participated in the battles of Fontenoy or Culloden. It is, however, certain that they took part in the campaign in Flanders of 1747—48, and at Laffeldt distinguished themselves under Colonel Seymour Conway, who was taken prisoner. In 1755 they went to America and shared in the disaster which overtook our forces at Fort Duquesne, afterwards—such as were left—being ordered to Albany. Two years after they were at Louisburg, and in 1759 were with Wolfe in the immortal struggle of Quebec. After seeing some service at Martinique and the Havannah, the regiment returned home in 1763 and were next employed under Abercromby in the West Indies. As a two-battalion regiment, they were represented (by the 1st battalion) in the war in Portugal in 1809, and were present at the passage of the Douro, the name of which only three regiments besides the

---

* The Northamptonshire Regiment bears as badges the Castle and Key, with the name "Gibraltar" above, and "Talavera" below, on the cap, and the Cross of St. George with a horseshoe on the collar. The motto is *Montis insignia Calpe*. On the colours are the Sphinx and the names of the following battles: "Louisburg," "Quebec, 1759," "Gibraltar," "Egypt," "Maida," "Douro," "Talavera," "Albuera," "Badajoz," "Salamanca," "Vittoria," "Pyrenees," "Nivelle," "Orthes," "Toulouse," "Peninsula," "Sevastopol," "New Zealand," "South Africa, 1879." The uniform is scarlet with facings of white.

Northamptonshire bear on their colours. In July of the same year was fought the bloody battle of Talavera, which yielded to the 48th perhaps the fairest flower in their chaplet of honour. It was at the critical moment of the fight, "when the British centre was absolutely beaten, that Colonel Donellan, who fell mortally wounded a few minutes later, led up the gallant 48th Regiment. Wheeling back into open columns of companies to let the disordered masses of the Guards pass through, the 48th assailed the enemy's flank with heavy volleys." The effect was to give the gallant Guards time to reform, and before long the enemy were in headlong retreat. As Wellesley declared, the day was saved by the "advance, position, and steadiness of the 1st battalion of the 48th under Major Middlemore," who had taken command of the regiment on the death of Colonel Donellan. With regard to the last-named officer, the account of the incident given by Grant has a certain pathos. He was the last officer in our service who adhered to the old Nivernais, or three-cornered cocked hat, and on the order to succour the Guards being given, executed the requisite manœuvres with consummate skill. At the moment of advance " he fell mortally wounded, and lifting his old Nivernais to Major Middlemore, requested him to take the command." Both battalions were at Albuera, where the second was with Stewart's first brigade, which, under Colonel Colborne, was " almost annihilated," while the 1st battalion charged under General Houghton and its own officers, Colonel Duckworth and Major Way, to "turn the doubtful day again." At Badajoz, to the 1st battalion under Major Wilson was assigned the storming of the San Roque, and such was the fury of their assault, that " resistance was almost instantaneously overpowered;" at Salamanca they gained yet another distinction for their honour-heavy colours. At Vittoria, St. Sebastian, Nivelle, at Orthes, Toulouse, and the battles of the Pyrenees they fought, ever foremost in the fray. At the close of the Peninsular War they repaired to India, where, in 1834, they served "in the brief but arduous campaign of Coorg," which was the last warlike service demanded of them till the Crimea, the intervening years being spent in Malta, the West Indies, and Jamaica. They landed in the Crimea in April, 1855, and from that date to the close of the war were actively engaged. Since then their time has been spent chiefly in India, but no active service of importance has fallen to the lot of the gallant 48th.

The 2nd battalion of the Northamptonshire Regiment, the 58th Foot, dates from 1755, and is the third regiment which has borne that number. In 1758 they joined the expedition against Louisburg under General Amherst, and the year following were in the famous British line which, on the heights of Abraham, gained Quebec and " the princely dominion of Canada" for the crown of Great Britain. In 1762 they fought in the Havanna, and during the following years were variously engaged. In 1781 they shared in the memorable defence of Gibraltar, being one of the five regiments which bear the "Castle and Key" in commemoration thereof. While engaged here they received the territorial designation of the Rutlandshire Regiment. When peace was concluded the 58th spent ten years at home, during which time amongst the captains appointed to the regiment was "Arthur Wellesley, from the 12th Light Dragoons." In 1794 the 58th were with the forces under Sir Charles Grey in the West Indies, and shared in the conquest of Martinique. After seeing some service in Minorca and the Mediterranean, the Rutlandshire Regiment were ordered to Egypt, and were placed in the reserve under Major-General, afterwards Sir John, Moore. On the occasion of the landing at Aboukir the fire of the 58th effectually checked the French cavalry which were seriously harassing the Guards. At the battle of Alexandria they, with the 28th, were posted amongst some ruins on the right of our line and here it was that the heaviest of the fighting took place. Under Colonel Crowdjye the 58th "manned the breaches in the ruined wall, and after three rounds of ball cartridge rushed on the enemy with the bayonet." But the struggle was by no means over. So impressed was the French General Menou with the importance of the position, that he promised a louis d'or to every soldier who should penetrate within the enclosure. At last, attacking on three sides at once, they got in—but few got out again. Our men closed up behind them; "when powder and shot lasted no longer, our people had recourse to stones and the butt-ends of their muskets. It was a hand-to-hand fight, a *mêlée* in which the French found they had not a chance either of victory or escape. They were knocked down in heaps, they were transfixed with the bayonet against the walls of the old building; the entire area was covered with their blood and their bodies. Seven hundred Frenchmen were slain amongst these dismal ruins, scarcely a man of them that entered got off, for the few who were not killed or prostrated by their wounds surrendered and cried for mercy." (*Low.*)

On the renewal of the war with France, a second battalion was enrolled and fought in many of the famous battles of the Peninsular War. The 1st battalion, meanwhile, was in Sicily, and under Sir John Stewart took part in the memorable battle of Maida. Here they were commanded by Sir John Oswald, and, with the 78th, formed Acland's brigade, which so splendidly seconded the brilliant efforts of the Light Infantry under Kemp. The 2nd battalion fought at Salamanca and at Burgos, during the disastrous retreat from which they suffered very heavily. After this they were attached to General

Barnes' Brigade. At Echellar they gained the praise of Lord Wellesley for the share they took in that splendid charge, which ended in "the astonishing spectacle being presented of fifteen hundred men driving, by sheer valour and force of arms, six thousand good troops from ground so rugged, the numbers might have been reversed and the defence made good without much merit." The Nivelle and Nive, Orthes and Bordeaux, witnessed their prowess and discipline, and at the close of the war the 2nd battalion was disbanded, having done well for its country and the honour of the regiment. The 1st battalion was engaged in Canada, and so were unable to share in the victory of Waterloo; they formed part, however, of the army of occupation. For the next twenty-two years or so their sphere of service lay in Jamaica and Ceylon, and during their sojourn at the latter station, they were engaged in quelling one of the periodic outbreaks of the Candians. In 1843 they were ordered to New South Wales, and took part in the first New Zealand War, returning home in 1859. After a peaceful interval of about twenty years they joined the British forces engaged in the Zulu War, during which—and the subsequent operations against the Boers—few regiments gained greater renown or suffered more severely. They were with the reinforcements which arrived in April, 1879, and were placed in the Second Division under General Newdigate. After the melancholy death of the Prince Imperial of France, it was by a party of the 58th that his body was escorted to Pietermaritzburg. On the 6th of June, occurred a somewhat regrettable incident—yet one to which, as history tells us, the best troops are liable—from a false alarm given by a sentry. Under the impression that the camp was surrounded, the officer in command ordered a random fire, from which the only victims—for no Zulus were near —were some nine men of the regiment. At the battle of Ulundi they were at the right rear angle of the square, on which the Zulu force desperately hurled itself, but the steady fire of the 58th and their comrades repulsed them just when a fierce hand-to-hand fight seemed imminent. When the war with the Boers broke out the 58th were amongst the three British regiments then in the Transvaal, and in January, 1881, some of the regiment were with Sir Pomeroy Colley at the disastrous affair of Laing's Nek. Terrible was the upshot of the day to the gallant Rutlandshire! They led the way up the steep slope, the grass of which was wet and slippery, the surface swept with bullets. For five minutes, the men endured a scathing fire from front and flank; then Colonel Deane gave the word to charge. Scarcely had he uttered it than he fell, mortally wounded; the command devolved upon Major Higginson, but ere long he, too, fell. Major Poole and Lieutenant Dolphin were shot dead; " Captain Lovegrove was wounded and nearly every non-commissioned officer was killed or wounded;" the colours were taken. "Lieutenant Bailie, a mere boy subaltern, but a gallant one, who carried one of the colours, on falling mortally wounded, was succoured by Lieutenant Peel who carried the other. 'Never mind me,' he exclaimed, while choking with blood, 'save the colours.'" Peel then took both colours, but he, too, soon fell; then Sergeant Brindstock seized them, and they were at last rescued by a desperate sally. The command of the regiment devolved upon Captain Hornby, who had been acting with a mounted body, and besides the casualties before referred to Lieutenant O'Donnell was wounded. Lieutenant Peel, it appeared, had not been shot when he fell, but had stumbled into a hole, and he was one of the ten officers who survived that terrible day. The accounts of fiendish cruelty on the part of the Boers were so frequent, that it is with a certain amount of grim satisfaction one reads that "Private Brennan bayoneted a Boer when in the act of shooting at a wounded soldier who lay helpless on the ground, and calling out for mercy." At Majuba Hill there were one hundred and fifty of the terribly attenuated regiment. The tale of that mad but heroic struggle has been before told: of the 58th, Captain the Hon. C. Maude (attached) was killed, Captain Morris and Lieutenants Hill and Lucy wounded, and Captain Hornby prisoner. Of these Lieutenant Lucy was specially complimented in the dispatches of Sir Evelyn Wood for his conspicuous valour. Meanwhile, Captain Saunders of the regiment had been gallantly holding Wakkerstroom, aided by Captain Power and Lieutenant Read, while a detachment under Lieutenant Compton had been with the force, which for twelve weeks had been besieged in Standerton.

Since the war in the Transvaal, in which they suffered so terribly, and fought so bravely, the 58th have not been engaged in any warlike operations which call for notice.*

THE NORTHUMBERLAND FUSILIERS †—Regimental District No. 5—consist of the famous old 5th Foot, and date their corporate existence as a regiment from 1674, though it was not till eleven years later that they were permanently placed on the British

---

* The sobriquets of the 58th are "The Black Cuffs" and "Steelbacks." The former recalls the original facings; the latter is said to have originated in the old flogging days, when the men of the 58th used to pride themselves on bearing the lash without wincing.

† The Northumberland Fusiliers bear as badges on cap and collar St. George and the Dragon on a grenade. The motto is *Quo fata vocant*. On the colours are the Rose and Crown and the King's Crest, with the following distinctions: "Wilhelmstahl," "Roleia," "Vimiera," "Corunna," "Busaco," "Ciudad Rodrigo," "Badajoz," "Salamanca," "Vittoria," "Nivelle," "Orthes," "Toulouse," "Peninsula," "Lucknow," "Afghanistan, 1878—80." The uniform is scarlet with facings of white, and Fusilier's cap with red and white feather.

Establishment. The British legion, which at the first-named date was in Holland, was formed into four regiments—"two English, one Scots, and one Irish. The latter is now designated the 5th Regiment of Foot, or Northumberland Fusiliers" (*Cannon*). They soon, however, dropped the Irish appellation and nationality, and as Fenwick's Regiment gained a high reputation in the wars fought by the Prince of Orange. On this period of their career, however, it is not our purpose to linger, as they were not at that time, strictly speaking, a regiment of the British Army. They accompanied the Prince of Orange when he landed in England, previously to accepting the Crown abandoned by his father-in-law, and from that date the career of the Northumberland Fusiliers is wholly identified with this country. They fought in the Irish Wars against the adherents of James II., and in the abortive foreign expeditions undertaken about that time. In 1693 they went abroad, where they served till the peace of Ryswick. After passing some nine years at home, principally in Ireland, the 5th were ordered, in 1706, to Portugal, where the mere fact of their presence imbued the enemy with a wholesome awe. At Caya, in 1709, the regiment is reported to have "acquired great honour by its signal gallantry;" later on, the attempt made by the Spaniards in 1727 to capture Gibraltar provided another opportunity for the gallant 5th to distinguish themselves. They took part in the expeditions against St. Malo and Cherbourg in 1758, and in 1760 joined the army in Germany and fought at Corbach, Warbourg, Zierenberg, Campen, Kirch-Denkern, Copenhagen, and other places. At Wilhelmstahl they gained their first "distinction," an honour rendered the more valuable since the 5th are the only regiment which bear that name on their colours. An artillery officer, writing at the time, says: "The 5th Foot behaved nobly, and took above twice its own number prisoners." They were allowed to change their caps for those of the French grenadiers they had conquered, and from that time dates the unique privilege they enjoy of wearing a red and white hackle feather on their fusilier caps. This was originally white, but when all infantry regiments were ordered to wear a white feather, the distinctive character of the badge in the case of the Northumberland Fusiliers was perpetuated by theirs being changed to red and white. It is illustrative of the tardiness which characterizes official recognition of military merit that though Wilhelmstahl was fought in 1762, it was not till 1836 that the 5th were allowed to bear the name on their colours. Visitors to Brighton will remember seeing in old Hove Churchyard the tombstone to the memory of Phœbe Hassell. This veritable Amazon had a share in the glories of Wilhelmstahl, having fought in the ranks of the 5th on that occasion. The regiment returned to England in

1763, remaining at home for some ten years, during which time they acquired the nickname of the "shiners," from their remarkable smartness of appearance. In 1767, the regimental order of merit, which has been found to work so well, was instituted. They were dispatched to America in 1774, and came in for the full of the fighting to be had there, taking part in the battles at Concord, Lexington, Bunker's Hill (where it was said that "the 5th behaved the best, and suffered the most"), Long Island, Brooklyn, Whiteplains, and Germantown. They distinguished themselves greatly at St. Lucia, where Brigadier-General Meadows, taking the colours and planting them in the ground, addressed the 5th in the following words: "Soldiers, as long as you have a bayonet to point against an enemy's breast, defend those colours."

The next eighteen years were passed at home and in Canada, and in 1799 the Northumberland Fusiliers were ordered to Holland, where, at Egmont-op-Zee and Winkle, under Colonel Bligh, they earned special praise. In 1806 they served at Buenos Ayres, and two years later joined Wellington's army in Portugal. At Roleia, they were to have formed one column with the 9th and 29th. The two latter regiments, however, by their "fierce neglect of orders" (referred to in treating of the Norfolk Regiment), took another path; the 5th, adhering to the plan marked out, appeared at the critical moment on Laborde's left, and he was eventually forced to retire. They fought at Vimiera; at Corunna the names of Mackenzie and Emes of the regiment were not dimmed even by the brilliant glory which surrounded that of Moore. They were at Flushing. Under Colonel Copson a detachment fought at Talavera; at Busaco they did sterling service; at Redinha and Sabugal they fought. At El Bodon Major Ridge led them forward to charge the French cavalry, retaking the Portuguese artillery that had been captured; later on in the day they successfully resisted, in conjunction with the 77th Regiment, the furious charge of the French horsemen. At Ciudad Rodrigo Ridge again led them to the desperate conflict. At Badajoz, again, though for the last time, he fought at their head, in the thick of the unholy turmoil that raged. The ladders put against the walls were, with their living freights, hurled backwards by the triumphant defenders. Shrieks, groans, oaths, the sickening thud of live, writhing bodies dashed against stone or earth, the clash of steel, the clang of stormers' axes, the crash of musketry, the clamour of cries and curses—amidst all this, " the British, baffled yet untamed, fell back to take shelter under the rugged edge of the hill. There the broken ranks were reformed, and the heroic Colonel Ridge, again springing forward, called with stentorian voice on his men to follow, and, seizing a ladder, raised it against the castle to the right of the former attack, where the wall was lower, and an embrasure offered some facility. A second ladder was placed alongside by the grenadier officer Canch, and the next instant he and Ridge were on the rampart, the shouting troops pressed after them, and the garrison, amazed and in a manner surprised, were driven fighting through the double gate into the town. The castle was won. Soon a reinforcement from the French reserve came to the gate, through which both sides fired, and the enemy retired; but Ridge fell, and no man died that night with more glory—yet many died, and there was much glory." (*Napier*). The 5th fought at Salamanca, and it would seem that it was at this battle that the glorious deception practised by one James Grant, a bandsman, was discovered. According to custom, the bandsmen were invariably left to guard the baggage during an engagement. This did not suit Grant, who was a fine man physically as morally, and, accordingly, he was wont to steal after the combatants, appropriate the first uniform whose wearer was *hors de combat*, and fall in with the grenadier company of the regiment. He fought with the most reckless courage throughout all the battles in which the 5th were engaged, but, strange to say, was never wounded. The 5th fought at Vittoria, at Nivelle, at Orthes and Toulouse. They were then ordered to Canada, the operations in which caused them to miss Waterloo. After serving in the army of occupation for some time, they were quartered in the West Indies, and their next active service (for they were in the Mauritius during the Crimean War) was in India at the Mutiny. They were with Havelock in his march to relieve Lucknow, and vied with the gallant Madras Fusiliers in their splendid courage. They remained in garrison at Lucknow till its final relief by Colin Campbell, and many are the acts of individual heroism recorded of men of the 5th. One of the regiment, Private McManus, was with the gallant little band which, under Surgeon Home, fought so nobly against such overwhelming odds in guarding and rescuing the wounded; at the fight at the Alumbagh, Sergeant Ewart, with some more men of the 5th, rescued their comrade, Private Deveney, who was lying, with a leg shot away, at the mercy of the rebels, who knew not what the term mercy meant. Private McHale on several occasions distinguished himself by his dauntless courage. His speciality seems to have been capturing guns, for at the Alumbagh, and again on the occasion of a sortie from the Lucknow Residency, he took some pieces from the rebels. "On every occasion of attack," says the official report, "Private McHale has been the first to meet the foe, amongst whom he caused such consternation by the boldness of his rush as to leave little work for those who followed to his support. By his habitual coolness and daring and sustained bravery in action, his name has become a household word for gallantry amongst his comrades."

After the relief of Lucknow, the 5th served in Oude, and throughout proved themselves worthy of their lofty traditions. Passing over the intermediate years, during which no active service of note fell to their lot, we find them with the Peshawur field force in the Afghan War of 1878—9, and with the Khyber line in 1880.*

The Oxfordshire Light Infantry† consist of the 43rd and 52nd Regiments. The former—the 43rd—date from 1741, the year following which they embarked for Minorca, where they stayed till 1749, though without seeing any active service. In 1757 they were ordered to Louisburg, having passed the intervening eight years in Ireland, and on the temporary abandonment of that expedition repaired to Nova Scotia. Various skirmishes of no great importance occupied their time here, and the regiment were getting weary of the comparative inaction when the welcome news arrived in 1759 that they were to join the army under General Wolfe. At first it seemed as though their initiation into the severe mysteries of warfare was to be identified with a failure, but the happy inspiration of scaling the heights of Abraham did more than nullify failure, it transformed it into success. At the battle of Quebec the position of the 43rd was in the centre of the first line. The incident and result of that battle are matter of general history. What may not be so generally known is the compliment—recorded by Sir R. Levinge, the historian of the 43rd—made to that regiment by the defeated French. "Never had they known," they admitted, "so fierce a fire or such perfect discipline; as to the centre corps, they levelled and fired *absolument comme un coup de canon*." Another testimony from our foes is recorded by Sir R. Levinge. Almost the last words of the brave Montcalm were, "If I could survive this wound I would engage to beat three times the amount of such forces as I commanded with a third of their number of British troops." After the fall of Quebec the 43rd fought at Sillery, and on peace being signed remained at the former station, from whence in 1762 they proceeded to Mar-

---

* In addition to the nickname above mentioned, the 5th were, during the Peninsular War, known as "The Old Bold Fifth," "The Fighting Fifth," and "Lord Wellesley's Body-Guard"—the last referring to some supposed preference of Lord Wellesley for the gallant regiment.

† The Oxfordshire Light Infantry bear as badge the bugle characteristic of Light Infantry. The motto is that of the Garter. On the colours are the Tudor Rose with the following names:—"Quebec, 1759," "Hindoostan," "Vimiera," "Corunna," "Busaco," "Fuentes d'Onor," "Ciudad Rodrigo," "Badajoz," "Salamanca," "Vittoria," "Nivelle," "Nive," "Orthes," "Toulouse," "Peninsula," "Waterloo," "South Africa, 1851-2-3," "Delhi," "New Zealand." The uniform is scarlet with facings of white. The officers wear shirt collars in "undress" uniform.

THE 43rd—OXFORDSHIRE LIGHT INFANTRY.

tinique.* They fought there and in the Havannah, and in 1764 returned to England, where they remained for ten years, when the troubles of the War of Independence summoned them to America, which they reached the first of all the regiments from England. Under Captain Lawrie they fought at Lexington and Concord; at Bunker's Hill they fought side by side with their future comrades and present 2nd battalion, the 52nd,† and suffered severely. They fought at Long Island with but little loss, at White Plains, Fort Washington, and New York Island, they shared in the victories won by the Royal troops. At Quaker's Hill, in 1778, they particularly distinguished themselves, as, indeed, they did throughout the unfortunate war which resulted in the independence of America. After the termination of the war they remained in England ten years, and in 1794 were ordered to Martinique, where they suffered terribly from the climate, an experience which was renewed three years later when they again served in the West Indies. Despite, however, the hostility of the climate, not a few—when the regiment was, in 1800, ordered home—elected to stay and volunteer into the West India regiments. In 1803 they received the formal denomination of Light Infantry, which in the case of the 43rd, more perhaps than in that of any other regiment, has remained as an especially distinctive appellation. In the following year there joined the ranks of the 43rd, as captain, their future commander and eulogist, Sir W. Napier, from whose brilliant pages we have so often quoted. The regiment was amongst those stationed at Shorncliffe during the scare of the threatened French invasion, and, like their companions of the Rifles, acquired considerable proficiency as marksmen. Under Colonel Stewart they took part in the expedition against Copenhagen in 1807, and with the 52nd and 92nd were brigaded under Sir Arthur Wellesley. On their return to England the ship, in which a considerable number of the regiment were, struck and for some time it seemed as though all on board would be lost. With Ensign Neale, however, the approach of death in no wise abated either his pluck or sense of the proprieties. Amongst his baggage was a flute on which he was no bad performer; routing it out he proceeded to play the "Dead March in *Saul*." *Abfuit omen!* The crew and soldiers were saved, and Ensign Neale, some years after, exchanged the sword for the stole and took holy orders.

* A curious incident is related by the writer above quoted. In 1761 the 43rd, under Major Elliott, were wrecked on Sable Island. In 1842 a violent storm swept over the island and completely swept away a big pyramid of sand, which had always excited curiosity. Huts were disclosed, and on investigation countless relics of the dead-and-gone warriors of the old 43rd were discovered—furniture, boxes, bullets, clothes, shoes, and innumerable smaller articles, including "a tiny brass dog collar with 'Major Elliott, 43rd Regiment,' engraven."

† Sir R. Levinge states that each regiment had at one time been numbered 54th.

With the Peninsular war proper the most brilliant glories of the 43rd may be said to commence. There was scarcely a combat or a skirmish in which they were not engaged, scarcely—if, indeed, even that limitation is not too exclusive—a report in which they were not praised. With the 52nd and 95th they formed the famous Light Division, to whose splendid prowess so much of the success of the British Army was due. It scarcely needs an apology under any circumstances to quote from a writer like Napier, but in dealing with the 43rd—his own regiment—quotation ceases to be merely allowable and becomes obligatory. It is not our province to attempt nicely to discriminate between the relative merits of strategic movements, or to question how far the loyalty of the warrior to his own corps may instinctively guide the pen of the military historian; in Napier's pages the deeds of the Light Division, and notably of the 43rd, are portrayed in colours brilliant and undying, and the Peninsular record of the 43rd will be best given, by presenting that portraiture as it came from his pen. At Vimiera the attack of the regiment was well timed. The steadfast hail of our artillery had thrown the French into some confusion; "the moment was happily seized by the 43rd; they poured down in a solid mass and with ringing shouts dashed against the column, driving it back with irrecoverable disorder, yet not without the fiercest fighting. The loss of the regiment was a hundred and twenty, and when the charge was over, a French soldier and the Sergeant-Armourer, Patrick, were found grimly confronting each other in death as they had done in life, their hands still clutching their muskets, and their bayonets plunged to the socket in each manly breast! It is by such men that thousands are animated and battles won." It was about this time that Sergeant Newman of the regiment gained his commission. He had been left behind in charge of a company of invalids, and by his energy and endurance beat off continued charges of French cavalry. As an example of the martial ardour that animated the regiment may be instanced the fact that, in their eagerness to be in time for the fight at Corunna, many men came to take their places in the ranks *crawling on hands and knees*, so fearfully lacerated were their feet!

The 2nd battalion—for the 1st had not hitherto been engaged in the Peninsula—was ordered home to recruit, and subsequently took part in the Walcheren expedition. The disastrous nature of that exploit has been before referred to: the historian of the 43rd throws an additional light on the ghastly picture when he tells us that, so fatal was the climate, in a fortnight no fewer than twelve thousand men were stricken down.

Fearfully sudden, too, were the attacks of the dread pestilence. Men would be marching gaily in the ranks or sitting idly in camp when they would reel and stumble, and a few hours afterwards only a livid corpse or a human wreck, whose days were surely numbered, remained to bear witness to the soldier that had been. Years after, when the terrible Crimean cholera was filling hospitals and cemeteries by that "dolorous midland sea," a writer*—whose works make us sigh regretfully "for the touch of a vanished hand"—wrote of two young soldiers who sat chatting together in the sweltering, death-fraught, heat. " And Charles told his comrade about Ravenshoe, about the deer and the pheasants and the blackcock, and about the big trout that lay nosing up into the swift places in the cool, clear water. And suddenly the lad turned on him, with his handsome face livid with agony and horror, and clutched him convulsively by both arms, and prayed him, for God Almighty's sake—There, that will do. The poor lad was dead in four hours." The passage is from a work of fiction—*oh, si sic omnia!*—it is true, but it was a faithful description of what took place in the Crimea, and might, with equally exact veracity, have been penned about Walcheren.

After this, both battalions of the regiment joined the allied forces in the Peninsula. The Douro was forced and Talavera won; and though the regiment was not at the latter battle, the march they made in their endeavours to be in time is reckoned one of the most remarkable in military annals. As a matter of fact, about a hundred of the regiment *were* present, having been earlier separated from the main body.

The combat on the Coa, where the 43rd were under command of Major M'Leod, "a young man endowed with a natural genius for war," may almost be said to have been won by them and the gallant 52nd. Two incidents related by Napier may be given, each illustrative of what manner of men the 43rd were composed. A soldier named Stewart, nicknamed "the Boy," because of his youth and gigantic stature and strength, was one of the last men who came down to the bridge, but he would not pass. "Turning round, he regarded the French with a grim look and spoke aloud as follows: 'So! this is the end of our boasting. This is our first battle, and we retreat. "The Boy" Stewart will not live to hear that said.' Then striding forward in his giant might he fell furiously on the nearest enemies with the bayonet, refused the quarter they seemed desirous of granting, and died fighting in the midst of them. Still more touching, more noble, more heroic, was the death of Sergeant Robert M'Quade. During M'Leod's

* Henry Kingsley, "Ravenshoe."

rush, this man* saw two Frenchmen level their muskets on rests against a high gap in the bank awaiting the uprise of an enemy. Sir George Brown, then a lad of sixteen, attempted to ascend to the fatal point, but M'Quade, himself only twenty-four years of age, pulled him back, saying, with a calm, decided tone, 'You are too young, sir, to be killed.' And then offering his own person to the fire, fell dead, pierced with both balls."

The 43rd fought at Busaco and Redinha; at Cazal Novo Napier was wounded; at Sabugal Captain Hopkins of the regiment did much to win the fight described by Wellington, "as one of the most glorious actions British troops were ever engaged in." Under Colonel Patrickson they captured a howitzer round which, when the battle ended, most of the slain were found heaped. Great was their glory at Ciudad Rodrigo, greater still at Badajoz, where the heroic Macleod, "whose feeble body would have been quite unfit for war if it had not been sustained by an unconquerable spirit," fell dead; where the "intrepid Lieutenant Shaw" stood for awhile alone on the ramparts he only had gained; and where Ferguson, "who having at Rodrigo received two deep wounds, was present, with his hurts still open, leading the stormers of his regiment, the third time a volunteer and the third time wounded." The loss of the 43rd exceeded that of any other regiment, twenty officers and three hundred and thirty-five sergeants and privates were killed and wounded. At Salamanca it is recorded of the regiment that the "43rd made a very extraordinary advance in line for a distance of three miles under a cannonade with as clear and firm a front as at a review." When, during the retreat from Madrid, the disgraceful ingratitude of the Spaniards culminated in wanton insults and outrages upon our troops—to whom they well-nigh owed their existence—the 43rd were conspicuous in teaching the insolent Don that the British and their allies were not to be thus treated with impunity. On one occasion, "the Prince of Orange remonstrating about his quarters with the sitting Junta, they ordered one of their guards to kill him; and he would have been killed had not Lieutenant Steele of the 43rd, a bold, athletic person, felled the man before he could stab." At the Huebra they and the Riflemen supported the guns defending the higher fords; at Vittoria the gallant regiment was for awhile "in a most extraordinary situation, at the elbow of the French position, isolated from the rest of the army, within a few hundred paces of Joseph with his 5,000 Guards." At Echellar—one of the battles of the "Pyrenees"—Sergeant Blood undoubtedly saved the British cause from the incalculable disaster that would have ensued from the capture of Wellington. The great general had taken half a company of the 43rd as an escort

* Both Stewart and M'Quade hailed from the North of Ireland.

while he examined his plans of the country. The French stealing on in force would inevitably have made him prisoner, had not Sergeant Blood, leaping headlong down the precipitous rocks adjoining the pass, given timely and effective warning.

Amongst the killed at St. Sebastian was Lieutenant J. O'Connell of the 43rd, a near connection of the Agitator. He had been in several storming parties before this, and seeking here again "in such dangerous service the promotion he had earned before without receiving—he found death." They fought on the Bidassoa; at Vera a strong force of Spanish was kept in check by a formidable abbatis, from behind which two French regiments poured a heavy fire. Despite all exhortations from their own officers they would not advance; "but there happened to be present," says Napier, "an officer of the 43rd regiment named Havelock. His fiery temper could not brook the check. He took off his hat, called upon the Spaniards, and, putting spurs to his horse, at one bound cleared the abbatis, and went headlong among the enemy. Then the soldiers, shouting for 'the fair boy,' so they called him, for he was very young and had light hair, with one shock broke through the French." The mere mention of "Nivelle" brings to mind the splendid heroism the regiment there displayed. The defences were well built and strongly manned, "but strong and valiant in arms must the soldiers have been who stood in that hour before the veterans of the 43rd." Throughout that day the famous Light Division fought, as even the heroes who composed it had scarcely fought before; pitted against overwhelming odds they forced the French back till the victory was won. Heavy was the loss, and amongst the slain were Freer and Lloyd of the 43rd, of whom their comrade in arms writes with a power and pathos all his own: "The first, low in rank, being but a lieutenant, was rich in honour, for he bore many scars, and was young of days. He was only nineteen, and had seen more combats and sieges than he could count years. Slight in person, and of such surpassing and delicate beauty that the Spaniards often thought him a girl disguised in man's clothing, he was yet so vigorous, so active, so brave, that the most daring and experienced veterans watched his looks on the field of battle, and would obey his slightest sign in the most difficult situations. His education was incomplete, yet his natural powers were so happy that the keenest and best-furnished intellects shrank from an encounter of wit, and all his thoughts and aspirations were proud and noble, indicating future greatness if destiny had so willed it. Such was Edward Freer of the 43rd, one of three brothers, who all died in the Spanish war. Assailed the night before the battle with that strange anticipation of coming death so often felt by military men, he was pierced with three balls at the first storming of the Rhune rocks, and the sternest soldiers in the regiment wept even in the middle of the fight when they heard of his fate."

The regiment fought at the Nive; at Arcangues, some of the regiment and a few Riflemen—about a hundred in all—were cut off by the French. The officer commanding the little British force was Ensign Campbell of the 43rd, a boy of eighteen, and the French seemed to entertain no doubt that so youthful a commander would surrender to their vastly superior number. But British pluck and dash, contempt of death and scorn of odds, do not "tarry till the beard be grown," or man's estate attained. Ensign Campbell was a brave gentleman and an officer of the 43rd to boot, so with shout and waving sword he led his seemingly doomed band against the astounded French, broke through them and reached a position of safety, though half of his followers were taken prisoners. There remained but a few more laurels to be won in the Peninsula; they were to gain "Toulouse" on their colours before the hardly won peace allowed of the return to England of her conquering army. But the stay there of the 43rd was little more than a flying visit. They were ordered to America, where dissensions were still rife, and thus missed being present at Waterloo. For a long time after that their victorious weapons were idle; in 1837 they took part in the suppression of the revolt in Canada, and fifteen years later were engaged in the Kaffir War. Here they were under Lieutenant-Colonel Skipwith, and in the attack on the Water Kloof formed part of the right column, losing in the assault a very promising officer, the Hon. H. Wrottesley, who fell mortally wounded. A sergeant and forty men under Lieutenant Giradot were on the ill-fated *Birkenhead,* and the Lieutenant was one of the fortunate few that escaped. From the Cape the regiment was ordered to India, and it is needless here to dwell on the sterling service they performed during and after the mutiny.* The next warfare in which "the fighting 43rd" were engaged was in New Zealand, 1861—3, and the campaign was in many respects a disastrous one for the regiment. The unfortunate repulse our troops experienced at the Gate Pah in April, 1861, caused at the time a bitter disgust amongst the troops, and none deplored it more keenly than the men of the 43rd. Lieutenant-Colonel Booth commanding the regiment was mortally wounded; amongst the killed were two brothers, R. C. Glover and F. S. G. Glover, both subalterns of the 43rd. The elder fell "in the foremost of the fray, and the younger, who loved him with more than a

* Amongst the Victoria crosses gained by our soldiers during that eventful time was one presented to Private H. E. Addison of the 43rd for gallantly defending a political officer in an engagement near Kunereah in January, 1859. Addison, besides losing a leg, received two serious wounds.

brother's love, rushed forward with a loud and bitter cry. It was in vain that he raised him in his arms and strove to bear him from the field; a hostile bullet brought both the brothers to the ground, and left them side by side with the tide of life ebbing fast away." Captain Hamilton, "one of a race of soldiers, and who had marched with Havelock to Lucknow," was shot through the head; seven men were taken prisoners by the fierce foe. When New Zealand was quiet again the regiment returned to England, leaving again a few years later for India, where, in 1873, they shared in the fighting consequent on the troubles in Malabar. Since that time no campaign of note has claimed the services of the 43rd.

The 52nd Regiment, the 2nd battalion of the Oxfordshire Light Infantry to which it gives the title, dates from 1775, when it was formed and numbered the 54th. Immediately after its completion the regiment was ordered to America, and throughout the war the gallant Oxford Light Infantry of the near future gave ample promise of the fame they were to win. At Bunker's Hill they won particular distinction, the whole of the grenadier company, with the exception of eight men, being either killed or wounded. It is not our purpose to follow the fortunes of the 52nd throughout the war. In all the battles they fought well and bravely, and when, in 1778, they returned home, it was acknowledged that few regiments with only a history of three years could show its page more fairly writ. Five years later—by which time they had received the title of the Oxfordshire Regiment—they were ordered to India, and participated in the siege of Cannanore, at which the forlorn hope supplied by the regiment had nearly every man killed or wounded. They fought in the subsequent campaign against Tippoo Sahib, being frequently brigaded with the 36th Regiment under Major Shelley. Lieutenant J. Evans of the 52nd was second in command of the storming party which forced its way into Bangalore; at Savendroog they were hotly engaged; at Seringapatam they not improbably saved the day by rescuing the Governor, Lord Cornwallis, from the imminent danger in which he was placed. After seventeen years of service in India the regiment returned home in 1800, many of the effective rank and file being transferred to the 77th and 80th Regiments. In 1803 a 2nd battalion which had been formed was constituted, as has been before mentioned, the 96th Regiment, and the remaining battalion received the distinctive appellation of "Light Infantry."

They were brigaded under Moore at Shorncliffe, and on the occasion of a review by the commander-in-chief, His Royal Highness was so impressed with their soldierly appearance that he recommended to the King that "promotion should be more extensive in that corps than had been usually granted." They served in Sicily and at Copenhagen; they were amongst the troops ordered to form General Moore's force for the defence of Sweden; and then the 2nd battalion, at that time recently formed, commenced the tale of Peninsular triumphs by its participations in the battle of Vimiera, where the 52nd and their present 1st battalion fought together under Anstruther. Both battalions were at Corunna, where they made some prisoners, and lost in the brilliant general, to whom the famous victory was due, the Colonel-in-chief of their regiment. After returning home the 1st battalion repaired to Portugal, and formed with the 43rd and 95th the famous Light Division.

It will be seen, from what has been said in dealing with the 43rd, that to write anything like a full account of the doings of this division would be to transcribe the history of the Peninsular War. We must be content with noticing here and there some—and those but a few—of the incidents in which the 52nd were more particularly concerned. At the combat on the Coa, they and the 43rd particularly distinguished themselves at the bridge, and after the battle was over, Lieutenant Dawson of the regiment gained great credit by the masterly manner in which, after being isolated from the main body of the army, he effected a junction with it, though to do so necessitated passing through the enemy's posts. At Busaco their splendid charge resulted in the defeat of the French, whose General Simon surrendered to Privates Hopkins and Harris. At Redinha, by some oversight they were placed in a position of extreme danger, being ordered to move forward blindly into a mass of fog, which, when it rose, "disclosed the 52nd on the slopes of the opposite mountain closely engaged in the midst of an army." They fought with great credit at Caza Nova and Sabugal, and a somewhat amusing anecdote is related of a private of the regiment in the latter battle. Private Patrick Lowe, though he had, as beseemed a 52nd man, the soul of a hero, was, in his physical formation, round and small and fat. During a skirmish his company, being threatened by a cavalry charge, fell back, but Pat, unfortunately, could not beat a sufficiently speedy retreat, and an impetuous dragoon was rapidly gaining on him. Undismayed, however, he faced about and covered his pursuer with his musket. Vainly did the dragoon try to disconcert his aim; wheel and curvet as he would that grim piece of gun metal and Pat's grimmer face behind it threatened him with certain death if he came on. So he fell back, and Pat rejoined his comrades without—to every one's surprise—shooting his antagonist. An officer took him roundly to task for this omission: "You were a fool to let the man go without shooting him." "Och, then, an' is it shooting ye mane?" responded Pat; "shure an' how could I shoot him *when I wasn't loaded at all, at all!*" At Marialva Captain Dobbs, with a single bayonet company and some riflemen, held the bridge against two thousand French; at Fuentes d'Onor the enemies' cavalry strove in vain to break the resolute squares of the Light Division. At Ciudad Rodrigo the ardour of the stormers of the Division would not allow them to wait for the hay-bags; they "jumped down the scarp, a depth of eleven feet, and rushed up the *fausse braie* under a smashing discharge of grape and musketry." Lord Wellington, in his dispatches, was betrayed into praises of a degree unusually high for him. "I cannot," he wrote, "sufficiently applaud the conduct of Colonel Colborne and of the detachment under his command." Napier and Dobbs and Gurwood were the other officers of the 52nd that forced themselves to the front at Ciudad Rodrigo; to the last named surrendered the French commander, Barrie, whose sword Wellington publicly presented to his gallant captor "on the breach by which Gurwood had entered, a fitting and proud compliment to a young soldier of fortune." At Badajoz—the assault of Picuria—Stewart and Nixon greatly excelled, while at the final storming the splendid gallantry of the Oxfordshire may be gauged by the fact that the 43rd and 52nd Regiments of the Light Division alone lost more men than the seven regiments engaged at the Castle. They fought at Salamanca and the Huebra; at Vittoria the 52nd Regiment, with an impetuous charge, carried the village of Margarita; the courage of the stormers at St. Sebastian has passed into a proverb; at Schelar and Vera and throughout the battles of the Pyrenees, the Oxfordshire Light Infantry were ever foremost; at the Nivelle, under their gallant leader Colborne, they were severely and gloriously engaged. An untoward occurrence cost the lives of many of their brave band to be needlessly sacrificed. A staff officer, acting on some misunderstanding, ordered Colborne to advance against the signal redoubt which was being obstinately defended by the enemy. "It was not a moment for remonstrance; on the top of the hill the troops made their rush, but then a ditch, thirty feet deep, well fraised and palisaded, stopped them short, and the fire of the enemy stretched the foremost in death." Colborne—who escaped by a miracle, as he was ever at the head of his men on horseback—made three different attempts to carry the work; then, calling the fox to the aid of the lion, he advanced alone with a white flag of truce, and showing the French commandant that he was completely surrounded, persuaded him to surrender. This he did, "only having one man killed, but on the British side there fell two hundred soldiers, victims to the presumptuous folly of a young staff officer." At Orthes, "Colonel

Colborne, so often distinguished, led the regiment across the marsh under a skirmishing fire, the men sinking at every step above the knees, in some places to the middle; yet still pressing forward with that stern resolution and order to be expected from the veterans of the Light Division, soldiers who had never yet met their match in the field." They fought at Toulouse; at Waterloo "the fate of the battle seemed to hang in the balance when the gallant 52nd, under Colborne of Peninsular glory, moved down upon the left flank of the Imperial Guard." The fire of such a regiment gave pause to the splendid column of the foe; the Rifles and other regiments coming up joined their volleys with those of the 52nd; the enemy wavered and swayed, and ere long their colonel's well-known voice called upon the regiment to charge, and the last great battle between the English and French had been fought and won.

The 52nd went into battle probably the strongest numerically of any regiment present, numbering, as they did, upwards of a thousand men; the casualties were one officer, one sergeant, and thirty-six rank and file killed; eight officers, ten sergeants, and a hundred and fifty rank and file wounded.

The 2nd battalion meanwhile had been engaged in Holland under Lieutenant-Colonel Gibbs. They distinguished themselves at Merxem, and Captain Diggle, who commanded on that occasion, mentions in his account that King William IV., then Duke of Clarence, was often to be seen "riding about the village, the skirts of his great-coat perforated by a bullet and wholly regardless of danger, as is the wont of the Royal family."

After Waterloo the 52nd were stationed in various places, including America, Canada, the West Indies, and India. At the time of the mutiny, they showed that the forty years which had passed since Waterloo had wrought no deterioration in their matchless efficiency. It is impossible to dwell upon all the varied proofs they gave of this; one will speak for all, and their deeds at the capture of Delhi rank with any in the long struggle in the Peninsula. The blowing open of the Cashmere Gate was entrusted to a party amongst which was Bugler Hawthorne of the 52nd. Under a heavy fire they proceeded to lay the powder against the gates; officer after officer fell before the massive gate was blown up; then Hawthorne was ordered to sound the advance to his regiment. Three times had he to sound before the notes could be heard amidst the din; then, under Colonel Campbell, the regiment dashed forward like greyhounds from the leash, and secured the barrier. For this feat Hawthorne received the Victoria Cross, and on the same occasion Corporal Henry Smith gained the same distinction for gallantly bearing off a wounded comrade. The histories of the mutiny teem with the deeds of the regiment, telling how Seymour and Blane, Vigors, Synge, Monsoon, Crosse, and Bayley were brave amongst the brave, but our sketch must here cease. No important service has since then fallen to the lot of the old Oxfordshire Light Infantry—"a regiment never surpassed in arms since arms were first borne by men."

THE RIFLE BRIGADE,* the Prince Consort's Own, takes precedence after the Argyll and Sutherland Highlanders, its number when first formed being the 95th. In the case of such a "regiment" as the Rifle Brigade, the compiler of any *short* account suffers from a veritable *embarras de richesses*. The Rifle Brigade, under its present or former designation, has fought everywhere; its doings have been chronicled by an enthusiastic historian,† it is a *corps d'élite*, and the various battalions of which from time to time it has been composed —the present number is four—have been, each of them, practically distinct regiments in all but name. In 1800 the commanders of fourteen regiments (2nd battalion Royals, 21st, 23rd, 25th, 27th, 29th, 49th, 55th, 69th, 71st, 72nd, 79th, 85th, and 92nd) received a communication from the Horse Guards, to the effect that it was intended to form a corps "to be instructed in the use of the rifle," and requesting them to select four non-commissioned officers and thirty men, and to recommend three officers for the purpose of forming the corps. This was in January, and so favourably was the project viewed, and so apt in their new duties did the new regiment prove, that in the following August three companies embarked with the expedition under General Pulteney against Spain. Shortly after this service—in which the chosen companies most creditably acquitted themselves—the regiment was formed, and the commissions of the officers dated the 25th August, the day on which they had a skirmish with the Spanish. The first duty of the corps as a perfected body seems to have been a sort of marine service at the bombardment of Copenhagen. In December, 1802, they were numbered the 95th, and

---

* The Rifle Brigade bear as badges a bugle on the glengarry. On the helmet plate is a bugle with strings on a Maltese Cross "surmounted by a wreath of laurel, with which is intertwined a scroll bearing the battles of Sebastopol, Alma, and Inkerman. The other battles are recorded on the arms of the cross, the whole is surmounted by the Prince Consort's coronet with 'Waterloo' below it. A lion is placed between each division of the cross." The motto is "Treu und fest." The following are the battles inscribed: "Copenhagen," "Monte Video," "Roleia," "Vimiera," "Corunna," "Busaco," "Barossa," "Fuentes d'Onor," "Ciudad Rodrigo," "Badajoz," "Salamanca," "Vittoria," "Nivelle," "Nive," "Orthes," "Toulouse," "Peninsula," "Waterloo," "South Africa, 1846—7," "South Africa 1851—2—3," "Alma," "Inkerman," "Sebastopol," "Lucknow," "Ashantee," "Ali Masjid," "Afghanistan 1878—9." The uniform is dark green with facings of black. The black racoon skin caps were exchanged for the helmet three or four years ago, but it is hoped that before long the more distinctive head-dress will be resumed.

† Sir Wm. Cope.

the following year, in Sir John Moore's camp of instruction at Shorncliffe, " first met and were brigaded with, as their compeers, the 43rd and 52nd, in united action with whom, as the Light Division in the Peninsula, so many of their laurels were won." In 1805 a second battalion was formed, and the first battalion was ordered to Germany, where, however, nothing more arduous than a military promenade occupied its attention. In 1807 the 2nd battalion joined the force under Sir Samuel Auchmuty destined for South America, and greatly distinguished itself at the taking of Monte Video. In 1807 the regiment* fought at Monte Video with the most marked valour, losing ninety-one of all ranks killed, and having double that number wounded and missing. Meanwhile, other companies of the regiment joined Lord Cathcart's expedition against Copenhagen, " where they first served under the immediate command of the great chief who commanded the advance; under whose eye they were so often to fight, whose praise they were so often to receive, their future Colonel, then Major-General Sir Arthur Wellesley," and during the campaign their " gallant style," their " conduct and steadiness," were more than once referred to in dispatches. The following year they joined the British Army in Portugal, and first engaged the enemy at Obeidos, in conjunction with their comrades of the King's Royal Rifle Corps. They fought with great dash and spirit at Roleia; at Vimiera the historian of the regiment relates that " three brothers of the name of Hart, privates in the 2nd battalion, pressed on the French with such daring intrepidity that Lieutenant Molloy, who himself was never far from his opponent in action, was obliged repeatedly to rebuke them. ' D—n you !' he cried, ' keep back and get under cover. Do you think you are fighting with your fists that you run into the teeth of the French ? ' " The 2nd battalion suffered very severely that day, one fourth of their number being put *hors de combat.* During the retreat to Corunna, under Moore, the 95th proved themselves invaluable, covering the movements of the other troops, and holding positions against the utmost efforts of the foe. During the battle at Corunna itself, the 1st battalion had a sort of duel with two battalions of Voltigeurs. The 95th had just made a brilliant charge against the enemy's artillery, when the Voltigeurs came to the rescue, causing them to fall back for a moment. They soon rallied, and for two hours kept up a sharp skirmish with their opponents, and in the end gained a complete victory, taking prisoners seven officers and one hundred and fifty-six men. The 95th was the last corps to enter Corunna, having acted as the rear-guard, and almost before they were embarked the enemy were firing on the ships. Their losses during the past

* Space will not allow of the battalions being in all cases particularized.

twenty days were one hundred and thirty-six killed or prisoners and thirty-five wounded.*

About this time—such was the popularity and evident value of the regiment—a third battalion was raised, the command of which devolved upon Andrew Barnard of the Royals, whose name in connection with the deeds of the Brigade is so familiar to all readers of the history of the Peninsular War. In May, 1809, the 1st battalion were brigaded with the 43rd and 52nd into the Light Brigade, to relate whose prowess would be to write anew the campaign which ended at Waterloo. Very severe were the hardships which the battalion experienced from the very first. In addition to the enemy, they had daily to reckon with that terrible foe—threatening Starvation. The discipline enforced by Crauford, their brigadier, was "Draconic" in its severity. Almost their first feat was, in their haste to reach Talavera, "in heavy marching order, under a burning sun, and with a most insufficient supply of food, to march upwards of fifty miles with only two short halts in twenty-five hours." Soon afterwards, at Barta del Puerco, they elicited praise even from the stern Crauford; in the battle on the Coa, they again fought splendidly and suffered severely. At Busaco, the charge of the Light Division was one of the most brilliant episodes of the war. Meanwhile, the 2nd battalion had been fighting in the Walcheren expedition, on its return from which, detachments were sent to join their comrades in Portugal, whither the 3rd battalion, under Barnard, proceeded in July, 1810. At Barossa, this battalion and some of the 2nd particularly distinguished themselves, the brave Barnard being twice wounded. After Redinha, an incident occurred which shows in a marked way the courteous feeling reciprocated by the English and French. The 1st battalion were driving the French before them, when the officer commanding the latter waved his handkerchief at the end of his sword. On the officer of the 95th coming up, the Frenchman suggested that both sides would be the better for a night's rest, and proposed a truce. The Rifles consented, and invited the French officers to share their mess, an overture which was gladly accepted, though the menu only disclosed ration beef, and little enough of that, with rum to wash it down. After dinner they separated, and the next morning the French resumed their retreat, and the Rifles their pursuit. The 95th distinguished them-

* In the account of the battles one is apt sometimes to lose sight of the less romantic aspect of the horrors of war. The following description shows it in all its naked hideousness. "The appearance of the battalion on their arrival in England was squalid and miserable. Most of the men had lost some of their appointments; many were without shoes, and their clothing was not only tattered and in rags, but in such a state of filth and so infested with vermin that on new clothing being served out it was burnt at the back of Hythe barracks."

selves at Sabugal; at Fuentes d'Onor, the repulse they inflicted on a strong body of French infantry was mentioned in Lord Wellesley's dispatches. In the various engagements which preceded the storming of Ciudad Rodrigo they rendered sterling service. At that storming, there is no need here to dwell upon the brilliant achievements of the Rifles—how Uniacke was killed, and Cox and Hamilton, Mitchell, M'Gregor, and Bedell were wounded; how Crauford, the gallant though stern commander of the Light Division, fell, cheering on his men; or how many brave men of the 95th slept that night the "sleep that never wakes." At the storming of Badajoz, again, the part they played is well known. Some led the Light Division; seven officers and a hundred men of the 95th formed part of the storming party. With the forlorn hope were nine non-commissioned officers of the regiment. The incidents of that direful day are history; twenty-three officers and two hundred and ninety-two non-commissioned officers and men of the Rifles were killed or wounded. Napier's splendid description is aptly quoted by Cope in its relation to the regiment. "Who shall measure out the glory of . . . . O'Hara of the 95th, who perished in the breach at the head of the stormers, and with him, nearly all the volunteers for that desperate service? Who shall describe . . . . the martial fury of that desperate soldier of the 95th who, in his resolution to win, thrust himself beneath the chained sword-blades, and there suffered the enemy to dash his head to pieces with the ends of their muskets?" To these might be added—only to mention the names of the killed—Stokes and Diggle, Hovenden, Cary, Alix, Crondace, Macdonald and Macpherson, of the last of whom it was said that "he had been true to man, and true to his God, and he looked his last hour in the face like a soldier and a Christian." It might be mentioned here that Sir Harry Smith, the hero of Aliwal in after years, gained his wife in a way that recalls the pages of some romance. After the terrible sack which followed the capture of Badajoz, two Spanish ladies of rank, the younger about fourteen, approached Smith, then a captain in the Rifles, who was talking with another officer, and threw themselves on the protection of the English. Their appearance showed the cruelty to which they had been subjected; their ears were bleeding from the brutal gash which had torn away their earrings, and to avoid worse and nameless shame, they had resolved to confide to the honour of the first British officer they met. The younger of the two ladies became, ere two years had passed, the wife of the officer who had saved her. In the battle of Salamanca, the brigade was not very actively engaged, and from that date till the battle of Vittoria, though privation and arduous labour, enough and to spare, fell to their lot, their participation in actual warfare was limited to a few skirmishes. Their historian claims for them that theirs was the regiment which commenced the battle of Vittoria, during which their dark uniform more than once exposed them to the fire of our own men, who mistook them for the enemy. They also captured the first guns which were taken from the French in the engagement, and throughout the day fully merited the enthusiastic praise which has been awarded to them. Their loss was twelve of all ranks killed; seven officers and sixty men wounded.

During the pursuit of the flying foe, some of the Riflemen were mounted behind the troopers of the Royal Dragoons, and it is interesting to note that in the sharp skirmish which they had on the Camino Real, they were fortunate enough to take "the last and only gun which the French carried off from Vittoria." At Schelar, one of the battles included in the "Pyrenees," they greatly distinguished themselves; but perhaps the combat at the Bridge of Jansi, where they had marched under a hot sun, and with frequent want of water, about eight leagues, "considering that it was made in the heat of an August sun, and that at the end of the march the men had four or five hours' hard fighting, may hold its place with the famous march from Calzada to Talavera . . . . It was said that two hundred men of one regiment of the Light Division fell out. But the Riflemen had a resolution to excel, and many held on till they died." At the storming of St. Sebastian, the regiment was represented by a subaltern and fifty men from each battalion. The names of the officers were Percival, Hamilton and Eaton, and the two former were desperately wounded. At the Bridge of Vera, the regiment suffered terrible loss, which their historian attributes in great measure to the ill-advised order of General Skerrett, by which Captain Cadoux, whose company held the bridge, was compelled to withdraw. The order was so peremptory that he had no choice left, but even while obeying, he remarked that "but few of his party would reach the camp." And so it proved. Up till then he had not lost a man; before many minutes had elapsed, Cadoux himself and sixteen others were killed, three officers, nine sergeants and thirty-four rank and file wounded out of a total of a hundred, all told. Again, at the battle of the Nivelle, where their gallant leader Sir Andrew Barnard was severely wounded, the regiment incurred very heavy loss. Sundry sharp skirmishes preceded the battle of the Nive in which the regiment played a leading part. They were not very actively employed at Orthes, the 1st battalion, indeed, being absent altogether. At the hard-fought battle of Tarbes, however, on the 20th of March, 1814, they had most of the fighting to themselves, and after a fierce struggle, during which "they fought muzzle to muzzle, and it was difficult to judge at first who would win," drove the French before them in disordered flight. At a skirmish which took place a few days afterwards a most extraordinary incident occurred, which—were it not for the character of the narrators and the evidence adduced—one would be tempted to ascribe to some latter-day Munchausen. "A Rifleman of the name of Powell was shot in the mouth, the ball knocking several of his teeth out. One of these struck a Portuguese and wounded him in the arm. The surgeon of the 43rd, who happened to be at hand, dressing the wound of the Portuguese, found in it not a bullet but a tooth. On this the cry went among the Riflemen that 'the French were firing bones and not bullets.'" At the battle of Toulouse the regiment was again actively engaged, and on the termination of the war returned to England. Meanwhile the 95th had been represented by detachments which gloriously upheld the honour of the regiment at Bergen-op-Zoom, Merxem, and other places in Holland. Scarcely had peace been secured with France than some of the regiment—the 3rd battalion—were ordered to New Orleans, and in the very arduous and not altogether satisfactory campaign which was sandwiched in between the war in the Peninsula and Waterloo proved themselves of the utmost value. At Quatre-Bras the 1st battalion enjoyed the distinction of being the first to engage with the enemy. At Waterloo the 1st battalion was with Picton, and the 2nd and part of the 3rd with Sir Frederick Adams. Very early in the day did the former come into action, while the latter were engaged in the fierce fighting that raged round Hougoumont, and in the splendid charge which completed the discomfiture of the Imperial Guard.* The losses of the regiment during the day were very severe, and their conduct was most highly praised. They stayed with the army of occupation, and in the February following Waterloo were removed from the regiments of the line, ceasing to be known as the 95th and receiving their present appellation of the Rifle Brigade.

The years following Waterloo must be passed over rapidly. There were disturbances in Ireland, *émeutes* in Birmingham, sundry and divers other occasions on which the Rifle Brigade was engaged, but it was not till 1846 that they were again employed in foreign service. At that date troubles arose in South Africa, and we wish that space would allow us to recount in detail all the brave deeds and services performed by the Rifle Brigade. It

---

* Another remarkable occurrence is narrated by Sir W. Cope, quoting Kincaid, which, he adds, has been confirmed to him by independent testimony. Lieutenant Worsley, of the 3rd battalion, "had at Badajoz received a shot in his ear which came out at the back of the neck, which on his recovery had the effect of turning his head to the right; at Waterloo he received exactly a similar wound in the left ear, the ball coming out near the exit of the former, which restored his head to its original position."

must suffice to repeat the dictum of an historian quoted by the chronicler of their deeds. "It was the useful green jacket, the untiring Rifle Brigade, who worried Sandilli out of his hiding place among the mountains." After fighting the natives it became necessary to teach the Boers a lesson, and this was most effectually done at Boemplatz, though the result to the representatives of the Rifle Brigade was that the command of both companies devolved upon second lieutenants. The general orders issued on the departure of the Rifles for England contained the following paragraph: "In 1805 the commander-in-chief, Sir H. Smith, joined this (1st) battalion. . . . He has served with it during the most eventful period of its career, and has never worn the regimental uniform of any other corps." The Rifles are to be congratulated on being thus complimented by a chief who had not learnt the lessons enforced by politicians of after years, that these same rebel Boers whom he hanged with such good will were, because they had beaten us, to have all they asked for. Then again the Kaffirs had to be dealt with, and the share the Rifle Brigade (with the sister corps, the 60th) had in the lesson taught is written large in the annals of the war. Gladly would we quote from the graphic accounts which exist of this arduous campaign,* but we must leave them to tell their own tale of the achievements of the Brigade and pass on to the war in the Crimea, in which the 1st and 2nd battalions gained so glorious a renown. At the Alma it was the 2nd battalion that was principally engaged, and amongst the many names which might be singled out are those of Colonel Lawrence, Major Norcott, Captain Syers, Captain the Earl of Errol, and Lieutenant Ross. Major Norcott was recommended for the Victoria Cross, and Sir George Brown testifies that "Major Norcott's conduct was not only conspicuous to the whole division but attracted the notice of the enemy, for the officer in command of the Russian battery, who was subsequently made prisoner, informed Lord Raglan that he had laid a gun especially for "the daring officer in the dark uniform on the black horse." In the approach to Balaclava, at which no serious fighting occurred, a rather amusing incident happened. As Captain Vigers was taking his men into the town "a baker, evidently in great terror, came out of his house and, notwithstanding the early hour of the morning, produced a roast turkey which he offered him, and a great number of loaves. These Vigers desired him to break into two and to give half to each man, so that all the men of his company had a good meal." Many were the incidents of daring which are to be credited to the Brigade during the battle of Inkerman and the first stages of the siege of Sebastopol: Wheatley's presence of mind,

* Notably from those of Mrs. Wood and Captain King.

in flinging a live shell over the parapet, Herbert's wonderful shooting, Harman's and Ferguson's close struggle with the Russians, the brave deeds of Powell, Godfrey, Alrington, Hewitt, and Markham. Some were officers, some privates, but no distinction is necessary where each and all added to the proud record of their regiment. At Inkerman the 1st battalion—recommended by their leader as one "which could do anything"—fought splendidly, and their fierce struggle may be estimated by the fact that the 2nd company was brought out of action by a colour sergeant.* The "affair at the Ovens" was one in which the 1st battalion was almost exclusively engaged, and Lieutenants Tryon, Bourchier, and Cuninghame, with four sergeants and a couple of hundred men, performed the arduous task which was not only eulogised by the commander-in-chief of the British army but formed the theme of an *Ordre Général* published by General Canrobert.† At the storming of the Redan a detachment of the 1st battalion under Stuart and Boileau and Sanders, and one of the 2nd under Blackett, Macdonell, Forman, and Freemantle, were engaged, and with the Rifles to be "engaged" is to be distinguished. Amongst so much that is worthy of record the account given of the deaths of Captain Hammond and Lieutenant Ryder claims mention. "Hammond had only been in the Crimea forty-eight hours when he was killed. When the Rifles were forming for the assault on the Redan a young subaltern addressed him, 'Captain Hammond, how fortunate we are! We are just in time for Sebastopol.' Hammond's eyes were gazing where the rays of the sun made a path of golden light over the sea, and his answer was short and remarkable, and accompanied by the quiet smile which those who knew him so well remember. 'I am quite ready,' he said." He was seen afterwards fighting like a hero at the embrasures, his gleaming sword flashing, his form conspicuous even in the awful hurly-burly from amongst which brave men's souls flew thick and fast to the gates of "the hereafter." "The next morning he was found in a ditch beneath a dozen of the slain with a bayonet wound through his heart." Ryder was scarcely eighteen when he fell. He had been severely wounded, but could not brook the necessary delay in attending to him. Binding his wound himself as best he might he again mounted the scaling ladder, "and when he was found next day in the ditch a bayonet thrust had transfixed his forehead."

After the fall of Sebastopol came peace, and with it the thanks of the Sovereign and the gratitude of the nation for the heroism which, at the cost of so many

---

* Colour-Sergeant Higgins, afterwards Captain W. Higgins.
† Bourchier and Cuninghame received the V.C., and Colour-Sergeant Hicks the French war medal.

brave lives, had added yet more names to the long roll of the Brigade's distinctions.*

On the outbreak of the Indian Mutiny, the 2nd and 3rd battalions of the Brigade were ordered to embark, and on arriving in India were pushed on to Cawnpore. It was soon found that not only their fighting but their marching powers were destined to be tried to the uttermost. One wonders as one reads of the long marches under blazing sun, with the heavy European clothing unchanged for days together, while want of sleep caused men now and again to stumble through sheer drowsiness even while marching in the ranks—one wonders how it came to pass that when they met the enemy, these weary, footsore, sleep-bereaved men brightened as with a flash into that activity the rebels found so deathful. When they fought at Cawnpore the 3rd battalion were almost starving, and frequently a biscuit and ration of rum formed the only meal during the day. The regiment captured Etawah, fought on the Ramgunga, and under Colonel Horsford engaged in the resultless pursuit of Nana Sahib. Under Outram they fought at the capture of Lucknow, and earned that commander's highest commendation for their spirit and dash. Two hundred men from the regiment with the same number of Sikhs were formed into a camel corps under Major Ross, and proved a most useful addition to the effective force of the British army. After the capture of Lucknow, the Rifles were engaged in constant skirmishes and sudden and fatiguing marches, during which many deaths occurred from disease and sunstroke. At the battle of Nawabgunga they gained special praise for the splendid manner in which, unaided, they kept at bay a vastly superior force of the enemy. At last, when their sorely-taxed strength was well-nigh failing, the 7th Hussars, with Sir C. Russell at their head, came thundering to the rescue. Their losses were heavy that day; far worse than the injuries done by the enemy's fire were the sufferings of the men from exposure to the sun. Numbers of the gallant Rifles lay seemingly dead—with many, alas! it was no mere seeming—others were raving mad. Had they not deserved it by their valour, it might almost be said that their sufferings alone merited the laudatory reference they received in the dispatches of Sir Hope Grant. At Jamo, Lieutenant Andrew Green engaged in a conflict which recalls something of the warrior tales told in 'chronicles of eld.' Rushing to the rescue of some men of his party who were surrounded by the enemy, he found himself attacked by six rebels. Two he shot; he was then cut down by the others, who hacked viciously at him while prostrate. Springing up he knocked down

* At the first distribution of V.C.'s no fewer than eight fell to officers and men of the Brigade.

two more with the butt of his revolver, and was keeping the others at bay with his sword when he was attacked by three fresh arrivals. Again he was cut down, and again he struggled to his feet and shot another of his assailants. When found by Colour-Sergeant Mansel, who gallantly fought his way to the rescue, Green was lying bathed in blood, having received fifteen wounds, of which all except one were sword cuts.

The Brigade captured Birwah, again suffering heavy loss; they fought at Hyderguh; Mejidia fell before their conquering arms. But it is impossible even to mention the names of all the places where they fought, or to tell of the sterling service rendered by the camel corps under Ross. When the mutiny was over no regiment had better earned the "Well done!" that echoed through the length and breadth of the Empire. Four of the Victoria Crosses fell to the share of the Brigade; while, in addition to those who were killed in action, two officers and a hundred and thirty-two men fell victims to disease. Afterwards—in 1861-2—the 1st battalion was ordered to Canada during the alarm caused by the "*Trent* affair," while the 2nd and 3rd battalions were engaged in various encounters with the Mohmunds and other hostile Indian tribes. Later on the 1st and 4th battalions assisted in teaching the Fenians a salutary lesson in Canada. The next operations of any magnitude in which the Brigade were represented was the Ashanti war in 1874, throughout which the 2nd battalion served. To quote the words of Sir Archibald Allison, "it is needless to speak of the steadiness and high discipline," of the courage and cheerfulness they displayed. The campaign was emphatically a trying one, and King Koffee's terrible ally, Disease, vanquished many a brave rifleman, whom shot and spear passed by. The final exploits of the Brigade are commemorated by "Ali Musjid" and "Afghanistan." In concluding this notice of the Rifle Brigade we cannot summarize its character and achievements better than in the words of King William IV., who, when Duke of Clarence, reviewed them at Plymouth: "What more can I say to you, riflemen, than that whenever there has been fighting you have been employed, and wherever you have been employed you have distinguished yourselves."

THE ROYAL FUSILIERS* (City of London Regiment)—Regimental district No. 7—are comprised of the old 7th Foot. In 1685 a large regiment was formed, chiefly from

---

* The Royal Fusiliers bear as badges " The White Rose of York (in the Garter) on a grenade, the flame of which is crowned," on cap and collar, with the White Horse on the helmet plate. The mottoes are those of the Garter and *Nec aspera terrent*. On their colours is the White Horse and "Martinique," "Talavera," "Albuera," "Badajoz," "Salamanca," "Vittoria," "Pyrenees," "Orthes," "Toulouse," "Peninsula," "Alma," "Inkerman," "Sevastopol," "Kandahar, 1880," "Afghanistan, 1879—80." The uniform is scarlet with facings of blue, and Fusilier's cap.

the old London bands, and designated the Ordnance Regiment, receiving at the same time the appellation of Royal Fusiliers. Their first service was at Walcourt, then in the Irish wars consequent on William's accession to the throne. After this they joined the troops in Holland, where they experienced some severe fighting. They were represented at Steenkirke; at Landen they fought with unexampled courage, nearly all their officers being either killed or wounded; for their gallantry in storming Namur they received the special thanks of William. They took part in the Duke of Ormond's expedition against Vigo, and in 1703 served as marines. Hurrying over the following years—during which we note that the regiment served as marines on board the fleet of the unfortunate Byng, which did *not* relieve Minorca—we come to the era of the war in America and Canada, during which they experienced some severe reverses, though throughout their consistent courage gained them unqualified praise. In the defence of St. John's a great number were made prisoners; they fought at Staten Island; at the capture of Fort Clinton—where our troops, unsupported by artillery, "crossed ground swept by ten guns, and without firing a shot pressed forward to the foot of the works, climbed over each other's shoulders on to the walls and drove the enemy back"—the 7th gained great distinction. At Cow Pens, in December, 1781, the regiment suffered severely from the unfortunate repulse experienced by our troops under Colonel Tarleton; their colours were taken, and many of their number killed and wounded. Shortly after that they returned to England and were on duty in various places, being for some time under the command of the Duke of Kent, father of Her present Majesty. In 1807, they were with the forces dispatched against Copenhagen, and a couple of years later under Colonel Packenham to Martinique. Here, at the stubborn fight on the heights of Surirey, the Royal Fusiliers gave striking evidence of their splendid fighting capacity. Meanwhile, the 2nd battalion of the regiment was with Wellesley in Portugal, and first met the foe at Talavera. Here, we learn from the Official Record, the Royal Fusiliers "met the storm of war with unshaken firmness," and succeeded in capturing seven guns. Both battalions were at Busaco; where, however, they did not come in for very much actual fighting. After a sharp skirmish at Burlada, the 7th and 23rd were formed into the famous Fusilier Brigade, under Pakenham, the command of the battalions being given to Vigers and Blakeney. At Albuera, the account of the magnificent charge of that Fusilier Brigade still kindles into enthusiasm the most listless and unemotional. The tide of war seemed turning steadily against us: "we had lost a whole brigade of artillery; a large number of our men were prisoners; a deep gully prevented the British from using their bayonets, and affairs wore a most unpromising appearance." As the history of the Royal Fusiliers expresses it, a crisis had arrived, and a mighty, a determined, a desperate effort alone could save the allied army from defeat. Sweeping onward in seemingly resistless force were three columns of exultant French, supported by cavalry and artillery, each column mustering about twice the number of the force that was about to check their insolent progress. That force was the Fusilier Brigade. In front of the advancing French were their lancers surrounding our guns that they had captured.

Their pride was short-lived; the stern, avenging British line swept them aside and recovered the guns, then moved forward against the dense columns of the enemy. "Such a gallant line startled the enemy's masses, which were increasing and pressing forward as to an assured victory; they wavered, hesitated, and then vomiting forth a storm of fire, hastily endeavoured to enlarge their front, while the fearful discharge of grape from all their artillery whistled through the British ranks. Myers was killed, other officers fell wounded, and the Fusilier battalions struck by the iron tempest reeled and staggered like sinking ships. Suddenly and sternly recovering they closed on their terrible enemies, and then was seen with what a majesty the British soldiers fight! . . . . Nothing could stop our astonishing infantry. No sudden burst of undisciplined valour, no nervous enthusiasm weakened the stability of their order, their flashing eyes were bent on the dark columns in front, their measured tread shook the ground, their dreadful volleys swept away the head of every formation, their deafening shouts overpowered the dissonant cries that broke from all parts of the tumultuous crowd, as foot by foot, and with a horrid carnage, it was driven by the incessant vigour of the attack to the farthest edge of the hill. In vain did the French reserves . . . . endeavour to sustain the fight. Their efforts only increased the irremediable confusion, and the mighty mass, like a loosened cliff, went headlong down the ascent. The rain flowed after in streams discoloured with blood, and fifteen hundred unwounded men, the remnant of six thousand unconquerable British soldiers, stood triumphant on the fatal hill" (*Napier*). Well may the record of the Royal Fusiliers assert that they "exceeded anything that the usual word 'gallantry' can convey." Thirty-two officers, thirty-four sergeants, six hundred and thirty-eight soldiers, express the loss in killed and wounded the 7th sustained that day.*

* Amongst the killed was Myers, Lieutenant-Colonel of the 1st battalion. The depreciators of "boy officers" may be interested to note that he was only twenty-eight years of age.

They fought again with great credit at Aldea de Pont and at Ciudad Rodrigo, though in the latter operations they were not largely engaged. At Badajoz it was Captain Mair of the 7th who led the storming party against the Trinidad bastion, while others of the regiment under Captain Cholwick attacked the breach in the curtain. Two hundred and thirty-two were killed and wounded during the assault. At Salamanca Captain Crowder gained his majority for dislodging, with only two companies of the regiment, a force of five hundred Frenchmen from a village they occupied. At Vittoria their position was against the enemy's centre, and materially assisted in the crushing defeat of Joseph's army; while, as evidence of the splendid state of discipline which they had attained, it may be mentioned that amidst the dazzling temptations which surrounded them, no case of that plundering on which the British commander commented so severely was reported in the ranks of the 7th. They fought in the battles of the Pyrenees, notably at Roncesvalles and Villalba, on the Bidassoa and at Orthes. At Toulouse they were not seriously engaged, and with this battle ended their glorious Peninsular record, for their services in the West Indies prevented their participating in Waterloo. In the expedition against New Orleans, which, barren of profitable result as it was, reflected nothing but credit on the troops engaged, the Royal Fusiliers again distinguished themselves, at the same time incurring considerable loss. From that time till the war with Russia in 1854 the 7th were not engaged in any warlike service. In the Crimea they were in the Light Division under Sir George Brown. Their splendid charge at the Alma, under Lacy Yeo, will long be remembered—how in the teeth of a storm of bullets they pressed on, though those who bore the colours were shot down in terrible succession, and how Private Lyle of the regiment helped Captain Bell to capture the Russian guns. At the famous sortie from Sebastopol of the 26th October and at Inkerman they fought, and throughout the prolonged siege acquitted themselves as might have been expected from their history and tradition. In the "affair at the Quarries" Captain Mitchell Jones gained the V.C. for the dauntless way in which, despite his receiving a wound in the early stage of the fighting, he led his men to the numerous attacks, and at the assault of the Redan Lieutenant Hope and Private Hughes gained the same priceless decoration. In the following September a non-combatant officer of the regiment, Assistant-Surgeon Hale, gained another Cross for his unremitting care of the wounded whom the heavy fire, which drove all but himself and Lieutenant Hope away from the spot, could not induce him to leave for a moment. During the Indian Mutiny the 7th were employed in Scinde, and a few years later in the disturbances on the

North-west Frontier. Passing over fifteen years, during which the history of the 7th was that of any distinguished regiment in times of peace, we find them next employed in the Afghan campaign of 1878—80. In the sortie from Candahar of 16th August, 1880, under General Brooke, the Royal Fusiliers were commanded by Major Vandaleur. The admirable courage and dash they displayed were unable to prevent the effort from being a failure, a failure, moreover, which cost the lives of Major Vandaleur and Lieutenants Wood and Marsh — "two gallant officers, mere lads," — and numbered Lieutenant de Trafford amongst the wounded. But Lieutenant Case and Private James Asford each earned the Victoria Cross for rescuing a wounded comrade under a searching fire. With Afghanistan ends the long roll of warlike achievements which are to be credited to the Royal Fusiliers.

THE BLACK WATCH (ROYAL HIGHLANDERS)*—Regimental District No. 42—are composed of the 42nd and 73rd Regiments and date from 1729, when six companies were raised for "local service." Originally, doubtless, care was taken to enlist none except those unfriendly to the Jacobite cause; after a time, however, this restriction was dropped as regarded the rank and file, though the officers were still chosen from Whig families.† The proposal made in 1743 to send the regiment abroad gave rise to some disturbance, the Highlanders being not unnaturally keenly jealous at anything that looked like sharp practice. But it is not our purpose to dwell upon these earlier years of a regiment, whose historians are both numerous and enthusiastic, interesting as such early records undoubtedly are. The disturbance was terminated, and shortly after the battle of Dettingen had been fought the Black Watch,‡ then consisting of ten companies,

---

* The Black Watch have as badges St. Andrew and Cross on Star of the Order of the Thistle over the Sphinx on glengarry, St. Andrew and Cross on collar. The mottoes are those of the Order of the Thistle and—*Am freiceadan dubh*—The Black Watch. On their colours are the royal cypher within the Garter and the names, "Mangalore," "Seringapatain," "Egypt," "Corunna," "Fuentes d'Onor," "Pyrenees," "Nivelle," "Nive," "Orthes," "Toulouse," "Peninsula," "Waterloo," "South Africa, 1846—7," "South Africa, 1851—3," "Alma," "Sevastopol," "Lucknow," "Ashantee," "Egypt, 1882, 1884," "Tel-el-Kebir," "Nile, 1884—5," "Kirbekan." The uniform is scarlet, with facings of blue, feather bonnet, and kilt.

† The privates were in most cases men of good social position. On one occasion George II. expressed a desire to see some of these famous soldiers, and two privates were sent to St. James's Palace, where they showed some of the national sword exercises. On leaving they were given a guinea apiece, but these *private* soldiers as they strode out threw the guerdon to the porter at the door.

‡ The Black Watch is the English equivalent of the Gaelic *Frieceadan Dugh*, which they were called in distinction to the *Saighdearan Dearg*, Red Soldiers. Their uniform at this time was a scarlet jacket and waistcoat with buff facings, with a tartan plaid of twelve yards long wound round the middle of the body, the upper part being fixed on the left shoulder, with flat beaver bonnets, bordered by the fess check of the Royal Stuarts, with a tuft of black feathers.

THE 42nd—THE BLACK WATCH (ROYAL HIGHLANDERS)

joined the allied forces in Flanders. At Fontenoy they fought with such marked heroism as to be saluted by the Duke of Cumberland himself with a loud cheer in acknowledgment of their chivalrous devotion. Their colonel, Sir Robert Munro, seemed to bear a charmed life. Suiting their tactics to the exigencies of their position the Highlanders, after delivering a volley, threw themselves flat on the ground while the return fire passed over them, but Sir Robert's enormous bulk, which had necessitated his being hauled out of the trenches by his own men, rendered this manœuvre impossible for himself to practise. He had perforce to stand there "like an invincible Ajax, and guarding the colours of his regiment faced unmoved the enemy's fire." In 1756 the Black Watch were ordered to America, and at Ticonderoga elicited unstinted praise for their valour. In that disastrous combat they lost six hundred and fifty killed or wounded. Others of the regiment* served in 1759 at Martinique, and greatly distinguished themselves by the "characteristic impetuosity" with which they fought. Their next service was in Canada, where they fought under General Amherst, and two years later they took part in the expedition against the Havannah. Many of the laurels of the Black Watch have been gained in America. In 1763 and subsequently they fought against the Indians, particularly distinguishing themselves at Bushey Run, and again in 1776 when the War of Independence gave them severe and constant work. "In every field," writes a chronicler of the regiment, "the Black Watch maintained their hardly-earned reputation," and numerous are the instances recorded of deeds of individual courage and readiness. As an example may be quoted the following:—

"In a skirmish with the Americans in 1776 Major Murray of the 42nd, being separated from his men, was attacked by three of the enemy. His dirk had slipped behind his back, and, like Colonel Munro before referred to, being very corpulent he could not reach it. He defended himself as well as he could with his fusil, and, watching his opportunity, seized the sword of one of his assailants and put the three to flight."

This same Major Murray found his Falstaffian dimensions again embarrassing at Fort Washington.

"The hill on which the fort stood was almost perpendicular, but the Highlanders rushed up the steep ascent like mountain cats. When halfway up the heights they heard a melancholy voice exclaim, 'Oh, soldiers, will you leave me?' On looking down they saw Major Murray, their commanding officer, at the foot of the precipice; his extreme obesity prevented him from following them. They were not deaf to this appeal;

---

* A second battalion had been raised consequent on the severe loss experienced at Ticonderoga.

it would never do to leave their corpulent commander behind. A party leaped down at once, seized him in their arms and bore him from ledge to ledge of the rock till they reached the summit, where they drove the enemy before them and made two hundred prisoners."

"In a skirmish with the American rebels in 1777 Sergeant Macgregor of the 42nd was severely wounded and remained insensible on the ground. Unlike Captain Crawley, who put on his old uniform before Waterloo, the sergeant, who seems to have been something of a dandy, had attired himself in his best as if he had been going to a ball instead of a battle. He wore a new jacket with silver lace, large silver buckles in his shoes, and a watch of some value. This display of wealth attracted the notice of an American soldier, who, actuated by no feeling of humanity, but by the sordid desire of stripping the sergeant at leisure, took him on his back and began to carry him off the field. It is probable that the American did not handle him very tenderly, and the motion soon restored him to consciousness. He saw at once the state of matters and proved himself master of the occasion. With one hand he drew his dirk, and grasping the American's throat with the other he swore that he would stab him to the heart if he did not retrace his steps and bear him back in safety to the British camp. The *argumentum ad hominem* in the shape of a glittering dagger before his eyes was too much for the American. On the way to the camp they were met by Lord Cornwallis, who thanked him for his humanity; but he had the candour to admit the truth. His lordship, who was much amused at the incident, gave the American his liberty, and, on Macgregor retiring from the service, procured for him a situation in the Customs at Leith."

In 1794 they fought in Holland, and in that terrible march through Westphalia rendered great service, especially at Gildermalsen, where they scattered a regiment of French Hussars. A Scotch officer records the fact that though the Highlanders all wore the kilt, and the men of the 42nd were principally very young soldiers, the loss they experienced from the terrible cold and privations " was out of all comparison less than that sustained by other corps." The following year they again served in the West Indies, and fought with their usual courage at St. Lucia and St. Vincent, and in 1800 joined Sir Ralph Abercrombie, with whom the following year they landed in Egypt. Here they were brigaded under Sir John Moore, and at the landing at Aboukir vied with the Welsh Fusiliers in their gallant onslaught on the French. The story of the battle of Alexandria has too often been told, and in the telling the deeds of the Black Watch enumerated, to need dwelling on here; it will suffice to say, that they undoubtedly are second to none of all the regiments that bear on their accoutrements the eloquent emblem of the Sphinx. It was to Major Sterling of the 42nd that the standard of the "Invincible Legion" was delivered; it was a corporal of the 42nd who shot one of the dragoons that attacked Abercrombie, and it was on the blanket of Donald Roy of the 42nd, that the loved general was borne away to die.

In 1808 the Black Watch joined the army in Portugal, and were with Sir John Moore at Corunna, and a tradition, tinged with the weird superstition of the Highlands, tells that there were not wanting those in the ranks of the Black Watch who, even as their gallant commander turned to them with the confident exhortation—"Highlanders, remember Egypt!" saw rising before his manly form the prophetic, shadowy shroud which foretold his coming death. The 2nd battalion of the regiment took part in the Walcheren expedition, while the 1st joined the allied army in Portugal. At Fuentes d'Onor, under Lord Blantyre, they vigorously repulsed and swept backward in disorder a formidable charge of French cavalry; at Burgos Major Dick, with the men of the Royal Highlanders under his command, were praised in dispatches for their gallantry at the assault. They fought in the picturesque battles of the Pyrenees and Nivelle, at the Nive and Orthes. At Toulouse General Pack, who commanded the Brigade, addressed the regiment as follows: "I have just now been with General Clinton, and he has been pleased to grant my request that in the charge which we are about to make upon the enemy's redoubts, the 42nd regiment shall have the honour of leading on the attack. The 42nd will advance!" Such a regiment needed no repetition of such an order; they advanced with a magnificent charge, and the redoubt was taken, but so terrible was the fire, that "out of about five hundred men which the 42nd brought into action, scarcely ninety reached the fatal redoubt from which the enemy had fled." At Quatre Bras they were subjected to a furious charge from the French Lancers, which came upon them before they could form square. The two flank companies were ridden down, but then the Highlanders formed square, and hemming the cavalry within, killed or made them prisoners. So fierce was this brief conflict that in the space of a few minutes the command of the regiment devolved upon four officers, of whom two were killed and one severely wounded. At Waterloo it suffices to say that they were in Picton's division. The two days' fighting cost the Black Watch in killed and wounded three hundred men.

Interesting though it would be to dwell on many of the occurrences of the intervening years, we must pass on to 1854, when the 42nd formed part of the famous

Highland Brigade in the Crimean War. Throughout the fascinating pages of the author of "Eothen" are numerous mentions of this splendid regiment, of which one of the earliest is the passage which tells how on that first trying march which preluded the Alma, when the troops arrived gasping and fainting with heat and thirst and weariness at their resting-place by the Bulganak River, the stern discipline of Sir Colin Campbell "would not allow even the rage of thirst to loosen the high discipline of his splendid Highland regiments. He halted them a little before they reached the stream, and so ordered it that . . . . they gained in comfort, and knew that they were the gainers." The next day was to be known throughout the centuries as the Battle of the Alma, and in the sweet, quiet fragrance of the morning air, while, though the enemy was in sight, nature seemed unready for war, and stillness pervaded the warrior-covered slopes, the quiet tones of Sir Colin were heard, remarking, "This will be a good time for the men to get loose half their cartridges." Before the day ended many pouches were empty, and their owners refilled them, recalling with pride "the deeds they did that day;" others were well-nigh full, but the hands that had so gleefully opened them in the morning, lay stiff for ever on the Russian hills. When the time came for the Highlanders to charge, matters were looking serious. Thistlethwaite and Lindsay of the Scots Guards had saved their colours, though torn and pierced with shot. The Guards, like wounded demi-gods, were resting, scornfully defiant, despite the terrible gaps in their ranks. Twelve battalions were before the Highland Brigade, which numbered three, yet there was no thought of the possibility of failure in Campbell's mind, as he wound up his short address to his men with the words: "Now, men, the army is watching us. Make me proud of my Highland Brigade!" Then the historian of the war tells us:— "Smoothly, easily, and swiftly, the Black Watch seemed to glide up the hill. A few instants before, and their tartans ranged dark in the valley; now their plumes were on the crest." A few deadly volleys, and the Russians fled in sheer confusion, followed by the exulting shout of the triumphant Scots. Neither Balaclava nor Inkerman are amongst the distinctions borne by the Black Watch, but the comprehensive "Sevastopol" covers many a deed of heroism done during the long months that elapsed before it fell. At the storming of the Redan, they were in reserve at the right attack, and, had it been necessary, would have shared with the Guards the renewed attack that was planned for the following morning.

Again passing over some years, we take up the thread of the record of the 42nd in 1873, when, under Colonel MacLeod, they served in the Ashantee War. At the battle of

Amoaful in January, 1874, the Black Watch were in the leading column under Alison, their own officers present being Majors Macpherson and Scott.* They soon experienced to the full the severe nature of the combat in which they were engaged. A correspondent wrote at the time that so hot was the fire, had the enemy used bullets instead of slugs, "scarcely a man of the Black Watch would have been left to tell the tale." Major Band was severely wounded, Major Macpherson was hit in several places, nine officers and nearly a hundred men were shot. For some time the firing was heavy and seemingly confused; at last the time came for a charge. Sir Archibald, at the head of the Black Watch, bade the pipes strike up "The Campbells are coming," and with a dash and a cheer the regiment charged straight for the foe. Throughout the fighting that preceded the taking of Coomassie, they were to the fore whenever fighting was to be done. In the advance on the capital, a well-known "Man of the Time"†—whose opinion on daring and self-possession is to be valued as coming from one who combines both qualities in so rare a manner—said, " their audacious spirit and true military bearing challenged admiration." "One man—Thomas Adams—exhibited himself eminently brave among brave men." After the town had fallen, the 42nd remained for a time as rear guard.

Their next—and concluding—campaign took place in Egypt, and it may well be imagined that we do not propose to dwell upon what is practically history of to-day. They were again under the command of Sir Archibald Alison, and at Tel-el-Kebir gave evidence that they were still the same formidable " Black Watch " as of yore. We learn from the official dispatches that the Highland Brigade was the first to reach the works, and that the fighting there was no mere child's play is evidenced by the fact that nine of all ranks were killed and forty-one wounded or missing. Amongst the former may be reckoned Lieutenant Graham, Sergeant-Major MacNeill, and Lieutenant Allen Park, though the last-named did not succumb to his wounds on the spot. They were engaged at El Teb and Tamai; at the latter place experiencing some very severe fighting, in which they lost, amongst others, Major Walker Aitken and Lieutenant Ronald Fraser, and nearly ninety others of all ranks. Private Edwards earned the Victoria Cross for "conspicuous bravery" in defence of a gun. Still later on they again won the distinction of Kirbekan on their colours.

The 2nd battalion of the Black Watch, the 73rd Regiment, dates its separate existence from 1786, when the 2nd battalion of the Black Watch was formed into a distinct

---

* Colonel M'Leod led the left column, and Captain Furse of the regiment was in command of a native regiment in the right column.

† Mr. H. M. Stanley.

regiment with the number 73. It is to the 2nd battalion that the Black Watch owe "Mangalore" and "Seringapatam." The defence of the former—described as one "that has been seldom equalled and never surpassed," and "as noble an example as any in history"—might of itself be sufficient to entitle the 73rd to the epithet "distinguished." At this time, however, they were the 2nd battalion of the 42nd. The Europeans fit for duty were about two hundred and fifty, and there were fifteen hundred natives. Against this handful Tippoo brought ninety thousand men, exclusive of two corps of European infantry, and one—under Lally—of Europeans and natives. He had besides eighty pieces of cannon. Mangalore was invested by this army about the 16th of May; for nine months Colonel Campbell and the 73rd, with the Sepoys, kept this huge host at bay; then they capitulated, but not before "the natives became so exhausted that many of them dropped down in the act of shouldering their firelocks, while others became totally blind." Food was exhausted; for some time the bill of fare had been dependent on frogs, dogs, crows, and similar delicacies; small wonder that even from the savage Tippoo they were granted "highly honourable terms." Of the 250 which the regiment numbered in May, nine officers and seventy rank and file were killed or wounded. As the 73rd the regiment fought at Pondicherry, were in Ceylon in 1793 under General Stuart, and at Seringapatam aided in the brilliant victory won over Tippoo. In the accounts of this most important battle the name of Colonels Sherbrooke and Major M'Donald, with other officers of the 73rd, are referred to in most laudatory terms. After this they were employed under the future Duke of Wellington in completing the subjection of the hostile tribes. Returning to England in 1806, the following eight years were passed in this country and New South Wales. A second battalion meanwhile had been formed, and under General Gibbs served in the Stralsund expedition of 1813, and was "the only British regiment present in the victory gained by Count Walmoden over the French in the plain of Gohrde, in Hanover, 16th September, 1813, to which the 73rd materially contributed." After serving under Sir Thomas Graham, the 73rd (2nd battalion) fought at Quatre Bras and Waterloo.

How well they fought at Waterloo may be gathered from the fact—referred to in our notice of the 30th Regiment—that the Duke at one time during the day sent to Halkett, in whose brigade they were, to inquire which of his regiments it was that was formed in square so far in advance. The answer revealed the actual state of the case, the square was formed of the dead warriors of the 30th and 73rd. "The last-named regiment sustained no less than thirteen charges from Cuirassiers, and seven hours of a cannonade,

THE 21st—ROYAL SCOTS FUSILIERS.

and so greatly were both corps cut up, that at half-past seven their colours were sent out of the field and taken to the rear." After Waterloo peaceful duties occupied the 73rd till the Cape War, which commenced in 1846. They served throughout the campaign, which did not practically terminate till 1853, and to Lieutenant-Colonel Eyre of the regiment was given the command of the right wing in the operations in the Amatolas. Space will not permit of a detailed account of the doings of the 73rd during the war, their valuable services in which consummated in the dashing attack on the fastness of the rebel chief Macomo, which, despite its seeming impregnability, was taken by storm by the regiment and their gallant companions. Their next service was in the operations in Nepaul immediately following the suppression of the Mutiny, in which they earned great credit. Since then their career has been unimportant, but it is interesting to note that on the resumption of their original position as the 2nd battalion of the Black Watch, they again adopted the kilt, which since 1809 had been discarded.

THE ROYAL SCOTS FUSILIERS*—Regimental District No. 21—date from 1678, though they were not put on the English establishment till ten years later. Their first experience —as a regiment, for the stalwart recruits were no novices in the art of fighting—of actual warfare, seems to have been Bothwell Bridge, where the Earl of Mar's Fusiliers, as they were then styled, with the battalions of the Scots Guards under Lord Livingstone, shared in all the varied fortunes of the day. At the time of the Revolution the then colonel of the 21st adhered to King James, and was accordingly superseded by the new Government. The regiment fought with distinction at Walcourt; at Steinkirke they were in the advanced guard and were one of the "five fine regiments" that were entirely cut to pieces owing to the infamous behaviour of Count Solmes, the Dutch Commander; they were represented in the bloody conflict of Landen; at Blenheim they were with the gallant Lord Cutts in the splendid infantry charge which hurtled against the well-defended village; it was the gallant colonel of the Scots Fusiliers—General Rowe— who, ere he fell mortally wounded, " struck his sword into the enemy's palisades before he gave the word ' Fire!'" After the battle, the 21st were amongst the regiments which escorted the enormous band of prisoners to Holland. At Ramillies again they fought,

* The Royal Scots Fusiliers bear as badges the thistle on a grenade on cap and collar. On the waist-plate is St. Andrew with the cross, and on the cap-plate the Royal Arms. The motto is that of the Order of the Thistle. On the colours are the Royal cypher, and "Blenheim," "Ramillies," "Oudenarde," "Malplaquet," "Dettingen," "Bladensburg," "Alma," "Inkerman," "Sevastopol," "South Africa, 1879." The uniform is scarlet with facings of blue and Fusilier's cap.

VOL. II.   L

distinguishing themselves by their extraordinary gallantry; at Oudenarde they were with those stern, immovable bodies of foot before whom the French cavalry fled, broken and demoralised; at Lisle and Wynendale they shared in the glories of the victories won. At Malplaquet six of their officers fell, and the records of the time are eloquent over the heroic bravery they there displayed. At Sheriffmuir the Fusiliers, then known as Orrery's Regiment, found themselves opposed to the son of their first colonel, the Earl of Mar, under whose command the Jacobite army was drawn up.

The 21st, then General Macartney's Regiment, were with the Force under General Wade in 1724, though their share was limited to enforcing the due payment of taxes in Aberdeenshire. In 1742 they were ordered to Flanders, and the following year fought at Dettingen, the first occasion, it is said, when the Fusilier Regiments wore those peculiar conical caps which came into vogue with the Prussian tactics. They suffered severely at Fontenoy; at the fratricidal conflict of Culloden they were one of the four Scottish regiments present in the army of King George. In 1761 the Scots Fusiliers, then the Earl of Panmure's Regiment, greatly distinguished themselves under Major Purcell at Belleisle, where they were amongst "the first on shore, and attacked the enemy with great intrepidity."

The campaign in America and Canada next claimed their services, and throughout the war their conduct elicited unstinted praise, especially at Stillwater, where they remained with the 10th and 62nd Regiments under a heavy fire for over four hours. At Saratoga they shared the fate of the remainder of the garrison, and were made prisoners of war.

In 1793 they repaired to the West Indies, and were represented in the fighting which centered about Martinique, gaining particular praise in the capture of Guadeloupe, in which Captain M'Donald of the regiment was killed. Then after a period of comparative inaction, they served in Sicily, and at Ischia, Scylla and Genoa gave evidence of the sterling qualities which have ever distinguished them. In 1814 they were with the army under Sir Thos. Graham which effected the reduction of Bergen-op-Zoom, and the same year fought again in America. At Bladensberg and Baltimore they gained great credit, at the latter place being opposed by the flower of the American army, and as a result suffering severe loss. The 21st were not at Waterloo, and the next distinction on their colours belongs to the wars of our own day. Between Baltimore and the Crimea their time was passed principally in the West Indies and Australia, in the last named of which stations they had a good deal of exciting employment in connection with the convict establishments.

In the Crimea they were in the Fourth Division, and were present at the Alma, at Inkerman, and in the various actions which preceded the fall of Sevastopol. At Inkerman General Cathcart, who led the Division, fell almost at the head of the 21st as he gave the word to charge. In the assault on the Redan, on the 18th of June, 1855, they were again engaged, and despite the unsuccessful nature of the attempt, elicited most favourable comments. After the Crimea the Royal Scots Fusiliers were again employed in the West Indies, and also in Burmah. The last name on their colours recalls the yet recent war in South Africa. They were amongst the reinforcements which reached Zululand in April, and a month or so after their arrival took part in the battle of Ulundi. Two companies, it may be added, had been previously left to garrison Fort Newdigate, under Colonel Collingwood of the regiment, while the rest of the regiment had occupied Fort Marshall. At Ulundi they were at the right rear angle of the square under Major Hazelrigge, and materially aided in repulsing the threatening charge made by the foe; later on, in the operations agaist Sekukuni, they were again employed, and bore a prominent part in the proceedings in November, a detachment on one occasion being under arms "twenty-four hours consecutively and without food." In the attack on Sekukuni's town, they were in the centre column under Major Murray of the 94th. The two regiments, we are told, made a rush at the stronghold in splendid order, vying each with the other which should be first, the pipers of the Fusiliers "filling the air with the breath of battle while playing with infernal energy." Under Captain Auchinleck they were actively employed in hunting and capturing the Basuto chieftain, and were fortunate enough to suffer comparatively little loss. At the outbreak of the Boer rebellion Captain Lambart was treacherously taken prisoner, and a treacherous and barbarous attempt made to kill him, under the circumstances mentioned in our notice of the 94th Regiment.

Fifty men of the Fusiliers had been before this organized as mounted infantry, and the remainder of the regiment were stationed at Pretoria and Rustenberg, where they were shortly afterwards besieged. A hundred or so were with Colley at the battle of Laing's Neck, and held the camp during that disastrous engagement. The garrison at Pretoria were under Colonel Gildea of the regiment, and during a sortie the Boers hoisted a flag of truce, and on the Fusiliers coming from cover, imagining they were dealing with civilised foes, fired upon them, killing or wounding twenty-one. "Colonel Gildea and his orderly while both bearing white flags in response were fired upon within sixty yards range, but both escaped. This was the third time the Boers had made a treacherous use of the white flag." It is satisfactory to record that on this occasion fourteen of the rebels were shot down and twenty taken prisoners. This was only one of the many gallant sorties made by the 21st from Pretoria, on one occasion Colonel Gildea being severely wounded. It is not remarkable that amongst the gallant soldiers who were fighting for life and honour against insolent and treacherous foes " a very bitter feeling was manifested against the conditions of peace concluded by the British Government with the Boers." Meanwhile at Rustenberg sixty of the 21st under Captain Auchinleck, who was wounded, were cooped up in a fort only twenty-five yards square, and kept the foe at bay for more than three months. It was by a detachment of the Fusiliers under Captain Burr that the heroic little band at Fort Mary was relieved. At Potchefstroom the regiment greatly distinguished themselves. Hostilities commenced by the Boers attempting to pull down the British flag. Captain Lambart of the 21st shot him in the arm, but was unfortunately taken prisoner. Then a regular fusilade began, and Captain Laurence Falls was shot dead. The commandant at Potchefstroom was Colonel Bellaris, and the officers of the 21st who were with him were Lieutenant-Colonel Winsloe, Lieutenants Lindsell, Dalrymple Hay, Kenneath Lean, and P. Brown. Major Thornhill and Lieutenant Rundle of the Royal Artillery were also present. On the 16th of December the Boers sent to demand surrender, but the only reply they received was two cannon shots. Throughout December, January, February, and the greater part of March the little force of three hundred men held the fort against an overwhelming number of the enemy.

On the 23rd of March, Lieutenant Dalrymple Hay with only ten men undertook to dislodge a party of some thirty rebels who had posted themselves in an annoying position. Three of his men were shot down at once; with the other seven he charged with fixed bayonets and drove the rebels away, killing about sixteen of them. From this incident may be gauged the value of all the nonsense written about the "courage" of the Boers. They were bold enough at a distance when they could bring their deadly marksmanship into play, but at close quarters *eight* men of the Fusiliers were more than sufficient to completely rout thirty of them. At last, when more than a third of the garrison were killed or wounded, when all provisions were exhausted, and after the allowance for each man had been some time reduced to "a pound of mealies and half a pound of Kaffir corn daily, with a quarter of a pound of tinned meat on alternate days," the garrison surrendered, claiming and obtaining full honours of war. The Boers knew that an armistice had been concluded *two full days before the capitulation.* Since the Transvaal war the Royal Scots Fusiliers have not had the opportunity of adding any distinction to their colours, though their recent achievements in Burmah give good evidence how well they still deserve the high estimation in which the regiment has ever been held.

THE CAMERONIANS (SCOTTISH RIFLES)*—Regimental District No. 26—which next engage our attention, consist of the 26th and 90th Foot. The 26th, from which the name is derived, were raised in 1689 from amongst those bands of stern Covenanters whom religious predilections had attracted to the cause of William and Mary. Their first colonel was the Earl of Angus, then apparently only eighteen years of age, and the conditions on which the men enlisted were curiously characteristic of their temperament. The officers were to be such men "as in conscience they could submit to;" a captain was appointed to the regiment, and an "elder" to each company; in each man's haversack was to be found a Bible. Their first engagement was at Dunkeld, where their gallant defence was for long the theme of universal praise. They were 1,200, whilst their assailants were more than four times as many; for four hours they fought desperately in street and house, by wall and market-place; when ammunition fell short they tore the lead from the roofs and converted it into slugs. At last the attacking force drew off, declaring that they "could fight men but not devils," and the Cameronians remained victors, having killed three hundred of the enemy and wounded "a vast number," while their own loss was under fifty. A Jacobite song of the period, quoted by Grant in his account of the siege, is higher praise than the compliments of troops of friends. Addressing the Cameronians, the poet says:

> "For murders too, as soldiers true,
> You were advanced well, boys;
> For you fought like devils, your only rivals,
> When you were at Dunkeld, boys."

At Steinkirke the Cameronians were in Mackay's brigade, and suffered severely in the terrible slaughter inflicted on them by the French Mousquetaires, their young colonel being killed at their head; at Namur they distinguished themselves under the brave Lord Cutts; at Blenheim their brigadier, the gallant Rowe, in whose division they were,

---

* The Cameronians bear as badge the Thistle on the glengary, and on the helmet-plate a mullet with bugle and strings. Surrounding this is a laurel wreath, on the leaves of which are the battles. On either side of the wreath are the sphinx and dragon. The whole has a coronet above. The motto is that of the Order of the Thistle. The battles inscribed are: "Blenheim," "Ramillies," "Oudenarde," "Malplaquet," "Mandora," "Egypt," "Corunna," "Martinique," "Guadeloupe," "China," "South Africa, 1846-7," "Sevastopol," "Lucknow," "Abyssinia," "South Africa, 1877-8-9." The uniform is green, with facings of dark green.

led them—as has been recorded—right up to the palisades, which he struck with his sword before giving the order to "Fire!" "At the battle of Ramillies the regiment, after being much exposed throughout the fight, was engaged in pursuit of the beaten foe till midnight;" they fought at Oudenarde and Wynendale, and in the battle of Malplaquet had four officers killed. Shortly after their return home they adopted the tartan trews, and, after serving in England for a few years, were ordered to the defence of Gibraltar in 1727. In 1767 the Cameronians were ordered to Canada, and throughout the American war fought under Lieut.-General Clinton.* They served at Alexandria, and at Corunna, where they were in the thickest of the fighting. A period of service with the Walcheren expedition so enfeebled the regiment through sickness that they were unable to take a very active part in the Peninsular war. But the chance for distinction came with the Chinese war of 1840, and they gladly seized it, though here again they suffered cruelly from sickness, losing their colonel and two hundred men. At Amoy Colonel Mountain, leading a body of the 26th, was the first of our forces actually over the wall, and at the capture of Chapoo distinguished himself by a hand-to-hand combat with a Tartar warrior. At the time the Tartar rushed at him "three balls struck him the same instant and three more passed through his haversack; of the former one furrowed the muscles of the spine, another hit him on the left side and passed out under the lower rib, the third struck him in the thigh, ran down the leg and came out at the knee; yet he killed his opponent and was soon fit for service." As an example of the severe loss the regiment incurred from fever, etc., may be mentioned the fact that scarcely one of those who started for the China war returned. Their number was nine hundred to commence with, nine hundred recruits were sent out, "yet only the original number remained when the regiment marched into the Castle of Edinburgh in 1843."

We must pass rapidly over the following years, during which the 26th served in Canada and India, and come to 1868, in which year they were with Napier's little army in Abyssinia. But even here their lot it was to learn that—

"They also serve who only stand and wait;"

for their duties did not bring them within actual fighting distance of the enemy. Since the Abyssinian war, though duty has been ever well performed, and the credit and high

* It is recorded that during this war a detachment of the regiment which had been embarked for some secret science was overpowered, but when capture appeared inevitable the colours were wound round a cannon shot and sunk in the river.

standing of the regiment well and thoroughly maintained, no foe has called for the stern lessons which these successors of the old Covenanters know so well how to give.

The 2nd battalion of the Scottish Rifles is the 90th, the Perthshire Volunteers of many a well-fought field. They date from 1794, when they were raised by Mr. Thomas Graham, somewhat to the annoyance of the 'Powers that be' near the Throne, who did not fancy a non-military man having too much to do with raising regiments. But "nice customs curtsey to great kings," and this volunteer of the Toulon expedition was to prove a veritable "king of men" in those Peninsular battles, where that "daring old man of a ready temper for battle" was to win renown as Sir Thomas Graham, afterwards Lord Lynedoch. Their first service was at Isle Dieu and Quiberon, and three years after they were at Minorca. Their first distinction was won in Egypt, where they won widespread praise for their gallant conduct at Mandora. Here, owing to their wearing brass helmets, they were mistaken by the enemy for dismounted dragoons, over whom an easy victory was to be anticipated. The withering fire with which they received the French cavalry proved the error of this surmise, but the fight was a stubborn and a severe one. Colonel Rowland Hill of the regiment was hit on the head and had to be taken off the field; at one time Abercrombie himself would have been taken prisoner but for the magnificent stand made by the 90th. Colonel Hill, it may be remarked, was taken on board the *Foudroyant*, and into the cabin occupied by him, slowly rallying from his severe wound, was the brave and well-loved Abercrombie brought to die. After Egypt the 90th served at Martinique, whence Captain Preedy of the regiment brought to the King the tidings of victory, and at Guadeloupe, where they captured an eagle. The following years were passed at home, at Malta, and in America. The records of the regiment contain an interesting account of the steadfast courage and discipline of the regiment on the occasion of a terrible shipwreck, and in 1846 they served under Lieutenant-Colonel Slade in the South African war of that date. Returning home in 1848, they landed in the Crimea in December, 1855, when amongst the Lieutenants was one Garnet Joseph Wolseley. On the occasion of the sortie of the 22nd of March Captain Vaughan, with about a dozen gallant fellows of the Perthshire Volunteers, beat back a formidable body of Russians; in the assault of the 7th of June, Colonel Campbell and Captain Wolseley were specially mentioned; a few days later Private Alexander won the Victoria Cross for bringing in wounded men, conduct which he repeated on the 6th of September following, when he helped to bring back the body of Captain Buckley of the Scots Guards.

In the final assault on the Redan a working party of one hundred men were under Captain Perrin. Colonel Handcock fell mortally wounded; inside the Redan were found the bodies of Captain Preston and Lieutenants Swift and Wilmer; Sergeant Moynihan "slew five Russians with his own hand" before it became necessary to retire. On the capture of the town Captain Vaughan of the regiment was found, terribly ill, in one of the hospitals. He said he had been brutally treated, and was about to be bayoneted in cold blood, but fortunately bethought him to make the Masonic sign, which was recognised by his would-be assassin who spared his life. Only for a few days, however, did Vaughan live after his rescue.

Scarcely was the Crimean War ended ere the 90th were ordered to India to assist in quelling the Mutiny. Their first exploit was the disarming of the disaffected cavalry at Berhampore. From there they were sent to reinforce Havelock, and with him marched to the relief of Lucknow. The first shot from the Alumbagh killed three officers, and about the same time, though elsewhere, fell the brave man Alexander, who had not yet received the V.C. he had so gallantly won in the Crimea. The splendid charge made by the 90th and 78th is recorded in any history of the events—how the Perthshire Light Infantry captured two guns, and how Colonel Campbell was saved from death by the Prayer-Book he carried in his breast arresting the course of a shot. Well known, too, is the gallant devotion to duty which earned the coveted Cross for Drs. Home and Bradshaw of the regiment, who, with only a handful of men, kept at bay hundreds of the rebels for nearly twenty-four hours. Three similar Crosses were won at the second relief of Lucknow by Major Guise, Sergeant Gill and Private Graham, when the regiment, under Major Barnston, did such great things. Throughout the Mutiny the 90th vied with the gallantest there in their endurance and courage, and before returning home had some further fighting in the Euzuffuzie expedition. Though the regiment itself did not participate in the Ashantee war, they may certainly claim a credit of connection in that campaign, for Wolseley and Evelyn Wood, and the gallant young Eyre, who fell at Ordahsu, were or had been all members of the Perthshire Light Infantry. In 1878 they were in South Africa, and early in the following year constituted the bulk of the infantry in No. 3 column under their own officer, Evelyn Wood, and served throughout the campaign; specially did they distinguish themselves at Inhlobane, where Lieutenant Lysons and Private Fowler were awarded the V.C., in clearing out a cavern whence the Zulus kept up a dangerous fire. Again at Kambula they were hotly engaged, eventually routing the foe with great loss, though Major Hackett was terribly

THE 72nd -- SEAFORTH HIGHLANDERS.

wounded, and—trying to assist him—Lieutenant Bright, one of the most popular officers in the regiment, lost his life. They were with the flying column that fought so well at Ulundi, after which their more active participation in the operations going on in Zululand terminated, and with that termination we must perforce close our notice of the Perthshire Light Infantry, now the 2nd battalion of the Cameronians.

THE SEAFORTH HIGHLANDERS *—Regimental District No. 72—consists of the 72nd and 78th Foot. The former date from 1778, when they were raised by the then Lord Seaforth in recognition of the graceful act of the Government in restoring to him the forfeited title of his ancestors. By a somewhat strange coincidence the first number borne by the regiment was that of their present 2nd battalion, 78. The first years of the regiment were somewhat tempestuous; the relations between England and the Scottish Highlanders were still somewhat strained, and each side was only too eager to allege bad faith on the part of the other. From this feeling originated the affair of "the wild Macraes," a sept or small clan who had enlisted under Lord Seaforth. They refused to embark for foreign service, and with colours flying and pipes playing betook themselves to Arthur's Seat, where they continued for some days in a state of inaggressive mutiny. But this was got over by a little tact, and before long the brave Highlanders marched back to their regiment with their colonel and other officers at their head. They then set sail for India, but on the voyage out lost their Colonel—Seaforth—from illness, an occurrence which exercised a most depressing and fatal effect on his men, many of whom sickened and died. On arriving in India they joined Stuart's force and marched against Cuddalore, and at that place, as at Palghantchery, Savendroog and Outra Durgum, proved how valuable an acquisition the Seaforth Highlanders were to the British Army. Palghantchery and Outra Durgum may indeed be said to have owed their capture chiefly to the "heroic ardour" of the 72nd. At Seringapatam they were in the third column, to which was entrusted the storming of the Pagoda Hill, under Colonel Maxwell, and not a little of the credit of the day is due to the dashing manner

* The Seaforth Highlanders bear as badges the Coronet and Cypher of the late Duke of York and Albany on the Star of the Thistle, and the Elephant, with "Assaye," on cap and collar. The mottoes are "Cabar Feidh"—the clan cry of the Seaforth; "Tulach Ard," that of the Mackenzies of Kintoul; and "Cuidich'n Righ" ("Cuideachd an Righ"). On their colours are "Hindoostan," "Assaye," "Cape of Good Hope," "Maida," "Java," "South Africa, 1835," "Sevastopol," "Persia," "Koosh-ab," "Lucknow," "Central India," "Peiwar Kotal," "Charasiah," "Kabul, 1879," "Kandahar, 1880," "Afghanistan, 1878—80" "Egypt, 1882," "Tel-el-Kebir." The uniform is scarlet with facings of yellow, with feather bonnet and kilt, the feather bonnet having a white hackle feather.

in which he carried out this plan. They also served at Pondicherry, and in Ceylon; after which, in 1798, they returned home.

In 1805 they embarked for the Cape of Good Hope, and at the Blaw Berg in the following year suffered somewhat severely, the list of casualties including Colonels Grant and Campbell of the regiment, while Lieutenant M'Arthur and thirty men distinguished themselves by engaging and repulsing a very superior force of Dutch. Three years later, in accordance with a "fad" of the government, the Seaforth Highlanders discontinued the wearing of the Highland costume, which, however, they have subsequently re-adopted. After this, for again we must pass over much, the 72nd were employed in the Mauritius and in India, about the time of Waterloo being employed in South Africa. During their sojourn here a somewhat characteristic incident occurred with the Boers. The latter appealed to the British for aid against the Kaffirs who were making raids upon their homesteads, and accordingly Captain Gethin of the regiment with some men went to the scene of a recent disturbance. Here they were surrounded by a body of Kaffirs in ambush and cut to pieces, Captain Gethin himself receiving no fewer than thirty-two wounds. It will surprise no one who has studied the history of the Boers to learn that the people whom Gethin came to help looked placidly on while he and his gallant men of the 72nd were being butchered. The regiment returned home in 1821, and two years after received the title of the "Duke of Albany's Highlanders," after the then Commander-in-Chief, his Royal Highness the Duke of York and Albany, at the same time receiving the Highland costume, only with trews instead of kilt. Their next service was again at the Cape of Good Hope, and during the operations against Macumo, the hostile Kaffir chief, they greatly distinguished themselves. After another interval of rest the Duke of Albany's Highlanders were dispatched to the Crimea, where they arrived in May, 1855, and from that date to the close of the war served in all the duties which our troops were called upon to perform. After the Crimea followed with deadly haste the Mutiny, where the 72nd earned lasting praise. Their chief exploits were while serving with Sir Hugh Rose's force in Central India, and at Kotah the fortune of war decreed that their chief opponents should be the revolted 72nd native regiment, whose uniform in some degree resembled that of the Duke of Albany's. The storming party was to abide the blowing up of the great gate, and owing to the unexpected delay in doing this found themselves exposed for some time to the fierce fire of the enemy. But when the explosion was heard, and the pipes struck up their martial tune, it required but a very few minutes to capture the town, thanks to the impetuous ardour of the 72nd and their comrades, who with a ringing shout—"Scotland for ever!" literally drove all before them. Throughout the struggles in Baroda the 72nd, who were subsequently with the Rajpootana Field Force, fought well and successfully, well meriting the unstinted meed of praise awarded to them. The next important campaign in which the 72nd were engaged was in Afghanistan in 1878. Here they were brigaded under General Roberts, and rendered most signal service at the storming of the Peiwar Kotal. Here the 72nd and the "brave little Ghoorkas" fairly divided the honours of the day between them, though Lieutenant Munro and several rank and file were in the list of casualties. During the march through the Sappri defile Sergeant Green gained his commission for the gallant defence he made of Captain Goad, and it is recorded by a Scotch writer that "a sick Highlander (of the 72nd), who was being carried in a dhooley, fired all his ammunition, sixty-two rounds, at the enemy, and as he was a good marksman, he never fired without getting a fair shot."

The following year they were still more actively employed, and round and about Cabul, under Roberts, came in for much fierce fighting, from which they gained a full sheaf of honours. Sergeants Macdonald, Cox, and M'Ilvean distinguished themselves at the assault of the Takt-i-Shah; Lieutenant Ferguson was twice wounded; Sergeant Jule (who was killed the next day) was the first man to gain the ridge, capturing at the same time two standards. Corporal Sellars, the first man to gain the top of the Asmai heights, gained a Victoria Cross; before that day's sun had set Captain Spens and Lieutenant Gainsford of the regiment had fallen fighting like heroes to the last; Lieutenant Egerton was badly wounded, and several rank and file put *hors de combat*. The regiment fought well in the attack on Sherpur, and in Roberts's famous march to Candahar were brigaded with the Gordon Highlanders and 60th Rifles. In the attack on Candahar Sir Frederick reported that "the 72nd and the 2nd Sikhs had the chief share of the fighting;" of the Second Brigade Colonel Brownlow, Captain Frowe and Sergeant Cameron were among the killed; Captain Stewart Murray and Lieutenant Munroe were badly wounded. In 1881 the regiment resumed the kilt, adopting the Mackenzie tartan, and were engaged in the Egyptian war of the following year, when they served with Macpherson's Indian Contingent; under Colonel Stockwell they brilliantly inaugurated their campaign by the capture of Chalouffe. At Tel-el-Kebir they were leading on the extreme left, "advancing steadily and in silence until an advanced battery of the enemy was reached, when it was gallantly stormed by the Highlanders" (*Sir G. Wolseley's Dispatch*), and after this they pursued the flying enemy and occupied the important town of Zagazig. Their losses were very slight, two men killed and three wounded, owing "to the excellent arrangements made by General Macpherson," and to the fact that the earlier attacks had so shaken the enemy that they could not withstand "the impetuous onslaught of the Seaforth Highlanders."

The 2nd battalion of the Seaforth Highlanders, consisting of the 78th regiment, the Ross-shire Buffs, also owes its existence to the loyal family of Seaforth, being raised in 1793 by the then head of the clan. Their first service was under the Earl of Chatham in the disastrous Walcheren Expedition, after which they took part in the campaign in Holland under the Duke of York. The value of the service rendered by the Highlanders during the terrible retreat to Bremen has been before mentioned; at Gildermalsen, however, the 78th ran a somewhat serious risk. "A regiment of the enemy's hussars, dressed in a uniform similar to that worn by the Emigrant regiment of the Duke de Choiseul in our service, pushed on, treacherously shouting 'Choiseul! Choiseul!' and got close to the 78th Highlanders undiscovered." They were, however, repulsed by some scathing volleys from the Black Watch. The 78th then served for a time at the Cape of Good Hope, and in 1797 were ordered to India,[*] where they gained the first of their many distinctions. Under Wellesley they assisted in the capture of the strong town of Ahmednughur, and under the immediate command of the same great leader fought with splendid courage at Assaye; they were on the left of the first line, and at the close of the day were led forward by Wellesley in person to clear out the village, which they did at the point of the bayonet after some desperate fighting. They fought at Argaum, and in 1811 were with the forces under Sir Samuel Achmuty in the operations in Java. On returning home they experienced the misfortune which our troops seem so often to have suffered, namely, that of being shipwrecked; the reports at the time speak in the most energetic terms of the courage and endurance displayed by the 78th, of whom, fortunately, not a man was lost. But the regiment had been reaping its harvest of honour in the West as well as in the East. Under Stuart they had been serving in Sicily, and are amongst the regiments whose colours bear the name "Maida." The record of the regiment narrates that the aspect of the regiment caused the general some apprehension, they looked so very young; quite six hundred of their number were under twenty-one. But there was nought of weakness or youthful instability in that splendid charge they made, led by their gallant Colonel, Patrick Macleod. Opposed to them was the French 42nd regiment of Grenadiers, led by a brave and skilful commander. But commander and

[*] A 2nd battalion.

troops alike were hurled back by the 78th. The retreat became a headlong flight, and so far did the Highlanders with fierce slaughter pursue the flying foe that an aide-de-camp was sent to bid them halt. "At the moment the order was delivered to Macleod he was incapable of speech, and was stooping from his horse on the shoulder of a sergeant of his regiment; a rifle ball had passed through his breast within an inch of the heart, inflicting a painful and perilous wound;" yet he never quitted his saddle or the field, but remained at the head of his Ross-shire Buffs during the remainder of the battle and the long pursuit that followed it. Again and again they charged during that day, and no regiment more nobly acquitted itself. In 1807 they fought in Egypt and gained undying fame at the disastrous conflict at El Hamet. Colonel Macleod with one company of the regiment and some of the 35th were surrounded and assailed by an overwhelming force. The colonel was killed; "there also fell Lieutenant Macrae with six more of his name; Sergeant John Macrae slew seven assailants with his claymore before his head was cloven from behind. Of Macleod's detachment, consisting of two hundred and seventy-five, all were killed to thirty, of whom fifteen only were unwounded." Strangely enough two of the prisoners of the 78th rose to high eminence in the land of their captivity. Ibrahim Aga, the famed governor of Medina and one of the Sultan's most able generals, was Private Thomas Keith on that dreadful day when his officers and comrades fell around him in El Hamet; Osman, "the learned leech" of Alexandria, who acquired a large practice and larger fortune, was a drummer boy in the 78th, whose medical training had been limited to assisting the regimental surgeon to tie bandages and mix medicines.

The Ross-shire Buffs have 'Persia' and 'Khoosh-ab' on their colours, words which recall their conduct in a campaign in which they earned a very high encomium from Sir Henry Havelock: they "behaved remarkably well at the battle of Khoosh-ab, . . . and during the naval action on the Euphrates and the landing, their steadiness, zeal, and activity were conspicuous. They . . . never seemed to complain of anything, but that they had no further chance of meeting the enemy. I am convinced that the regiment would be second to none in the service if their high military qualities were drawn forth; they are proud of their colours, their tartan, and their former high achievements." On the night preceding the battle of Khoosh-ab, the enemy attempted a surprise on our forces, but thanks to steadiness and discipline, the only result was to somewhat lessen the number of the morrow's assailants. During this midnight attack the 78th were exposed to a somewhat bewildering ruse on the part of the Persians, one of whose buglers had learned the "calls" used in our service, and repeatedly sounded "cease firing" close to the Ross-shires—fortunately, however, he entirely failed to mislead them. When the Mutiny broke out "the high military qualities" of the regiment were called forth with a vengeance, and the result proved how admirably General Havelock had gauged the calibre of the corps. We shall not attempt to follow *seriatim* the services the 78th rendered throughout the Mutiny; these services are matter of history, and will be recalled whenever the Indian Mutiny is mentioned. They were with Havelock in his march to relieve Cawnpore and Lucknow; marching in eight days a hundred and twenty-six miles, fighting four battles, and capturing a score of guns. As is sadly well known the force arrived too late at Cawnpore, despite their heroic efforts and splendid victories, and the terrible sight that met their eyes—mangled bodies, torn clothing, children's little frocks and toys, tresses of long hair torn out by the roots, all bedabbled with blood—lives yet, an awful memory. Not many years before, a poet had put into the lips of a singer of old Rome the stirring couplet which spoke of

> ..."the inexpiable wrong, the unutterable shame
> That turns the coward's heart to steel, the sluggard's blood to flame.'

There were neither cowards nor sluggards in this band of heroes, and men told at the time how the Ross-shire Buffs, finding amongst the blood-boltered débris a tress of black hair torn from the head of one of poor, murdered General Wheeler's daughters, divided it amongst their number, each vowing, like the Knight of Snowdon, to stain it deep in rebel blood. Splendidly did they fight at the Alumbagh, when, at last, Lucknow was taken. Two incidents are recorded by a countryman, each having for its hero a piper of the 78th. In one case the piper was wounded and a couple of his comrades were carrying him off, when they saw, to their dismay, a rebel trooper approaching with drawn sword. The position was critical, but the piper was equal to the occasion; "going through the ordinary manœuvres of loading a gun, he lifted the longest shank of his pipes to his shoulder and pointed it at the Sepoy's head." As a result the latter "turned tail and ran off." On another occasion—the capture of Lucknow—a piper found himself alone, lost in the tortuous streets, with gun discharged and bayonet unfixed. "To him enter," round a sudden corner, one of the rebel cavalry, who forthwith made at him. Whatever views may be held of the relative merits of sword and bayonet, there can be but one opinion as to the superiority of the former when the latter is not fixed. The days of the brave 78th man seemed numbered. "Suddenly," he wrote, "a bright idea struck me; all at once I seized my pipe, put it to my mouth, and gave forth a shrill note which so startled the fellow that he bolted like a shot, evidently imagining it was some infernal machine; so my pipe saved my life."

The 78th gained too many of those crosses inscribed "For Valour," for us to be able to do more than quote some of the circumstances. Private James Hollowell, 78th Highlanders, received the Victoria Cross for conduct officially described as follows:— "A party on the 26th September, 1857, was shut up and besieged in a house in the city of Lucknow by the rebel Sepoys. Private James Hollowell, one of the party, behaved throughout the day in the most admirable manner; he directed, encouraged, and led the others, exposing himself fearlessly, and by his talent in persuading and cheering, prevailed on nine desperate men to make a successful defence in a burning house, with the enemy firing through four windows."

"Assistant Surgeon Valentine Munbee M'Master, 78th Highlanders, was recommended for the Victoria Cross for the intrepidity with which he exposed himself to the fire of the enemy in bringing in and attending to the wounded on the 25th September, at Lucknow. He had served in the Persian War and in all Havelock's operations for the succour of the Residency. After arriving at the latter place he accompanied many sorties and was wounded. He was with Outram's force at the Alumbagh, and took part in the Rohilcund campaign."

"Surgeon Joseph Jee was selected by his brother officers for the Victoria Cross. On September 25th, 1857, the 78th Highlanders had been left behind to protect the passage of the Char Bagh Bridge. The enemy, seeing their isolated position, gathered round them from every quarter, occupying all the neighbouring buildings. From the tops of these came a perfect hail of musket-bullets, while two heavy guns were enfilading the regiment with deadly accuracy. Ordered not to move till every bullock had crossed the bridge, the regiment for a long time remained halted. At length, becoming desperate, they charged the guns, dashing up the street with a loud cheer, led by their Adjutant, whose horse had been shot under him. They were received by a volley, and men dropped in numbers; but the survivors persevered, reached the guns, and after a short, sharp struggle captured them. Dr. Jee contrived, by great personal exertions, in getting the wounded who had been hit in the charge carried off on the backs of their comrades, till he had succeeded in collecting the dhooly-bearers who had fled. He is said to have exposed himself in the most devoted manner. Later on, while trying to reach the Residency with the wounded under his charge, he was obliged to throw himself into the Moti Mehal, where he remained besieged the whole of the following night and morning."

The official account says that he repeatedly exposed himself to a heavy fire "in proceeding to dress the wounded men who fell while serving a 24-pounder in a most exposed situation. He eventually succeeded in taking many of the wounded, through a cross-fire of ordnance and musketry, safely into the Residency, by the river bank, although repeatedly warned not to make the perilous attempt."

The gallant Adjutant who led the 78th Highlanders in the brilliant charge abovementioned was Lieutenant Herbert Taylor Macpherson, afterwards the Sir Herbert Macpherson who commanded the Indian contingent in the Egyptian War, and is now a C.B.

After Lucknow the 78th joined the Rohilcund Field Force, where they, needless to say, did yeoman's service. The following years were passed in Gibraltar, Canada, and Ireland; after this they served under General Phayre in Afghanistan, but were not actively engaged. No important operations coming within the scope of this sketch have since that date fallen to the lot of the gallant Ross-shire Buffs.

The King's (Shropshire) Light Infantry*—Regimental District No. 53—is composed of the 53rd and 85th Regiments of the line. The former, the 53rd, date from 1755, when they were raised by Colonel Whitmore, and first numbered the 55th. The first duty on which they were engaged was that of garrisoning Gibraltar, where they stayed twelve years. In 1776 occurred the fighting under Burgoyne in and about Quebec, and in this campaign the 53rd gained considerable credit, especially at Crown Point and Ticonderoga, where the flank companies were engaged, and shared, with so many others of the royal troops, the discomforts of imprisonment. Returning to England in 1789 they fought, four years later, in Flanders, where they gained their first distinction in "Nieuport," previously to which, however, they had made an honourable name for themselves at Famars and Valenciennes. The 53rd are the only regiment that bear Nieuport on their colours, and it is recorded that Major R. Matthews of the regiment "particularly distinguished himself," while their conduct was such as to elicit very eulogistic mention in the dispatches of the commander. The following year they fought at Vaux, Prémont, Landrécies, Cateau, Tournay, and other less notable engagements,

---

* The King's (Shropshire) Light Infantry bear as badges the monogram K.L.I., with a bugle on a star on the cap, and a bugle on the collar. The motto is "Aucto Splendore Resurgo." On the colours are: "Nieuport," "Tournay," "St. Lucia," "Talavera," "Fuentes d'Onor," "Salamanca," "Vittoria," "Pyrenees," "Nivelle," "Nive," "Toulouse," "Peninsula," "Bladensburg," "Aliwal," "Sobraon," "Punjaub," "Goojerat," "Lucknow," "Afghanistan, 1879–80," "Egypt, 1882," "Suakin, 1885." The uniform is scarlet, with facings of blue.

and with the 14th and 37th Regiments were known as the "Fighting Brigade." Right well did they earn the sobriquet! On one occasion, on the road between Lisle and Roubaix, the fighting Brigade kept at bay an overwhelming mass of the enemy, but for close upon *half* their gallant number it was the last of all their glorious fields. At Tournay, again, the regiment, under Major Wiseman, was severely engaged and suffered considerable loss; their conduct, however, earned the special praise and thanks of the Commander-in-Chief. They returned to England in 1795 after sharing in that terrible retreat so often, perforce, referred to, and shortly after were ordered to the West Indies. At St. Lucia they were with the future hero of Corunna in the splendid attack which captured Morne Chabot, after which they rendered signal service in the Carib War in St. Vincent, and added the capture of Trinidad to their already crowded list of achievements. They returned to England in 1802, and the year following a 2nd battalion was formed, which represented the gallant Shropshire in the Peninsular Campaign. We will, however, before dealing with them, pursue the career of the 1st battalion, which, in 1805, was ordered to India, and for many years bore a conspicuous part in the many fierce encounters fought with the native princes. At the storming of Callinger, for instance, a fortress of immense strength, surrounded by seemingly impassable defiles and ravines, and itself recalling the lonely hamlet which the poet describes as being—

> "Like an eagle's nest
> Perched on the crest
> Of purple Apennine,"

Colonel Mawby, who commanded them, declared that "he had not words to express his admiration of the conduct of every officer and soldier in the 53rd," while the General Orders echoed his eulogy in their reference to "the exemplary exertions, zeal, and persevering courage of officers and men." In 1813 and the following year, the 53rd were with Sir Robert Rollo Gillespie in Nepaul, and at the capture of Kalunga—another fortress standing, as Sir Robert himself described it, "on the summit of an almost inaccessible mountain and covered by an impenetrable forest"—again won universal praise. Colonel Mawby, Major Ingleby, Captain Coultman, Lieutenants Young, Anstice, and Harrington are some of those of the 53rd whose names were in men's mouths as those who had done gloriously, and had in many cases won honour only at the cost of life or limb. For many years they fought in India and returned home in 1823, having lost 350 officers and 1,167 privates, who had been killed or had succumbed to wounds or disease, and nearly 500 of all ranks invalided.

We must now retrace our steps somewhat and glance at the doings of the 2nd battalion, which, as has been said, was formed in 1803. The first six years of their existence were passed in Ireland, whence, in 1809, they were dispatched to the Peninsula. Here they were brigaded with the 7th Fusiliers under General A. Campbell, and commenced their warlike career with the combats about Oporto. It was not to be long before they added the famous name of "Talavera" to the roll of the regiment's honours. The historian of the war records that on Campbell's division the French fell with infinite fury, yet "the English regiments, putting the French skirmishers aside, met the advancing columns with loud shouts, broke their front, lapped their flanks with fire, and giving them no respite pushed them back with a terrible carnage." They were not actually attacked at Busaco, but took part in the investment of Almeida and in the battle of Fuentes d'Onor. They were employed in covering the siege of Badajoz and the operations at Almaraz; in the capture of the fortified convents before Salamanca they elicited unstinted admiration; at the battle of Salamanca itself no regiment was for a time more hardly pressed than "that brave regiment," as Napier styles the 53rd. In vain Boyer's Dragoons thundered down upon their flank, exposed by the retreat of the Portuguese regiments; though many of the 53rd were actually cut down by their sabres, steadily and unflinchingly did they stem the surging tide; the crisis of the day thus passed favourably to the British, and before many hours the important battle was won. The regiment served in the siege of Burgos, Lieutenant Frazer distinguishing himself in one of the assaults; they fought in the centre column at Vittoria, took part in the blockade of Pampeluna, and showed how stubbornly they could struggle till they conquered in the wild warfare that took place on the slopes of the towering Pyrenees. The regimental record states that there were volunteers from the regiment present at St. Sebastian; at Nivelle they "evinced great courage" and captured a field-piece; at Toulouse, that "needless battle," they suffered very severely. The last duty of the 2nd battalion of the 53rd was to garrison St. Helena, where the Emperor—officially known as 'General Buonaparte'—was placed that the world might have peace. Here they gained the respect and admiration of their mighty captive, and we cannot better bid farewell to this brave regiment—which was disbanded in 1817—than by quoting the words used by a Minister in his place in Parliament. "Whatsoever," averred Lord Bathurst, "the General could say in praise of that corps was not adequate to its merits."

For twenty-one years the 53rd (1st battalion) served at various home stations, and in 1844 returned again to India, there to win fresh honours. Plenty of fighting had they on the Sutlej. At Aliwal they were on the extreme left and carried the village of Boondree at the point of the bayonet, being referred to by Sir Harry Smith as 'a young regiment, but veterans in daring gallantry and regularity.' At Sobraon the 53rd were in Sir Robert Dick's Division under Brigadier Stacy. The attack made by the brigade in the teeth of a withering fire will long be remembered by the eulogists—and they are many—of British Infantry, and the official records of the regiment show how highly the General esteemed their share in the warfare. At Goojerat they were in reserve, and for the following years were engaged in the desultory fighting along the Peshawur frontier. During the mutiny they were, as beseemed men with such traditions, of invaluable service. After being for some short time at Fort William they were attached to Campbell's force which marched to relieve Lucknow. In the attack made by the enemy on the advance guard on the 12th of November, the 53rd were foremost in inflicting the repulse which resulted, and in the assault on the Secunderbagh the regiment, under Captain Walton, vied with the Sikhs and Highlanders in exacting a terrible recompense from the merciless, murderous foe. At Furruckbad they were attacked while crossing the river to support an advanced picket, and shared in inflicting the crushing defeat on the rebels. In the battle of Cawnpore, the siege of Lucknow, the subsequent operations in Oude, and the final crusade under Colonel Walker of the Bays, which completed the subjugation of the terror-stricken rebels, the 53rd were well to the fore. At the assault of Meangunge they especially distinguished themselves.

"The Light Company of the 53rd, under Captain Hopkins, were thrown forward in a plantation which approached the walls near enough to check the musketry fire from the fort, and some Punjaubees to the right of the guns in another plantation. About a couple of hours' pounding brought down a piece of the wall large enough to let four men abreast enter, when the 53rd were ordered up to be ready to assault, and the General spoke a few encouraging words to them. Soon Anson was sent to order the 53rd to the assault, the cannonade ceased and they immediately debouched from the plantation, headed by their gallant Colonel, and marched as steadily as if on parade towards the breach. In a second the leading files of the 53rd were up, Hopkins getting first to the breach, and turning to our left down a street, we were directly among the enemy, chopping and sticking as hard as we could. About this time poor Brockhurst of the 53rd was shot through the body."

The 53rd were, indeed, well to the fore. It would be a lengthy task to detail in full the many instances of valour which the regiment and individual members of it displayed, but in the annals of those who have won the Victoria Cross few accounts are more eloquent in their plain unadorned narration than the following:—

"At Chota Nagpore, on the 2nd October, 1857, the mutineers were, after a hard struggle, defeated, but not till they had killed or disabled one-third of our weak force. Two of the enemy's guns caused great havoc and affairs looked critical, when, with Sergeant Denis Dynon of the 53rd, Lieutenant Daunt rushed forward and, pistolling the artillerymen, drove them from their guns. Again on the 2nd November, at Nomeelah Behar, Daunt, with a few of Rattray's Sikhs, pursued a large body of mutineers of the 32nd Bengal Native Infantry into an enclosure, in driving them from which he was severely wounded. The Victoria Cross was awarded both to him and Dynon."

"The 53rd regiment at the capture of the Secunderbagh did not enter by the breach, but by a gate which was opened for them after the 93rd and Sikhs had got in. Nevertheless, in driving the Sepoys out of the numerous buildings in which they had taken refuge the 53rd had a good deal of fighting, for the enemy was only conquered by being absolutely exterminated. The regiment also distinguished itself on the 17th November. To it, therefore, were assigned four Victoria Crosses, the recipients to be selected by their comrades. The names of those thus decorated were Lieutenant Alfred Ffrench, Sergeant-Major Charles Pye, and Privates J. Kenny and C. Irwin. Lieutenant Ffrench, in command of the Grenadiers, was one of the first to enter the building. The whole company bore testimony to his conspicuous gallantry on this occasion. Sergeant-Major Pye was remarked for the steady and fearless manner in which he brought up ammunition under fire on the 17th November, and on every occasion on which his regiment had been engaged. Kenny obtained the Cross for conspicuous courage at the taking of the Secunderbagh, and for volunteering to bring up ammunition to his company under a very severe cross-fire. Irwin also displayed great bravery at the capture of the Secunderbagh and, though severely wounded, was one of the first men of his regiment who entered the building under a heavy fire." (*Victoria Cross in India.*)

The 53rd returned home in 1860, and from that time to the commencement of the Egyptian War of 1882 were quartered in the United Kingdom, Canada, and the Bermudas. In the disposition of the forces at Alexandria the 53rd were in the Second Division under General Hamley, and shared in the various operations which culminated in the capture of the lines of Kafr Dowar and the surrender of Damietta. It was by an escort of the 53rd under Major Rogerson that Abdellah, the Pasha who had vowed that he would never yield to the infidels, was conveyed to Cairo. At the conclusion of the war the 53rd remained for a time to garrison Cairo, and in the operations of 1885 added to their list of distinctions, under circumstances of too recent date to need enumeration here.

The 2nd battalion of the King's (Shropshire) Light Infantry, the 85th, dates from 1793, when it was raised, and known, from the place of recruiting, as the Bucks Volunteers. The first service of the regiment was in 1794, when the Bucks Volunteers were ordered to Walcheren and had their share of fighting; they were then for a time at Gibraltar, and after again visiting Holland, where they very greatly distinguished themselves, returned home. After being employed in Madeira and Jamaica they again served at Walcheren in the discreditably planned expedition of 1809. They then repaired to the Peninsula, and fought with credit at Fuentes d'Onor, having been previously engaged in many of the less known combats and skirmishes which so frequently took place. On the occasion of the first storming of the Fort Christoval at Badajoz, the stormers were led by Major McIntosh of the 85th; the effort was fruitless, but if valour alone could have won that terrible breach, of a surety it would have been won that night. They fought at the Nive and at Barrouilhet, and then proceeded to America. Perhaps seldom have troops fought under greater disadvantages than those which here confronted the 85th and their comrades. "These troops, badly provisioned, slenderly supplied even with ammunition, and, after their hardships in the Peninsula, many of them requiring repose and attendance in hospital, rather than exposure in battle," numbered perhaps four thousand; "except those belonging to General Ross and the staff officers, there was not a single horse with our troops;" and the three "toy guns" which constituted our artillery were drawn by seamen. During the march towards Bladensburg, many fell out of the ranks, faint and utterly exhausted; nine thousand Americans with twenty guns occupied a position of great strength and commanding altitude; yet in a few minutes this force—double ours in numerical strength, and composed of fresh, unwearied men, fighting in their own country and protected by the fire of their own well-placed guns—fled before the impetuous charge of the British, headed by "the gallant 85th under Colonel Thornton." They fought at Baltimore, the following September, with similar gallantry though with heavy loss, and at New Orleans again acquitted themselves in such wise that the records of that unfortunate expedition mention again and again the brave deeds of "Colonel Thornton and the gallant 85th."* For many years after this, only peaceful duties engaged their services. They served in England, Ireland, Canada, the Mauritius and other places till 1856, when they were ordered to South Africa, where the growing power of Panda, father of Cetewayo, compelled the Imperial Government to observe a watchful attitude. In 1868 the 85th were ordered to India, and eleven years later took part in the operations of the Cabul Field Force, their services in which are evidenced by the distinction, "Afghanistan, 1879—80."

The Prince Albert's (Somersetshire Light Infantry),†—Regimental District No. 13—consisting of the famous old 13th Foot, date from 1685, when the threatened invasion by Monmouth induced the King to increase the strength of the army. At the time of the Revolution the sympathies of the regiment were divided, their Colonel, Lord Huntingdon, remaining loyal to King James, while others of the officers advocated the cause of the Prince of Orange. When the country had settled down under the new régime the 13th were employed in Scotland, taking part in the operations against Edinburgh and in the battle of Killiecrankie. On the latter occasion, under Colonel Hastings, they shared with the 25th the praise of being the only regiments that did not behave badly,‡ the commander stating that in the thick of the fight he saw "Hastings on the right sustaining the reputation of the British lion."§ They fought at the Boyne and other Irish battles, and in 1701 commenced the career of foreign service in which they have won so great a renown. They fought at Mineguen and assisted at the sieges of Venloo, St. Michaels, Ruremonde, Liege, and others. In 1704 Barrymore's Regiment, as the 13th were then called, were sent to Gibraltar to assist the Prince of Hesse Darmstadt who was defending Gibraltar, and during the siege Major Moncall of the regiment rendered most important service. A selected party of French Grenadiers forced their way some distance into the defences when Major Moncall led his men to the charge and

---

* It was a few months previous to this that they received their motto of the Duke of York's Own Regiment of Light Infantry. This was subsequently changed to the King's Light Infantry Regiment, a title which obtained till the most recent change gave to the amalgamated corps the name they now bear.

† The Prince Albert's Somersetshire Light Infantry bear as badges a mural crown with "Jellalabad" over it, underneath it a bugle with the cypher of the late Prince Consort on cap and collar. The motto is that of the Garter. On the colours are: "The Sphinx," "Dettingen," "Egypt," "Martinique," "Ava," "Afghanistan," "Ghuznee," "Jellalabad," "Cabool," "Sevastopol," "South Africa, 1878—9." The uniform is scarlet with blue facings; on the gold lace of the officers' tunic is a black stripe.

‡ See *ante*, page 286.

§ This brave officer, it is sad to relate, was subsequently cashiered for irregularity connected with the supplies which it was then the duty of colonels of regiments to provide.

drove the bold assailants off. The 13th then served at the siege of Barcelona and the relief of St. Matheo. Shortly after the bulk of the regiment were, at the instance of Lord Peterborough, converted bodily into dragoons. The nucleus returned home to recruit, and the following year returned again to Portugal, when they fought most gallantly at Caya. In 1727 they took part in the defence of Gibraltar, after which they remained comparatively inactive till 1743, when they fought at Dettingen, the first name they bear on their colours. They suffered heavy loss at Fontenoy, after which they returned home and took part in the engagements with the adherents of Prince Charles Edward. In 1746 they went abroad, and at Roucoux and Val were distinguished for their "heroic conduct." Passing over the intervening years, during which they were not engaged in any war of importance, in 1790 we find the 1st Somersetshire Regiment—to use the title given in 1782—ordered to the West Indies, where, notably at Fort Bizzeton, in St. Domingo, they very greatly distinguished themselves. They returned home "a regimental wreck" in 1796, and after taking part in the suppression of the Irish rebellion went, in 1800, to Egypt. Here they were brigaded under General Cradock, their own Colonel being Colonel Colville, and at the battle and blockade of Alexandria earned high praise. Their next fighting of importance was at Martinique, where, as well as at Guadeloupe under General Skinner, they again distinguished themselves. The 13th were not engaged in any of the Peninsular battles, but in 1813 were ordered to Canada, where they had their full share in what fighting was to be had. After a few years at home they were ordered, in 1823, to India, and the following year played a glorious part in the Burmese War. Most interesting would it be to follow at length the brave deeds which are commemorated by "Ava," but a very brief recapitulation of them must perforce serve our purpose. In the capture of Rangoon Major Sale of the regiment killed the Burmese commander in single combat, and took his gold-hilted sword and scabbard. When fear lent prudence to the councils of the "Lord of the White Elephant" the European captives were released, but "Major Sale, of the 13th Light Infantry—the future hero of Jellalabad—found Mrs. Hudson, of missionary celebrity, bound to a tree and immediately released her."

Throughout the campaign Major—soon afterwards Colonel—Sale was with his brave 13th, foremost wherever fighting was, and almost invariably the same dispatch that recorded his courage added the ominous words, "severely wounded." At Melloone the 13th, with the 38th, formed the storming party. "By these two British regiments, weakened in numbers by war and pestilence to nearly half their proper strength, fifteen thousand well-armed men were hunted, in one confused mass, from the strongest works they had ever constructed." So fierce and irresistible was the assault that the total casualties of the storming column were only five killed and twenty wounded. Returning to India, the 13th had a period of repose for twelve years or so, after which their prowess found another opportunity for assertion in the Afghan War of 1839. Well, indeed, may the regiment glory in the recollection of Jellalabad, and, like their ancestors of Agincourt,

"Stand a-tiptoe when that day is named."

At Ghuznee they captured two standards. There were a few of the 13th amongst the unfortunate captives from Cabul; Lady Sale, the wife of their gallant Colonel, was wounded by a musket-ball, and sent back—happily for her—as a hostage; it was Colonel Dennie* of the 13th who, when rumours of trouble first came from Cabul, foretold with such terribly literal accuracy the ghastly catastrophe that came to pass:— "You will see that not a soul will escape from Cabul *but one man, and he will come to tell us that the rest are all destroyed.*" Meanwhile, at Jellalabad, the gallant Sale and the 13th were stemming the fierce torrent of murder and conquest, and when the time came for the Army of Vengeance to start on its righteously stern mission, the command of one of the divisions was given to him. At Jugdulluck, the 13th, with whom were the 9th, "scaled the heights, turned the position, and bayoneted the defenders with dreadful slaughter, neither side asking quarter nor hoping for it." At Tizeen, that decisive battle that occupied only a few minutes, and where the might of the British power was indelibly written in grim and blood-red letters, the 13th operated in extended order on the right, and when the central gorge was passed, "closed in by companies, fixing their bayonets as they came cheering down to the charge." When the rescued captives were brought in under an escort led by Sir Robert Sale in person, it is difficult to read without emotion how "the gallant 13th Light Infantry crowded with loud cheers round the wife and widowed daughter" of their beloved chief. On their return to India, the brave regiment that had fought so splendidly were received everywhere with praise and applause; garrisons presented arms to them as they passed; public and private bodies vied in doing them honour; and they received from their Sovereign the title of her Consort's regiment, the right to wear the Royal facings, and the special badge of the "Mural Crown."

Many were the officers of the 13th who distinguished themselves in that Afghan

* Colonel Dennie was killed in the famous and brilliant sortie from Jellalabad.

War,* and amongst them was one whose name a few years later was on the lips and in the hearts of all his countrymen—Sir Henry Havelock.

The 13th returned to England in 1845, and for a few years enjoyed well-earned repose. In the Crimean War they were attached to the Fourth Division, but did not take part in any of the three famous battles whose names appear on the colours of other regiments; they bear, however, the comprehensive distinction of "Sevastopol." In October, 1857, they arrived in India, where they shared in the relief of Azimghur, and "subsequently saw some service in the Jugdespore jungle, and in the Trans-Gogra districts during the years 1858—9." After a sojourn at home and in Gibraltar, the Prince Albert's Light Infantry were ordered to the Cape, and were in the third column of Lord Chelmsford's army, under Sir Evelyn Wood—subsequently the Flying Column—their own chief being Colonel Victor Gilbert. At the battle of Kambula, on the 29th of March, 1879, they experienced some severe fighting, and greatly distinguished themselves, they and the 90th "vying with each other in noble rivalry, and beating back the hordes of Zulus upon the two most exposed flanks." They fought gallantly at Ulundi, where they unfortunately lost Lieutenant Pardoe, who was mortally wounded, and in July received orders to return to England, their departure effecting the disintegration of the famous Flying Column which had done such great things.† Since the Zulu War, the only active service in which the Somersetshire have been engaged has been with the Burmah expeditionary force, the details of which are of too recent date to come within the scope of this work.‡

THE PRINCE OF WALES'S (NORTH STAFFORDSHIRE REGIMENT§)—Regimental District No. 64—is composed of the 64th and 98th Foot. In 1758 the 2nd battalion of the 11th Foot was constituted the 64th Regiment, and the newly formed corps were speedily under orders for the West Indies, where they were engaged at Martinique. Returning home in 1763, they went to America in 1770, and served there till 1782, during which period occurred the revolt of the colonies against British rule. After a short time at

---

* The gallant Sir R. Sale was killed at Moodkhee, where, by a strange coincidence, also fell Sir John M'Caskill, who commanded the other division of Pollock's Army of Vengeance.

† Amongst the Victoria Crosses gained in the Zulu War was one awarded to Captain Knox, late of the 13th, serving with a body of Irregulars, for gallantly rescuing Lieutenant Smith at Inhlobane.

‡ The 2nd battalion of the Thirteenth dates from 1858.

§ The Prince of Wales's North Staffordshire Regiment bear as badges the Prince of Wales's Plume with Staffordshire Knot on cap, and Staffordshire Knot on collar. The motto is that of the Prince of Wales. On the Colours are the Dragon and "St. Lucia," "Surinam," "China," "Punjaub," "Persia," "Reshire," "Bushire," "Koosh-ab," "Lucknow." The uniform is scarlet with facings of white.

home, they went in 1793 to Barbadoes and again took part in the operations directed against Martinique and Guadaloupe, subsequently gaining the distinction of "St. Lucia" on their colours. They were engaged a few years later under Brigadier Hughes at Surinam. Duties elsewhere prevented their taking part in any of the Peninsular battles, but they were for some time in the army of occupation in France, from which time till 1856 only peace duties occupied their services. In the latter year, however, the Persian War broke out, and brought to the 64th an opportunity of showing they were no whit behind regiments which had been more actively employed. "Bushire," "Reshire," "Koosh-ab,"—all speak to the courage and endurance of the 64th, in the operations in which they were engaged. A yet more serious warfare awaited them in India; the moment they landed they marched under Havelock to Cawnpore, and had some sharp fighting at Futtehpore. At the capture of Cawnpore, the conduct of the 64th under Major Stirling provoked the greatest praise. After capturing four villages and seven guns, our wearied troops were checked by a 24-pounder which the rebels had placed in position on the road. The 64th were ordered to take it, and, despite the heavy loss they had incurred, they charged up to the grinning muzzle, captured it, and dispersed the rebels. In the General Order issued by Havelock, he addressed the 64th in the following words: "Your fire was reserved till you saw the colour of your enemies' moustaches—this gave us the victory."

It is impossible to avoid mentioning in connection with this incident the somewhat aggrieved feelings that were naturally aroused amongst the officers and men of the 64th by the fact of Lieutenant Havelock—now Sir H. Havelock Allen—heading them at the final charge, and being, therefore, recommended by his father for the Victoria Cross. No one who remembers the General's previous reticence as to his son's valour will accuse him of paternal bias. No one who recalls the previous and subsequent career of Lieutenant Havelock will deny that he was brave amongst the brave. But it is not difficult to understand that the 64th were hurt at even an apparent suggestion that their own officers were not competent to lead them, no matter how desperate the venture. Perhaps the most dispassionate account of the incident is that contained in the work, "The Victoria Cross in India," from which we have before quoted.

"At the final action previous to the entry into Cawnpore, affairs at one time looked rather bad. The British guns, owing to the fatigue of their cattle, could not come up quickly enough to reply to a 24-pounder placed on the road, which was doing great execution. This gun was guarded by a large body of rebel infantry. Havelock ordered his exhausted infantry to make a last effort. They responded to the appeal, and advanced. The 64th regiment was more immediately opposite to the gun than the other regiments. Major Stirling commanding the 64th had lost his horse, but was gallantly leading his men on foot. No other mounted officer was present. Perhaps observing this fact, perhaps only obeying the dictates of his own courage, Lieutenant Havelock placed himself in front of the regiment, and steered steadily for the 24-pounder, which fired round-shot up to 300 yards, and grape afterwards, with great precision and rapidity. Coolly the 64th drew nearer, losing men at every step, and equally coolly did Lieutenant Havelock ride at a foot's pace straight for the muzzle of the gun. At length, with a rush, the latter was captured; the enemy then fled, and the day was won."

They remained under General Wyndham to garrison Cawnpore, and in the attack made by the rebels on the 28th of November were greatly distinguished. Encouraged by a temporary success they had obtained, the rebels fought with redoubled vigour, hoping, doubtless, to revel in another massacre. The 64th frustrated the fiendish hope. "Captain Wright, with only thirty men of the 64th, held the Baptist chapel and the old burial ground. Finding that the enemy were surrounding him he drew off his men in skirmishing order and stopped the advance of the Sepoys by a fire of musketry. About this time he saw a wing of his own corps, about two hundred and fifty strong, commanded by Colonel Wilson, marching by order of General Wyndham to capture four guns that were playing with fatal precision on the British left. Rallying his small force, Wright instantly led it as a sort of advanced guard to Wilson, on whose men the enemy now turned, their guns doing terrible execution. The brave 64th never wavered, but with a ringing shout rushed on the cannon, spiking three of them before the gunners had recovered from their surprise; but it was alike impossible to retain or carry them off, for the foe were ten to one. Colonel Wilson and Major Stirling were shot, Captains Murphy and M'Crea were cut down at the guns, while Captain M'Kinnon and Lieutenant Gordon were severely wounded, taken prisoners, and murdered in cold blood. The slaughter was great among the 64th." During this episode, Drummer Thomas Flinn, of the 64th Regiment, was wounded; but, nevertheless, he persisted in remaining with his comrades, and engaged in a hand-to-hand encounter with two of the rebel artillerymen. Later on the regiment was engaged against Tantia Topee and in Rohilcund, and throughout the mutiny gained deservedly the reputation of being a gallant and dashing regiment. Since then no warlike duties of importance have fallen to their lot.

The 98th, the 2nd battalion of the North Staffordshire, dates from 1824, and is, according to Colonel Archer, the sixth regiment which has borne that number. Their first duty was in South Africa, where they served for several years, after which they fought in the China War of 1840—41, their officer being Colonel Campbell. In 1846 they repaired to India and bear the distinction "Punjaub" in commemoration of the services they rendered during that anxious time. In 1850 they took part in the campaign against the fierce Afridis, and in the fighting in the Kohat Pass rendered signal and meritorious service. Returning home in 1855, a couple of years later saw them again in India, sharing in the operations under General Cotton against the Eusufzies. For many years the 98th remained in India, finding from time to time plenty of occupation in the occasionally irksome duties devolving upon the army in "our Great Dependency;" and after a stay in England, whither they returned in 1867, the Afghan troubles of 1879—80 caused them again to seek "the tented field," though their participation in the operations was limited to the steps taken after the taking of Candahar. No subsequent warfare has fallen to their lot, but amongst the minor military services which from time to time occupy our forces, the Zhob Valley Expedition of 1884 broke for the 98th the spell of inaction.

THE SOUTH STAFFORDSHIRE REGIMENT*—Regimental District No. 38—is composed of the 38th and 80th Regiments of the line. The 38th Regiment dates from 1702, when it was raised in Ireland, and for many years known as Colonel Luke Lillingstone's Regiment of Foot. Five years after its formation the regiment went to the West Indies and served there "an unprecedented period of, it is said, nearly sixty years, during which detachments of the corps served at the capture of Guadaloupe in 1759, and of Martinique in 1762." (*Archer*.) On their return home the 38th—as they were numbered in 1751—served in the American War, after which the flank companies were employed at Martinique in 1794, and subsequently at St. Lucia. The regiment as a whole, after taking part in the campaign in Holland, served under Sir D. Baird at the Cape of Good Hope in 1805, and the following year at Buenos Ayres. At Monte Video in 1807, under Colonel Vassal, they formed part of the assaulting party, and greatly distinguished

---

* The South Stafford Regiment bear as badges the Sphinx and "Egypt" over the Staffordshire Knot on the cap, and the Staffordshire Knot on the collar. On the waist-plate is borne Windsor Castle between these two badges. The Motto is that of the Garter. On the colours are "Egypt," "Monte Video," "Roleia," "Vimiera," "Corunna," "Busaco," "Badajoz," "Salamanca," "Vittoria," "St. Sebastian," "Nive," "Peninsula," "Ava," "Moodkee" "Ferozeshah," "Sobraon," "Pegu," "Alma," "Inkerman," "Sevastopol," "Lucknow," "Central India," "South Africa, 1878—79," "Egypt, 1882," "Nile, 1884—85," "Kirbekan."

themselves, Colonel Vassal being mortally wounded. The 38th then took part in the Peninsular War, fighting at Roleia and Vimiera, sharing in Moore's splendid victory at Corunna, and gaining for their colours the eloquent legend of "Busaco." At Badajoz, when a temporary discomfiture caused Walker's brigade to fall back, the pursuing French found themselves checked by "two hundred men of the 38th, who had been kept well in hand by Colonel Nugent," and who, after a fierce volley, charged with the bayonet. They fought at Salamanca and Burgos under Graham, they conquered at Vittoria, they shared in the ghastly victory at San Sebastian, forced the passage of the Bidassoa, and fought in the conquering ranks at the Nive. They were not at Waterloo, but joined the army of occupation after it was won. In 1818 they served in South America, and in 1822 repaired to India and were engaged in the first Burmese War, gaining the distinction of "Ava" for their colours. Returning to England in 1836, the following fifteen years were spent in various places, including Central America. In the Crimea the 38th were in Sir Richard England's (Third) Division, and—for we must needs leave much untold—bear "Alma," "Inkerman," and "Sevastopol" on their heavily emblazoned colours. From the Crimea they were ordered to India, where they arrived in November, 1857, and after fighting valiantly at Lucknow, took part in the subsequent campaign in Oude. They returned to England in 1872, and enjoyed a peaceful interval between that date and 1882, when they were ordered to Egypt.

Few regiments can boast a better record than the South Staffordshire during the campaigns of 1882, and 1884—85. The 38th, with the 3rd battalion of the 60th, were the first regiments to land in Egypt after Sir Beauchamp Seymour's ultimatum, and on the 22nd of July took part in the first skirmish of the war in connection with the destruction of the Ramleh Isthmus. In the final arrangement of the forces they were in the 4th brigade (Second Division), and took part, under Colonel Thackwell, in the reconnaissance at Mahalla, where they had one man wounded.* During the whole of the operations they ably carried out their part in the various duties which devolved upon the Second Division, duties none the less important because they did not include the more familiarly known of the engagements. They formed part of the force under General Earle, and at Kirbekan they highly distinguished themselves. Early in the day fell their gallant Colonel Eyre,† leading his men against a ridge held by an overwhelming force of fierce fanatics; "the Arabs fought

---

* He was shot through the cheek, "but went on fighting as if untouched."
† Colonel Eyre had been promoted from the ranks in recognition of his valour in the Crimea.

at bay with the courage of desperation, having the vantage-ground everywhere. And thus, against desperate odds our gallant soldiers, in spite of a withering fire all round, gained rock after rock, fastness after fastness, behind which the well-directed aim of the Arabs dealt death at every shot. Inch by inch, with fearful odds against them, do the Highlanders on the left and the South Staffordshire men on the right press forward and gain ground." After General Earle had fallen the 38th were ordered by General Brackenbury to storm "a steep and rocky hill four hundred feet high, held by a body of the Soudanese," a difficult task which they brilliantly accomplished after incredible toil and severe fighting. And so, with the freshly added lustre shed by the latest Egyptian War, ends the record of the services of the brave South Staffordshire.

The 2nd battalion of the South Staffordshire, the 80th Regiment, dates from 1793, when it was raised by Lord Paget. The following year, the Staffordshire Volunteers, as the regiment was then called, joined the Duke of York's army in Flanders, and during their sojourn there lost more than half their number. A few years later they formed part of Baird's army, which, with a view to joining Abercrombie, made the march across the desert which has been before referred to, and by this participation in the campaign gained the Sphinx and "Egypt" for their colours. After this they were for several years in India, gaining warriors' craft in the many battles by which the British rule was consolidated, and thus missed participation in any of the Peninsular battles, as they did not return to England before 1818. After a stay here of some sixteen years or so, they were ordered to Australia, and during the years 1836—1844, were more or less busily employed in the not very congenial task of suppressing convict riots. Their next station was in India, during their voyage to which occurred a most extraordinary incident. "Part of the corps," says Colonel Archer, "during the voyage was shipwrecked under very remarkable circumstances, being cast high and dry by a storm-wave in the dead of night on the top of a wood or jungle in the Little Andamans." Arrived in India, they were fortunate enough to participate in some of the most important events which the stirring history of British arms in India has to chronicle. They fought at Moodkee, where night alone saved the foe from total destruction. At Ferozeshah they earned a reputation for courage and discipline of which any regiment might be proud.

"About twelve o'clock at night, the Sikhs finding that Sir Harry Smith had been forced to retire from the village, and that their batteries were not occupied, brought some guns to bear upon our column, the fire from which was very destructive. The Governor-

General mounted his horse and called to the 80th Regiment, which was at the head of the column, 'My lads, we shall have no sleep until we have those guns.' The regiment deployed immediately, advanced, supported by the 1st Bengal Europeans, and drove a large body of Sikhs from three guns, which they spiked. The regiment then retired, and took up its position again at the head of the column as steadily as if on a parade, much to the admiration of the Governor-General and Commander-in-Chief, the former of whom exclaimed, as they passed him, 'Plucky dogs! plucky dogs! we cannot fail to win with such men as these.'"

To the brilliant victory of Sobraon they contributed not a little, and it was at the head of the 80th that the gallant Sir Robert Dick received his death wound. They bore a brilliant part in the second Burmese War in 1852. In the attack on the Grand Pagoda four companies of the 80th under Major Montgomery formed the advance, driving the enemy steadily before them, while in the attack on the eastern entrance the assaulting force comprised a wing of the 80th under Major Lockhart. In the attack on Pegu, the one company of the 80th that were present were commanded by Captain Ormsby, and ably performed their part in the singularly easy and bloodless victory achieved by our troops. After the war in Burmah, the next fighting in which the 80th shared was in India, where they gained "Central India" as a distinction. Those familiar with the military history of that time know how much severe and splendid fighting those words commemorate. They assisted at the capture of Calpee, shared in the arduous task of the pacification of Oude, and a few years later took part in the Bhotan Expedition,* which was found so much more difficult than had at first been anticipated. The regiment returned home in 1866, and were represented nine years later in the expedition to Perak. The next important war in which they were engaged was that in South Africa of 1878—79. They were in garrison at Luneburg under Major Charles Tucker, and in March, 1879, a company under Captain Moriarty was ordered to meet some supplies which were being forwarded. Owing to some delay the Intombe River which had to be crossed grew swollen with the rains, and some question seems to have been raised as to the judgment with which the encampment was laid. However that may be, in the early morning of the 12th some four thousand Zulus, led by the Chief Umbelini, swept down upon the little band of seventy-one. Across the river, Lieutenant Harward had been posted with some thirty men; in a few moments all that remained of the entire company scarcely numbered more. Captain Moriarty was killed the moment he left

* Three companies only were engaged at the commencement of the campaign.

his tent; in some cases his men were assegaied before they could leave theirs. Lieutenant Harward's party opened a brisk fire on the Zulus, but naturally it could have no effect on such a mass, and at least two hundred of them crossed the river. Lieutenant Harward ordered his men to fall back upon a farmhouse, and then he did a thing which, fortunately, is without a parallel in military history—rode off himself to obtain succour from Luneburg! Probably the severest critics of this infatuated action would acquit Lieutenant Harward of anything approaching cowardice, but the error was none the less a terrible one. Fortunately, dark though the Hour was, with it came the Man.

"Sergeant Booth, the senior non-commissioned officer present, now assumed command, rallied the small group of men, and endeavoured to cover the retreat of the few soldiers upon the opposite bank, who were trying to escape across the river towards him. The little band, to avoid being assegaied at close quarters, were compelled to fall back. This small knot of gallant men fought the Zulus for three miles in retreat, but Sergeant Booth and his men showed a bold front on every side. They kept close together, firing volleys at their pursuers as they prepared to rush upon them. The party gallantly checked the Zulus, and finally completed its retirement without losing a man. Sergeant Booth's heroic conduct enabled several fugitives who had safely crossed the river without arms or even clothes to escape and reach Luneberg."

The *Gazette* informed his countrymen "that had it not been for the coolness displayed by this non-commissioned officer, not one man would have escaped."

The observations made by Lord Chelmsford in commenting on the decision of the Court Martial held on Lieutenant Harward included some remarks which deserve a place in any record of British regiments. After referring to the "monstrous theory that a regimental officer, who is the only officer present with a party of soldiers actually and seriously engaged with the enemy, can, under any pretext whatever, be justified in deserting them," his Lordship went on to say:—"The more helpless the position in which an officer finds his men, the more it is his bounden duty to stay and share their fortune, whether for good or ill. It is because the British officer has always done so, that he occupies the position in which he is held in the estimation of the world, and that he possesses the influence he does in the ranks of our army. The soldier has learned to feel that come what may, he can in the direst moment of danger look with implicit faith to his officer, knowing that he will never desert him under any possible circumstances. It is to this faith of the British soldier in his officer that we owe most of the gallant deeds recorded in our annals."

On another and previous occasion had a V.C. been gained in this savage African warfare, by a man of the 80th. "On the 22nd January, 1879, when the camp at Isandhlwana was taken by the enemy, Private Wassall, 80th Foot, retreated towards the Buffalo River, in which he saw a comrade, Private Westwood of the same regiment, struggling and apparently drowning. He rode to the bank, dismounted, leaving his horse on the Zulu side, rescued the man from the stream, and again mounted his horse, dragging Private Westwood across the river under a heavy shower of bullets."

Some five companies of the 80th were at Ulundi, where they led the advance, and subsequently the regiment was represented in Colonel Clarke's column. In the operations against Sekukuni, Major Creagh did valuable service, and in the final attack upon the chief's stronghold, the 80th were in the centre column. The regiment returned home in 1880, and have not since then been engaged in any important warfare.*

THE SUFFOLK REGIMENT †—Regimental District No. 12—is composed of the two battalions of the old 12th Foot. In 1661, Windsor Castle was garrisoned by several independent companies, from which was formed the 12th Regiment, which, however, did not receive the numerical distinction till twenty-four years later. It was with the 12th Regiment that James II. made the experiment which was to give him such unwelcome proof of the unwillingness of the army as a whole to assist in his contemplated return to subservience to Rome. Advancing to their head he called upon all who would not support the proposed repeal of the Test clauses to lay down their arms. With a very few exceptions the whole regiment complied with most disconcerting alacrity. James paused for a few minutes and then bid the soldiers take them up again, moodily observing he would not do them the honour of consulting them again. The Colonel of the 12th—Lord Lichfield—remained, however, loyal to his misguided sovereign.

Till after the Revolution no particularly important service seems to have fallen to the lot of the 12th; in 1689 Wharton's Regiment, as they were then generally called, followed the veteran Schomberg to Ireland, where, the following year, they fought in the battle of the Boyne. After this they were employed on the coast of France and in

---

* It is to the 80th that the South Staffordshire owe the badge of Windsor Castle, which was granted by William IV.

† The Suffolk Regiment bear as badges the Castle and Key in a laurel wreath with a Crown above and "Gibraltar" below on cap and collar. The motto is "Montis insignia Calpe"—"The badges of Mount Calpe" (Gibraltar). On the colours are "Dettingen," "Minden," "Gibraltar," "Seringapatam," "India," "South Africa, 1851—53," "New Zealand," "Afghanistan, 1878—79." The uniform is scarlet with facings of white.

Flanders, being amongst the regiments which the cowardice of the Dutch governor compelled to surrender at Dixmude. Colonel Brewer of the 12th vehemently protested against this shameful action, counselling that the fortress should be defended to the last extremity; he was, however, overruled, but his protest secured his immunity from the disgrace and punishment awarded to the other officers who supported the governor's views. Their next service was in the West Indies, on returning from whence they were employed in the dyke-cutting operations about Ostend, and in Minorca. They were then ordered to Scotland, where they formed part of General Wade's expedition, and, twenty years or so later, gained their first distinction at Dettingen. Splendid was their courage at Fontenoy, while they were in Ingoldsby's Brigade, where their loss was more than that of any other regiment.* Three hundred and seventy-one officers and men fell, yet when their colonel and half their number were *hors de combat*, the splendid English regiment fought on, refusing to believe till the last that the army to which they belonged was beaten. The 12th subsequently repaired to Germany, where they took part in the Seven Years' War, being one of the six British Infantry Regiments who bear Minden† on their colours, and of whose bearing at that battle it was written—"Such was the unshaken firmness of these troops that nothing could stop them, and the whole body of French cavalry was routed."‡ They fought at Kirch Denkern, Grobenstein, Lutterberg, Homburg and Cassel, after which their next important service was that from which is derived the badge of the "Castle and Key," the ever-memorable defence of Gibraltar. Though the adage that "the world knows nothing of its greatest men" holds true, *mutatis mutandis*, with regard to achievements, yet the story of this defence of Gibraltar, the endurance, the heroism, the indomitable British pluck it called forth, is, we are glad to think, familiar to all. Under Colonel Trigge the regiment, numbering 29 officers and 570 rank and file, rendered sterling service, notably in the famous sortie, and thanks to them and their brave comrades the mountain Tarif§ still remains a mighty witness to the power of Britain. During the siege the total loss of the regiment was a hundred and seventy-four of all ranks. It is noted as a coincidence that on the occasion of the sortie of the night of the 26th of November, 1761, the only two complete regiments were the 12th and Hardenberg's, which had fought side by side at Minden. Lieutenant Tweedie of

* Of the line; the Scots Guards are said to have lost 437 of all ranks, killed and wounded.
† At Minden the 12th were commanded by Lieutenant-Colonel Robinson.
‡ About this time the 2nd battalion of the 12th was formed into the 65th regiment.
§ Such is the derivation of the word Gibraltar, Gib-el-Tarif, "Tarif" being a renowned Moorish chieftain.

the regiment was the only officer wounded in this enormously successful operation, which effected destruction to the value of £2,000,000 sterling. As indicative of the straits to which, in the earlier part of the siege, the garrison was reduced, the following extract from Major Drinkwater's history may be of interest:—

"Provisions of every kind were now becoming very scarce and exorbitantly dear: mutton, 3s. and 3s. 6d. per pound; veal, 4s.; pork, 2s. and 2s. 6d.; a pig's head, 19s.; ducks, from 14s. to 18s. a couple; and a goose a guinea. Fish was equally high, and vegetables were with difficulty to be got for any money; but bread, the great essential of life and health, was the article most wanted. It was about this period that the Governor made trial what quantity of rice would suffice a single person for twenty-four hours, and actually lived himself eight days on four ounces of rice per day."

After Gibraltar the 12th served for some time as Marines, while the flank companies were engaged at Martinique and Guadaloupe, where they were almost annihilated. They fought again in Flanders and shared in the disastrous retreat of Bremen, after which, in 1796, they proceeded to the Cape, and thence to India. Here they were the senior King's Regiment, and were required by General Order to be always ready to turn out, night or day. At Seringapatam, under Lieutenant-Colonel Shaw, they were the leading regiment in Baird's column, and on one occasion were ordered forward to occupy an important position midway between our camp and the fortress. Scarcely had they approached the required posts when the enemy sent off showers of rockets and blue lights which illuminated the surrounding country and showed the movements of our men with alarming distinctness. Twenty thousand of the enemy are said to have been showering these missiles, at one time "no hail could be thicker; with every blue light came a shower of bullets, and several rockets passed through the column from head to rear, causing death and dreadful lacerations. The cries of the wounded were awful." Yet still the 12th pressed on, firing not a shot, in obedience to the order of "brave old Colonel Shaw"—"All must be done with the bayonet." At last, when a fresh attack was commenced on his flank, the Colonel ordered his men to lie flat down, with the result that the enemy, supposing their withering fire had destroyed the column, "ventured forward to make sure with the bayonet, to be greeted with the words, 'Up 12th and charge,'" and to be driven back to their positions. At the final assault the 12th formed part of the storming party, and by their adroit rear attack on Tippoo's desperate band undoubtedly saved much loss to our force. In the attempted sortie made by the fierce tyrant, a volley from the light company of the 12th gave him his mortal wound. "Covered with blood and dying now, the fallen Sultan was raised by a faithful few and placed in his palanquin, where he lay faint and exhausted, till some of the 12th, climbing over the dead and dying, reached him. A servant who survived the carnage related that one of the soldiers seized Tippoo's sword-belt, which was exceedingly rich, and attempted to drag it off, and that the Sultan, who still grasped his sword, made a last cut with it, wounding in the knee the soldier, who shot him through the temple and killed him on the spot."

The career of the regiment after the fall of Seringapatam may be shortly epitomised by stating that they were actively employed in "Wynaad, in the Carnatic, against the Polygars, in Cochin and Travancore—services commemorated by the word 'India' on their colours." The mention of these places recalls the prowess displayed by the 12th at Quilon in 1808, under circumstances which read like a romance. When the hostile attitude of the Rajah of Travancore threatened Quilon, the 12th, who were stationed at Cannamore in Malabar, were ordered to the support of the garrison, and under Colonel Picton, brother of the Peninsular hero, they embarked. On the way more than half of the regiment were belated, and on arriving off Quilon with the rest, Colonel Picton was received with the intelligence that the whole country was in arms, and that to land would be to court absolute annihilation. "In defiance of this the 12th landed in small boats that would only convey three or four men at a time," and proceeded to make good their position. The next morning—utterly regardless that they numbered units as against the hundreds of the enemy—the gallant Suffolk proceeded to storm the palace of the Rajah's prime minister, after accomplishing which they returned to their camp. This, however, they were compelled to evacuate, as a force of some forty thousand of the enemy, led by European officers, were advancing against them, and they accordingly took possession of an old fort. By this time the 12th were reduced to two hundred and fifty men; there were about twelve hundred Sepoys and some ten thousand followers; and to add to their discomfort a terrible tropical storm came on directly they got into the dismantled fort, "rusting the fire-arms, and rendering much of the ammunition unfit for service." Despite this it was determined to regain the camp at the bayonet's point, and at that critical juncture the missing six companies were hailed approaching with some native troops they had picked up *en route*. They brought with them tidings which stimulated to fever point the already furious rage of the 12th against the barbarous foe. Some thirty men of the regiment under Sergeant-Major Tilsby had been in a small vessel and so escaped the hurricane which had delayed the others. They had landed near Alepe, and mistaking it for Quilon had marched in. They were beguiled with falsehoods, induced to pile their arms in what they were told was the English barracks, and invited to drink and fraternise with their foes. The arrack was drugged : "They soon became intoxicated and stupefied, and while in this state were easily secured by the Travancorians, one of whom, with a heavy iron bar, broke the two wrists of each soldier, smashing the bones hopelessly to atoms ; then, tightly tying their hands behind them, and binding their knees and necks together, they precipitated them into a loathsome dungeon." They were left like this four days and nights, without food or drink, the savages around them derisively mimicking their groans; then they were taken out, and dragged to a deep pool, into which—with heavy stones tied to the neck of each—they were flung in to drown "amid shouts, laughter, and the clapping of hands." No wonder that when the day of battle came the avenging fury of the 12th was irresistible. They carried a strong battery of guns, and hurled aside a force of at least ten thousand of the enemy who strove to retake them. "The 12th were inspired by a degree of fury beyond description, and never ceased to shout 'Remember Alepe! Remember Alepe!' One thrust his bayonet with such force into his adversary's body as to fix it in the back-bone so firmly that he had perforce to leave it. "Lieutenant Thomson of the 12th charged five thousand of the enemy, with only fifty men, three times, and fell to rise no more, covered with wounds."

The 12th served in the Mauritius, and the years that elapsed between the warfare signalised by "India" and 1851 were passed in various places, no fighting of any magnitude coming in their way. In 1851 they were ordered to South Africa to take part in the Kaffir War, in which they greatly distinguished themselves.* For some time they were employed in Australia, and took part in the Maori War in New Zealand.

Passing over the following few years we come to the Afghan Campaign of 1878—80, the last in which the gallant Suffolk have been engaged, and in which they acquitted themselves in such manner as to win the final distinction for their colours, and to give evidence of the fact that one of Her Majesty's oldest and most efficient regiments has deteriorated no whit from the heroes of Minden and Gibraltar.

* It was the 2nd battalion engaged in South Africa. Sixteen men of the regiment went down in the *Birkenhead*.

THE EAST SURREY REGIMENT*—Regimental District No. 31—is composed of the 31st and 70th Regiments. The 31st were originally Marines, and were formed into a regiment of foot in 1715. Their first important fighting was at Dettingen, where they gained the approbation of George II., and at the same time as a consequence the sobriquet of the Young Buffs, the king having mistaken them for the famous 3rd Regiment. Fierce fighting, too, did they have at Fontenoy, where, it is recorded, only eleven men of the grenadier company came out of action. Four years later they served at Minorca, then, after a short sojourn at home, in Florida, and the Carib War in St. Vincent, where they did good service. In 1776 they were quartered in Canada, some garrisoning Quebec, others participating in the misfortunes which attended General Burgoyne's army at Saratoga.† In 1794 the flank companies served at Martinique, Guadaloupe and St. Lucia, and returned home in 1797, "reduced to a mere company." Soon after a 2nd battalion was formed, which obtained, for the East Surrey the Peninsular distinctions on their colours.

They fought at Talavera; at Albuhera the 31st alone of the four splendid regiments that charged against the advancing column of the enemy "being formed in column, stood their ground," and escaped the disastrous onset of the French cavalry. Yet their loss was very heavy, and—as has been recorded in connection with the "Die-hards,"— "at the close of the action the dead and wounded men of our gallant 31st and 57th Regiments were found lying in two distinct lines on the very ground they occupied when fighting." In his account of the action, Lord Wellesley wrote: "This little battalion alone held its ground against all the *colonnes en masse.*" The story of "Vittoria" and "The Pyrenees," of "Nivelle" and the "Nive," has before been told, and the 31st bear these names on their colours. At St. Pierre they formed part of the right wing under General Byng, and the important part they played in that most brilliant victory may be gauged by the fact that when their gallant leader was elevated to the peerage as Earl of Strafford, the regimental colours of the regiment formed a portion of his coat-of-arms. They fought at Orthes, and bear that name as well as the "Peninsula" on their colours. Like many other 2nd battalions they were disbanded at the Peace, leaving a record

* The East Surrey Regiment bear as badges the arms of Guildford surrounded by the Garter surmounted by the Crown on a star of eight points on the cap, and the arms of Guildford on the collar. The motto is that of the Garter. On the colours is the Tudor Rose, and "Dettingen," "Guadaloupe," "Talavera," "Albuhera," "Vittoria," "Pyrenees," "Nivelle," "Nive," "Orthes," "Peninsula," "Cabool, 1842," "Moodkee," "Ferozeshah," "Aliwal," "Sobraon," "Sevastopol," "Taku Forts," "New Zealand," "Afghanistan, 1878—79," "Suakim, 1885." The uniform is scarlet with facings of white; a black line is worn in the officers' gold lace.

† During this period they received the county name of "Huntingdonshire."

of services of which any corps might be proud. The 1st battalion meanwhile had been serving in Sicily, Egypt, Spain, Genoa, and various other places, all of them witnesses to the courage and discipline of the regiment, though the names of none of them are found amongst the distinctions. In 1824 they were ordered to India under Colonel Pearson and Major McGregor, and were on the ill-fated *Kent* East Indiaman when she foundered. As the official record expresses it: "In the midst of dangers against which it seemed hopeless to struggle—at a time when no aid appeared, and passively to die was all that remained—each man displayed the manly resignation, the ready obedience, and the unfailing discipline characteristic of a good soldier." Fortunately the great majority were saved, only seventy-six out of a total of nearly five hundred being lost. During their stay in India they took part in the Afghan and Sikh Wars, and were with Pollock's avenging army after the massacre of Cabul. They fought at Moodkee; at Ferozeshah fell Major Baldwin of the regiment; at Aliwal they were remarked as being "emulous for the front;" "Sobraon" gives the final gleam to the lustre of their Indian achievements. Then followed a period of comparative peace till, in May, 1855, they arrived in the Crimea. In this war they took part in the assaults on the Redan of the 18th of June and 8th of September, and bear "Sevastopol" in commemoration of their gallant conduct. After peace was declared they were dispatched to the Cape and in 1858 to Bombay, their next service of note being the China Campaign of 1860. Here they were in the First Division, and after the fall of the Taku Forts marched to Tientsin, detachments being subsequently stationed at Ho-see-woo and Yung-tsan to keep the road clear between that city and our camp. The regiment returned home in 1863, since which date they have not been engaged in any operations which call for notice.

The 70th—the 2nd battalion of the East Surrey Regiment—was formed in 1756 from the 2nd battalion of the 31st, so that the recent amalgamation has replaced it in its original position. Colonel Archer cites the fact that a few years after the incorporation of the regiment, "five companies were embarked on board a naval squadron as reinforcements for Madras, but nothing more is known of them." In 1764 the 70th were ordered to the West Indies, where they remained for some ten years, subsequently serving for four years in Canada, during which time they received the territorial designation of "The Surrey Regiment." To anticipate for a moment the order of events, we find that in 1812 they were officially styled the "Glasgow Lowland Regiment," but during a subsequent sojourn in Canada—namely in 1825—they received their original and present title again. In 1794 they took part in Sir Charles Grey's expedition in

Martinique, and during the operations connected therewith gained the distinction of "Guadaloupe." For many years following their sphere of duty lay mainly amongst our various colonies and possessions, chiefly in Canada. In 1848 the 70th were ordered to India, and during the Mutiny were engaged on the Peshawar frontier. In 1863 they were with Sir Duncan Cameron in New Zealand, and took part in the attack on the Gate Pah, the evacuation of which by the Maories was discovered by Major Greaves of the regiment, who, regardless of the possible fatal result to himself, made a reconnaissance of the position. Returning to England in 1866, they remained in this country for some five years, in 1871 being again ordered to India. In the Afghan campaign of 1878—79 the 70th were in the Candahar column, and afterwards served with the Thull Field Force. Their last active service was in the Egyptian campaign of 1884, during which they acquitted themselves with great credit, under General Graham, in the fighting which took place round Suakin, Hasheen, and Tamai.

It is a very famous Regiment that next calls for notice, being none other than the QUEEN'S (ROYAL WEST SURREY REGIMENT)*—Regimental District No. 2.

One of the oldest, as it is one of the most famous of Her Majesty's regiments, its proud title, *The Queen's*, recalls the epoch of the Merry Monarch, when Tangiers became the property of the crown of England, as the marriage portion of Catherine of Portugal. So valuable a possession necessitated an efficient garrison, and accordingly, in 1661, Lord Peterborough's regiment was raised for the purpose, and the following year received the title of "The Queen's," with the badge of the Paschal Lamb, one of the armorial bearings of Portugal, and started for our new African possession. Here the Queen's was recruited from the garrison of Dunkirk, composed of veterans who had fought for the King during the late rebellion, and the First Tangier Regiment, to use the alternative title, became in a military sense a *corps d'élite*. They soon had opportunity to prove their metal. A body of twenty-four thousand Moors, notwithstanding a treaty of alliance, made, in June, 1663, an attempt to surprise the Tangier garrison, and would probably have succeeded, but for the stubborn defence made by Major Ridgert of the Queen's, who with

---

* The Queen's Royal West Surrey Regiment bear as badge the Paschal Lamb, granted by Queen Catherine, wife of Charles II. and daughter of King John of Portugal. The mottoes are "Pristinæ Virtutis Memor" and "Vel exuviæ triumphant." On the colours are the Royal Cypher in the Garter, and the Sphinx, with the following names: "Egypt," "Vimiera," "Corunna," "Salamanca," "Vittoria," "Pyrenees," "Nivelle," "Toulouse," "Peninsula," "Afghanistan," "Ghuznee," "Khelat," "South Africa, 1851-2-3," "Taku Forts," "Pekin." The uniform is scarlet with facings of blue. "The Queen's are the only regiment that still possess a third colour." Some other regiments, such as the 5th and 74th, also preserve a third colour, but do not carry it on parade.—(*Perry.*)

THE 2nd—THE QUEEN'S (ROYAL WEST SURREY).

only forty men held the foe at bay till the garrison could turn out in force. From this time skirmishes, sometimes assuming the proportions of battles, were of frequent occurrence, and in one of them the Earl of Teviot, who had succeeded Lord Peterborough in the colonelcy of the regiment and governorship of the garrison, was killed. In 1668, Lord Middleton became colonel, and during his tenure of the post, the Queen's had the honour of numbering amongst its volunteers the man who afterwards became the most successful and most celebrated general of his age, " the man who never fought a battle which he did not gain, or besieged a town which he failed to reduce—John Churchill, Duke of Marlborough." Mr. Churchill was at this time about twenty years of age, and held an ensign's commission in the Foot Guards, but made his first essays in actual service beneath the walls of Tangiers. Passing over the intermediate years, during which " the Queen's Regiment had, almost single-handed, maintained the important fortress, and many and various had been their warlike exploits against the barbarians," we come to 1682, when the colonelcy of the regiment was given to Colonel Piercy Kirke, whose name was for so long connected with the Queen's.

Four years later, as Parliament most unaccountably failed to provide for the support of this most important possession, the King was reluctantly compelled to destroy the fortifications at Tangiers, and recall the garrison, and the Queen's arrived in England in 1684. The following year at Sedgemoor, we read that "Kirke's regiment did good service." Then followed the period of repression, to which common tradition attributes the origin of the nickname of "Kirke's Lambs," with an implied character for cruelty. It is indeed more than probable that the colonel did not unduly temper justice with mercy, but the historian of the regiment well points out that had the cruelty of the regiment been so excessive as commonly reported, " it is not very probable that in the short space of four years it would have been so lost sight of, as to admit a demonstration of joy on the occasion of Kirke relieving Derry, when the people of Taunton devoted an evening to drinking his health in public." With regard to the epithet "Lambs" as applied to the regiment, assumedly in an unfavourable and ironical sense, the assumption is entirely demolished by the fact, noted by writers of the time, that the sobriquet was in use long before the alleged "atrocities" in the West. Shortly after the Revolution,* the Queen Dowager's Regiment, as they had been called after the death of Charles II., were ordered to Ireland, where they fought at the Boyne, Limerick,

* It is recorded that when overtures were made to Colonel Kirke to embrace the Roman Catholic faith, he replied that " he was pre-engaged, for he had promised the Emperor of Morocco that if ever he changed his religion, he would turn Mahommedan."

Athlone, Aghrim, and other places, and in 1692 joined the army in Flanders. At Landen they fought with signal gallantry. The Royal Scots were being forced back by the brilliant charge of the French, when "the Queen Dowager's Regiment, through smoke and flame and a storm of shot, came rushing with charged pikes to the succour of their Scottish comrades." Soon, though after desperate fighting, the enemy were driven back, and the two splendid regiments which before now had stood side by side at Tangiers when the dense hordes of the Moorish Cavalry swept round them like a whirlwind, once again "stood triumphant at the end of the village they had won, and were thanked for their gallantry by the King." They were with the army which took Nassau, where they lost several officers, and where their colonel, Selwyn, was promoted to the rank of Brigadier-General. Early in the next reign they shared in the operations at Cadiz and Vigo,* and the following year joined Marlborough's army in the Netherlands. Here, at Tongres, they gained the status of a *Royal* Regiment and their motto, "Pristinæ Virtutis Memor."†

The Queen's and another regiment, since disbanded, were the only force garrisoning Tongres, the speedy reduction of which was necessary to the plans of the French. Accordingly *forty thousand men*, under Marshals Villeroy and Boufflers, made a night march to seize it, and "attacked it with great vigour; but the two regiments defended themselves with extraordinary bravery for *twenty-eight hours;* and when at length reduced to surrender they had secured time for Marshal D'Auverquerke to collect his forces in so strong a position that the enemy declined a general engagement." They were shortly after exchanged, and took part in the various battles in Spain under the Earl of Galway, at Almanza losing twenty-two officers killed or prisoners. Portmore's Regiment (as the 2nd Foot were at this time called) had suffered so much during the campaign, that after Almanza their serviceable men were transferred to other regiments, and the headquarters sent to England to recruit. With the exception of an abortive attempt on Quebec in 1711, and some garrison duty in Gibraltar in 1740 and subsequently, the Queen's had no active service till 1793, when they were employed as Marines in Lord Howe's fleet, and, in the glorious victories gained over the French, experienced some slight loss.‡ In 1794, a 2nd battalion was formed, and under Lord

* Colonel Bellasis, who then commanded the regiment, made rather too free with the plunder, for on his return he was tried by court-martial and dismissed the service.

† Such is the generally accepted view; it has, however, been suggested that the second and unexplained motto, "Vel exuviæ triumphant," may commemorate Tongres, while the former may, as in the case of the 8th Royal Irish Lancers, allude to their prowess in Spain.

‡ On the accession of George I. the regiment was called "Her Royal Highness the Princess of Wales's own Regiment of Foot," receiving its former and present designation of "The Queen's Own" on the accession of George II.

Dalhousie proceeded almost immediately to the West Indies, where, so great had been their sufferings, at the end of 1795 all that remained of the ten companies which originally composed the battalion were a hundred and sixty-two men. In that year the 1st battalion was also ordered to the West Indies, but owing to a tempest only six companies arrived, under Lieut.-Colonel Harris, where they were incorporated into the 2nd battalion, which after the capture of Trinidad returned to England. The 1st battalion, which had been reformed, served in Ireland during the rebellion there, and afterwards joined the Duke of York's army in Holland, where they greatly distinguished themselves at the Helder and Egmont-op-Zee. During one of the incursions on the coast of France, then so much in vogue, the Official Record relates that "Major Ramsay, of the Queen's, seized several sloops and gun-vessels and burned a corvette of 18 guns."

The following year, 1801, was to gain for the regiment the first of their "distinctions," if we except the motto before referred to, in the sandy plains of Egypt, when "the fate of Asia was to be decided on the shores of Africa, by the two most powerful European nations." They besieged Aboukir and fought at Alexandria, Rosetta and Rahmanie, and on the conclusion of the treaty of Amiens repaired to their familiar quarters at Gibraltar, returning to England in 1805. In 1808 they were ordered to proceed to the Peninsula, in General Acland's brigade, and arrived there a few hours before Vimiera, the second name they bear on their colours. In the winter campaign in Spain which terminated in Corunna, the Queen's bore a gallant part, being brigaded on that eventful 16th of January, 1809, under General Hill, on the left of Moore's position.* The rearguard, to which was assigned the duty of covering the retreat of the army and keeping the enemy in check till the embarkation was completed, was under the command of Colonel Kingsbury of the regiment. After Corunna the regiment returned to England, though a detachment under Captain Gordon was fortunate enough to share in the battle of Talavera. The regiment as a whole shared in Lord Chatham's Walcheren expedition, and in 1811 joined the Sixth Division of Wellesley's army. After some sharp service round Salamanca, they participated in the memorable battle which bears that name. The advance of the Sixth Division to restore the wavering fortunes of the day forms one of the most dramatic scenes of that glorious war piece. Despite

The numerical title was given in 1751. In 1783, the regiment was for a while commanded by the Duke of Kent, father of Her present Majesty.

* An occurrence preserved by the Official Record is of sufficiently extraordinary a nature to merit mention. A private named Samuel Evans was wounded at Corunna. "He was landed in England, and died in the Military Hospital at Plymouth, on the 30th of January. A post-mortem examination showed that he had been *shot through the heart*, yet had survived *sixteen days*. His heart is preserved in the museum of the above hospital.

the concentrated fire of twenty-one guns, and a perfect tempest of well-directed musketry, the Queen's and their gallant companions pressed on, and the battle of Salamanca was won. So heavy was the loss to the Queen's, that "towards the close of the action, a subaltern officer, Lieutenant Borlase, had the honour of commanding the regiment." In consequence of the loss on this occasion the head-quarters of the regiment with six attenuated companies returned to England, the remaining four companies being attached to Lowry Cole's Division, and sharing with it the honours of "Vittoria" and the "Pyrenees." At "Nivelle" the Queen's particularly distinguished themselves, leading the attack of the centre columns against the enemy's position, and before the war ended, once more rendered themselves splendidly conspicuous at the battle of Toulouse. The regiment was in England when Waterloo was fought, and early in the following year proceeded to the West Indies, where the gallant heroes of Egypt and the Peninsula found in the terrible climate a foe more deadly than the legions of Napoleon, losing in three months, from fever, eleven officers and two hundred men. They returned to England in 1821, and four years later were ordered to India, where they remained for many years, during which they were enabled to add "Afghanistan" to their distinctions, with the sequent names of Ghuznee and Khelat. They were also engaged in the intermittent warfare with the Mahrattas. After this, their next warfare of note was in South Africa, where they rendered signal service. In the attack on the Waterkloof the Queen's were brigaded with the 6th and 91st, under Colonel Michell, and experienced some severe fighting, Captain Addison of the regiment being severely wounded. Passing over the following few years, which were spent in South Africa, the gallant Queen's were next engaged in the war in China, where they were in the second brigade of the First Division, which was the first to disembark. A reconnaissance was determined on, and the Queen's were the British regiment chosen to perform this arduous undertaking. For three-quarters of a mile their road lay over a "flat of soft, sticky, slippery mud," into which the men sank ankle-deep. "Nearly every man was disembarrassed of his lower integuments, and one gallant brigadier led on his men in no other garment than his shirt." In the final advance on the Taku Forts the Queen's were on the left of the advance column, and in the comparatively bloodless victory then gained, admirably performed the important duties allotted to them, at Tangku and Chang-chai-wan especially distinguishing themselves. Before they quitted the Celestial kingdom the Queen's had seen Pekin surrendered to the allied forces, and gained thereby the last name which appears on their colours. Since the campaign in China

THE 35th—ROYAL SUSSEX.

they have not been engaged in any war, their services having been those of peaceful occupation in the East and West Indies, Canada, and the Ionian Islands.

THE ROYAL SUSSEX REGIMENT*—Regimental District No. 35—consists of the old 35th and 107th Regiments. The 35th was raised in Ireland in 1701, and in the following year placed on the British establishment as a "Regiment of Foot for sea service." Before long Lord Donegal's Regiment, as the 35th were then styled, had plenty of active work at Cadiz and the West Indies, and in the defence of Gibraltar in 1704. The following year they served "with Peterborough in Spain," and at the capture of Barcelona—"one of the most gallant actions performed by that little army in Spain"—and its subsequent defence suffered severely, losing their colonel in one of the stubbornly contested engagements. The disastrous battle of Almanza ended for a long time their career of foreign service, the next forty years or so being passed in Ireland. In 1758 the 35th formed part of General Amherst's expedition against Louisburg, where they acquitted themselves in such wise as to gain the first distinction on their colours. At Quebec, the following year, they won the distinctive badge of the Feather for their heroic conduct in defeating the Royal Roussillon Grenadiers of France. Throughout the war which resulted in the subjugation of Canada to the British Crown the 35th were engaged, remaining in the Dominion till 1761, when they were ordered to Martinique, and rendered good service there and at the Havannah. After a short sojourn at home they were ordered to America, and took part in many of the engagements between the royal troops and colonists. They fought at Bunker's Hill, Brooklyn, New York, and other places, the flank companies being with General Burgoyne in the expedition to Ticonderoga in the spring of 1777. For sixteen years or thereabouts they were quartered in the West Indies, after which they were represented—by two battalions—in the fighting in Holland in 1799. Passing over a few years we find the Sussex Regiment—as they were called in 1805—gaining for themselves a lasting reputation at Maida, where a hundred and fifty picked men of the regiment, under Major Robinson, were in that famous right wing which Colonel Kemp led against the French Light Infantry with the result that "the enemy became appalled; they broke and endeavoured to fly, but . . . . were overtaken with most dreadful slaughter." Some of the regiment,

* The Royal Sussex bear as badges the Cross of St. George on an eight-pointed star placed on a feather on cap, and the Cross of St. George in a wreath on a Maltese cross placed on a feather on collar. The motto is that of the Garter. On the colours is the Tudor Rose with the following names: "Louisburg," "Quebec, 1759," "Maida," "Egypt, 1882," "Nile, 1884-85," "Abu Klea." The uniform is scarlet with facings of blue.

too, formed part of the little band of two hundred, which, under Colonel Robertson, held the castle of Scylla against the overwhelming forces of Regnier. On one side was the sea, whose terrors were attested by fact and fable alike; on the other a force of six thousand French, "with five 24-pounders, four battering mortars, and many field-pieces." Yet, when after three days and nights of desperate fighting the heroic garrison was embarked by the war-ship *Electra;* cries of derision and mockery from the retreating boats greeted the ears of the enraged enemy, who "purchased only a pile of ruins at the expense of several hundred lives, while the loss of the British was only eleven killed and thirty-one wounded." The following year they fought in Egypt, where they lost more than half their numbers. Under Stuart and Oswald they marched against Rosetta, and when the attacking force, having lost two-fifths of its number, had to fall back, a company of the Sussex were with Colonel Macleod, of the 78th, when he was surrounded by the Albanians.* For the following seven years the 1st battalion of the 35th were busily employed in various duties on the Continent, distinguishing themselves in the capture of Santa Maura in the Ionian Isles, the conquest of Lissa, and numerous other engagements, which, owing to the Titanic struggle waging in the Peninsula, are apt to be lost sight of. A second battalion, which had been raised on the renewal of the war, took part in the Walcheren expedition, and, after serving in Holland, were in reserve at Huy during the battle of Waterloo, after which they joined the army of occupation. For many years the record of the 35th, though indicative of plenty of hard work, does not present any very noteworthy incident. From Waterloo till just before the Mutiny in India their duties were divided between Italy, the West Indies, Corfu, and the Mauritius. In 1854 they were ordered to Burmah, and during the latter half of 1857 were in garrison at Calcutta, subsequently taking part in the sundry engagements incident to the final suppression of the Mutiny. The years which intervened between the Mutiny and the recent Egyptian war were passed by the Royal Sussex at home, in our West Indian and European dominions. When military operations in Egypt were resolved upon, the 35th were assigned to the Second Division, under Sir Evelyn Wood, and occupied the Antoniades estate at Alexandria, which they transformed into a most effective and strong position. It will be noted that by a strange coincidence the Royal Sussex of our days found themselves, under Colonel Vandeleur, Major Grattan, and other officers, quartered not far from the spot where, three-quarters of a century ago, their predecessors had fought and died under the brave Macleod. After Kafrdowar

* *See* p. 85.

they remained in garrison at Ramleh, and when the first phase of the war terminated were amongst the troops left to occupy Cairo. When hostilities again broke out they were ready to hand and proved themselves worthy successors of the heroes of Maida. Under Major Sunderland they were on the right flank of Stewart's square at Abu Klea, where there was need, if ever there was, for British soldiers to heed well the counsel of the valiant Philistine of old—to "be strong and quit themselves like men." After the battle a hundred and fifty men of the regiment were left to guard the wells of Abu Klea. Again at Abu Kru they fought, and throughout the remainder of the war rendered sterling service, returning home on its termination.

The 2nd battalion of the Royal Sussex Regiment, the 107th, was originally the 3rd Bengal European Infantry in the employ of the East India Company, and dates from 1854. Needless to say that their matriculation in the stern school of war was provided by the Mutiny, during which they were widely employed. At Agra, in October, 1857, the 107th were in garrison when the enemy, ignorant of the fact that Greathead's column had arrived, attempted a surprise. "As soon as the firing was heard in the fort of Agra, the 3rd Bengal Infantry rushed forward to the assistance of their comrades (of Greathead's force) and eagerly joined in the pursuit, which lasted for twelve miles." Throughout the Mutiny they were of the utmost service, and in 1861 were incorporated into the Imperial army. It was not, however, till 1875 that they came to England. The subsequent services of the 107th have been confined to garrison duty at Malta and Cairo.

The SOUTH WALES BORDERERS*—Regimental District No. 24—are composed of the 24th Foot. Despite their Welsh designation, they were raised in Ireland in 1689, almost immediately after which they were transferred to England. Under Sir Edward Dering, their first Colonel, they fought at the Boyne and probably at all the Irish battles. They are said, too, to have served with King William's army in the Netherlands, and to have taken part in the siege of Namur. In 1702, the famous Marlborough was appointed to the colonelcy of the regiment, which, under his generalship, fought at Schellenberg, Blenheim and Ramillies, Oudenarde, Lisle, and Malplaquet. In 1791,

* The South Wales Borderers bear as badges the Red Dragon of Wales in a laurel wreath with Crown over on cap, and the Sphinx with "Egypt" on collar. The motto is that of the Garter. The Queen's Colour has a silver wreath on the Staff in memory of Isandhlwana. On the Colours are the Sphinx and "Blenheim," "Ramillies," "Oudenarde," "Malplaquet," "Egypt," "Cape of Good Hope, 1806," "Talavera," "Fuentes d'Onor," "Salamanca," "Vittoria," "Pyrenees," "Nivelle," "Orthes," "Peninsula," "Chillianwallah," "Goojerat," "South Africa, 1877-8-9." The uniform is scarlet with facings of white.

they took part in the expedition under Lord Cobham against Vigo, and after a comparatively uneventful period of something over twenty years, fought as "Wentworth's Regiment" at Carthagena. After this most unsatisfactory performance, they were for some time in Cuba, with the result that they lost four-fifths of their number. After a short stay in Jamaica, they returned home, and found their next active employment, with the exception of the attempted capture of St. Malo in 1758, in the Seven Years' War in Germany, where they fought under Lord Granby at Warbourg, Corbach, Kirch Denkern, and Wilhelmstahl. After a few years at Gibraltar, they were ordered in 1776 to Canada, where they fought at Stillwater and the subsequent actions. After a brief sojourn in England, the 24th, then called the South Warwickshire, again repaired to America, where they remained till ordered to join the army in Egypt, where they gained another distinction by the part they took in the siege of Alexandria. Their next employment was in South Africa in 1806, when the 1st battalion formed part of Sir David Baird's force, after which they proceeded to India, incurring the misfortune of having a considerable number of their body taken prisoners by a French fleet. This, however, was not accomplished without a struggle. The transports were three East Indiamen named respectively the *Ceylon*, the *Wyndham*, and the *Astell*, and the last named probably owed its escape to the gallantry of the 24th under Major Foster, with whom were Captains Gubbins, Craig, and Maxwell, and Ensign D'Aine.

Meanwhile the 2nd battalion had joined the British army in the Peninsula, and fought with distinction at Talavera, Fuentes d'Onor, Salamanca, Burgos, and Vittoria, experiencing such heavy losses "that only four weak companies remained, which were formed, with four others similarly situated, as the 2nd battalion of the 58th, and so fought throughout the remainder of the war." They greatly distinguished themselves under Colonel McLean at the siege of St. Sebastian. They had to ford the Urumea River, which ran so deep that the men had to hold their cartridge-boxes above it. A terrible shower of grape was poured upon them when they were in mid stream, "many were killed, and more sank wounded to drown miserably. But closing in shoulder to shoulder the survivors moved steadily on." Their point of attack was the great breach, where the struggle raged with fearful ferocity, so that "it could hardly be judged whether the hurt or unhurt were most numerous." Then came the explosion which opened the mighty walls of the stubborn fort, and the 24th with their comrades poured in through the chasm, victors at last. When peace was declared, the 2nd battalion of the South Warwickshire was disbanded. The 1st battalion had during this time been engaged in India, notably on the Nepaulese frontier. After a short stay in England they were ordered to Canada, where they stayed some years, and were of great service during the troubles in 1837. Sterner warfare awaited them in India, whither they were sent in 1846. After fighting at Sadoolapore early in December, 1848, they were present in Colin Campbell's division at the disastrous conflict of Chillianwallah, the following month. Under Colonel Brooks, they effected a most brilliant charge on the enemy's guns. Despite the six hundred yards across which they had to double, they drove away the gunners, and were in the act of spiking the guns, when several regiments of the enemy lying in ambush poured upon them "a concentrated fire that no troops could withstand." They fell literally in heaps, and at this critical moment the Sikh Cavalry swept down upon them. "Pennycuick and his son, both officers of the 24th, fell just as they reached the guns. A stalwart Sikh was seen leaning over the helpless father, prostrated by a shot, and inflicting fresh gashes on his body, when the boy ensign of seventeen, worthy of such a noble father, stepped forward and dealt an avenging blow. The heroic boy strode across his parent's corpse, and bade defiance to the savage multitude; but numbers soon overwhelmed him, and he fell dead." (*Thackwell*). Not the least of the disasters of the day was the loss of the colours of the gallant 24th, but, as if in melancholy anticipation of a similar heroic episode of more recent date, "one was afterwards found, wrapped round the dead body of the ensign who had borne it into action." That day no fewer than 13 officers and 227 men of the regiment were killed, and 310 of all ranks wounded. A month later was fought Goojerat, the last Indian distinction which the 24th bear, though for many years after the North-west Frontier and the Punjaub witnessed innumerable evidences of their courage and warlike prowess. The years which intervened between the suppression of the Mutiny and the Zulu War were passed by the 24th in various places, in most of which something of active service fell to their lot. India, Burmah, West Griqua-Land, and the Gauka country were severally the spheres of their duty.

While they were in Burmah, a detachment was despatched to the Little Andamans to rescue the captain and some of the crew of a British vessel, who it was but too truly surmised had fallen victims to the savages. About twenty men formed the small force under Lieutenant Much, who was accompanied by Surgeon Douglas and Lieutenant Glassford, the last-named as a volunteer. On arriving at their destination, they landed under a discharge of arrows, and soon found conclusive evidences that their unfortunate countrymen had been barbarously murdered. When they wished to return it was found that their boats were so seriously damaged as to be useless. Efforts were made to get off on a raft, but the nature of the coast rendered this impossible. "Seeing the evil plight of their comrades, Dr. Douglas, Privates Murphy, and Cooper, Bell, and Griffiths, of the 24th Regiment, manned the second gig, and made their way through the surf almost to the shore. Finding their boats half filled with water, they returned, but only to make a second attempt which proved successful, Dr. Douglas and his crew managing to convey five of the party which had landed safely, through the surf to the boats outside. On a third trip he removed the remainder, all being rescued with the exception of Lieutenant Glassford, who was drowned." The official report eulogises the "intrepid," "cool," and "collected" manner in which Dr. Douglas and his companions achieved their heroic task, and it is satisfactory to record that the statutes of the Order were for this occasion a little strained, to enable these five gallant men to receive the guerdon of the Victoria Cross.

It is a mere truism to say that wherever and whenever the Zulu War is mentioned, two names spontaneously suggest themselves. One, immortalised by the melancholy romance of his life and death, is that of the Prince Imperial of France, the other is that of the 24th Regiment individually and collectively. It is with the latter part of the Zulu War that we shall chiefly deal, premising that the 1st battalion of the 24th was already *in situ* when hostilities began (having been, as has been mentioned, engaged in Griqualand), and that the 2nd battalion arrived in 1879. Both battalions were attached to the second column, the command of which was entrusted to Colonel Glynn of the regiment, and, in January, 1879, were encamped at Rorke's Drift on the Buffalo River, where they had one or two successful skirmishes with the enemy. Two companies were left at Helpmakaar, and two at Rorke's Drift, when, on the 20th of the same month, the column moved on to the hill of Isandhlwana. By dint of false reports the enemy succeeded in disarming all suspicion, and the camp at Isandhlwana was weakened by the dispatch of various parties on reconnaissances. Before there was a suspicion of danger, with the awful suddenness of a tropical tempest, the Zulus, numbering many thousands, swept down upon the devoted garrison. Before "Mostyn's and Cavaye's companies of the 24th had time to form rallying squares, or even to fix their bayonets, they were slaughtered to a man." No hope was left; death at the hands of a savage foe was inevitable, yet probably never throughout their long and brilliant career had the 24th more nobly vindicated the honour and valour of British warriors. Calmly, as if the yelling savages were but a London crowd thronging to see a review, Colonel Pulleine turned to Melvill with the words: "You, as senior lieutenant, will take the colours, and make the best of your way from here," and, with a farewell hand-shake with his subaltern, addressed the handful of his gallant regiment who were about him: "Men of the 24th, here we are, and here we stand to fight it out to the end." The end was terribly near. "The light was darkened with flying assegais thrown from near with deadly effect. In a few minutes Colonel Pulleine, every officer, and every man of the gallant 24th lay upon the ground dying or dead. The two companies* who had been skirmishing on the left by the skirts of the 'Ngata Range, were never seen or heard of again . . . . Instantly surrounded, every man was laid dead upon the ground. Not one was left alive."† Lieutenants Melvill and Coghill, with Private Williams, dashed on till they came to the Buffalo River. Here Williams was drowned. Melvill's horse was shot, and the colours slipped from his hand. Coghill had reached the other side in safety, when, looking back, he saw his companion clinging to a rock, trying in vain to recover the colours. He rode back to his assistance, and then his horse, also, was shot, and the two doomed officers struggled on, literal targets for the enemy. Let us quote Captain Parr to learn the last of these heroes of our own days. "There are, not many hundred yards from the river's side, two boulders within six feet of each other, near the rocky path. At these boulders they made their last stand, and fought until overpowered. Here we found them lying side by side, and buried them on the spot where they fought and fell so gallantly." Ten days after, the colours were found in the bed of the river by Major Black of the regiment. Many are the incidents gathered, some of them from the Zulus themselves, relating to that terrible struggle. A corporal of the regiment "slew four Zulus with his bayonet, which stuck for a moment in the throat of his last opponent; then he was assegaied." The Zulus described how the "red soldiers taunted them to come on," and how when our ammunition was all exhausted, the cunning savages hurled the bodies of their own dead against the gleaming fence of bayonets, and then rushing in, assegaied every man. Another account describes the tortures and mutilations inflicted on the wounded: "The men who returned with the General saw enough of it—one poor little drummer-boy held up on a bayonet."

Of the 24th there fell that day five entire companies of the 1st battalion with ninety men of the 2nd. Meanwhile one company of the 2nd battalion had been left at Rorke's Drift under Lieutenant Bromhead. The splendid defence made by him and Lieutenant Chard has been before referred to,‡ so we will here only notice a few of the deeds of valour performed by men of the 24th. When the enemy set fire to the hospital,

* Under Lieutenant Younghusband. † Major Elliott. ‡ See p. 137.

the garrison defended it step by step as they brought out as many of the sick as possible. Privates Williams and Hook held a room in the hospital for about an hour, " one holding the enemy at bay with his bayonet, while the other broke through three more partitions to the inner defence, and got eight sick men safely out of the hospital. Privates Williams and Robert Jones in like manner rescued six men; Corporal Allen and Private Hitch held a most dangerous post commanding the communication between the hospital and inner defence. Exposed to fire from both sides they were severely wounded, yet when their injuries rendered them incapable of handling their arms, they had their wounds dressed by the surgeon, and then returned to the defence and handed out cartridges to their comrades." Throughout the war the gallant 24th, who were subsequently reinforced, rendered sterling service, and in the retreat from Inhlobane, Lieutenant Brown of the 1st battalion gained the Victoria Cross for rescuing under heavy fire two soldiers who would otherwise have been captured by the closely pursuing Zulus.

Since the Zulu War the South Wales Borderers have not been engaged in any warfare which comes within the scope of this work. The silver wreath on the Queen's colour of the regiment is a permanent memorial of the wreath of immortelles fastened by Her Majesty on the colours, to save which Melvill, Coghill, and Williams gave their lives, and will remain to all time an eloquent testimony of the honour in which Sovereign and nation hold one of the most gallant and distinguished regiments of the Queen's army.

THE ROYAL WARWICKSHIRE REGIMENT *—Regimental District No. 6—consists of the old 6th Foot, and dates from 1673, when a body of English soldiers was raised for the service of the States General, and placed under the command of Sir Walter Vane, Colonel of the Buffs. Of this body of troops, the regiment now known as the Royal Warwickshire formed part. It is not within our province to follow the deeds of the regiment while fighting purely as auxiliaries in the service of another power. The histories of the time have few more enthralling passages than those which tell of the prowess of those gallant English who alike in court and camp, in battlefield and Presence Chamber, held their own against all comers, and gained honour and fair fame as well for themselves as for the imperial Island, " compassed by the inviolate sea," whose warrior sons they

* The Royal Warwickshire bear as badges a white antelope with gold collar and chain (in the Garter), surrounded by a laurel wreath, on cap; and the Bear and Ragged Staff, the cognisance of the Earls of Warwick, on collar. The motto is that of the Garter, though it would seem that "Nec aspera terrent" and "Vi et Armis" have also been used as mottoes. On their colours are the Tudor Rose on crown, and "Roleia," "Vimiera," "Corunna," "Vittoria," "Pyrenees," "Nivelle," "Orthes," "Peninsula," "Niagara," "South Africa, 1846—7," "South Africa, 1851—2—3." The uniform is scarlet with facings of blue.

were. When Monmouth's claims began to alarm King James, he required the return of the regiments in the service of the States, and the 6th, then known as Bellasis' Regiment, arrived in England in July, 1685, returning, however, shortly after to the Netherlands. When they next came to England it was in the train of the Prince of Orange, who a few weeks later assumed the style of King of England. On the voyage hither, four companies of the regiment were captured by Captain Aylmer, whose ship, the *Swallow*, had not yet migrated to the new *régime*. The next employment of the 6th was in Ireland, where the adherents of King James still held together, and in this service they fought at Charlemont, the Boyne, Athlone, Ballymore, Aghrim, and other battles. In 1692 the 6th—then known as Hesse d'Armstadt's Regiment, the Prince of that name being appointed to the colonelcy—were ordered to Holland, and fought in Holland. "The 6th nobly sustained their reputation, and fought manfully, resisting the superior numbers of the enemy with signal firmness: their commanding officer, Lieutenant-Colonel Foxon, fell mortally wounded. The French legions—dragoons, musketeers, pikemen, and grenadiers—crowded round this devoted corps in great numbers, and it sustained considerable loss." When at last a retreat was ordered, the 6th withdrew from the field "a mere skeleton." After being recruited, they served at Namur, again with considerable loss, and after various unimportant operations, took part in the expeditions against Cadiz and Vigo. They joined Lord Peterborough's army in Spain in 1705, and greatly distinguished themselves at the siege of Barcelona, the grenadiers of the regiment, under Lieutenant-Colonel Southwell, leading the assault upon the strong detached fort of Montjuich. After most strenuous and gallant fighting, the attack proved successful: the garrison surrendered to the "intrepid Southwell," who was embraced by King Charles of Spain and appointed Governor of the citadel. Barcelona fell soon afterwards, and the regiment continued, under the immediate direction of Lord Peterborough, to share in all the exploits performed by our troops, exploits so brilliant and heroic as—to quote the words of the historian—to "carry with them the appearance of fiction and romance rather than sober truth," but which nevertheless are as well attested as any other historical fact. Two years later they fought at Almanza, needless to say with gallantry, but with heavy loss: nine officers, including the lieutenant-colonel, were killed, and fourteen wounded or prisoners. In 1708 they took part in the subjugation of Minorca, Fort St. Philip—the only fortress which made any serious resistance—being captured by the headlong gallantry of "the grenadiers of the 6th and another corps."

They fought at Saragossa, their colonel, Thomas Harrison, being commissioned to carry home the news and spoils of the victory to Queen Anne. It is probably to their achievements in Spain that the 6th owe their badge of the Antelope. So at least says tradition, which, however, is not supported by any documentary evidence. They fought at Brihuega in 1710, where several were taken prisoners, soon, however, to escape or be exchanged, and in 1714 the regiment returned home. In 1719 they took part in the Vigo expedition, after which their next service of importance seems to have been in the West Indies in 1741, from whence they returned the following year sorely reduced by pestilence. They were actively engaged in the "affair of '45," fighting at Ruthven and Preston Pans, where they were amongst those battalions of infantry who stood their ground, and as a consequence "had nearly every man killed, wounded, or taken prisoner." After this, with the exception of garrison duty in Gibraltar, the 6th were chiefly at home till 1772, when they received orders to proceed to St. Vincent, where they were engaged with credit to themselves in the operations against the Caribs. After a sojourn in England and in Canada they went to Martinique in 1794, and took part in the fighting which there took place. After assisting in suppressing the rebellion in Ireland, during which irksome service—notably at Castlebar—they most gallantly acquitted themselves, the 6th proceeded, in the summer of 1808, to join Lord Wellesley's army in Portugal. They were brigaded with the 32nd Regiment under General Bowles, and on the 17th of August took part—though not "seriously"—in the battle of Roleia, the first name which, despite their long and arduous service, appears on their colours. Two days later followed Vimiera, after which they were attached to the army under Sir John Moore, "the only general," as the vaunting Buonaparte declared, "worthy for him to contend against," and under him fought in the ill-fated field of Corunna. Their losses here were about four hundred, and the Walcheren expedition, in which they took part, still further swelled the list of casualties. In 1812 they again joined the Allied Army in the Peninsula, being brigaded under General Barnes in Lord Dalhousie's Division. They arrived at Vittoria after the battle had begun, but their gallant conduct there was conspicuous, as it was in the subsequent sanguinary engagements in the Pyrenees. At Echelar in particular they were the observed of all observers—and they were not a few—of that "terrible drama called war." "Barnes," wrote an officer present, "set at the French as if every man had been a bull-dog, and himself the best bred of all;" "The attack on the enemy," wrote Lord Wellesley, "is the most gallant and finest thing I ever witnessed."

THE 23rd—ROYAL WELSH FUSILIERS.

The regiment were partially engaged at the Bidassoa, and under Beresford carried the strong redoubts on the enemy's left centre at the Nivelle. The next year at Orthes they suffered severely, and on the termination of the war in the Peninsula proceeded to Canada, where they immediately took part in the siege of Port Erie, particularly distinguishing themselves under Major Taylor in the repulse of a sortie in force made by the Americans in September, 1814. Joining the Duke of Wellington after Waterloo, the 6th remained for some months with the army of occupation, returning to England towards the end of 1818. From that date till 1846 they were stationed in various places, including South Africa and India. In 1846 they were engaged in the Caffre war, and a few years after in the renewed hostilities with the same gallant but barbarous foes. In the latter campaign they were in Colonel Michell's brigade, and had their full share of the severe fighting that ensued. In the attack on the Waterkloof, Lieutenant Morris of the regiment was mortally wounded, and in the final assault the 6th formed part of the centre column, and by their courage and endurance well deserved their final distinction in South Africa, 1851—2—3.* In 1857 they were ordered to India, and were actively engaged in the Oude campaign of 1858, and many of the subsequent years have been passed by the regiment in the same country, the Hazarah expedition and the "little war" on the Punjab frontier providing something of active service. A second battalion was raised in 1858, but has not yet been engaged in warfare of any magnitude.

Foremost amongst the famous regiments of Her Majesty's Army are the ROYAL WELSH FUSILIERS,†—Regimental District No. 23—the old 23rd of warlike renown. The Royal Welsh Fusiliers were raised almost immediately after the Revolution had transferred the royal authority from the hands of King James to those of his daughter

* At Fort Cox the Grenadier company particularly distinguished itself.
† The Royal Welsh Fusiliers bear as badges the Red Dragon of Wales on a grenade on cap, and a grenade on collar. On the cap plate, waist plate, and buttons is the Prince of Wales' Plume. The mottoes are "Ich Dien" and "Nec aspera terrent." The Royal Welsh Fusiliers are the only regiment that retain the "flash" (five black ribbons some nine inches long, hanging from the back of the collar), a survival of the days when queues were worn, and when the flour and grease used in them played havoc with the tunics. The 23rd were abroad when the queue was abolished, and on their return their commanding officer obtained leave to retain the "flash." The "Regimental Goat" is also accorded by Royal Warrant. Grose, in his "Military Antiquities," says that the Royal Welsh Fusiliers "have a privileged honour of passing in review preceded by a goat with gilded horns, and adorned with ringlets of flowers . . . and the corps values itself much on the ancientness of the custom." On the colours are the Rising Sun, the Red Dragon, the White Horse, the Sphinx, and the following names: "Blenheim," "Ramillies," "Oudenarde," "Malplaquet," "Dettingen," "Minden," "Egypt," "Corunna," "Martinique," "Albuhera," "Badajoz," "Salamanca," "Vittoria," "Pyrenees," "Nivelle," "Orthes," "Toulouse," "Peninsula," "Waterloo," "Alma," "Inkerman," "Sevastopol," "Lucknow," "Ashantee." The uniform is scarlet with facings of blue, and fusilier cap.

and son-in-law. Raised in Wales and the adjoining counties in 1689, the 23rd in August of that year arrived in Ireland, where the aforesaid transfer of power was not yet an accomplished fact. At the battle of the Boyne they satisfied the critical eye of William, who is reported to have watched with some anxiety the effect of their first fire on his newly raised regiments; and to the present day the Welsh Fusiliers preserve a memento of this their first battle. "The spurs won by Major Toby Purcell (of the 23rd) at the battle of the Boyne are still preserved in the regiment, in possession of the senior major for the time being" (*Cannon*). After the fall of Aghrim, at which the regiment suffered severely, Major Toby Purcell became colonel, *vice* Colonel Herbert, their first commander, who fell into the hands of the Irish and was inhumanly murdered. Passing over the melancholy category of the battles in Ireland, we find the 23rd—then known as Ingoldsby's Regiment—amongst the reinforcements which joined King William's army in Holland in the early part of 1694, and the following year they took part in the siege of Namur, during which they suffered very severely. On the final capitulation the 23rd were ordered to take possession of the gates. After the peace of Ryswick the regiment returned to Ireland, remaining there till June, 1701, when they again embarked for Flanders, to take part in the memorable campaigns of Marlborough. After sharing in numerous battles and sieges they were present at the battle of Schellenberg, where they vied in gallantry with the Foot Guards and Royals, losing five officers and sixty-six rank and file killed, eleven officers and a hundred and sixty others wounded. Then came Blenheim, where the 23rd were in Rowe's brigade, which commenced the action, and where, "amidst the storm of war, they had repeated opportunities of distinguishing themselves." They fought at Huy and Neer Hespen, and after some less important engagements were in the right of the British line at Ramillies. Again—passing over subordinate incidents in the long war—we come to Oudenarde, to which few regiments can refer with greater pride than the Royal Welsh Fusiliers. It was they who, under Brigadier Sabine, headed the brilliant attack on the village of Heynem, when seven battalions of the enemy were taken prisoners; and it was they who, after driving another body of French from their position, repulsed a body of cavalry which attacked them in front and flank. At the siege of Lisle the attacking force included the 23rd, again led to victory by the brave Sabine; they shared in the siege of Tournay, and in September, 1709, took part in the battle of Malplaquet, where the loss of life was greater "than at the battles of Blenheim, Ramillies, and Oudenarde put together." On this occasion they were in Count Lothum's Division, to which was allotted the severe and trying task of forcing the entrenchments in the wood of Taisniere. Mons and Pont-à-Vendin next occupied their attention; at Douay they had fifty-six of all ranks killed and a hundred and fifty-six wounded.

Shortly after the return of the regiment to England they received the title of the "Prince of Wales's Own Royal Regiment of Welsh Fusiliers," and enjoyed a time of repose till 1742, when they joined Lord Stair's army in Flanders, and fought at Dettingen, where they "wore for the first time those peculiar conical caps which came into vogue with the Prussian tactics." At Fontenoy the losses of the 23rd were very severe, no less than 324 being killed, wounded, or missing. At Laffeldt they again suffered severely, chiefly from the misconduct of the Dutch cavalry. "These troopers suddenly gave way, went threes about, and at full gallop bore down upon five battalions of the reserve, and trampled them under foot. One of these regiments proved to be the 23rd, who resented this unforeseen catastrophe by pouring upon the Dutch two rattling volleys that were intended for the French." The 23rd were one of the four regiments which defended Minorca "against such numbers of the enemy, by sea and land, for such a length of time, as can perhaps scarcely be paralleled in history," and their loss exceeded that of any of the other regiments. After taking part in the expeditions against St. Malo and Cherbourg, their next great warlike achievement was at Minden, in 1759, where, under Lieutenant-Colonel Sacheverel Pole, theirs were among the tempest of bullets that struck in mid-onset the "line of French Cavaliers, gay in splendid uniforms, and formidable in numbers," and hurled them back a broken and routed rabble. Part of the regiment was engaged at Warbourg; at Campen the "23rd were engaged in a desperate musketry fight for many hours, opposed to very superior numbers;" they fought at Kirch Denkern; they assisted in the victory at Graebenstein. Before peace was declared they were engaged in very many actions, and no regiment merited better the ten years' rest they enjoyed consequent on the Treaty of Fontainebleau. In 1773 the 23rd were ordered to America, and fought at Concord, Lexington, and Bunker's Hill. Terribly they suffered at this last, though scarcely to the extent alleged by the enemy. Fenimore Cooper, the well-known novelist, asserts that the regiment, "distinguished alike for its courage and its losses, had hardly men enough left to saddle their goat;" while the wife of John Adams, afterwards President of the United States, declared that "but *one* officer of all the Welsh Fusiliers remains to tell his story." Space will not permit to do more than record the brief fact that the Royal Welsh Fusiliers fought at Long Island, New York, White Plains, Ridgefield (where they received the particular thanks of the Brigadier-General), Brandywine, Monmouth Court House, and other places known to the students of the history of the war—fighting against terrible odds and under great privations, but ever foremost among the brave.

Returning to England in 1784, the Welsh Fusiliers remained at home for ten years, when they took part in the operations at Dominique, and a few years later were represented in the expedition against Ostend. In 1799 they embarked for Holland, and shared with the 55th Regiment the chief fighting at the landing, afterwards taking part in the sharp combats of Alkmaar and Egmont-op-Zee. On their return to England, one of the ships in which about two hundred and sixty men of the regiment were embarked was wrecked, and Lieutenant Hill, who was in command, found—after himself escaping death by a miracle—that out of "four hundred and forty-six souls which had sailed, only twenty-five survived—himself, nineteen men of the Royal Welsh Fusiliers, and five Dutch sailors." The next important fighting in which they were concerned was the ever-memorable campaign in Egypt, when the 23rd were in the reserve under Sir John Moore. The story of the landing is familiar to most—how the reserve jumped on shore and formed line as they advanced, and how the 23rd and 40th "rushed up the heights with almost preternatural energy, never firing a shot, but charging with the bayonet . . . . breaking and pursuing the enemy, and . . . taking at the same time three pieces of cannon." They fought in the battle of Alexandria, being, with the rest of the reserve, the part of our force against whom the principal attacks of the enemy were directed; and, with their comrades, "conducted themselves with unexampled spirit, resisting the impetuosity of the French infantry, and repulsing several charges of cavalry." After the capitulation of Alexandria they repaired to Gibraltar, and a couple of years later returned to England. About this time a second battalion was added, and the 1st battalion took part in the bombardment of Copenhagen, subsequently proceeding to Canada. The 2nd battalion joined General Baird's army previous to the battle of Corunna, at which they were in reserve, and subsequently formed the rearguard on the embarkation of the troops. In the same year the 2nd battalion received what may be described as its death-blow in the fatal swamps of Walcheren; "it was never afterwards employed on foreign service, and, indeed, never attained to such a degree of efficiency as to be able to repair the casualties of the 1st battalion during the Peninsular War." Before engaging on the career of glory indicated by those words, the 1st battalion won the distinction of "Martinique" for the colours. Here, under Lieutenant-Colonel Ellis, they very greatly distinguished themselves. The grenadier company drove the enemy from their position, and repulsed—though with heavy loss—a very superior force. The next day the attack on Fort Bourbon commenced, and again did the gallant Welsh Fusiliers show of what mettle they were. The following year they joined Wellington's army in the Peninsula, forming with the 7th the splendid Fusilier Brigade under Pakenham, in the Fourth Division under Lowry Cole. The first "big battle" in which they were engaged was Albuera. The famous advance of the Fusilier Brigade at the crisis of the battle has been immortalized by Napier, and before referred to. Of that "gallant line," that "astonishing infantry," the 23rd formed part; theirs was the strength and majesty with which the British soldier fights, theirs the flashing eyes, the measured tread, the dreadful volleys, the deafening shouts, and they were amongst those unconquerable British soldiers who "stood triumphant on the fatal hill." Seventy-eight were killed and two hundred and sixty wounded: "so numerous were the casualties amongst the officers and sergeants that one company was, at the conclusion of the action, commanded by a corporal. At Aldea de Ponte the Fourth Division remained as a rearguard. When it was necessary for it to retreat, Wellington asked General Pakenham for a stop-gap regiment to cover the operation. To this the latter answered "that he had already placed the Royal Welsh Fusiliers there." "Ah," replied Wellington, "that is the very thing." At the storming of Badajoz their losses were again severe, four officers and sergeants being killed and twenty-one wounded. They fought at Salamanca; at Vittoria "they did not come in immediate collision with the enemy;" at Pampeluna, "a contest only second to that of Albuera in severity," the 23rd charged four different times. So terrible by this time had been their losses that Lieutenant-Colonel Ellis, commanding the regiment—who had, be it remarked in passing, been wounded in *every one* of the above-mentioned engagements—wrote: "The battalion has only the semblance of one. I commenced the action of the 25th with only two hundred and fifty-four; so, with the loss of one hundred and five . . . . I am reduced to a hundred and sixty bayonets. On the morning of the 30th, when formed for the pursuit of Marshal Soult, I only stood one hundred and twenty-one, and by the 3rd of August I was reduced to one hundred and eight." There were volunteers from their number, under Lieutenant Griffiths, amongst the stormers of St. Sebastian. They fought at Nivelle and the Nive; at Orthes the Fourth Division commenced the battle; at Toulouse "the 23rd were under a heavy cannonade the whole day;" at Waterloo the 23rd were at first in reserve, but were more actively engaged as the day wore on. Here fell, as doubtless he wished to fall, their gallant colonel, Sir Henry Ellis. Struck in the breast with a musket-ball, he rode to the rear to have his wound dressed: his horse threw him while leaping a ditch. When found shortly afterwards he was taken to a neighbouring shed, which took fire in the night. Though rescued by Surgeon Munro of the regiment, he was unable to rally after these accumulated shocks. After Waterloo the regiment served with the army of occupation, and from that time till the Crimean War rested on the laurels they had so gloriously earned, passing the time at home, at Gibraltar, in the West Indies, and Canada.

In the Crimea the 23rd were in the Light Division under Sir George Brown, and at the battle of the Alma were on the extreme left. "Nothing could exceed the coolness of the Welsh Fusiliers as they swept forward under a volleying fire." At the commencement of the famous up-hill charge the regiment was nearly decimated by a murderous fire, yet they and the Rifle Brigade pressed steadily on. One who was present thus describes the scene: "As we clambered out of the river the enemy gave us a fierce fire, the cannon belching forth murderous volleys of grape and round shot, while musket balls fell thick as hail . . . . . Half way up the heights we reached the cannons' mouths which were planted on the entrenchment. Our regiment was about to cross the stockade into the enemy's position, when the commands were given, 'Cease firing. Retire!' because we were in danger of firing on the French. Our colonel (Colonel Chester) rushed in front of us, shouting 'No, no! On lads, on!' He fell with the word on his lip, and never spoke or raised his head again, but lay dead with a scornful frown, his sword clutched in the death-grasp." Ensign Henry fell dead, Lieutenant Anstruther "sprung on to the parapet, and digging the butt of the colour-staff into the ground paused to take breath. In another instant he fell dead, dragging the colours down with him: a glorious pall." They were snatched from his hand by Private Evans, and ere long were flying above the great redoubt. But the Russians advanced in overwhelming masses, and for a brief moment our gallant troops wavered, the "temporary repulse proving terribly fatal to the Welsh Fusiliers, who lost nine of their officers."* Amongst the gallant deeds done at the Alma was that performed by Captain Bell of the 23rd, at the Great Redoubt. "He was charging at the head of his company at the moment when the Russians were retreating with those guns which had dealt such havoc among our men. Farther on, in the rear of the Redoubt, Bell saw a Russian driver urging on with whip and spur three horses which were dragging a brass 16-pounder gun; in a moment he was alongside the driver, and held a revolver to his head. The latter understood the significance of such an act, and, slipping from

* The total loss was 204 of all ranks killed and wounded.

his horse, took to his heels. Bell seized the bridle of one of the horses, and aided by a soldier of the 7th Fusiliers named Pyle, led them round the shoulder of the parapet to the rear of our line, where he met Sir George Brown, the general in command of the Light Division. Now, it is the duty of a captain to be at the head of his company, and the general is said to have reminded him of this fact in language of considerable emphasis. There was no help for it; Bell had to relinquish his prize, and to return to his company. But the gun was safe; the horses drew it down the hill, where it remained till after the battle. The gun is now to be seen at Woolwich, and the horses were put into our "Black Battery." At the close of the war, Captain Bell's heroism was not forgotten; he was decorated with the Victoria Cross." The Light Division were hotly engaged at Inkerman; throughout the siege of Sevastopol the 23rd were in the thick of the fighting. When Brigadier Shirley was incapacitated from leading the assault on the Redan of the 8th September, it was Lieutenant-Colonel Bunbury of the regiment that took his place. "Colonel Lysons of the 23rd, though wounded in the thigh, remained on the ground, and with brandished sword cheered on the stormers." Lieutenant O'Connor, who, as a sergeant,* had rescued the colours of the regiment at the Alma, again "displayed conspicuous courage, and was again severely wounded." For tending and rescuing Lieutenant Dynely, who was mortally wounded, Surgeon Sylvester and Corporal Shields received the Victoria Cross. After the Crimean War the 23rd were amongst the regiments ordered to India, and took part in the relief and subsequent siege of Lucknow, under Sir Colin Campbell, in the battle of Cawnpore (where they were in reserve), and in the operations on the Goomtee and in Oude. It would be unfair, in referring to the Mutiny services of the regiment, to omit all allusion to the gallant action which gained for two men of the regiment the Victoria Cross. At the Secunderbagh, Lieutenant Hackett and Private Monger "saw a wounded corporal of the regiment lying out in the open, and exposed to a very heavy fire. Hackett, assisted by Monger, disregarding the danger, went out and brought their comrade in. The same day Hackett ascended the roof of a bungalow, amidst a storm of bullets, and cut down the thatch to prevent its being set on fire, thus rendering a very important service." Their next campaign of note was the Ashantee War of 1873, in which they were represented by the 2nd battalion, raised in 1858. They reached Cape Coast early in December, landed on the following New Year's Day, and shortly afterwards marched to the front. A company of the regiment, under

* He subsequently rose to the rank of major-general.

Lieutenant-Colonel Mostyn, was attached to the column under Sir Archibald Alison, and at the battle of Amoaful were ordered to "advance along the main road and clear the bush;" an arduous and dangerous duty which they admirably performed. The following day they supported the force told off to attack Bequah, and drove off the foe, who attempted to retake that place. During the final advance on Coomassie they were directed to defend the village of Ordahsu, which was threatened by the enemy. The 23rd were the first regiment that, on the close of the war, landed at Portsmouth, "where, among other graceful gifts, a regimental goat was presented to them in lieu of the famous Indian one which died at Cape Coast."* The 1st battalion served in Burmah, under Sir Henry Prendergast.

THE WELSH REGIMENT†—Regimental District No. 41—is composed of the 41st and 69th Regiments of Foot. The 41st Regiment dates from 1719, when a royal warrant authorised the formation of a "Regiment of Royal Invalids,"—a sort of first reserve,—which was mainly composed of veteran soldiers from the regiments of Guards, and known as the 41st Royal Invalids. Not for many years was the latter title dropped, and it was not till so recently as 1831 that the territorial designation of "Welsh" was given to the regiment. For some considerable time after their formation the 41st had a comparatively uneventful record. Towards the close of the century, however, they exchanged the peaceful quarters of their own county for the West Indies, which offered at that time a busy sphere of action for military prowess. They were engaged at Dominique and Port au Prince, and at Fort Bizotten won deserved applause. During the whole time of the Peninsula War the 41st were in Canada, where they earned those distinctions, some of which sound so strange to us of to-day, and two of which—"Detroit" and "Miami"—are borne by no other regiment. At Detroit, in 1812, they were with the forces under General Brock, who captured that place from the Americans under Hull; at Queenstown they—under the same brave leader, who was unfortunately killed—repulsed a determined attack; at Miami, under Colonel Proctor, they played an important part in the victory which resulted in the capture of the American General, Harrison; in

---

* The bulk of the regiment was not actively engaged during the campaign, being in the rear at Cape Coast.

† The Welsh Regiment wear as badges the Prince of Wales plume and motto on cap, and the Red Dragon of Wales on collar. The mottoes are "Gwell Angaunen Chwilydd"—"Better Death than Shame"—and "Ich Dien." On the colours are the united Tudor Rose and Thistle, within the Garter, and the Royal Cypher, with the following names:—"Bourbon," "Java," "Detroit," "Queenstown," "Miami," "Niagara," "Waterloo," "India," "Ava," "Kandahar," "Ghuznee," "Kabul, 1842," "Alma," "Inkerman," "Sevastopol." The uniform is scarlet, with facings of white.

December, 1813, they shared in the capture of Fort Niagara. Returning to Europe almost immediately after, they joined the army of occupation in France, and from that time till the Burmese War of 1825 were not engaged in any important warfare. The campaign commemorated by "Ava" has been before described; suffice it to say that the 41st were amongst those regiments of whose achievements the Governor General recorded his "unbounded admiration" for the way in which they had established the "renown of British troops in a new and distant region?" The description given by Major Snodgrass affords a vivid idea of the nature of the difficulties with which the 41st and their comrades had to contend. "Hidden from our view on every side in the darkness of a deep and—to regular bodies—impenetrable forest, far beyond which the inhabitants and all the cattle of the Rangoon districts had been driven, the Burmese chiefs carried on their operations, and matured their future schemes with vigilance, secrecy, and activity. Neither rumour nor intelligence of what was passing within their posts ever reached us. Beyond the invisible line which circumscribed our position all was mystery or vague conjecture." When the forward march began, says another writer, "The headquarter-staff, with the first division, proceeded across a dismal and deserted country, interspersed thickly with wild jungle, deep swamps, gigantic reeds, and elephant grass, fifteen feet in height, amidst which even the standard poles of the regiments disappeared. The 41st and the other regiments—with the exception of the Royals, who went by water—proceeded in two divisions by land. On the 12th (of December, 1825) the cholera broke out amongst them, as they were frequently delayed by rain, and the miasma of the swamps was intolerable. By the wayside, they frequently passed the mouldering remains of Burmese soldiers who had been crucified on gibbets for wandering from their posts." Their next distinctions were gained in a kindred country. "Kandahar" and "Ghuznee" tell of the share the gallant Welsh had in the fierce fighting which followed the disaster at Kabul, and by which General Nott vindicated the ability of Britain to conquer and avenge. After their stay in India they returned to take part in the Crimean War. Here the Welsh were brigaded under Adams, with the 47th and 49th, in the Division of Sir de Lacy Evans, and crossed that "perilous ford" at the Alma under a galling fire, and were soon engaged in a "close and murderous strife." At Inkerman they charged in the nick of time to save the 55th, who had been gallantly resisting overwhelming numbers, from utter destruction. Forming line as they advanced the Welsh and 49th Regiments charged up the hill towards the redoubt and attacked the enemy with brilliant gallantry. Storming they came, shoulder to shoulder, and hurled back the Russians. They fought at the Quarries; at the final assault on the Redan, four hundred men of the 41st were included in the storming party under Colonel James Ewan of the regiment, "one of the best officers in the army, a man of singular calmness and bravery, and beloved by officers and men." Amongst those who followed Wyndham into the Redan were Hartready, Kennelly, and Dan Mahoney of the 41st, "the last, a fine, tall grenadier, fell dead in the embrasure by Colonel Wyndham's side, shot through the heart as he was shouting 'Come on, boys, come on.'" While waving his sword in the act of encouraging his men, the brave Ewan was shot through the lungs, and died that night; with him fell Captains Corry and Lockhart.

Many were the acts of individual heroism performed during the war by men of the Welsh Regiment.

"Of Sergeant-Major Ambrose Madden it is related that, heading a party, he cut off and captured a Russian officer and fourteen privates, three of whom he took with his own hand. He was rewarded with the Victoria Cross."

"When the Regiment was driven back by an overwhelming force, Colonel Carpenter, commanding, fell from his horse severely wounded by a bullet. So great was the stress on his men that for several minutes Colonel Carpenter remained in the enemy's hands. During that time he was repeatedly stabbed by the brutal Russian soldiers. Seeing his commanding officer thus ill-treated, Private Thomas Beach rushed out of the retreating ranks, slew two of the foe, and kept the others at bay till the arrival of more men of the 41st. Colonel Carpenter was then carried to the rear, but he soon died. For this exploit Beach received the Victoria Cross."

"Captain Hugh Rowlands, of the 41st, was sent with his company on picket before daybreak on the 5th November. At the first glimmer of light they advanced from the night position to one more advanced, and for a time not a sound was heard. At length, however, one of Rowland's sentries on Shell Hill thought he perceived a Russian column advancing through the mist. Rowlands ran forward and, seeing that he was confronted by two battalions, opened fire. Taken by surprise, the Russians fell back a short distance, but, being reinforced, they faced about and pressed forward. Rowlands still declined to give way, and for half an hour stood his ground. At the end of that time the Russians had placed twenty-two guns in battery on Shell Hill; but even then, though forced to retreat, Rowlands continue to gall the Russian artillerymen with his fire. At a later period of the battle he, with some few men of his own regiment and the 47th, rescued Colonel Haly, commanding the latter, who had been wounded and surrounded. For these acts of gallantry Captain Rowlands received the Victoria Cross."

Since the Crimea the 41st have not been engaged in any warfare that calls for notice, having been engaged in peaceful duties in Jamaica, India, the Cape and Egypt.*

The 2nd battalion of the Welsh Regiment (the 69th) was raised in Lincolnshire in 1760, and first known as Colville's Foot. The first foreign service of the newly raised corps was in America, then in Gibraltar, and later still at St. Lucien in 1778. In 1782 began a period of abnormal but glorious service; the 69th were ordered to serve as Marines in the fleets under Rodney and Hood; and in the famous victory gained over De Grasse won a laurel wreath to encircle the number "69" on their colours. A few years later they were amongst the defenders of Toulon, when amongst their foes was a young Corsican captain of artillery, known to after years as Napoleon the Great. The following year they were with the expedition against Bastia, of which the command was vested—jointly with Colonel Vitelles, of the regiment—in the "Mighty Seaman, tender and true," whose *vale* to his countrymen from amidst the battle din of Trafalgar rings ever with clarion clearness. On their return home the transports were captured by the French, but Captain O'Dogherty, of the 69th, sank the honoured colours of the regiment, and afterwards escaped with his men. In 1796 the 69th were struggling against the climate and the foe at St. Domingo, and the following year played a part—and that a glorious one—in the famous victory off Cape St. Vincent. Some of the 69th were on the *Captain* when Nelson performed the magnificent feat of boarding two hostile vessels, one *across the deck of the other*. Lieutenant Charles Pierson led the detachment of the 69th; a soldier of the regiment smashing with the butt end of his musket a galley window, found a way for his commodore to follow, and the *San Nicolas* was won. But almost at the moment that Nelson was receiving the swords of its officers a fire was poured on the English from the *San Josef*. Then it was that the great sea captain gave utterance to the familiar "Death or Westminster Abbey!" and, ably seconded by the 69th, boarded the *San Josef* from the deck of her own consort. From the reports made by Nelson we know that Lieutenant Pierson and Privates Stevens and Ashcroft distinguished themselves in a strife where all fought as heroes—Ashcroft aiding not a little to the victory by the splendid impudence which prompted him to haul down the enemy's colours even before the boarders had fairly gained a footing on the deck. In the picture in Greenwich Hospital of this most memorable day, the figures "69" can be distinguished on

* The sobriquet of the 41st was for some time the "Invalids."

the breast-plate of the officer standing by Nelson—Lieutenant Pierson of the regiment; and from the frequent and confident reference made by Nelson that day to his "old Agamemnons" of the 69th, did the regiment acquire the sobriquet they have since borne.* In 1799 the 69th were with Sir R. Abercrombie in Holland, and formed part of the brigade under General Coote; then they served in Jamaica, and afterwards assisted in the construction of the Martello Towers around the English coast. In 1805 we find them in India, gaining unstinted admiration by their valour at Vellore. Four companies of the 69th were in garrison here when a mutiny arose: many were murdered in their sleep, but the others—foremost amongst whom were Captains M'Loughlin and Barrow, Sergeant M'Manns and Private Bottom—held out manfully. So sore were their straits that at one time they were reduced to firing *rupees*; but though they were but a handful against a host, the mutineers were kept at bay, their insolent flag torn down—though in the tearing brave men fell quickly in succession—and the position held till his Majesty's 19th Dragoons swept down to the rescue. In 1809 they were at Travancore, and the following year won "Bourbon" for their colours. Colonel Macleod of the regiment had landed with some hundred and sixty men, but owing to the tempestuous weather found himself, for want of supports and directions, in a precarious position. In this emergency a subaltern officer—Lieutenant Foulkstone—volunteered to *swim* to him with information—a splendid feat, which he successfully achieved. The following year the 69th were at Java; and at the desperate assault on Fort Cornelis again distinguished themselves under Colonel Macleod, eleven officers and seventy-six men being killed or wounded. A second battalion meanwhile was playing its part in the European strife then raging. They fought at Merxem; at Bergen-op-Zoom Colonel Morice fell, badly wounded, at the head of one of the assaulting parties; Major Muttlebury led the regiment to the timely succour of the Guards, which, however, was only effected at the cost of their own subsequent surrender. At Quatre Bras they were in Halkett's Division, and later on were placed at the disposal of Sir Denis Pack. Seeing them threatened by a charge of Cuirassiers, Sir Denis ordered them to form square. By some unfortunate misconception the Prince of Orange countermanded this order, with the result that as they were reforming line the French cavalry fell upon them, and they were nearly cut to pieces.† At Waterloo they were in the Fifth Brigade, than which no part of the army, according

* About 300 men of the 69th served as marines on board the *Agamemnon*, when they came particularly under Nelson's notice.

† Grant records that a volunteer, named Clarke, "afterwards an officer in the 42nd," received twenty-three wounds in defence of the colours.

to Creasy, had more severe fighting. Colonel Morice was early wounded, but refused to retire; a shot through the head terminated his brave career. When the Old Guard prepared to charge, the 69th were pushed forward by Halkett to resist their terrible progress. Since Waterloo no important fighting has fallen to the share of the 69th. During the Crimea they were in the West Indies, and during the anxious time of the Mutiny, in Burmah; and their subsequent service, though diversely located, has not brought them again upon the "tented field."

THE DUKE OF WELLINGTON'S WEST RIDING REGIMENT*—Regimental District No. 33—is composed of the 33rd and 76th Regiments of Foot. The 33rd were raised in Yorkshire, in 1702, by Lord Huntingdon, and soon exchanged the familiar surroundings of home for the battle fields of Holland and Spain. At Valentia d'Alcantara they "advanced with great courage and conduct, restored all things, and bravely pushed with colours flying into the breach"; at Almanza, Wade's Regiment, as they were then called, were with the 6th on the left of the British line, and checked by their steady fire the pursuing French cavalry. Spendidly as the British infantry fought, the day went against us, and, like many other regiments, the 33rd were nearly annihilated. They fought at Dettingen; at Fontenoy they again suffered heavy loss; gallantly did they acquit themselves during the campaigns of 1746-47, especially in a fierce combat on the Jaar, near Tongres. They fought at Val, again with loss, and took part in the descents upon the French coast, with which the authorities of that day were wont to amuse themselves. They served in the campaign in Germany under Lord Granby, and in the American War of Independence, during which the British commander, Lord Cornwallis, filled the position of Colonel of the 33rd. At Long Island they led the advance and, but for the order to retire, would doubtless have captured the redoubt; at Fort Washington they were with the Second Division which landed at Island Creek, and after some stiff fighting forced the enemy from the rocks and trees up the steep and rugged mountain. So steep was the hill that the assailants could only climb it by grasping the trees and bushes. At the battle of Camden, or Rugeley's Mills, fought on August 16th, 1780, the 33rd were on the left of the First Division under Colonel Webster, and in conjunction

* The Duke of Wellington's West Riding Regiment bear as badges the Duke of Wellington's Crest (a Red Demi Lion, in a Ducal Coronet, holding the St. George's Pennon) on the cap, and the Elephant on the collar. The motto is that of the Duke: *Virtutis fortuna comes*. On the colours are "Dettingen," "Hindoostan," "Seringapatam," "Ally Ghur," "Delhi, 1803," "Leswarree," "Deig," "Nive," "Peninsula," "Waterloo," "Alma," "Inkerman," "Sevastopol," "Abyssinia." The uniform is scarlet, with facings of white. The West Riding Regiment is the only one named after a subject other than one of the Blood Royal.

with the 23rd chiefly assisted in gaining what has been described as "one of the most decisive victories ever won, where the *loss* of the Americans in killed, wounded, and prisoners exceeded the number of British regular troops engaged by at least three hundred." Again at Guildford Court House, did Cornwallis's Own, under the brave Colonel Webster, behave with signal valour; and when the surrender of the army at York Town put a virtual end to the melancholy warfare, no regiment had deserved better of their King and country than the 33rd. At the commencement of the French war the flank companies of the Regiment, according to Archer, went to the West Indies, "and are said gradually to have died out." The remainder of the regiment joined the army in Flanders and shared in the miseries of the Bremen retreat." The retreat of the British, through all the horrors of an inclement winter, from the Scheldt to the Waal, which they crossed upon the ice, and from the Waal to the mouth of the Elbe, was something more than creditable to the men. Taking into account the inexperience and want of scientific skill of their officers, the fraudulency of their commissariat, and the incompetency of the medical department, it is amazing, where so many were wounded, and so many invalided by cold and cutting frost, that any of them should ever have returned alive to England. Except in the number of its victims, the French retreat from Moscow in 1812 was not more terrible than this. Our allies had deserted us; the people of the country, if not openly hostile, were unfriendly and churlish to the last degree, closing their doors to the sick and wounded, refusing food for money, and doing nothing for us; and the French General Pichegru was in pursuit with a force five times more numerous than our shattered army. Yet whenever the French trod too closely on our rear, they were beaten back with loss." On the 30th of December our infantry drove back the French and captured some guns; on the 8th of the following month they hurled back the approaching enemy with fearful loss; on the 11th of the same month they again taught the French that even in retreat the British lion is fatally terrible to his foes. They then joined the army in India in the campaign in which their chief, Colonel Wellesley, as a "General of Sepoys," laid the foundation of his splendid fame. At Seringapatam they experienced some terrible fighting in the wood on the right bank of the river, and at one time a report was current that they had been overpowered and that their Colonel (Wellesley) with at least a company of the regiment were missing. When, however, Major Shea, the next in command, arrived in camp with the disastrous intelligence, he found his colonel, with the missing company, there before him. In the final storm the 33rd, mustering 413 bayonets in all, were on the left of the assaulting column and were second to none in the furious courage which carried the fortress. When it was reported to Sir David Baird that some men of the 33rd, who had been taken prisoners, had been put to death with horrible torture, he is said to have declared that if the report proved true he would " deliver Tippoo over to be dealt with by the grenadiers of the 33rd as they might chose." On the fall of Seringapatam the post of Governor was, much to the—not unnatural—chagrin of Sir David Baird, conferred upon Colonel Wellesley of the 33rd Regiment.

Passing over the next few years, we find the regiment in Holland towards the end of the campaign. At Quatre Bras they were in Halkett's Brigade, where they suffered heavy loss; at Waterloo they and the 69th sprung up with the Household Troops when the famous order was given, " Up Guards, and at them!" Sir Colin Halkett waving the regimental colour of the splendid West Riding Regiment in front of the line. The journal of a brave officer of the 30th contains a narrative of what took place in this part of the field. "Hougomont and its wood sent up a broad flame through the dark masses of smoke that overhung the field; beneath this cloud the French were indistinctly visible. Here a waving mass of long red feathers could be seen; there, gleams as from a sheet of steel showed that the cuirassiers were moving; four hundred cannon were belching forth fire and death on every side; the roaring and shouting were indistinguishably commixed— together they gave me an idea of a labouring volcano. Bodies of infantry and cavalry were pouring down on us, and it was time to leave contemplation, so I moved towards our columns, which were standing up in square. The 30th and 73rd formed one, and 33rd and 69th another. In a few minutes after, the enemy's cavalry galloped up and crowned the crest of our position. Our guns were abandoned, and they formed between the two brigades, about a hundred paces in our front. Their first charge was magnificent. As soon as they quickened their trot into a gallop, the cuirassiers bent their heads, so that the peaks of their helmets looked like vizors, and they seemed cased in armour from the plume to the saddle. Not a shot was fired till they were within thirty yards, when the word was given, and our men fired away at them. The effect was magical. Through the smoke we could see helmets falling, cavaliers springing from their seats with convulsive springs as they received our balls, horses plunging and rearing in the agonies of fright and pain, and crowds of the soldiery dismounted, part of the squadron in retreat, but the more daring remainder backing their horses to force them on our bayonets. Our fire soon disposed of these gentlemen. The main body re-formed in our front, and rapidly and gallantly repeated their attacks. In fact, from this time (about four o'clock) till near six we had a constant repetition of these brave but unavailing charges. There was no difficulty in repulsing them, but our ammunition decreased alarmingly. At length an artillery waggon galloped up, emptied two or three casks of cartridges into the square, and we were all comfortable. The best cavalry is contemptible to a steady and well-supplied infantry regiment; even our men saw this, and began to pity the useless perseverance of their assailants, and as they advanced would growl out, 'Here come these fools again!' One of their superior officers tried a *ruse de guerre* by advancing and dropping his sword, as though he surrendered; some of us were deceived by him, but Halkett ordered the men to fire, and he coolly retired, saluting us. Their devotion was invincible. One officer whom we had taken prisoner was asked what force Napoleon might have in the field, and replied with a smile of mingled derision and threatening, 'Vous verrez bientôt sa force, messieurs.' As the Duke came near us late in the evening, Halkett rode out to him and represented our weak state, begging his Grace to afford us a little support. 'It's impossible, Halkett,' said he. And our general replied, 'If so, sir, you may depend on the brigade to a man!'"

From the time of Waterloo till the Crimea the 33rd, in common with many other regiments, were not engaged in any actual warfare, being quartered in Jamaica, Gibraltar, and Canada.* In the Crimea they were in Sir George Brown's—the "Light"—Division, and at the Alma proved with what justice they have been considered a *corps d'élite*. In the temporary repulse at the redoubt (referred to in the account of the 23rd) the Duke of Wellington's suffered very severely; "no less than nineteen sergeants fell, chiefly in defence of the colours." At one time the 33rd Regiment, with the rest of the brigade under the command of General Codrington, had advanced too far, and actually got into one of the Russian batteries, when the enemy swarmed round their ranks in such numbers that they were compelled to retire and reform. At Inkerman and "The Quarries" they were again hotly engaged; on the 19th of April a wing of the regiment under Lieutenant-Colonel Munday, with some of the 77th, captured, without firing a shot, but by the bayonet alone, two of the rifle pits which so harassed our forces. Throughout the siege they were ever to the fore, in skirmish, in trenches, and assault. The 33rd were sent to India, arriving there, however, after the Mutiny; and their next service of note was in Abyssinia. Here they were the first troops under orders to land in that well-nigh unknown region,

* The title, "Duke of Wellington's," with their former Colonel's crest and motto, were given to the Regiment on the Duke's death in 1852.

whose barbaric sovereign claimed lineage from Solomon the Wise and the Queen of Sheba, and hidden beneath whose sullen and stupendous rocks, tradition averred, lay gold compared with which the hordes of Midas were but a collection of specimens, and gems amongst which the Kohinoor and the "Mother of Emeralds" would have been noticed only as foils. To the 33rd, too, was assigned the honour of advancing first on Magdala, and the speedy fall of a citadel which might have been invulnerable tells how well they fulfilled their task. During the advance, Colonel Locke ordered six men of the regiment, with three gunners, to occupy a path down which it was thought Theodore was endeavouring to escape; and the little party, while moving forward, captured no fewer than twenty guns. The actual storming proved somewhat sterner work than had been anticipated.

The 33rd was marching in fours, firing right and left as they went up the steep road, which led to the summit of the rock on which Magdala is situated, headed by the Engineers. All of a sudden it became known that the blasting powder had been forgotten, and that the stormers must dispense with its assistance. On receiving the intimation, the 33rd broke off from the road and clambered up the hill under the fire of the enemy. "On reaching the foot of the wall they found that it was, in fact, a scarped cliff, about seven or eight feet high, with a hedge of prickly bushes about a foot high at the top. Private Bergin, who was a tall man, six feet in height, contrived with his bayonet to make a gap in the hedge. Drummer Magnor, of the 33rd, was by his side, and Bergin said, 'Let me help you up, and then you can pull me up.' Magnor agreed, and getting on Bergin's shoulders caught hold of the top of the cliff with his hands, and being shoved up by the butt of Bergin's rifle, got to the top, and then pulled up Bergin, who was assisted in mounting by Ensign Connor and Corporal Murphy. Bergin saw a cluster of the enemy standing at the gate, which was about forty yards off. Ensign Connor asked Bergin to give him a hand, but Bergin replied that he wanted to have a shot at the enemy, and that the drummer, having no rifle, had better help the rest of the party up. Meanwhile, the enemy had been firing at Bergin, who lost no time in replying, advancing as he fired. Some of the enemy kept on firing, but others ran away. By the time he had fired ten or twelve rounds Bergin had reached the gate, the enemy falling back before him, at least such of them as were not killed by his breech-loader, which caused several to drop. It was then that some officers and men came up, and the whole party advanced towards the inner circle of fortifications. All of the enemy, save one, had disappeared through an open gate. The one exception stood his ground, and tried to fire four or five rounds at Bergin and an officer who accompanied. It had been raining heavily that afternoon, and the Abyssinian's gun snapped each time. The officer, saying, 'I'll make him a prisoner!' rushed forward to seize the man. The latter drew a sword, and in another instant would have cut the officer down, when Bergin promptly shot the Abyssinian through the head. The officer might have easily protected himself, for he was armed with sword and revolver, but he was so intent on capturing his gallant foe, that but for Bergin he would have been slain. Notwithstanding his narrow escape, this officer, with the true spirit of an English gentleman, exclaimed, when he saw the man fall, 'It was a pity to kill him, for he was a brave soldier!' Bergin and his comrades then entered the gate, and skirmishing through the inner town soon put an end to all resistance. For this exploit both Magnor and Bergin were given the Victoria Cross."

The flank movement of the 33rd practically achieved the capture of Magdala. At the top of a flight of steps remained one obstacle, a gate, which the rifles of the 33rd soon blew in. Within the gate lay the corpse of Theodore, habited as a simple chieftain, slain by his own hand. With the fall of Magdala ended for the time the warlike achievements of the famous 1st Battalion of the Duke of Wellington's West Riding Regiment. The 33rd Foot used to be known as "Have-a-cake Lads," from Sergeant Snap's manner of enticing recruits by displaying an oatcake spitted on a sword.

The Second Battalion of the Duke of Wellington's regiment, the 76th, was raised in 1787 at the cost of the East India Company. Two other regiments had borne the same number, the first Irish, the second Scotch—the well-known Macdonald Highlanders, disbanded in 1784. The present 76th proceeded almost immediately to India to fight against Tippoo Sahib. They fought at Savendroog; they were with the army which captured Bangalore; at Seringapatam they fought and conquered side by side with the 36th Regiment. These two regiments found themselves in front of a redoubt held by the flower of the Indian army. "Advancing with the bayonet alone, the grenadiers of the 36th and 76th Regiments carried the covered way; but when attempting to enter the gorge, they encountered a dreadful fire of grape musketry, which cut them down in heaps, and compelled all who survived to recoil. Thrice the brave fellows rushed on to renew the attack, and thrice they were repulsed; but as the ammunition of the enemy was becoming expended a fourth attempt was attempted, and proved successful, and with the fury of madmen the surviving grenadiers rushed into the work, and three hundred and fifty Mysoreans perished under their bayonets." A few years later they again distinguished themselves, at Allyghur and Delhi, and in the signal victory won by Lord Lake at Leswarree. "On the side of the British," says an account of the battle, "the brunt was borne by the King's 76th Regiment, which, with a battalion and five companies of Sepoys, had to sustain a tremendous fire of canister-shot and a massive charge of cavalry. 'This handful of heroes,' as Lake called them, though thinned by the enemy's artillery, stood firm, and repulsed the horse." It was the 76th who led the way through jungle and over nullah, "and assailed the legions of Scindiah with the bravery that never dreams of defeat." They claim to share with the 8th Hussars the honour of capturing the standards and guns that fell to the spoil of the victors, and the absence from their colours of this distinction has given rise to some comment. At Deeg the 76th were in the first line. With one furious charge they drove the enemy out of the village, and pressing furiously onward, attacked the line of guns which were pouring a continuous and deadly fire on our men. As the 76th came up "the guns were abandoned, the gunners flying to others in the rear; so that by the time the second line passed through the fortified village, they saw the brave 76th far ahead in the thickest of a vast multitude, and almost lost; but they came to the rescue with a mighty rush." The command now devolved upon Colonel Monson of the regiment, and the foe were pressed right up to the walls of Deeg. Some of the enemy's cavalry by this time had wheeled round and retaken their first line of guns, which they turned against our troops; but Captain Henry Norford of the 76th, with only twenty-eight men, charging with the bayonet, drove them off and recaptured the cannon, in which brilliant exploit he was unfortunately killed. Their splendid exploits in India, which are commemorated by the badge of the Elephant, were terminated by the siege of Bhurtpore; after which, in 1807, they returned home, only two men, Lieutenant Montgomery and Quartermaster Hopkins—both of whom had risen from the ranks—remaining of those who had left England twenty years before. The 76th took part in the Walcheren expedition, and joined the army in Spain in 1813, being assigned to Lord Aylmer's brigade. They fought on the Bidassoa, at Nive, in the battles of the Pyrenees, and at Bayonne. They then proceeded to America and fought at Plattsburg and other places, not returning to England till 1827. Since then they have served in India, Burmah, the West Indies, and Canada, but have not been engaged in any fighting requiring notice.

The 76th are credited with the sobriquet of "The Pigs," owing to their Elephant badge at one time—thanks to a clumsy draughtsman—somewhat resembling a boar.

Another name was "The Immortals," from most of the men having been wounded in 1806; while a third was the "Old Seven and Sixpennies," from their number.

The Duke of Edinburgh's Wiltshire Regiment *—Regimental District No. 62—is composed of the 62nd and 99th Regiments.

The 62nd Regiment date their separate existence from 1758, when the second battalion of the King's Own was formed into a distinct regiment. Their first experience of warfare was under General Amherst, at Louisbourg,† after which some of the regiment were with Wolfe at Quebec. Their next sphere of service was in Ireland, where they greatly distinguished themselves at Carrickfergus, when it was besieged by the famous French corsair, Thurot. Four companies only were present, and these, it is recorded, were raw recruits, and "were actually at instruction drill when the boats of Thurot suddenly landed the French infantry." Colonel Jennings recalled them by sound of bugle, but the French followed before the gates could be closed. Colonel Jennings, Lord Wallingford, Captain Bland, Lieutenants Hall and Ellis, with fifty soldiers and some volunteers, drove them back, and for a long time the little garrison held the foe at bay, though they had but little ammunition, and were reduced to throwing stones and bricks. But further defence was useless and impossible, and the four companies of the 62nd—those "raw recruits"—marched out from this, the scene of their first battle, with all the honours of war.‡

After a short time passed in the West Indies, the 62nd were ordered to America, where they served under General Burgoyne. At Stillwater the whole brunt of the fierce attack made by the Americans fell on the 62nd, with whom were the 20th and Scots Fusiliers. Deserted by their native allies, almost without provisions, and opposed by vastly superior forces, these gallant regiments maintained the fight for four hours, and remained at the last masters of the field. The following month saw the surrender at Saratoga, previous to which, in a brilliant but unsuccessful attempt to force the enemy's position, the 62nd obtained their familiar sobriquet of the "Springers," having acted as light infantry, with whom in those days the command "Spring up" meant to

---

* The Duke of Edinburgh's Wiltshire Regiment bear as a badge the coronet and cypher of the Duke of Edinburgh on cap and collar. The motto is that of the Garter. On the colours are "Nive," "Peninsula," "Ferozeshah," "Sobraon," "Sevastopol," "Pekin," "New Zealand," "South Africa, 1879." The uniform is scarlet with facings of white.

† Archer.

‡ The 62nd used to have a "splash" on their buttons, commemorative of the tradition that when bullets failed the men supplied their place with coat buttons.

advance. "It exceeds," says Botta, "the power of words to describe the pitiable condition to which the British Army at Saratoga was now reduced. The troops were worn down by a series of toil, privation, sickness and desperate fighting. They were abandoned by the Indians and Canadians, and the effective force of the whole army was now diminished by repeated and heavy losses, which had principally fallen on the best soldiers and the most distinguished officers, from ten thousand combatants to less than one-half that number. Of this remnant, little more than three thousand were English.

"In these circumstances, and thus weakened, they were invested by an army of four times their own number, whose position extended three-parts of a circle round them; who refused to fight them, as knowing their weakness, and who, from the nature of the ground, could not be attacked in any part. In this helpless condition, obliged to be constantly under arms, while the enemy's cannon played on every part of the camp, and even the American rifle-balls whistled in many parts of the lines, the troops of Burgoyne retained their customary firmness, and while sinking under a hard necessity, they showed themselves worthy of a better fate. They could not be reproached with an action or a word which betrayed a want of temper or of fortitude. General Gates, in the first instance, demanded that the Royal army should surrender prisoners of war. He also proposed that the British should ground their arms. Burgoyne replied, "This article is inadmissible in every extremity: sooner than this army will consent to ground their arms in their encampment, they will rush on the enemy, determined to take no quarter." The following few years the 62nd spent at home, their next foreign service being in Jamaica, where they were engaged in quelling the Maroon rising, and lost during their sojourn there the greater part of their number from disease. In 1807 they were in Sicily, and a detachment of the regiment, under Captain Cruikshank, was amongst the defenders of the Castle of Scylla, while others shared in the operations at Rosetta in Egypt. In 1809 they joined the force under Sir John Stuart, and took part in his successful exploits at Naples, Ischia, Procida, and Palermo, at which last-named place they much distinguished themselves. In 1813 they joined Lord Aylmer's Brigade in Spain, and fought at the Bidassoa, Nivelle, Nive, and Bayonne. They then went to America, and were present at the surrender of Castine, returning to Europe to join the Army of Occupation in France. The regiment remained at home till 1830, when they went to India, where they remained for some years. They fought at Masulipatam and Moulmain; at Ferozeshah, under General Littler, they suffered more than any other European regiment, having seventeen officers and two hundred and thirty rank and file killed or wounded. "Unfortunately, in the hurry of the moment, Sir John Littler, in his despatch after the battle, used the words 'panic-struck,' as applicable to Her Majesty's 62nd Regiment, and attributed some irresolution on the part of the native regiments in his division to the example of the 62nd. The charges were groundless. Before the 62nd fell back, they had 7 officers killed and 10 wounded, 76 rank and file killed and 154 wounded. The regiment were numerically weak; their loss was greater than that of any other European regiment present. Both the Governor-General and Commander-in-Chief did all they could to remove the injurious impression, and at home, in the House of Lords, the Duke of Wellington stood manfully forward to vindicate the fame of the heroic band, and apply balm to their wounded pride." A detachment was at Aliwal, and they fought in Ashburnham's Brigade at Sobraon, where they supported the 10th and 53rd. The 62nd retired home before war broke out again in India, and enjoyed a period of repose till the Crimea, where, however, they did not participate in the earlier battles. They saw, nevertheless, plenty of service in the Quarries, and in the final assault on the Redan shared with the Buffs and the Welsh Regiment the honour of contributing to the stormers chosen from the Second Division. Since the Crimea they have served in America and India, but have not been engaged in any important warfare.

The Second Battalion of the Duke of Edinburgh's Wiltshire Regiment, the 99th, dates from 1824, when they were raised in Scotland, and were for some time known as the Lanarkshire Regiment. For the first twenty years, or thereabouts, the 99th were stationed in the Mauritius and Ireland, in 1845 being despatched to New Zealand, where they gained their first distinction by the part they took in the war there, notably at Ohaianai and Ruapekapeka. They remained in Australia and Van Diemen's Land for some years, their next service being in the Chinese war of 1860. Here they were in the Second Division and fought at Sinho, at the Taku Forts, at Changchai-wan, and were present at the capture of Pekin. The next eighteen years were passed in comparative quietness by the 99th; they were stationed for a considerable portion of the time in Natal, and were consequently familiar with the country when the Zulu troubles required their service. They were in the first column under Colonel Pearson, their own commander being Colonel Welman, and early in January fought at Inyezane, where they shared the honours of the day with the Buffs and Engineers. A day or so afterwards they reached Etschowe, and scarcely had they done so when tidings reached Colonel Pearson of the disaster at Isandlhwana. Despite its disadvantages the Colonel determined to hold Etschowe rather than retreat, and the defences were strengthened as much as possible. To the 99th was assigned the south face of the fort, and all was in readiness when Lieutenant Rowden of the regiment, who at the head of his mounted scouts had made an extended exploration, reported that a considerable force was collecting. Provisions soon became scarce, and raids, in which the 99th took part, broke the monotony of their state of siege. One of these raids was a very brilliant affair, and reflected great credit on the force which effected it, and which was in great part composed of men of the 99th. Early in the morning they made their way out of the little fort, down the almost precipitous glade that led to the river, along the course of which they pursued their way for some distance. After a long day's march they encamped in a favourable position, though sleep was out of the question, as they had several alarms, and it became evident from certain indications known to the experienced in Zulu warfare, that they were being reconnoitred by the enemy, though in all probability not in sufficient force to deliver an attack. In the grey light of the early morning they saw "the enemy hovering in large bodies on the opposite ridges, and evidently puzzled by the movements of this handful of white men, the more so as one of Rowden's scouts tied an handkerchief to an overhanging branch before leaving the spot, thus giving them the idea that a detachment occupied it, and that it was a signal they knew not what for." The exploring party were thus enabled to make an extended reconnaissance and soon discovered enough to convince them that the enemy would soon be reinforced, and that they must retire without delay if they wished to avoid capture. "Some of the soldiers cut long canes, fastened them between ledges of the rock, and fixed some coloured clothes thereto, leading watchers to believe that there was a garrison still on the kop, which was quitted silently and swiftly," and the party pressed on towards the kraal, on which it was intended to make the raid. Ere, however, they reached it the enemy had opened fire on them, but the quality of their arms fortunately prevented any casualty. The party of the 99th, with their comrades, preceded by some mounted men, now advanced at the double, and the kraal was swept from end to end, and set in flames, and two large packages of mealies were brought off, but the force was too slender to pursue the flying cattle, and the return to Etschowe became of instant necessity. As it was, a large body of the foe had gathered on the road, while some others were assembling in a position to attack the little body in flank. Soon a sharp volley was poured in at a distance of not more than fifty yards. This was answered with effect by our mounted infantry, but the foe kept up a running fire, not retiring, despite their heavy losses, till the fort was reached, and the 99th, with their brave companions, safe within its walls. Others of the regiment, meanwhile, were with Lord Chelmsford advancing to the relief of Etschowe, and on the 2nd of April, 1879, was fought the battle of Ghingilovo, which enabled a junction to be effected. The companies of the 99th who were with Lord Chelmsford were on the left front of the lager, and had their full share of the stubborn fighting that ensued. The victory over the Zulus accomplished the relief of Etschowe; some of the 99th under Major Walker of the regiment were left to garrison Ghingilovo, and on the 5th of April their comrades from the garrison joined them after ten weeks' blockade. After the first phase of the war was over the 99th stayed for some time in Natal, and have since been stationed in Bermuda and India.

The Worcestershire Regiment*— Regimental District No. 29—consists of the 29th and 36th Regiments of Foot.

The 29th Regiment dates from 1702, when Colonel Thomas Farrington was commissioned to raise a regiment. In 1704 Farrington's Foot were ordered to Germany, and fought at Neer Hespen, taking part, in 1706, in the famous battle of Ramillies. According to one account they were at Almanza, though this does not appear by any means certain. The early history of the regiment is, however, wrapped in considerable obscurity. A few years later they were at Gibraltar, and during the Seven Years' War were amongst the troops retained in England. In 1776 they went to Canada, and fought under Burgoyne, finding their next warlike employment as Marines on the Channel Fleet. In this capacity they were present at numerous actions, and on the "glorious first of June" suffered heavy loss. They then proceeded to the West Indies, and fought at Grenada, three years later joining the army in Holland. A few years more brings us to a period in which the doings of the 29th are recorded with no uncertain touch, being blazoned alike on their colours and in the histories of that war whose close was to see England supreme by land and sea, the saviour of Europe and the director of its destinies. At Roleia, under Colonel Lake, the 29th, with whom were the 9th (the brigade of General Nightingale), were ordered to force a pass through the dense groves behind

* The Worcestershire Regiment bear as badges a silver Lion crowned in a Garter on an eight-pointed star on cap and collar. The mottoes are "Firm" and "Honi soit qui mal y pense." On the colours are the Tudor Rose and "Ramillies," "Hindoostan," "Roleia," "Vimiera," "Corunna," "Talavera," "Albuera," "Salamanca," "Pyrenees," "Nivelle," "Nive," "Orthes," "Toulouse," "Peninsula," "Ferozeshah," "Sobraon," "Punjaub," "Chillianwallah," "Goojerat." The uniform is scarlet with facings of white.

which were thronged the French sharp-shooters. When the 29th were within a few yards of a thicket a terrific fire was opened on them, "which only the most resolute bravery could have withstood." That resolute bravery was theirs. Waving his hat and sword, Colonel Lake called on his men to follow him. He fell beneath the shower of bullets, but his commands and example were followed, and by a magnificent charge the 29th gained the position. Scarcely had they done so, and before they could form line, when a French battalion advanced against them. Once more the bayonet did its deadly work; many fell, but the French were forced to retreat, and the 29th—by this time joined by their comrades—remained the victors. The incident is well described in a recent work. "The conduct of Colonel Lake, at the head of the brave 29th, was admired by friends and foes, and his premature loss was deeply regretted in our camp. On leading his men up to the French 82nd, he said to them, 'Soldiers, I shall remain in front of you! remember that the bayonet is the only weapon for a British soldier!' That French regiment did not wait to try its effects. When Lake had cleared a ravine, and gained the top of a hill, he stood, as he was getting his fearfully thinned regiment into order, like a target to be shot at. It is said that one French officer declared afterwards that he had himself fired seven shots at him. Once he seemed to stagger as if he were hit, but it was only at the seventh shot that he fell. Upon his body were found two wounds, the mortal one being a ball which went through him from side to side. Sergeant-Major Richards stood over his fallen beloved officer until he was himself riddled with musket balls, and bayonets. As this poor fellow was dying, he said, 'I should not so much care if our Colonel had been spared.' Never had a regiment better right to ornament its flag than had the always gallant and well-doing 29th to inscribe on its banner the name of Roleia." At Vimiera they were again engaged, and—to quote Archer's enthusiastic reference—"the brunt of the fighting was borne by the 29th, which was, and ever has been, one of the finest corps in the army."* In the combats preceding Talavera the 29th again distinguished themselves, utterly routing a French regiment which advanced against them, and, under Stewart, holding their own in that terrible forty minutes in which no fewer than fifteen hundred British soldiers perished. They fought right well in the furious combat of Talavera; at Albuera, Napier records how the 29th, "terribly resolute, smote friends and foes in their onward progress"—though the "friends" were those from whom they might well pray to be

* The same writer states that the Regiment fought at this battle in the old-fashioned *queues*, the officers wearing the contemporary cocked hats.

preserved, the Spaniards whose blundering occasioned so much loss. Under Colonel Inglis the Worcestershire performed literal "prodigies of heroism," and the historic charge of the Fusilier Brigade completed a victory which every regiment had combined to gain. Amongst the studiously reserved reports made by the great English General, there is perhaps none more unstinted in its eulogy than that in which he refers to the deeds of the 29th on this day. From the Peninsula they repaired to Canada, and so missed Waterloo. After spending some years at home they were ordered to the Mauritius, where they remained about twelve years, and in 1842 went to India, where they were to reap fresh honours in the Sutlej campaign. On the day following the battle of Moodkee the 29th arrived there in charge of some guns, and two days later fought valiantly at Ferozeshah.

"Her Majesty's 29th and 1st European Light Infantry, with undaunted bravery, rushed forward, crossed a dry nullah, and found themselves exposed to one of the hottest fires of musketry that can possibly be imagined; and what rendered it still more galling was, that the Sikhs were themselves concealed behind high walls, over which the European soldiers could not climb. To remain under such a fire without the power of returning it with any effect would have been madness, the men would have been annihilated. Thrice did Her Majesty's 29th Regiment charge the works, and thrice were they obliged to retire, each time followed by the Sikhs, who spared none, and cut to pieces the wounded." "Her Majesty's 29th regiment alone, exhibited a loss in killed and wounded of 13 officers, 8 serjeants, and 157 rank and file."

They fought at Sobraon, where fell their brave leader, Colonel Taylor; at the desperate battle of Chillianwallah they were in Gilbert's Division, which formed the eighth column of advance. Terrible though the odds, the gallant Worcestershire more than held their own, forcing their way to the rear of the Sikh position and spiking several guns beneath a heavy fire. The latest of their well-fought fields is Goojerat, where the complete victory they materially assisted in gaining brilliantly closed a brilliant record of brilliant deeds. The subsequent years have been passed by the 29th chiefly in India and the West Indies.

The 36th—the second battalion of the Worcestershire Regiment—were raised in Ireland in 1701, and served the first few years on board ship. In 1705 they were amongst the stormers whom Lord Peterborough led into the strong castle of Monjuich, near Barcelona; and on the surrender of the city their Colonel, Lord Charlemont, was presented by the General to the King of Spain as one who had done his Majesty good service. After a sojourn of several months in Spain, during which some of the soldiers were converted into dragoons, the 36th, as Allnut's Foot, fought at Almanza, where they were almost destroyed, five officers being killed and thirteen made prisoners, amongst whom was Colonel Allnut. Eight years later, having during the interval been to America and back, they were engaged in repressing the Jacobite rising in Scotland, fighting with credit to themselves at Dunblain and Sheriffmuir. After a period of comparative inaction, they were ordered in 1741 to the West Indies, and took part in the operations at Carthagena, returning home in time to again fight for the established government against the adherents of the Stuarts. They fought at Falkirk and Culloden, and were doubtless rejoiced when the opportunity offered, in 1747, of engaging once more in foreign warfare. At Val they suffered very severely—so much so, indeed, as to have to return home to recruit, and we next find them taking part in the Duke of Marlborough's descents upon the French coast. In 1761 they took part in the operations against Bellisle, and three years later went to Jamaica, where they remained for about nine years. In 1783 they went to India, and in the fighting against Tippoo Sahib gained lasting renown. They fought at Mangalore, and at Cananore under Major Knox. In the defence of Sattimungulum in 1790 they bore the brunt of the fighting, on one occasion having no food and only a little tobacco from the evening of the 13th till late on the night of the 15th. When Tippoo upbraided his officers for their want of success, they declared that the "battalion wearing the colours of the prophet could not be vanquished by any troops in the world."* At Bangalore, under Captain Andrew White, they carried the Delhi Gate; they stormed Nundy Droog in 1791; at Seringapatam they were in the first column under General Meadows, and again were led by Captain Andrew White. Had there been need of an incentive to such troops as the Herefordshire (as they had been styled in 1782) to fight to the uttermost, it was supplied by the tidings that Dr. Home, the regimental surgeon, who had been taken prisoner some months before, had been murdered by Tippoo's order at Nundy Droog. The splendid advance they made has been referred to in the account of the 76th (2nd battalion West Riding Regiment), and the Worcestershire Regiment may well recall with pride their achievements of that day. "Midnight was close at hand; 'the moon, full and cloudless in all her Indian splendour, shone down on the broad and rapid Cavey, on the high white walls of Sri Runga, on the palaces and island gardens of Tippo'—shone too on the weird but splendid spectacle of three columns of warriors moving resistlessly forward to change the ownership of all these fair things, and to exact a terrible recompense for comrades and

* The facings of the regiment were then green.

countrymen ruthlessly murdered and tortured by the tyrant who rejoiced in his name of 'the Tiger Lord.'" It has been suggested that the regimental motto, "Firm," takes its origin from the use of that word in Lord Cornwallis' report of the regiment, but the correspondence preserved in the official record conclusively proves that it was in use for many years before the Indian triumphs of the regiment. Before leaving India they fought at Pondicherry, and returned home in 1799 after an absence of sixteen years.

The following year they were amongst the troops dispatched, under General Maitland, to the assistance of the French Royalists at Quiberon, and for the next seven years had a comparatively tranquil time, as, though they were ordered to Germany in 1806, they did not come in for any actual fighting. In June, 1807, the Herefordshire arrived at Monte Video under General Crauford, and took part in the disastrous operations at Buenos Ayres, and the following year saw them in the Peninsula with Wellesley's conquering army. In Seymour's Brigade they fought at Roleia and Vimiera, gaining from Lord Wellesley the high praise, that "the 36th is an example to any regiment;" at Corunna they were on the left of the British line; they took part in the bombardment of Flushing; they fought at Almeida; were present, though not engaged, at Fuentes d'Onor; took part in the sharp affairs of Especha and Ronda; and—greatly, we may be sure, to their disappointment—just missed the magnificent struggles at Ciudad Rodrigo and Badajoz. At Salamanca they were at first in reserve, but had their full share of hard fighting before "the effulgent crest of the won ridge became black and silent, and the whole French army vanished as it were in the darkness." They were at Burgos and Vittoria; fought in the wild, fierce struggles on the Pyrenees; charged with the resistless columns at Nivelle (carrying a formidable redoubt at Ainhoa); forced the passage of the Nive; and, with their comrades, hurled the columns of D'Amargnac from their ground at Orthes. At Toulouse it was the 36th that began the attack of the Sixth Division; and in this, their last battle for many years, they suffered somewhat severely. Practically the 36th have not been engaged in warfare since. They were not at Waterloo nor at the Crimea, and have been chiefly stationed in the West Indies and Canada, some slight skirmishing at Corfu in 1848 being the only interruption to their enjoyment of the "piping time of peace." *

* The nicknames of the 36th were "The Saucy Greens," and the "Firms."

THE YORK AND LANCASTER REGIMENT *—Regimental District No. 65 — consists of the 65th and 84th Regiments of Foot. The 65th Regiment was originally the 2nd battalion of the 12th and received the separate numbering in 1758. The year following their existence as a distinct regiment the newly-formed corps made their *début* on the war stage at Guadeloupe and afterwards at the Havannah. Their next service was in America during the War of Independence, when they fought at Bunker's Hill. For some years after that they appear to have been comparatively inactive, but in 1794 they formed part of the forces under Sir Charles—afterwards Earl—Grey at Martinique. On the occasion of the capture of Morne Bellevue the 65th were directed to support the storming party, and in the subsequent operations were fully and creditably engaged. In 1803 they were ordered to India, and after fighting at Guzerat and Malwa took part in the siege of Bhurtpore. For many years they continued identified with our struggles in the East. They fought in the Persian Gulf and Kattiawar, and again at Guzerat in 1814. They fought, too, in the Pindaree War of 1817, and two years later served with Sir William Grant in the Persian Gulf and in the chastisement inflicted on the Beni-Boo-Ali Arabs. In the final attack on their fortress in Aden it is reported that the brunt of the fighting was borne by the 65th and a native regiment, and that very serious loss was incurred. The following year the 65th returned home and were subsequently stationed in the West Indies and Canada. The next opportunity that offered of active service was in New Zealand, where they formed part of the forces under Sir Duncan Cameron. One of the most remarkable and noteworthy incidents of the war was connected with a skirmish in which many brave officers and men lost their lives, and in which one of the survivors gained the Victoria Cross. The narrative of the last named has been published.

"We had to cross," he said, "nine or ten miles of swamp, intersected by rivers scarcely practicable for regular troops, so as to strike the foot of the wooded range of hills on a spur of which stands the Pa of Camerontown. We had to creep through the dense bush, but there is no difficulty persistent pluck may not surmount. "McKenna took a direct course through the bush towards the spot where the natives were supposed to be." About five o'clock I reached a large opening, where I could plainly see the rebels' encampment in the bush about four hundred yards in advance. Crossing the

---

* The York and Lancaster Regiment bear as badges the Tudor Rose with the Royal Tiger below on cap and the Royal Tiger on the collar. The motto is that of the Garter. On the colours are "India," "Arabia," "Nive," "Peninsula," "Lucknow," "New Zealand," "Egypt, 1882—84," and "Tel-el-Kebir." The uniform is scarlet with facings of white. There is a black line in the lace of the officers' tunics.

clearing in a stooping position, and at a smart pace, I again made for the bush, followed by the whole detachment. Five minutes after, we could distinctly hear the sound of the rebels' voices; and Captain Swift, imagining that they were advancing by the same path to attack us, threw his men into ambush. On finding that they refused to advance, I crept stealthily up to within a few yards of them. Unlike most Maori war parties, they were laughing and chattering, which led me to think they had been making free with the rum they had seized in the canoes. I returned and reported this to Captain Swift, who came to the same conclusion as myself, that they were all drunk. The order was at once given to 'fix bayonets and charge.' Our men advanced—led by Captain Swift, Lieutenant Butler, and myself—three abreast, the path not admitting more. When we had stolen up to within a few yards of the rebels our leader gave the word 'Charge!' The word had scarcely passed his lips when, as if by enchantment, the whole bush was lighted up with a terrific volley. It seemed as if one of the extinct volcanoes, so common here, had suddenly opened its crater and begun to belch forth flames. The enemy were so close when they fired that some of their coarse powder was actually found sticking in the faces of our soldiers. For a moment our men staggered beneath this heavy fire; but it was only for a moment, for immediately recovering themselves they closed up in a line of skirmishers in the bush, and brought their rifles to bear on their dusky foes. I had taken cover behind a tree close to Lieutenant Butler for the purpose of reloading my rifle." Even in that terribly anxious time, McKenna goes on to say he was struck with the courage of Lieutenant Butler. "He stood at the left front, a little in advance, cheering on his men by his voice, and still more by his example. I saw him discharge his revolver right and left; three Maoris fell beneath his fire, and were dragged into the bush by their friends. All at once I saw him sink slowly to the ground . . . . . I sprang forward with two others to his assistance, and on raising him in my arms he said, 'Lead on the men, McKenna.' Surprised at such an order, I looked round to see where the captain was, and there he lay by his side, mortally wounded.

"'Are you wounded, sir?' was my first exclamation.

"'Oh, yes, McKenna; very severely,' he replied.

"On seeing me loading my rifle, he said—

"'Never mind loading. Take my revolver and lead on the men.'

"These were the last words he spoke. I mechanically took up the revolver, gave one last look at my dying officer, and then shouted, like one possessed—

"'Men, the captain is wounded. Charge!'

"I rushed on at the head of the men, and we drove the natives before us like sheep. We now found ourselves in a small opening on the crest of the hill. The natives found shelter in the bush, to our left and front, where they opened fire on our little band of thirty-eight men. Our position was critical. One of our officers was mortally, the other severely, wounded. Ten miles of swamp and bush lay between us and any succour; around us were three hundred savages thirsting for our blood. I ordered my men to extend in skirmishing order across the clearing, and to keep up a steady fire, so as to hold the place for a time till the wounded officers could be carried well on to the redoubt before the approach of night compelled us to retire.

"About four o'clock next morning we resumed our march through the bush; and pushing our way with difficulty through the dense masses of supplejack and creepers, we crossed over hills thickly covered with wood, we descended ravines that were almost perpendicular. No word of complaint was heard—all struggled on for their lives. At length, at eight o'clock A.M., our gallant little band emerged from the bush, and found themselves in the open country, about seven miles from the redoubt, which they could see in the distance. Rushing straight ahead, they met Colonel Murray with a hundred men of the 65th Regiment coming to their assistance."

When McKenna arrived at the Queen's Redoubt with his sad but heroic story he received the highest guerdon that a soldier can well receive. General Cameron, surrounded by his staff, advanced and shook the brave sergeant warmly by the hand. "Sergeant," he said, "you have done well." "And I am amply rewarded by this honour," was McKenna's answer. "Not to myself alone, sir, but to the brave fellows who were with me, is the credit due." "I know it," said the General. "There is not another corps in the Colony could have done as the 65th." "Nor was this all," adds McKenna: "in his dispatch to Governor Grey, General Cameron expressed his admiration and approval of our dear old regiment in the most complimentary terms, and it was on his recommendation that I received my commission and the Victoria Cross." Corporal Ryan—one of those who stayed with poor Captain Swift till he breathed his last—was also gazetted for the Victoria Cross, but never lived to wear it. "His death was in keeping with his life; he was accidentally drowned, near Tuakan, while trying to save a drunken comrade. Three months after their gallant conduct, Privates Bulford, Talbot, Cole, and Thomas received the medal for distinguished conduct in the field; the first two for remaining with the body of Captain Swift, and the two latter for waiting on Lieutenant Butler, and conveying him towards the redoubt."

Returning home in 1867 the 65th found their next warlike employment in the Egyptian War of 1884, when they were ordered to proceed to Suakim from Aden where they were stationed. They reached Trinkitat two days before the battle of El-Teb. At this battle they were on the left of the square on which the great force of the enemy's attack was directed. The battle began shortly after eleven o'clock, and the fire commenced to tell upon the advancing square. Thousands of the foe were then in front, and hundreds hanging on the flanks of the square, which now made straight for the enemy's position. "It is not a charge," wrote an eye-witness, " but a steady, solid movement in the formation which has all along been observed. It looks, however, all the more formidable, for enthusiasm and discipline are equally marked, as the whole of the troops are cheering while the square sweeps down towards the enemy." When the distance between the opposing forces—between this small compact square of British soldiers, and the thousands of the fierce Arabs—had lessened to a few paces, the enemy's fire ceased. They were about to make one of those headlong, desperate charges in which they excelled, with levelled spears and huge, double-handled swords; they came on, a yelling flood, careless of death themselves, so that they might exterminate, if possible, the hated, overmastering English. As has been said, the brunt of their onset fell on the 65th, with whom were some of the Black Watch and Naval Brigade. To quote the graphic description of the War Correspondent of the *Standard*, the Soudanese came on "in groups of thirties and twenties, sometimes of threes and twos, and sometimes alone. They dash forward against our ranks with poised spear, but not a man reaches the line of bayonets, for one and all are swept away by the terrible musketry fire. For a moment on the other side of the square the matter seems to be in some doubt. So hotly do the Arabs press forward that the troops pause in their steady advance. It becomes a hand-to-hand fight, the soldiers meeting the Arab spear with cold steel, their favourite weapon, and beating them at it. There is not much shouting, and only a short, sharp exclamation, a brief shout or an oath, as the soldiers engage with their foes. At this critical moment for the enemy the Gardner guns open fire, and their leaden hail soon decides matters." It was due to the timely bayonets of the 65th that the gallant Captain Knyvet Wilson, survived to wear the Victoria Cross he had so splendidly earned, by keeping at bay single handed the Arabs who were pressing on the Naval Brigade. When the York and Lancaster came to his assistance, he was already wounded, fortunately not seriously.

At Tamai the whole strength of the Arab onset was again directed against the face of the square where the 65th were stationed, and some unsteadiness ensued, though even in a moment of seeming disaster the York and Lancaster resolutely faced the foe and dealt shrewd bayonet thrusts in exchange for the havoc caused by the long spears and heavy swords of the furious Arabs. The skirmish at the wells of Tamanieh practically ended the operations under General Graham in the Soudan, and since that date the 65th have not been engaged in active warfare.*

The Second Battalion of the York and Lancaster—the 84th Regiment—dates from 1793. The first years of the regiment's existence were passed in India, Flanders, the Cape, and in the Red Sea. In 1809 the 84th were represented at Flushing, and later on at Goa and the Mauritius. A second battalion fought, in 1813, at the battles on the Bidassoa and at Nive. The 1st battalion meanwhile was pursuing much the same career as the 65th, upholding in far distant lands the threatened supremacy of England. For many years they were stationed in Jamaica and Burmah, and when the Indian Mutiny taxed to the uttermost the courage and endurance of the regiments at hand the 84th gave splendid evidence of their worth and valour. When the crisis arrived at Cawnpore, of the hundred and fifty Europeans who formed the garrison sixty men belonged to the 84th, others having been despatched by General Wheeler to Lucknow, where their services seemed even more urgently required. For over three weeks did the little band defend their desperate position against an overwhelming army provided with artillery and careless of numbers; at last disease—the fatal miasma from rotting corpses,—trifling wounds rendered deadly from foul air and neglect—compelled surrender. The sequel of that surrender is but too well known. Amongst the martyrs whose blood cried aloud to Heaven and their countrymen for vengeance were the gallant contingent of the 84th, of whom but one man, Private Murphy, escaped. Others of the regiment were with Havelock in the first relief of Lucknow, and were amongst the band of heroes that in the face of a deadly storm from cannon and musket surmounted every obstacle, stormed the palisade, bayonetted the gunners and took the cannon. In September Colonel Greathead of the regiment with his column commenced his pursuit of the enemy, already discovering that their rebellion was doomed. At Secunderabad it is recorded that the troops found a vast quantity of plundered property, including ladies' bonnets, laces, etc., the sight of which was sufficient for the 84th, so they set the whole place in flames. Never was distinction better earned than that of "Lucknow" by the 84th; seldom can any single regiment refer to so many recorded deeds of daring as can they.

* The 65th were known—from their badge—as the Royal Tigers.

We will quote a few of the instances:—

"In one of the murderous actions in which Captain Maude took part the fire was so heavy that nearly all the artillerymen of one of his guns had been killed or wounded. In this emergency Private Joel Holmes, of the 84th Regiment, volunteered to assist in working the gun, and for doing so was granted the Victoria Cross. Lance-Corporal Abraham Boulger of the same regiment also obtained this distinction for his courage as a skirmisher in all the twelve actions fought by Havelock between the 12th July and the 25th September, 1857. This gallant soldier was one of the party which stormed the bridge over the canal on the occasion of Havelock's relief of the Residency, and shot a gunner who was in the act of firing a 68-pounder in the face of our troops. He was also the first man to enter a masked battery. This feat was mentioned in general orders. In the subsequent defence of the residency he was severely wounded. Sergeant-Major George Lambert, of the 84th Regiment, obtained the Victoria Cross and an Ensign's commission for his distinguished conduct in three of Havelock's battles, namely at Oonao, on the 29th July, at Bithour on the 16th August—where the rebels were driven out of a strong position at the point of the bayonet,—and at the passage through Lucknow to the Residency on the 25th September. During Havelock's memorable campaign Private P. Mylot, of the 84th Regiment, conducted himself with great gallantry in every fight, particularly on one occasion, when foremost of all he rushed across a road swept by the enemy's fire to capture an enclosure. So conspicuous had his courage been that he was elected by the privates of the regiment as worthy of the Victoria Cross. He was subsequently promoted to the rank of Ensign." The Hon. Augustus Anson was another of the 84th who gained the Victoria Cross. The official record thus relates the occurrence. On the 28th of September, 1857, the 9th Light Dragoons had charged through the town of Bolundshahur and were reforming. "The enemy attempted to close the entrance by drawing their carts across it so as to shut in the cavalry, and form a cover from which to fire upon them. Captain A. Anson, taking a lance, dashed out of the gateway and knocked the drivers off their carts. Owing to a wound in his left hand received at Delhi, he could not stop his horse, and rode into the middle of the enemy, who fired a volley at him, one ball passing through his coat." Again at Lucknow he distinguished himself in the storming, at which his horse was killed, and he himself slightly wounded. "He has shown the greatest gallantry on every occasion, and has slain many enemies in fight."

The Regiment then served with the Assinghur Field Force, and from that time till the outbreak of the recent Egyptian War were stationed—when not at home—at Malta, in Jamaica, and Canada. In 1882 the 84th were in Graham's—the 2nd—brigade of the First Division, and came into action on the 24th and 25th of August, having, in the engagements round Tel-el-Mahuta, thirty men *hors de combat* from wounds and sunstroke. At Kassasin Lock they occupied a not very favourable position in advance, and on the arrival of the Egyptian reinforcements were deployed to meet the attack. Amongst the wounded in this successful engagement were Major Forrester, Captain Reeves, and Lieutenant Cunninghame, and the conduct of the regiment elicited deserved commendation. At Tel-el-Kebir they took part in that grand advance of Graham's brigade on the right before which the enemy wavered and broke, the casualties of the regiment being confined to twelve non-commissioned officers and men wounded. With Tel-el-Kebir ends the record of the active service of the 84th.

THE KING'S OWN YORKSHIRE LIGHT INFANTRY,* until recently known as the King's Own Light Infantry (South Yorkshire Regiment)—Regimental District 51—consists of the 51st and 105th Foot.

The 51st were raised in 1755 as the 53rd, but the disbanding of two prior regiments gave the present numerical rank. Two years after their formation the 51st took part in the expeditions made under Mordaunt against the French coast, and the following year went to Germany. They fought at Minden, being on the right of the British line, in this their first battle giving unmistakable earnest of their future fame, and before they returned home took part in the engagements at Corbach and Warbourg. Their next employment was at Minorca in 1771, where they very greatly distinguished themselves at St. Philip. The castle of this name, which commanded the harbour of Mahon, had been long considered impregnable, but at the time of the siege the upper works had been allowed to fall into decay. Parts, however, were bomb-proof and of massive strength. An Engineer officer present during the siege vouches for the following :—A shell falling without exploding upon one of the casemates produced a shock sufficient to throw to the ground a bottle and some glasses which were on a table in the building, without producing the slightest perceptible flaw in the arch ! In 1781 the attacking force numbered at least sixteen hundred men, with a hundred and fifty guns and mortars. By November

* The King's Own Yorkshire Light Infantry bear as badges the York Rose and a horn with a crown over on cap and collar. The motto is "*Cede nullis.*" On the colours are "Minden," "Corunna," "Fuentes d'Onor," "Salamanca," "Vittoria," "Pyrenees," "Nivelle," "Orthes," "Peninsula," "Waterloo," "Pegu," "Ali Musjid," "Afghanistan, 1879-80." The uniform is scarlet with facings of blue.

the place was closely invested on all sides, "and the little garrison thus cut off from all supplies of fresh food. The greater part of them had been long in the island, and were no doubt predisposed to the attacks of the scurvy which now appeared amongst them, of exceptional virulence. In January, 1782, things were even worse, for an aggravated form of typhus fever had also made its appearance. Nothing could exceed the devotion of the men. Scarcely a man could be persuaded to go into hospital if he could in any way avoid it, and the severity of by far the greatest number of cases was only discovered by men falling dead at their posts, or, when missed from their guards, by being found dead in some spot where they had gone to end their pain away from their comrades' gaze. Early in February, four hundred and ten men being on duty, it was found that—sick and wounded included—only two hundred remained to relieve them, nineteen hundred out of the original garrison of two thousand six hundred having actually died and been buried in the narrow precincts of the place within the space of six months. Only then was it determined to capitulate. As they sorrowfully laid down their arms, having marched out with the honours of war, 'an involuntary shout burst from the enemy as they passed, and many of the French officers were affected even to tears.'"

In 1794 they were ordered to Corsica, and were very actively concerned at the sieges of San Fiorenzo and Bastia. When the General, Sir D. Dundas, resolved on an assault, the 51st were directed to proceed along the seashore. Arduous though the march was, it was at last completed; the troops converged in front of the redoubt, and "without firing a shot, swarmed into the redoubt from three points, and by their bayonets alone swept the French and Corsicans down the slope, and within five 'minutes the British colours were flying from the redoubt, and the commandant, with a considerable portion of the garrison, were disarmed and taken." Then followed the siege and capture of Bastia, and, after a few less important engagements, Corsica was formally transferred to the British Crown. In 1797 they were with Sir John Stuart in Portugal, and the following year went to India. Before long, however, they were transferred to Ceylon, and in 1800 had some sharp fighting with the Candyans, in which "the gallantry of Ensigns Grant and Smellie and of Captain Pollock was conspicuous." Returning to England in 1807, they were present, two years later, at Corunna and Walcheren. They then joined Wellesley and fought at Fuentes d'Onor and Sabugal. "Salamanca" and "Vittoria," "Pyrenees" and "Nivelle" tell their own tale; "Orthes" and the "Peninsula" complete the record of their triumphs with the 'conquering army.' At Waterloo they were on the left of the British line, and acquitted themselves as might be expected from their traditions in that warring chaos from which was to arise a new-born Peace. It was in vain that the terrible squadrons of cuirassiers charged down again and again on the firm squares. The 51st had gauged the calibre of these dashing horsemen on many a Peninsular field before this 18th of June—

> "But on the British heart were lost
> The terrors of the charging host;
> For not an eye the storm that viewed
> Changed its proud glance of fortitude,
> Nor was one forward footstep stayed
> As dropped the dying and the dead.
> Fast as their ranks the thunders tear,
> Fast they renewed each serried square;
> And on the wounded and the slain
> Closed their diminished files again,
> Till from their line scarce spear's length three,
> Emerging from the smoke they see,
> Helmet and plume and panoply—
> Then waked their fire at once!
>
> * * * * *
>
> Then down went helm and lance,
> Down were the eagle banners sent,
> Down reeling steeds and riders went,
> Corselets were pierced and pennons rent."
>
> *Scott.*

They were engaged at Cambray, which was their last warlike achievement for many years. In 1837 they went to Australia, and nine years later to India. While here they were engaged in the Burmese War of 1852, and gained—not without hard fighting—the distinction of "Pegu." Some of the 51st were on board the *Sesostris,* which so ably assisted the operations on the Rangoon River.* In the attack on the Golden Pagoda, the 51st were in the right column, which were the first to land, and four companies under Major Fraser, with some sappers and miners, formed the storming party. Heavy firing met them as they forced their way through the surrounding woods, and up the ladders against the stockade. Captain Blundell, of the leading company, fell mortally wounded, nor did he fall alone; but the dash of the attack was irresistible, and the White House of Guadama was in our hands. Greatly, too, did the regiment, or rather the detachment present with Sir John Cheape in his operations against Myat-Htoon, distinguish themselves. "Lieutenant Trevor, of the Engineers, with Corporal Livingstone and Private Preston, of H.M. 51st Foot, first entered the enemy's breastwork (on the

* Colonel Archer.

19th March, 1853), the two former each shooting down one of the enemy opposing their entrance. The lead devolved on Serjeant Preston, of H.M. 51st."

The following May they took Bassein, on which occasion, reported the General Commanding (General Godwin), "the enemy appeared so completely surprised and paralysed by our approach that . . . nearly all the men of H.M. 51st Foot got on shore under the Pagoda before a shot was fired." But shots were fired soon, and as the gallant 51st stormed the Pagoda and Mud Fort, Major Errington fell wounded, and with him fell Captains Darroch and Rice and Lieutenant Carter. The 51st were again engaged in the defence of Martaban, which was subjected to an unexpected, but not very formidable, attack by the Burmese. The regiment came home in 1856, returning to India two years later, and during the following nine years were engaged in the Punjaub, and the disturbances in the Hayara district. After a short stay at home, 1872 saw them again in India, and five years later taking part in the Jowaki expedition. The Afghan War of 1878-80 completes—with the exception, too recent for mention here, of the records of the Burmese Expeditionary Force—the annals of the 51st. In the quasi-official account by Shadbolt, the doings of the 51st are set out with a minuteness which the signally valuable nature of the service they rendered amply warrants. In November, 1878, the 51st K.O.L.I., as part of the 4th Brigade, 1st division, Peshawur Valley Field Force, advanced into the Khyber Pass, and the same day were engaged in the front attack on Ali Musjid. Marching from Jamrud, the regiment, under the command of Colonel Madden, came within range of the enemy's guns about 1.30 p m., and two hours later went into action, six companies occupying various advanced positions on the surrounding heights, and remaining engaged until darkness closed in. The casualties of the regiment during the day were, one man killed and two wounded. Early the following morning, three companies, under Lieutenant-Colonel Ball Acton, crossed the river to support the projected assault of the 3rd Brigade on a ridge to the enemy's right. It was, however, discovered that the fort had been abandoned in the night, and Lieutenant-Colonel Acton's companies shortly afterwards entered it. In the meantime two companies of the regiment, under Lieutenants Seppings and Bennett, took possession of the enemy's camp by the river, capturing some twenty prisoners, two guns, and a quantity of ammunition.

The regiment remained at Ali Musjid on the further advance of the main body of the division. From the 24th to the 29th of November there was constant firing into the camp at night by the Afridis, considerable numbers of whom assembled on the adjacent ridges. On the night of the 25th November a daring attempt was made by some two or three hundred of these tribesmen to rush a small picket, consisting of one sergeant and fifteen rank and file, under Lieutenant Johnson, placed on a hill to the left of the Khyber stream. The attack was gallantly repulsed, the enemy being very roughly handled. Of the picket, Sergeant Binge was severely, and four men were slightly, wounded. In consequence of the unsettled state of the tribes, the 51st were constantly on duty, for some time getting only one night's rest out of four or five.

On the 19th December, 1878, three companies, under Lieutenant-Colonel Acton, left Ali Musjid on the first expedition into the Bazar Valley, and during the succeeding fortnight were engaged with the rest of General Maude's force in destroying the villages and towers of the hostile Zatra Khel. While leading the column during its retirement from the valley on the 22nd December, the companies were engaged in some sharp skirmishing with the enemy on the surrounding heights. In the second expedition into the Bazar Valley, at the latter end of January, 1879, the regiment was again represented, two hundred men under Major Burnaby marching from Ali Musjid on the 25th of that month, and after being engaged in the various operations of the expeditionary force, returning on the 4th February. In the meantime shots continued to be fired at night into the camp at Ali Musjid, severely wounding, on the 19th December, two sentries.

On the 8th March, 1879, the 51st K.O.L.I. were transferred to the 3rd brigade, 1st division, and on the 17th of the same month marched towards Jalalabad, where they arrived on the 24th. Three companies under Lieutenant-Colonel Acton took part, *en route*, in an expedition sent out from Basawal to Maidanak on the night of the 19th to punish a section of the Shinwari tribe who had attacked a survey party under Captain Leach, R.E.; and on the 1st April a company under Captain Kenneth accompanied the ill-fated expedition into the Lughman Valley, in which the greater part of a squadron of the 10th Hussars was swept away in the Kabul river and drowned.*

After being encamped a month at Jalalabad, the regiment advanced to Safed Sang, where they arrived on the 27th April, and remained until after the conclusion of peace. On the 8th May they formed part of the guard of honour which received H.H. Yakub Khan.

Commencing the return march towards India on the 5th June, 1879, the 51st L.I., after recrossing the frontier, made their way to Cherat. The excessive fatigue and

* See Vol. I., p. 80.

hardship endured on the march resulted in many casualties, no less than thirty-five deaths occurring in the month of June, and nine more in July.

In his report on the services of officers of the First Division Peshawur Valley F.F., the Lieutenant-General Commanding referred to the 51st as "a regiment excellent in its discipline, and excellent in the soldier-like spirit it has shown throughout."

On the renewal of hostilities in the autumn of 1879, the 51st K.O.L.I. were again ordered up for active service, and as part of Brigadier-General Arbuthnot's Brigade of Major-General Bright's Division, marched to Jelalabad, where they arrived on the 23rd October, 1879.

Four companies of the regiment escorted the ex-Amir Yakub Khan from that city to Basawal, starting on the 4th and returning on the 8th December, 1879.

In the middle of December the regiment advanced to Safed Sang, and on the 17th of that month, in response to a request for reinforcements from Brigadier-General C. Gough, who was then at Jagdalak, three companies under Lieutenant-Colonel Ball Acton marched for Peiwar. Finding, on arrival, that Colonel Norman, commanding at that post, was also *en route* to open communication with the advanced brigade, and had bivouacked five miles further on the road, Colonel Acton detached twenty-five men to the Peiwar Kotal, and the following morning continued his advance. After marching four miles, he came upon the enemy assembled in considerable force, and turning up a nullah to their right, drove them from the position they had taken up. Communications were then opened with Colonel Norman's force, and subsequently with that of General Gough, after which the Peiwar party returned. On the 28th one company of the regiment quitted Peiwar for Jagdalak, and was replaced by another company. The following day a mixed force under Colonel Acton, including two companies of the 51st, also marched for Jagdalak, and when within sight of its destination again came into contact with a dispersed and large body of the enemy. In this encounter one man of the regiment was wounded.

In the middle of January, 1880, the headquarters of the regiment marched from Safed Sang to Peiwar, where they were rejoined by one of the companies from Jagdalak, and shortly afterwards received a welcome addition in the shape of a draft of 215 men who had recently arrived from England. During this month they were placed, by a redistribution, in the 1st brigade, 2nd division, Kabul F.F., and on that force being broken up in March became a unit of the Gandamak moveable column.

In the attack on Ali Musjid, in November, 1878, the 51st were in the fourth brigade under Sir Samuel Browne, and were sharply engaged, and had to regret the loss under exceptionally sad circumstances of Lieutenant Thurlow. He and Lieutenant Reid, also of the 51st, were riding some three miles distant from their cantonments when they were attacked by some forty Afghans. Thurlow was killed and Reid's pony bolted, but directly he could master it the latter returned to attempt to bring off his friend's body. Unable to do this himself—he was again shot at and narrowly missed—he returned to camp and brought out a detachment, "by which the body of the deceased officer was recovered and saved from mutilation." For his gallantry on this occasion Reid received the Victoria Cross.

A few days afterwards a convoy, commanded by Lieutenant Pollock, while proceeding to Jagdalak Kotal, was attacked by a large body of marauders. The party was immediately reinforced by the company under command of Captain Nugent, with Lieutenant Reid, and the enemy were dispersed with considerable loss, eleven camels which had been driven off by them being recovered. On the 9th of April the companies at Jagdalak rejoined headquarters.

In the second week of April the regiment took part with the moveable column in the expedition into the Hissarak Valley, and were engaged in several sharp skirmishes with the enemy. On the night of the 12th, Sergeant McCarthy, a gallant and popular soldier, was shot while turning out his piquet; and in the course of the various operations which were conducted, six men of the regiment were wounded. Shortly after the return of the expeditionary force the regiment was moved up to Jagdalak.

On the 31st May, 1880, the 51st King's Own Light Infantry marched with the moveable column to Safed Sang, *en route* for the Lughman Valley, and for several days took part in carrying out the retributive measures with which that district was visited. On the 11th June, part of the rear guard, commanded by Major Burnaby, while recrossing the Kabul river, was hotly fired on, Major Burnaby receiving a contusion of the face by a spent bullet. The hard work and exposure to which the column was subjected were excessive, and during the return march many men fell out from the ranks from exhaustion. On the 4th July, headquarters and four companies assembled at Peiwar, another company arriving next day, after a slight skirmish *en route*.

The last expedition during the war, in which the regiment took part, was one led by Colonel Ball Acton against the Ghilzai villages, Arab Khel and Jokan, which were destroyed in the first week in July, as punishment for various raids committed by the tribes on convoys, &c.

On the 9th August, 1880, the 51st King's Own Light Infantry commenced its return march to India, and after arriving at Peshawur on the 23rd of the month, proceeded to Lawrencepur, and eventually to Bareilly.

The casualties of the regiment during the second campaign were, two officers and men killed, fourteen wounded, and 151 invalided, of whom twenty-two died.* (Shadbolt.)

The 105th—the 2nd battalion of the Yorkshire Light Infantry—dates, as at present constituted, from 1839, when it was raised as the Second Madras European Regiment. The precursors of the regiment were the Second Madras European Light Infantry, and as such did good service for many years in the various engagements which occupied our army. From 1839 to 1860 the 105th served in India and Burmah, and since then have served at Aden, making their first visit to England in 1874. It is from the 105th that the motto *Cede Nullis* is derived, but whence it comes is uncertain, no time apparently being known when it was not in use. Its first appearance in the Army List, however, is, according to Colonel Archer, in 1841.

THE PRINCESS OF WALES'S OWN YORKSHIRE REGIMENT †—Regimental District No. 19—consists of the old 19th Foot. Though so few names appear on the colours the 19th is a regiment possessing a notable and long record of varied services well performed. Raised in 1688 from the bands of pikemen assembled in Devonshire to assist the cause of William of Orange, they were sent four years later to Flanders, and fought at Steenkirk, though without loss. The following year they were at Landen, and were subsequently engaged in covering the siege of Namur. In 1702 they took part in the operations against Cadiz, leaving Europe shortly after for the West Indies. In 1710 we find them again in Flanders, where they fought at Douay and Bethune, and at Malplaquet, "the bloodiest action in the whole war." From 1714 they enjoyed a period of home duty for thirty years, repairing again to Flanders in 1745, when they took part in the battle of Fontenoy, and suffered severe loss there. Seldom, indeed, has an army in which the British were so strongly represented, sustained such a defeat. "Still, however, Cumberland, with his brave British and Hanoverian troops, persevered in his attack on the left, leaving the cavalry in the rear, and dragging some pieces of artillery

---

* The 51st were sometimes known as the "Kolis," from the initial letters of their title.

† The Princess of Wales' Own Yorkshire Regiment bear as badges the Princess of Wales' and coronet with "1875" on a Danish cross on cap and collar. The date commemorates the presenting of new colours by Her Royal Highness. The motto is that of the Garter. On the colours are the White Rose, and "Malplaquet," "Alma," "Inkerman," and "Sevastopol." The uniform is scarlet with facings of white.

with their own muscular arms; the foot crossed a ravine, and advanced full in front of the wood, the batteries and the abattis, and of the best part of the enemy's army, for Saxe had been allowed time and opportunity to gather strength from his right wing. The combat soon became close, and was terrific; our men were killed in heaps by the enemy's artillery, but still they went closer, sweeping away the French foot and the sturdy Swiss guards, and giving back death for death. . . . . From the necessity of the ground they now occupied, which was hollow and narrow, the British and Hanoverian foot were huddled together in compact masses. Saxe, by the advice of the Duke of Richelieu, brought four pieces of heavy artillery to play upon them in this condition; and while the cannon roared and inflicted death in the front, they were attacked in flank by fresh troops, both foot and horse. . . . . The Duke of Cumberland was the last in the retreat; he called upon the men to remember Blenheim and Ramillies. . . . . If the English soldiers had had their will and no enemy in their rear, it might have been difficult to prevent, that evening, a new kind of combat, for their fury against the Dutch amounted almost to madness." A Highland officer (Culloden Papers) wrote: "The action will, I believe, be found to be the bloodiest as to officers that has happened to the British in the memory of man. The Hanoverians behaved most gallantly and bravely, and had the Dutch taken example from them, we had supped that night in Tournay." They fought at Val and Roncoux; in 1761—as the Duke of St. Alban's, or Beauclerc's Foot—they formed part of the force of ten thousand men under General Studholm Hodgson, destined for the capture of Belle Isle, in Brittany. "The citadel of Palais, the capital of the isle, is a strong fortification fronting the sea, composed principally of a horn work, and is provided with two dry ditches, the one next the counterscarp, and the other so contrived as to secure the inner fortifications. This citadel is divided from the largest part of the town by an inlet of the sea, over which there is a bridge of communication. From the other part of the town, that which is most inhabited, it is only divided by its own fortifications and a glacis, which projects into a place called the Esplanade, where the reservoir is kept. Though there is a fine conveniency for having wet ditches, yet round the town there is only a dry one, and some fortifications which cannot in many places be esteemed of the strongest kind; indeed, the low country which lies to the southward can easily be laid under water." Taking advantage of the fact that the steep and formidable nature of the approaches on one side rendered the enemy careless at these points, the Grenadier Company of the 19th, under Captain Paterson, clambered up them, "and were in full possession of the rocks before the French were aware of the circumstance." Here they held their ground in a fierce contest with superior numbers, in which Captain Paterson lost an arm, and subsequent reinforcements enabled them to drive the French back. "In this affair a private, named Samuel Johnson, displayed remarkable bravery. On perceiving a subaltern of his regiment, to whom he felt grateful for some act of past kindness, overpowered by numbers, and about to be bayoneted by a French grenadier, he rushed to his assistance and rescued him, killing no fewer than six of his assailants." The Regiment spent several years at home and at Gibraltar, and in 1794 shared in the skirmishes and sufferings endured by our army in Holland. In May, 1794, Pichegru, who had continued to outwit the Austrians, swooped down with about fifty thousand men upon the British camp at Tournay. The Duke of York's army numbered, perhaps, thirty thousand, of whom, fortunately, only a small proportion was Dutch. "But though flushed with success, the French were repulsed in every attack they made, and compelled to retreat from a field which they left covered with their dead. The celerity of their movements and the superiority of their numbers were of no avail against the steadiness and determination of the Duke's troops. The latter were occasionally brought to fight when they ought not to have fought at all, but whether attacking or attacked, the British troops invariably proved their pluck and stamina."

"There was staunchness, there was heroism of the highest order in this fighting on the part of troops who had previously experienced every possible disaster; and after this there was a glorious fortitude in the manner in which they withstood cold and hunger, and the fierce war of the elements, and in the midst of an unceasing hurricane of wind, snow, and sleet. Many of the sick and wounded carried in open waggons were frozen to death, or perished of want, but not a living man in the army spoke of a halt or of a surrender."

In 1796 they were ordered to Ceylon, and in 1799 five companies took part in the important battle of Seringapatam. For many years after that their duties were in Ceylon, where the frequent risings of the Candyans afforded them plenty of active and dangerous service. In 1803 many of the officers and men were massacred in a rebellion of formidable proportions, and peace was not restored without some sharp fighting, of which the 19th bore the brunt. The Mauritius, the Ionian Islands, Corfu, North America, with a brief sojourn in England, occupied the attention of the regiment till the Crimean War, when the opportunity offered for them to add three famous names to their colours. They were in the Light Division under Sir George Brown; and at the Alma shared, with the Welsh Fusiliers and Connaught Rangers, the glory of that magnificent charge up-hill, during which, from rock and boulder, from thicket and vine-trellis, poured a devastating hail of Russian bullets. "The 19th, with the Grenadiers and the Fusiliers, the 95th, the 30th, and the 47th Regiments, pressed eagerly forward with the regularity and firmness of troops on parade. Just beyond the battery the heads of a strong body of Russians were visible, and these at last formed and charged down the hill in a compact mass upon the British troops toiling up the steep in face of the dreadful fire that was doing such execution in the ranks. Some guns that had been brought up by the English artillery, with much difficulty, now opened upon this Russian column, and, so true was the aim, that at every discharge a clear passage was made through the serried mass. This well-executed manœuvre decided the day, the Russians turned, broke, and fled over the hill."

In this trying and painful ascent the indomitable valour of our men—many of them in action for the first time in their lives—was fully displayed. Exposed to a continual roar of artillery, without being able for some time to return the fire, they kept on their course undaunted.

The men never quailed nor paused in their toilsome and perilous march. After the retreat of this formidable battalion of the enemy the battle was speedily won.

They fought like heroes at Inkerman, where confusion seemed to multiply the terrors of the strife. As the 19th with the rest of the Light Division pressed onward the scene was intensely bewildering. One thing only was terribly distinct in its doings: the grim Death which was so busy that drear November day. From the valley where seethed the battle in fullest fury rose a deafening din—boom of cannon, rattle of muskets, the clang of steel, the hoarse word of command, the hoarser cries of fighting men, shouts of triumph, and groans of pain. Men fell fast, yet oftentimes no foe was visible—only the lurid flash gleaming from the dense thicket, and the white smoke drifting hither and thither on the blood-laden breeze.

At the Quarries and the Redan they vied with the bravest. "One of the most heroic episodes at the last assault was connected with a mere youth, named Massey, a lieutenant in the 19th Regiment, who kept out in the open in the hope of inducing the soldiers to follow; and there, amidst the most dreadful fire, he stood with a reckless courage that excited the astonishment even of the enemy. He was dreadfully wounded, but won the sobriquet of 'Redan Massey.'" On the termination of the war he returned to the University of Dublin, exchanging "feats of broil and battle" for the "still air of delightful studies," though even to the retirement of the academic walls his fame had preceded him; his fellow-students fêted and belauded him, as well they might; and men who passed him in the street paused to point, with enthusiastic admiration, at the young hero of the Redan.

Amongst other individual instances of bravery of men of the 19th may be mentioned that of Private John Lyons, who on one occasion took up a live shell that had fallen amongst our men, carried it to the edge of the parapet and hurled it over the trenches. Again, there was Private Samuel Evans, who, seeing, on the 13th of April, a Sapper engaged singly in repairing an embrasure under a heavy fire, went with Private Callaghan to his assistance, and completed the work.

The 19th arrived in India at the end of the mutiny, and for years were engaged in the numerous tribal disturbances which threatened the peace of the empire. After a short sojourn at Bermuda and in Canada they took part in the last phase of the war in the Soudan, "being employed on the line of communications during the Nile campaign of 1884-5 and in the subsequent operations on the Soudan frontier including the battle of Giniss."*

THE EAST YORKSHIRE REGIMENT†—Regimental District No. 15—consists of the old Fifteenth Foot. The 15th date from 1685, in which year they were raised in Nottinghamshire by Colonel Tufton, who was one of the officers that remained loyal to King James, and was accordingly superseded at the Revolution. After serving for some time in Scotland the 15th went to Holland, and in 1695 fought with credit at Kenoque and Dixmunde. They were engaged at Kaiserwerth and Nimeguen, at Venloo and Ruremonde, at Liége and Schellenberg. In 1704 they fought at Blenheim, being in Rowe's famous brigade, and commanded by Lieutenant-Colonel Britton. It was an occasion to try to the uttermost the *morale* of the British troops. The position was critical, and rumours that a tremendous battle was inevitable had spread through the allied host. The absolute necessity for the battle of Blenheim to be fought, when and how it was, has been pithily put by Sir Edward Creasy. "Although the French army of Italy had been unable to penetrate into Austria, and although the masterly strategy of Marlborough

---

* The nickname of the 19th was the "Green Howards," to distinguish them from the Buffs, both regiments being commanded by colonels of that name.

† The East Yorkshire Regiment bear as badge the White Rose in a laurel wreath on a star on cap and collar. The motto is that of the Garter. On the colours are "Blenheim," "Ramillies," "Oudenarde," "Malplaquet," "Louisbourg," "Quebec, 1759," "Martinique," "Guadeloupe," "Afghanistan, 1879—80." The uniform is scarlet with facings of white, with a black line on the gold lace of the officers' tunics.

THE 15th—EAST YORKSHIRE.

had hitherto warded off the destruction, with which the allies seemed menaced at the beginning of the campaign; the peril was still most serious. It was absolutely necessary for Marlborough to attack the enemy before Villeroy should be roused into action. There was nothing to prevent that General and his army from marching into Franconia, whence the allies drew their principal supplies; and besides thus distressing them, he might by marching on and joining his army to those of Tallard and the Elector, form a mass which would overwhelm the force under Marlborough and Eugene. On the other hand, the chances of a battle seemed perilous, and the fatal consequences of a defeat were certain. . . . The consequences of a defeat of the confederated army must have broken up the Grand Alliance, and realised the proudest hopes of the French King. . . . Marlborough's words, at the council of war when the battle was resolved on, to the officers who remonstrated with him on the seeming temerity of attacking the enemy in their position, were remarkable. 'I know the danger, yet a battle is absolutely necessary; and I rely on the bravery and discipline of our troops, which will make amends for our disadvantages.'"

A curious incident relating to the regiment is quoted by a writer from an old book called "Advice to Officers." The 15th—then known as Howe's Regiment—were attacking the village of Blenheim, when the major—who on account of too great strictness was unpopular—addressed his men, confessing "that he had been to blame, and begged to fall by the hands of the French—not theirs." "March on, sir!" replied a grenadier. "The enemy is before us, and we have something else to do than think of you just now!" When the French gave way the officer waved his hat in his enthusiasm, exclaiming "Hurrah! gentlemen, the day is our own!" As he was saying the words he fell dead, shot through the brain. It would appear from the manner of recounting the incident, coupled with the significant title of the work in which it appears, that it was doubtful whether that fatal shot came from the front or the rear. The regiment suffered heavily that day, as they did at Ramillies and Oudenarde. They fought at Tournay in 1709, perhaps one of the most desperate sieges, from the point of view of individual suffering, of the many undertaken during this long war. Some estimate of the difficulties our troops had to contend with may be gathered from the following:—"The citadel of Tournay was situated on some high ground, with a gentle ascent from the town, and the siege proved a service of the most difficult character, arising from the multiplicity of the subterranean works which were more numerous than those above ground. The approaches were carried on by sinking pits several fathoms deep, and working from thence under ground, until the troops arrived at the casemates and mines. The soldiers engaged in these services frequently encountered parties of the enemy, and numerous combats occurred in these gloomy labyrinths. On some occasions the men at work under ground were inundated with water; at other times suffocated with smoke, or buried by the explosion of mines."

At the conclusive combat at Malplaquet the 15th were in the reserve, losing only one officer. In the various battles and skirmishes which followed they were well to the fore, returning home in 1714. In 1719 they fought at Glenshiel, following General Wightman in his skilful movement into the then almost inaccessible mountains, and showing their firm courage in combating and repulsing the brave McKenzies and McGregors. They were attacked in rear and flank, but gallantly held their own, though they lost Captain Downes and two subalterns.

After this they enjoyed a period of inaction for some twenty years or more, their next important service being at Carthagena in 1741. The same old book before referred to ("Advice to Officers") relates that the troops were very much annoyed during the night by continued reports from the outpost officer that a large body of Spaniards was approaching. No attack or demonstration was, however, made, and at last an aide-de-camp was sent to the front to ascertain the cause of the reports. There, sure enough, he saw what appeared to be a body of soldiers in the white uniform of the Spaniards, which now and again appeared and disappeared in the most perplexing fashion. A nearer investigation explained the mystery. Some white barked trees (the manchineel trees) had been cut down by the enemy to the height of five feet, and their tops burned, thus giving them black hats to their white clothes. Added to this the sky was full of flying clouds which darkened the moon. In 1746 the 15th fought at Quiberon and l'Orient, and eleven years later took part in the expeditions against the French coast. In 1758 they were with General Amherst in the attack on Louisbourg, and shared in that successful and not costly victory, though the loss to the 15th was somewhat severe. In 1759 we find them at Quebec, in the brigade of General Monckton. Very familiar amongst the household words of our military annals is the name Quebec. There is probably not an Englishman who does not regard it as one of the brightest flowers in the country's Honour Wreath: there is, probably, not one in a hundred who realizes to any degree the difficulty and importance of the action. "The position was an extremely strong one," says a competent writer; "the main force was encamped on the high ground below Quebec, with their right resting on the St. Charles

River, and the left on the Montmorency, a distance of between seven and eight miles. The front was covered by steep ground which rose nearly from the edge of the river, and the right was covered by the guns of the citadel of Quebec.

"A boom of logs chained together was laid across the mouth of the St. Charles, which was further guarded by two hulks, mounted with cannon. A bridge of boats, crossing the river a mile higher up, connected the city with the camp. All the gates of Quebec, except that of St. Charles, which faced the bridge, were closed and barricaded. A hundred and six cannon were mounted on the walls, while a floating-battery of twelve heavy pieces, a number of gun-boats, and eight fire-ships, formed the river defences. The frigates which had convoyed the merchant fleet were taken higher up the river, and a thousand of their seamen came down from Quebec to man the batteries and gun-boats. Against this force of sixteen thousand men, posted behind defensive works, on a position almost impregnable by nature, General Wolfe was bringing less than nine thousand troops. The steep and lofty heights that lined the river rendered the cannon of the ships useless to him, and the exigencies of the fleet in such narrow and difficult navigation prevented the sailors being landed to assist the troops." The 15th captured Point Levi, and were amongst the first troops that gained the memorable heights of Abraham, greatly distinguishing themselves in the famous battle that followed. The regiment remained in Quebec, defending it against the subsequent attacks, and in 1762 went to Martinique, where and at the Havannah they maintained their high reputation.

Returning to England in 1768, a few years later they were ordered to America, and took part in most of the battles during the War of Independence, including Charlestown, Long Island, Brooklyn, and Brandywine. In 1782, the year that they received their title, they experienced some sharp fighting at St. Christoval, in St. Lucia, and twelve years later took part in the still more important operations in the same neighbourhood. Under Sir Charles Grey they fought at Martinique, and led by Major Lyon and Captain Paumier, greatly distinguished themselves at the storming of Mount Mathurine. At Guadeloupe, where they were again hotly engaged, they had two officers and several privates killed. After a short stay at home they were ordered to Barbadoes in 1805, and for some time served as marines. In 1809 they took part in the successful operations under General Beckwith in Martinique, and the following year three hundred of the regiment served under Colonel Riall, who was commanding our forces at Guadeloupe, again taking part five years later in the summary action rendered necessary by the adherence of Linois and Boyer to the cause of Napoleon. After a few years spent at Bermuda and Canada the regiment returned home in 1821, and during the following years were occupied in quelling the Irish disturbances of 1826 and the more formidable movements in Canada in 1832 and at the commencement of Her Majesty's reign. They were next ordered to Ceylon, where the ever-recurring Candyan difficulties gave them some work to do, and the next important operation in which they were concerned was the Afghan War of 1879-80, where they were represented by the Second Battalion.

"The Second Battalion of the 15th Regiment," says Shadbolt, "formed part of the Reserve Division, Southern Afghanistan Field Force, which during the early part of March, 1880, was concentrated at Karachi, Suid. After the receipt of the news of the disaster at Maiwand, the headquarters, eight companies left Karachi on the 4th August for Sibi, and marching through the Bolan Pass in detachments, with inadequate transport, with insufficient water, and in burning heat, arrived at Quetta on the 29th of the month. Notwithstanding the great hardships they endured, the men worked with admirable spirit. The trying nature of the march is attested by the fact that some one hundred of them, chiefly young soldiers who had been recently sent out, were placed *hors de combat* by sunstroke, heat and apoplexy before reaching the Afghan frontier." The 15th advanced with Phayre's Division through the Khojak Pass, but arrived too late to participate in the battle of Kandahar, and returned to India the following December. Since that date they have been quartered in North America, Bermuda, and Gibraltar, but have not been engaged in any warlike service.

THE PRINCE OF WALES'S OWN WEST YORKSHIRE REGIMENT*—Regimental District No. 14—consists of the 14th Foot, which were raised in 1685 at the time of Monmouth's invasion by Sir G. Hales, chiefly in the neighbourhood of Canterbury. At the revolution Sir G. Hales remained faithful to King James, and was with him in his attempt to escape, being in consequence sent to the Tower. The first service of the regiment was in Scotland, whence in 1693 they went to Flanders. At Landen they were in Ramsay's

---

* The Prince of Wales Own West Yorkshire Regiment bear as badges the White Horse with the Prince of Wales' Feathers on cap and the Feathers on the collar. On the waist plate is the Royal Tiger with "India" and "Waterloo." The motto is "*Nec aspera terrent*." On the colours are, in addition to the White Horse, "Tournay," "Corunna," "Java," "Waterloo," "Bhurtpore," "India," "Sevastopol," "New Zealand," "Afghanistan, 1879—80." The uniform is scarlet with facings of white.

brigade and suffered severely, having five officers killed, seven wounded, and their Lieutenant-Colonel taken prisoner. The following year they were engaged in covering the siege of Hay, and the only British officer killed during this campaign was Captain Sacheverell of the 14th. In 1695 they were employed at various sieges, notably at that of Namur, where, as Tidcombe's Foot, they "crowned themselves with glory;" and throughout the later battles of that year they followed the dashing lead of the gallant Lord Cutts. For the following two or three years they were stationed in Ireland, whence, however, they sent detachments at various times to join the British army in Spain. When Prince Charles Edward made his attempt in 1715 the 14th were summoned to Scotland, and fought as Jaspar Clayton's Foot at Dunblane, and four years later at Glenshiel, where Captains Moore and Heighinton were wounded. In 1727 they went to Gibraltar, of which their Colonel, Jaspar Clayton, was Lieutenant-Governor, and assisted in its successful defence against the Spaniards, remaining there for several years. The 14th were not at Dettingen, but amongst those who fell there was their gallant Colonel, who was on the staff. They fought at Falkirk in 1746 as Price's Foot, and were in the first line in the division of General Cholmondeley. Complete though the defeat of King George's army was, the 14th have little to reproach themselves with, they and the King's Own made a determined stand and withstood the fury of the charging Highland host with astonishing firmness, "evincing most heroic valour under circumstances of peculiar danger and difficulty." At Culloden they were again in the first line, and fortunately did not incur much loss. They went to America in 1766 and five years later to St. Vincent, returning to America in 1773. Though the regiment was not as a whole engaged at Bunker's Hill, they lost in that battle two of their officers who were employed on the staff. A few months later the 14th distinguished themselves at an action known as that of Great Bridge, but do not seem to have been very actively engaged during the remainder of the War of Independence, and returned to England in 1777. After a short sojourn in Jamaica in 1782, they took part in the campaign in Holland eleven years later, being one of the first regiments to arrive. They fought at Famars in May, 1793. On this occasion it is related that the Bedfordshire Regiment, as they had been styled in 1782, being mainly composed of young men who had never been in action before, though evincing the most daring courage, got somewhat out of order. Colonel Doyle, seeing this, galloped to the front, called a halt, reinforced the ranks, and then, bidding the band strike up the French Republican air, *Ça ira*, led them on to the charge. The loss of the regiment, owing in great measure to this action of their Colonel, was slight, and they were specially thanked in General Orders. At Valenciennes a hundred volunteers were required from the 14th to join the forlorn hope. Colonel Doyle assembled his men and, pointing out the danger of the enterprise, requested that those who were prepared to undertake it should "recover" arms. Instantly the whole regiment "recovered" as one man, and their Colonel, with genuine pride and emotion, directed that instead of any volunteering, which all were ready to do, the first ten men of each company should be chosen. In the operations about Dunkirk—to quote an instance which is typical of the enthusiastic devotion which has ever characterised the 14th—when the deep ditch threatened to prove a formidable obstacle, Lieutenant Clapham jumped in and stood with the water up to his arm-pits, that the grenadiers might use his shoulders as stepping-stones to the other side! They fought at Landrécies and Cateau; at Tournay they particularly distinguished themselves, gaining the first name on their colours. They were for a long time isolated from the rest of the army and hemmed in on all sides "by the whole weight and power of the enemy's overwhelming numbers." Retreat became inevitable, though to retreat seemed almost to court annihilation. Yet, "surrounded by the enemy, fired on by artillery and infantry, and menaced by cavalry," the gallant 14th moved as though at a review. There was no hurry or excitement; in defeat as in victory they were, and knew that they were, one of the finest regiments of the finest army in the world; their retreat was dignified, deliberate, defiant. On the road by which they must pass was erected a strong barricade behind which the enemy had gathered in force. At this last disaster even the brave General expressed his fear that they must surrender. "No, sir," replied Captain Clapham, "the 14th can cut through them." And the 14th did cut through them, and received from friends and foes alike the meed of praise due to as gallant an action as any troops ever performed. Again at Guildermalsen they evinced the same heroic courage, and returned home in 1795, having gained a reputation second to none. In 1796 they fought at St. Lucia and St. Vincent, receiving the thanks of Abercrombie, who, when it was decided that the 14th were not to accompany him on his further expeditions, expressed his regret with the very distinguished compliment that "he did not think any service could go on well without them."

A second battalion which had been formed fought at Corunna, where, under Colonel Nicholls of the regiment, they greatly distinguished themselves in driving the French out of the adjoining village. They fought also at Walcheren with equal distinction. The 1st battalion were engaged in 1810 at the Mauritius, and the following year won "Java" for their colours by their splendid courage, under Colonel Watson, at the storming of Cornelis. The further disturbances in Java occupied them for some months, after which they experienced some active service amongst the pirates at Borneo. The 14th were represented at Waterloo by a third battalion, which, under Colonel Tidy, was brigaded with the 23rd and 51st in the Fourth Division. It is needless to recount again the oft-told tale of the victory at Waterloo; suffice it here to say that the General's Report declared that "the 3rd battalion of the 14th, in this its first trial, displayed a gallantry and steadiness becoming veteran troops." They were also engaged at Cambray; after which, in common with many others, the 3rd battalion of the 14th were disbanded. In the year of Waterloo the 1st battalion were serving in Nepaul, and for the following years were engaged in the almost constant struggle with the Pindarees and Mahrattas. Bhurtpore, in 1825, brought fresh honours to the 14th. Two lieutenant-colonels of the regiment—Colonels M'Combe and Edwards—were acting as brigadiers, and the regiment itself was commanded by Major Everard. At the terrible explosion which cleared the way for the stormers, Colonel M'Combe was severely struck by the falling débris, but the regiment, "in splendid order and high spirits," fought their way into the breach. When the stronghold surrendered, the Commander-in-Chief entered at the head of the 14th—a graceful compliment to the signal valour they had displayed. They returned home in 1831, and five years later went to the West Indies, where, and in Canada, their time was chiefly passed till the Crimean War. Early in January they landed at the Crimea, and took part in the assault of the 18th of June. The 2nd battalion, raised in 1858, was ordered to New Zealand, and served in the Maori Wars of 1860 to 1863, remaining abroad till 1870. The same battalion subsequently took part in the Afghan campaign of 1879—80, gaining thereby the last distinction on their honoured colours. The 14th (2nd Battalion) were at Lucknow when they received orders to join the Reserve Division of the force in northern Afghanistan. They proceeded to Peshawar, and thence, with General Hill's Brigade, to Jamrud, subsequently moving to Laudi Kotal and Pesh Bolak. In the following May they took part in the action of Mazina, where General Gile successfully encountered and dispersed the Afghans under Ghulam Ahmad. In the Order published by the General, he thus refers to the regiment: "The Second Battalion of the 14th, although composed chiefly of young soldiers, behaved with great steadiness, coolness and gallantry, and were kept well in hand by their commanding officer, Colonel Warren, assisted by the company officers. The action was well calculated to produce wild firing, but there was none. Captain Noyes (of the regiment) behaved with great gallantry in storming a sungah, in which he got wounded, and the Brigadier-General will have much pleasure in bringing his name to the notice of the Major-General Commanding." The next month four companies of the regiment joined a column commanded by their officer, Colonel Warren, and were employed in destroying some of the enemy's defences near Sunga Seraj, returning two months later to India.*

In treating of the ROYAL MARINES † we find ourselves treating of a corps which, so to speak, are in themselves,

"abstracts and brief chronicles of the time,"

during which, by sea and by land, the Island Empire has forced its way to the foremost place amidst the nations of the earth. Divided as they are into Artillery and Infantry it will not be necessary in these pages to do more than indicate the distinction: the record of glory, unique and conspicuous, applies to the corps as a whole. It has been said—and the definition has something of wit in it—that the chief characteristic of the Marines is their *amphibiousness*, their participation in the nature of both land and sea forces. Doubtless, indeed, some would claim them as belonging to the Navy. It is true that they are borne on the Navy Estimates, but for all that—to hazard in a brief phrase a definition devoid of technicalities—the Marines are SOLDIERS, albeit they serve at sea, and co-operate with the Navy of Great Britain. Her Majesty's Army could ill afford to lose such splendid contributors to its glories as the Marines; there are but comparatively few of the "distinctions" borne on the proud colours of its regiments, which the Marines may not claim: as time has passed, each year has added its testimony to their unrivalled discipline, dauntless courage, and loyal patience. Perhaps throughout their glorious chronicle there is no quality that so impresses itself on the mind of the reader as this last. For many years the "cold shade of opposition" seemed their habitual atmosphere; blunders in organization were accompanied by disregard in rewards and recognition. Even now there are not wanting many voices of weight which urge that the showers of honours and rewards following any campaign is somewhat arbitrary, not to say empirical, in its meteoric flight, and too frequently avoids by no indistinct curve the

---

* The 14th Foot used to be called the "Old and Bold," and "Calvert's Entire," from their having three battalions when Sir H. Calvert was Colonel, from 1806 to 1826.

† The Royal Marines bear as a badge the Globe, with the word "Gibraltar," with the Laurel, and the motto *Per Mare, per Terram*. The uniform of the Royal Marine Artillery is blue with facings of scarlet, and on the helmet-plate a grenade, on the ball of which is a globe with "Gibraltar" above it and an anchor below it. The Royal Marine Light Infantry have a scarlet uniform with blue facings, and have in addition to the globe and laurel the distinctive 'bugle' of Light Infantry. The helmet-plate has an eight-pointed star on which is a globe with "Gibraltar" above it and an anchor and cable below it; below the anchor is a bugle.

constellation of "The Royal Marines," which often stands the most direct in its normal course. No distinctions, save the transcendent one of "Gibraltar," are borne by the Marines, and the reason is somewhat analogous to that which, in court etiquette, prescribes the simple "Sir" as the address for the highest. The distinctions of the Marines are comprised in their badge and their motto. When the late Duke of Clarence, the General of the Royal Marines, gave a new stand of colours to the corps in October, 1827, his observations were to the following effect:—

"The list of actions in which the corps had been distinguished having been laid before the King, the list was so extensive, and the difficulty of selection so great, amongst so many glorious deeds, of such a portion as could be inserted in the space, that his Majesty determined, in lieu of the usual mottoes and badges on the colours of troops of the line, to direct that the 'Globe encircled with laurel' should be the distinguishing badge, as the most appropriate emblem of a corps whose duties carried them to all parts of the globe, in every quarter of which they had earned laurels by their valour and good conduct."

Bearing in mind the mixed character of the Royal Marines, the sketch embodied in the following pages will be illustrative more of the military part of their record; and even then, so full of brave deeds, of splendid courage, of uncomplaining endurance, of brilliant daring, and steadfast discipline is the record, the sketch must needs be but in barest outline, and will serve but to indicate the glowing colours and wealth of crowded and glorious detail which fill the completed picture.

The origin of the Marines must be sought for in the famous "Trained Bands" of London; a view of their lineage which is borne out by the fact that the Marines, with the Guards and the Buffs, alone, of the Regulars, enjoy the privilege of marching through the City with bayonets fixed and bands playing. In this connection the historian of the corps cites the following as evidences that the Marines are entitled to the precedence of the present 3rd Regiment in the British Line.

In the memoirs of Major Donkin, published in 1777, it is stated that "The 3rd Regiment of Foot, raised in 1663, known by the ancient title of the Old Buffs, have the privilege of marching through London with drums beating and colours flying. It happened in the year 1746, that a detachment of Marines beating along Cheapside, one of the magistrates came up to the officer, requiring him to cease the drum, as no soldiers were allowed to interrupt the civil repose. The captain commanding immediately said: 'We are Marines.' 'Oh, sir,' replied the alderman, 'I beg pardon, I did not know it. Pray continue your route as you please.'"

In 1664 a regiment which received the name of the "Admiral's Regiment" was raised for sea service, and after some service and a period of "suspended animation" reappeared in 1684 as "His Royal Highness the Duke of York and Albany's Maritime Regiment of Foot," after which, according to Colonel Arden, they became incorporated into the Coldstream Guards. In 1702 six regiments of the present 30th, 31st, and 32nd, and three since disbanded, were appointed as Marines, and six others—the 6th, 19th, 20th, 34th, and the battalions of the 36th—for "sea service," at which time their uniform, according to Cannon, consisted of high-crowned leather caps, covered with cloth of the same colour as the facings of the regiment, and ornamented with devices the same as the caps worn by the Grenadiers, scarlet frock-coat, buff waist-belt, black pouch carried in front, with bayonet belt attached, buff gaiters. After bearing well their part in the task allotted to them, these regiments were reabsorbed into the army, and from 1714 to 1739 there were no Marines, properly speaking, though a company or two of "Invalids" remained to preserve the succession. Need soon arose for the services of so useful a corps, and in 1747 a Royal Warrant was issued assigning the status of the force. The position and status of the Marines present so many points of interest in its relation to the constitutional theory of the Royal Forces, that we may be pardoned quoting the views of so well known a writer as Clode, summarizing as they do the various epochs in the history of the corps. "Their origin has already been given, but the troops raised in Charles II.'s reign as part of the army were disbanded with it. In the year 1694, by Order in Council of the 22nd February, two regiments of Marines were raised, to be under the direction of the Admiralty, and under the command of the naval officers when afloat. Only one of the two regiments was ever to be on shore. While the Marines were afloat they were governed by the Navy Act, 13 Car. II., c. 29; on shore by the Mutiny Act of 8 and 9 William and Mary (c. 13, sec. 8), and later Acts, until a Marine Mutiny Act was passed for their government. The establishment of these regiments was looked upon with great jealousy, as being, in fact, an increase of the standing Army; indeed, the House of Commons voted the supply on a resolution "that they were to be employed in the service of the Navy only." Half-pay was granted to the officers by Council Order of 18th January, 1697.

"In 1702 the 30th, 31st, and 32nd Regiments of the line were formed, and served as Marine regiments. Their establishment was under the charge of the Secretary at War, and they were governed by Orders of Queen Anne of the 1st July, 1702. On the peace of Utrecht being proclaimed they were to be disbanded at the end of the year 1713.

"In the year 1739 the Marine force was again established. It was provided for in the Army Estimates until the year 1745; and by Royal Warrant of the 28th February, 1746—7 (under the countersign of Chesterfield), the Lords of the Admiralty were directed to take the immediate and entire command of all the Marine Regiments then raised, or thereafter to be raised, and to prepare and publish such rules and ordinances as were fit to be observed by them. At the peace of Aix-la-Chapelle, in 1748, the force was totally disbanded.

"The Marine force on the present establishment dates from the year 1755. Commissions ceased to be purchasable, and the officers now rise to command by seniority. A Mutiny Act—28 Geo. II., c. 11—was passed for their government on land, the Act leaving them liable to the Navy Discipline Act while on board ship. When serving with the army, they rank between the 49th and 50th Regiments of the Line, and by Royal Order of the 29th April, 1802, they bear the style of the "Royal Marines." The corps is divided into Infantry and Artillery, the latter being formed under an Order in Council of the 18th August, 1804, by selection of the most intelligent and experienced men of the Infantry. The total number of both arms, as fixed by Order in Council of the 22nd October, 1859, was 16,986 (including commissioned and non-commissioned officers), but it has been reduced by subsequent Orders in Council."

A few years later this first-named Royal Warrant was acted on, and the year 1755 may, as has been said, be assigned as the commencement of the corps of Marines as at present constituted. And starting from that date we shall review, only too shortly, the deeds and triumphs of the corps.* But they can claim by inheritance a share in earlier triumphs than those that followed the warrant of George II. The Marines of that day had played no inconsiderable part in the capture and defence of Gibraltar in 1704, and gained therein "immortal glory." "Captain Fisher of that corps, with 17 men, attempted to check the advance of 500 Grenadiers of the enemy after the round tower had fallen into their hands. This gallant officer was taken prisoner, rescued, and again taken by the enemy, who, though ultimately repulsed, carried their prisoner into the Spanish lines."

In 1705—6 they took part in the bombardment of Ostend, and were with the troops which, under the chivalrous Peterborough, took Barcelona, and taught the Spaniards what English honour meant; in 1708 they took the well-laden galleons of Spain at Minorca; in 1719, under Lord Cobham, they helped to take Vigo, and with it booty

---

* In army precedence, as has been said, the Marines rank after the Princess Charlotte of Wales's Royal Berkshire Regiment, the 49th, and the 50th Foot.

valued at fourscore thousand pounds. Twenty years later the Marines played no inconsiderable part in the capture of Portobello, carrying the ramparts by assault, and forming *themselves* into a scaling ladder, whereby the summit might be reached.

At St. Lazar, in 1741, a thousand Marines formed part of General Guise's force, and at the storming, that splendid charge of the Grenadiers, before which the Spaniards were utterly demoralised, was led by Colonel Grant of the 5th Marines, who fell mortally wounded.

It was not long after the warrant of 1755 had been issued before the Marines had an opportunity of distinguishing themselves in some of the most important of the Indian wars. The eyes of England were straining towards those Eastern fields, where a handful of British warriors were overthrowing the dynasties of centuries, and founding the mighty Indian empire over which Her Majesty rules to-day.

Shortly after Colonel Coote had gained his victory at Wandewash, he was joined by a force of three hundred Marines under Major Monson, who before long effected the capture of Caricat.

Hannah Snell, who had served on board the *Swallow*, one of Admiral Boscawen's squadron, is said to have fought in the ranks at the siege of Cuddalore. " She behaved with conspicuous courage, and received a ball in the groin, which she herself extracted two days afterwards. Eleven other wounds in both legs rendered her removal to the hospital at Cuddalore absolutely necessary, and having returned home, her sex was not discovered until she obtained her discharge. She afterwards wore the Marine dress, and having presented a petition to H.R.H. the Duke of Cumberland, obtained a pension of £30 a year for life." She subsequently, it is said, owned a public-house at Wapping, where she " did her spiriting " clad in the uniform of the corps.

The Marines took part in the defeat of Thurot, the corsair; in the following year occurred the fighting at Belle Isle, for their conduct in which the Marines bear the laurel wreath. In May a formidable sortie was made by the enemy, who succeeded in making prisoners of General Crauford and two officers, and their onward course seemed for a time irresistible. " The contest remained doubtful until the arrival of a party of Marines under Captain David Hepburn, who drove them with the bayonet, and forced them to retire with considerable loss."

A few days later the Marines, under Captain Carruthers, stormed a strong redoubt of the enemy, and after a fierce bayonet struggle carried it, following up their success by driving the French from two more redoubts and forcing them to take refuge in the citadel. Colonel McKenzie commanded the Marines on this occasion, and both he and Captain Murray, who greatly distinguished himself, were wounded. Amongst the names of men who did valiantly are those of Captain Carruthers and Captain Wright, and it was generally allowed that the high praise awarded to the corps for their conduct was more than justified. Praise from an enemy is praise indeed, and the references of the defeated French to the terrible "petits grenadiers," as they styled the Marines, bore testimony to the important part the corps played in the capture. They served in the Havannah and Manilla campaigns, and it is pleasant to record the fact that the booty taken was sufficient to give to the captains not less than "£65,053, to the lieutenants, £39,014, and to a private marine, £484." In 1775 the Marines were amongst the first corps engaged in the War of Independence. The first outbreak was at Lexington, a village near Concord, to which latter place Colonel Smith of the 10th had been dispatched with orders to destroy the magazines. He "had not marched far when it was found, by the firing of guns and ringing of bells, that the country was alarmed; and Major Pitcairne, of the Marines, with six light companies, was dispatched double quick to get possession of two bridges on different roads leading off from the opposite side of Concord. At five in the morning the Major entered Lexington and found the militia of the town under arms on the Green. 'Disperse, you rebels,' cried the Major, riding boldly forward; 'throw down your arms, and instantly disperse.' They obeyed with evident reluctance, but, as they did so, several muskets were fired at the troops from the neighbouring houses and from behind a wall. More than one man was wounded, and Major Pitcairne's horse was shot under him." The corps were actively engaged at Bunker's Hill, the first battalion being amongst the regiments ordered forward to storm the enemy's fortifications. Splendid though the victory was, taking into consideration all the surrounding circumstances, it was dearly purchased, and the Marines suffered very heavily; five officers—amongst whom was the gallant Pitcairne—and seventeen men were killed; four officers and fifty-seven men wounded. "The reputation of the Marines," writes their historian, "was never more nobly sustained than in this sanguinary contest. Their unshaken firmness was conspicuous, and the valour they displayed in closing with the enemy when some part of the attacking column wavered, gained them, not only the admiration of their comrades, but the commendation of their distinguished Chief." At Charlestown, again, they suffered severely, and again gave sterling proof of their valour and value. They fought at St. Lucia, in the action off the Doggerbank, and shared in the glories of Rodney's victories.

The year 1794 was a busy and glorious one for the corps. There was Martinique with its brilliant successes following fast one after the other, gained by fierce hand-to-hand fighting amidst its wild, luxuriant vegetation, so deathful with all its beauty; St. Lucia, outbidding the sister island in beauty, with its rocks "feathered from the clouds to the waves with evergreen foliage;" Guadaloupe, with its chequered history of gallant struggles and ultimate defeat. There was yet another battle fought that year, which, though a naval one, is yet one of the fairest flowers amidst the crowded blossoms of the Marines' chaplet—the "glorious first of June." In all of these were the Marines engaged; in all of these did they win meed of honour and glory.

As evidencing the unflinching loyalty of the Marines may be instanced their conduct in the troublous times of the Mutinies at the Nore and Spithead; though they were often outnumbered, though if any regiment ever had reason to complain of official coldness and disregard the Marines were that regiment, yet, when authority was contemned or threatened, the King's Government could always rely upon the Marines. Doubtless the task was bitter as it was desperate. The mutinous seamen were not only their comrades with whom they were linked by the bonds of danger and victory, but they were the invincible sailors of the British fleet, before whose fierce prowess and dash the mightiest nations had been taught to quail. And it was against these men, heroes of the age and their own companions, that, when loyalty demanded, the Marines stood forward with bayonet fixed and muskets loaded, to assert the rights of authority against rebellion. It is related of Captain David Wilson of the Marines that when the men of the *Agamemnon* mutinied and demanded of him the keys of the arm-chest, "the gallant veteran, finding himself unsupported by the captain of the ship, threw the keys overboard, telling the mutineers' delegates that if they particularly wanted them they might go after them.' While on this subject—that of the loyalty of the Marines against disaffection—we may quote Mr. Davenant's account of the Mutiny in 1799 on board the *Impétueux* in Bantry Bay. "On Thursday, the 30th of May, at noon, Sir R. Pellew had gone—being engaged to dine with Sir Alan Gardner—to dress in his cabin, and had ordered the officer of the watch to call all hands at the usual time, one watch to clear hawse and the other two to wash decks. When the order was given it was obeyed by all the Marines but by very few of the seamen. A few moments afterwards signal was made to unmoor, whereupon cries of "No, no, no!" arose from the main hatchway, and the sailors pressed forward in a disorderly crowd, those in the rear encouraging the foremost with shouts of "Go on, go on!" The first lieutenant, Ross, and the officer of the watch, Lieutenant

Stokes, demanded the cause of their riotous behaviour, and were told after some hesitation that there was a letter. "Give it to me," said the lieutenant, "and I will deliver it to the captain." But a cry of "No, no, no!" was immediately raised. Lieutenant Ross then desired Mr. Stokes to inform the captain, upon which the mutineers shouted, "One and all! one and all!" At this moment Sir Edward, in his dressing-gown, appeared upon the quarter-deck, where upwards of two hundred and fifty seamen had collected. He was received with cries of "A boat, a boat!" His voice stilled the clamour, and in reply to his inquiries he was informed that they wished to send a letter to Lord Bridport complaining of tyranny and hard usage. Upon his undertaking to deliver it himself or send an officer with it, they shouted, "No, no—a boat of our own!" In vain he endeavoured to reason with them; some of the ringleaders exclaimed, with fearful oaths, they *would* have a boat. "You will, will you?" said Sir Edward, and whispering a brief order to Captain Boys of the Marines, he ran to the cabin for his sword. By the time he had returned, the Marines were drawn up with fixed bayonets on the poop; he immediately ordered them to clear the quarter-deck, a guard to be posted at various places, and the sentries to be doubled. Intimidated by their Commander's resolution, the mutineers threw themselves off the quarter-deck and ran down the hatchways, crying to their companions to dowse all the lights and clear away the ladders. Swift as the hound upon the hare were Sir Edward and his officers, and before the confusion could be increased by darkness, seized the ringleaders and threw them into irons. The letter, an unsigned one, was now given up, and the ship's company returned to their duty quietly."

We must pass over several years, rich with the record of Cape St. Vincent and Camperdown, of Teneriffe and the Nile, and take up the history of the corps in 1799, when Sir Sidney Smith gave the world evidence of what a British officer can do against odds which to any other would prove irresistible. The Marines were represented in that gallant body of men who held Acre, and their historian gives a graphic account of their doings.

"General Berthier, who commanded a division of the enemy, affords the best testimony of the merits of the Marines upon this occasion, and we therefore, without comment, give an extract from a letter of that gallant officer, dated from the French camp:—

"'On the 18th Germinal (7th of April) the enemy at break of day attacked our left and centre; each column was headed by British Marines belonging to the ships, and their colours were seen waving with those of the Djezzar, and the batteries were all manned by Englishmen. The enemy attempted to surprise our advanced posts, but their design was seen through: we received them with a brisk fire from our parallels, and all that appeared were either killed or wounded. The enemy ultimately retired without gaining an inch towards destroying our works. The central column acted with more obstinacy, and their object was to penetrate to the entrance of our mine; they were commanded by Major Thomas Oldfield, who advanced boldly towards the entrance of the mine at the head of some of his intrepid countrymen. They attacked like heroes, and were received by heroes—death only checked their bold career; the remainder retreated, and took refuge in the fortress. The approaches of our parallels remained covered with the dead bodies of English and of Turks. The body of Major Oldfield was carried off by our Grenadiers, who brought him to headquarters, but he had expired before their arrival. His sword, to which he had done so much honour, was also honoured after his fall: it remains in the hands of one of our Grenadiers. He was buried amongst us, and has carried with him the esteem of the whole French army.'

"This eulogium from an enemy, and a soldier whose proud renown is associated with that of Napoleon, is the noblest epitaph that the brave could aspire to."

But the praise of Major Oldfield and his Marines was not to be left only to a chivalrous enemy. Sir Sidney Smith, at a meeting of the anniversary of the Naval Asylum, held on the 2nd of June, 1802, offered a tribute to the memory of this gallant soldier. After speaking of the many virtues of Captain Miller, Sir Sidney thus enlarges upon the merits of his departed friend, Major Oldfield:—

"The next is Major Oldfield, of the Marines. I will tell the company where the body of this brave man was contended for, and they will judge where and how he died. It was in a sortie of the garrison of St. Jean d'Acre, when attacked by General Bonaparte, that Major Oldfield, who commanded a column, was missing. On our troops advancing, he was found—his body was found—at the mouth of one of the enemy's mines, and at the foot of their works: our brave men hooked him by the neckcloth as he lay dead, to draw him off; the enemy at the same time pierced him with a halbert, and each party struggled for his body. The neckcloth gave way, and the enemy succeeded in dragging to their works this brave man; and here I must do them the justice which such gallant foes are justly entitled to: they buried him with all the honours of war!"

Another gallant deed of the same year is recorded by Captain Nicolas, and may well claim a notice here. Lemmerton, in West Friesland, which was held by 150 seamen and Marines under Captain Boorder, of the *Espiègle*, was attacked in the early morning of the 11th of October by the advanced party of French and Batavians, consisting of an officer with thirty rank and file, who attempted to storm the North battery." The British soon got them between two fires, and so effectually surrounded them that they laid down their arms with the loss of two killed. The prisoners had scarcely been secured, when the main body, amounting to 670 men, attacked the British, who, after a contest of four hours and a half, routed the enemy in every direction, with the loss of five killed and nine wounded. The Marines continuing the pursuit, killed and wounded more than forty, and if the allied forces had not broken down a bridge in their retreat, they would have lost their colours and two field-pieces. Captain Boorder, in his official letter, says, "Lieutenants Wyburn, Howel, Higginson, and Gardner, of the Marines, behaved with honour to themselves and credit to their country, and their men distinguished themselves in the most gallant manner."

The Marines took part in the Battle of Copenhagen in 1801, and the same year shared in the victories gained in Egypt. When the troops arrived off Alexandria, with its old Pharos rising bleak and bare from the sea, a force of 600 Marines, under Colonel Walter Smith, were landed, and immediately entered into action. Admirably did they acquit themselves, but on this—as, unfortunately, on many a similar—occasion but few of the honours and rewards given freely enough to other regiments were bestowed upon the Marines. Some feeling was aroused, and representations made, with the gratifying result that a special compliment—that of the prefix "Royal" to their title—was accorded. Captain Nicolas thus expresses himself on the subject: "The distinguished services of the Marines, and their unshaken loyalty, had frequently obtained for them the public expression of their country's gratitude; but no particular mark of the royal favour was extended to the corps until the 29th of April, 1802, when the following gratifying communication was conveyed to their commandant by the Earl of St. Vincent:—

'Admiralty Office, 29th April, 1802.

'SIR,—The Earl of St. Vincent having signified to my Lords Commissioners of the Admiralty that His Majesty, in order to mark his royal approbation of the very meritorious conduct of the corps of Marines during the late war, has been graciously pleased to direct that in future the corps shall be styled the "Royal Marines:"

'I have great satisfaction in obeying their Lordships' commands to communicate this intelligence to you, and in offering their Lordships' congratulations on this testimony of the opinion His Majesty entertains of the very distinguished services of that part of his forces to which you belong.

'I am, Sir, &c., &c.,

(*Signed*) 'EVAN NEPEAN.

'Lieutenant-General Souter Johnstone,
  'Commandant of the Marines.'"

As a consequence of the change in title the facings of the Marines were changed from white to the blue characteristic of "Royal" regiments, and the lace on the tunics from silver to gold. In November, 1803, Lieutenant Nicolls, R.M., greatly distinguished himself in an attack on a French vessel under the guns of the batteries of Monte Christo, a splendid service, in which he was desperately wounded. As usual, the chief share of the praise and rewards fell to the lot of another officer—*not* a Marine, and it was not till long after that the claims of Nicolls were recognised. Before he died, however, the gallant Lieutenant of Marines had risen to the rank of General Sir Edward Nicolls, K.C.B.

In 1804 the Royal Marine Artillery was constituted,[*] a corps which, though disbanded in 1832, with the exception of "a couple of companies to serve as a nucleus," were the predecessors of the Royal Marine Artillery of our own day.

In 1804 was performed one of the most brilliant and daring feats recorded in that era of brave deeds—the capture and defence of the "Diamond Rock." About half a mile from the shores of Cape Diamond rises the Rock, which for several months was borne upon the estimates and appeared in the Navy List as "His Majesty's sloop of war *Diamond Rock*." "It was a rough-looking place," says a writer, "with little that was inviting about it—a great firm rock, the highest point of which might be something over five hundred feet above the level of the sea; the circumference of it less than a mile, and in its shape not at all unlike a haystack. On the west side there were bold rugged cliffs —precipitous, sheer up-and-down walls, seeming as though they would defy all approach to them; and the roar of the surf beating against the base of them was distinctly audible at the distance of a mile. Yet here was the only place where a landing could be effected. The other three sides of the Diamond Rock were simply inaccessible, presenting a perpendicular face from within a few feet of the summit. On the whole it looked uncommonly like a *noli me tangere* sort of place, reminding me of Lundy Island, in the British Channel, where, as old Holinshed quaintly says, 'there is no entrance but for friends.'"[†]

---

[*] Blue uniform with scarlet facings.
[†] Davenant.

The position of this rock had given much annoyance to our cruisers, as it enabled the enemy's ships, by running in between it and the shore, to escape. It was resolved, therefore, to annex and fortify it, and Commodore Hood accordingly did so, placing on it one hundred and twenty men, chiefly Marines, under Lieutenant Maurice. "The camp—for it was more that than anything else—was established at the top of the rock, in a little scoop or valley, where the only green things the place boasted, a grove of wild fig-trees, were situated. But before you could get to this some rough places had to be passed. Crannies where the stone had rotted away, or had yielded to the sea-water beating on it, had to be crawled through, and then the ledges of steep rocks, between which we afterwards made bridges of rafters, had to be clambered over." For five months the gallant little garrison held this miniature Gibraltar, working havoc with the enemy's ships—notably *La Belle Emélie*—till the French determined at all hazards to evict them, and accordingly in May of the same year *five* ships of war lay formal siege to the devoted band of Marines and seamen. They received a right British welcome, and, so far as the capture of H.M.S. *Diamond Rock* by a *coup de main* was possible, might be besieging it to this day. Unfortunately, however, provisions began to run short, and the greater part of the ammunition was spoiled, so Captain Maurice agreed to evacuate the rock on terms which reflect more honour on the garrison than many a victory. Captain Maurice and his Marines and seamen were to embark in their own boats, wearing their side arms, and were to row themselves to the French ships, till they reached which the British colours were to float undisturbed over the Rock. Moreover, they were not to be considered prisoners of war, but were to be sent under a flag of truce to Barbadoes. The Marines may well cherish the memory of their prowess at the Diamond Rock as one of the most brilliant actions which even they can boast.

Passing over Trafalgar and St. Domingo, victories which belong entirely to the naval service, we find the Marines in 1807 taking part in the bombardment of Copenhagen, an exploit which has before been fully described. In the same year Captain Brisbane, of the *Arethusa*, "put himself at the head of his Marines, mounted the walls of Fort Amsterdam, in Curaçoa, and presenting himself in person before the Dutch governor, demanded, sword in hand, the surrender of the island." The same year some Marines were brigaded under General Lumley in the attack upon Monte Video, and the gallant but unfortunate expedition against Buenos Ayres. In 1808 Lieutenant How, of the Marines, gained universal praise for his splendid defence of Fort Trinidad, and the following year the corps were represented in the victories and sufferings covered by the name of "Walcheren." In 1810 Captains Snow and Stuart led two companies of the corps to attack the strong defences in Santa Maura. These defences consisted of "a rampart with a wet ditch and abattis in front, armed with four guns and manned by 500 infantry." The Greek regiments in our service refused to face the withering fire poured in by the defenders, but the other troops, led by the Marines, burst through with the bayonet, and drove the enemy helter-skelter into the castle. "As the column," writes Captain Nicholas, "advanced left in front, the Calabrian free corps became the leading division of the battalion under Major Clark; but at the first discharge of a well-directed fire of grape and musketry from the enemy the Calabrese instantly threw themselves on the ground, and remained immovable in spite of every effort to rally them and the indignant treatment they received from the Marines, who now, cheering, passed over their bodies, and dashing forward broke through the abattis; then, rushing into the intrenchments, pursued the enemy until their gallant progress was arrested by an order for them to fall back to the redoubts they had so nobly carried.

"The conduct of the Marines elicited the admiration of the army, and the following appeared in the Orders issued on the occasion:—

'Headquarters, Santa Maura, 23rd March, 1810.

'Parole Cephalonia.

'Brigadier-General Oswald has to acknowledge the great gallantry displayed by the troops who accomplished the storming of three of the enemy's intrenched batteries. The intrepid manner in which the Royal Marines performed that service claims the highest admiration. He requests that Major Clark, who led them on, also Captains Snowe and Stewart, and the officers and non-commissioned officers, will be pleased to accept his tribute of approbation. He laments the brave officers and men lost on this occasion, but it is some consolation to think that their gallantry was rewarded by success.

(*Signed*) 'A. CUST, A.A.G.'"

A few weeks later Lieutenants Moore and Brattle led their men to the capture of Grova, which was effected after inflicting two defeats upon the enemy; and in 1810 the corps played a conspicuous part in the subjection of the Isle of Bourbon. In 1811 the Royal Marine Artillery formed the chief part of the small force—not exceeding 350 men—which, under Captain Maurice, R.N., defended the important Isle of Anholt, in the Baltic, against an attack of some 1,600 of the enemy. With a loss to our men of only two killed and twenty wounded, that of the Danes was prodigious. One lot of prisoners, which "were more numerous than the small garrison," were allowed to depart. When the fight was over three officers and nearly a hundred privates were found to have been killed; 'twenty-three wounded were taken into our hospital; sixteen officers and 504 rank and file were taken, with three pieces of cannon, 484 muskets, and 470 swords and other stores.'

The Marines fought at Washington and Bladensberg; under Captain Gordon a party of the corps destroyed Alexandria, on the Potomac; at Baltimore they were in both the right and the left brigade, and had their full share of the sharp fighting which culminated in so brilliant a victory. In 1816 the corps, both artillery and infantry, took a prominent part in the bombardment of Algiers, during which they suffered considerable loss. They fought at Navarino and in the first Chinese war; in the Syrian war two companies of Marines under Captain Childs were posted at Nahr-el-Kelb, while others were with the troops under Napier which operated against D'Jehaila. "The Marines advanced briskly to the assault . . . . and reached within thirty yards of the tower, when a destructive fire was opened upon them from a crenelated outwork, having a deep ditch in the front, which was completely masked from the fire of the ships. Finding that his men were falling fast, that the wall of the castle was impracticable, that there was no gate accessible, and nothing but the muzzles of the enemy's muskets visible through the loopholes, Captain Robinson very judiciously drew his men off."—(*Report of Captain Martin to Sir Charles Napier*). The Marines were re-embarked, and shortly afterwards, under Captain Morrison and Captain Fegan, were busily engaged at Ornagacuan and Sidon. Captain Wylock, with a company of Marines, effected a brilliant lodgment in an adjoining fort, an operation in which Lieutenant Hoskin of the corps and many men were killed and wounded, while Captain Henderson at the head of the first battalion of the corps "was landed on the beach to the northward of Sidon, where the men quickly formed their ranks and advanced cheering to the walls." " I put myself at the head of the British Marines," wrote Sir Charles Napier, "and broke into the barracks. Captain Henderson and another party lodged themselves in a house above the barracks. This being done, I marched the battalion along the line wall to the upper gate, broke it open, and seized the castle." Though our force was only a thousand men, and the garrison three times that number, not a man of the latter escaped, while our loss was only thirty-seven, including one Marine officer killed. The concluding remarks of Sir Charles Napier were as follows: " In taking a town by storm much confusion necessarily arises, accompanied by plunder and other barbarities, but to the honour of our Marines, the Austrians, and the Turks, I believe there never was an occasion where less blood was spilt, or disorder easier put an end to." After the fall of Acre two hundred and fifty men of the Marines, under Lieutenant-Colonel Walker, remained to protect the town. In 1846 they were engaged in the war in New Zealand, and in 1850 in Kafirland. In 1852 they served in Burmah, capturing the Pagoda at Dalha, and being actively engaged at Pegu and Prome, the latter place, indeed, being practically taken by the Marines single-handed. In the Crimean War the Marine Brigade rendered most efficient service. Some five thousand men were landed shortly after the battle of Alma, and throughout the protracted siege were active, *more suo*, wherever hard work was to be done. Many were the instances of individual valour recorded of the Royal Marines.

"Bombardier Thomas Wilkinson, Royal Marine Artillery, was one of a detachment which had been opposed at Balaklava. Captain Alexander and Lieutenant Gull, and fifty men, among whom was Wilkinson, volunteered for the trenches, and on the 5th of June began to do duty in the batteries. On the very first day Wilkinson attracted the attention of the officer commanding the artillery in the right attack by his gallantry in repairing the parapet with sandbags under a heavy fire. The officer in question specially reported this man's gallantry, and he in consequence received the Victoria Cross."

At Inkerman two companies of the Marines were present, and Corporal John Prettyjohn won the Victoria Cross for conspicuous gallantry, " placing himself in an advanced position and shooting four Russians." At Viborg, in July, 1854, Lieutenant Dowell, R.M.A., earned the same pre-eminent distinction for rescuing, under a heavy fire of grape and musketry, some of the crew of a cutter whose magazine had exploded. After placing the men in safety he returned and brought the disabled boat out from under a battery.

The Marines were employed at the bombardment of Sweaborg, respecting which it is recorded that "the duty and conduct of every officer and man was most arduous and meritorious—none more so, perhaps, than those of the Royal Marine Artillery." At Kinburn the Royal Marines formed, with the 63rd Regiment, the Second Brigade, and with the capture of that bravely defended fortress ended their achievements in the Crimea.

The war in China afforded fresh opportunity for the Marines. A wing of the corps was amongst the troops under Brigadier Reeves landed to occupy Tinghai, and afterwards saw plenty of fighting before Sinho. In the attack upon the Takoo Forts, one detachment of the Marines was under Colonel Gascoigne, and "another detachment of the same gallant corps," under Colonel Travers, carried a pontoon for the passage of the wet ditches. The mandarin in command of the first fort was pistolled by Captain Prynne of the Marines; and at Kaowle, Yon-chaiwei, Tientsin, and Pekin the corps shared, with the others of her Majesty's regiments, in the credit of the successful enterprise. The Marines were amongst the troops engaged in New Zealand in 1860 to 1863, where, at Mangatawhiri and the Gate Pah, they rendered signal service, Lieut. Gardiner and Gunner Baker, both of the R.M.A., particularly distinguishing themselves.

They were in Abyssinia in 1867; their next service of importance being with the expedition to Ashantee in 1873. In June, at the very nick of time, a detachment of the corps, numbering about one hundred and ten men, under Colonel Festing, R.M.A., arrived at Elmina, and five days later repelled, with the aid of some sailors, a determined attack made by some two thousand of the enemy. But the climate proved so fatal to the gallant Marines that they had, "with scarcely an exception, to be invalided and sent home," their place, however, being supplied by another detachment of one hundred and fifty men.* In October war began in earnest, and though but a few Marines were able to be attached to Sir Garnet Wolseley's force, their services were throughout of the greatest value.

"The force of Sir Garnet, as given in his despatch, consisted of only 29 blue-jackets, with one 7-pound gun; one rocket-trough; 20 Royal Marine Artillery; 129 Royal Marine Light Infantry; 205 of the 2nd West India Regiment; 126 Houssas; 10 armed Police, 30 axe men and 270 carriers. The Royal Marines were now thrown out in extended order, and the forward movement began again. Suddenly there was heard a single shot, followed by a heavy fire of musketry, mingled with wild yells on one side and cheers on the other. 'Steady, Marines!' shouted their commander; 'don't throw away a shot, my lads, and don't fire at random. Take ground to the left; get the steel gun on its carriage, and bring it to the front.' At this time a wild and continuous fire was flashing on all sides. On our left was a grassy plateau, with a thick wood distant three hundred yards. In our front the ground fell and was covered with low bush, breast-high. The din was deafening. Captain Fremantle, with the steel gun, the seamen, and some rockets, now assailed

---

* Lieutenant H. Earle, R.M.L.I., was sent as an envoy to the King of Dekra.

the wood on our left front, so as to turn the enemy's position. Captain Crease with the Marine Artillery, took it on the other flank.

"After a short halt the troops advanced again, and after a two hours' march reached another village, named Amguana, which was found to be abandoned and was instantly destroyed. The march lay then along the beach, so Sir Garnet was now joined by some seamen and Marines from the *Decoy*, under Captain Luxmoore of the *Argus*, the same officer who had been wounded on the Prah. He brought with him a case of claret for the thirsty Marines, and 'those who say the British soldier will not drink claret should have seen the pleasure with which these twenty men drank their allowance. Ten minutes' halt and they marched on like new men." Not long afterwards 150 Marines under Captain Allunt were detailed for an expedition into the bush, Colonel Festing being in command of a force which had some sharp fighting at Dunquah, in which he was wounded. Under Major Russell the Marines had some very severe fighting at a place called Abracrampa, which was attacked by a force of at least 10,000 of the enemy. The church was held by the Marines and seamen, and their well-directed fire successfully kept the ferocious foe in check. But the latter were speedily reinforced and the little garrison began to grow faint from continuous watching, and to wonder when relief would arrive. It arrived soon, however; Sir Garnet, with a force of about 650, including some Marines, marched to the rescue and soon drove off the besiegers. In his report he refers in eulogistic terms to "the admirable conduct of Major Russell and the officers under his orders, who, with only fifty Marines in addition to native levies, held the town against numbers at least twentyfold, during two most fatiguing days and nights, throughout which time none of them could rest for a moment." Reinforcements arrived from England and the march to Coomassie began, and here occurs another instance of the want of recognition of the Marines before referred to. "Some soreness, we are told, was felt in England at so little mention being made of the Royal Marines, but they were only eighty in number, and shared in the work of the Naval Brigade."—(*Grant*). They fought at Amoaful, charged in after the gallant Gifford at Bequah, and with the 42nd were in the rear on the march to the Ordah. Of the praise which was bestowed by sovereign and country on the brave troops that had fought so well in Ashantee, none was better earned than that accorded to the Royal Marines.

Six years after the salutary lesson taught to King Koffee, we find the Royal Marines engaged in the sterner warfare in South Africa. Here they were in the Naval Brigade of the First Column, commanded by Colonel Pearson, and were the first troops to cross the Tugela when war was decided on. They fought at Inyezane, and then under Pearson occupied Etschowe. Their position here, as has before been mentioned, soon became that of a blockaded force, and to the Marines was confided the charge of the rocket tubes, a most important weapon when dealing with barbarous foes. Marines were, too, in the divisions under Low and Pemberton that marched to the relief of the beleaguered garrison, and fought at Ghingilovo. Egypt has been the latest field on which the gallantry of the Royal Marines has been displayed. Alexandria, Kassassin, Tel-el-Kebir, Suakim, El Teb, Tamai, Hasheen, Abu Klea, the Nile—each of these names may be claimed as a "distinction" included in their globe. At the end of July, seven companies, numbering a thousand strong, under Colonel Tuson, took part in a reconnaissance in force made by Sir Archibald Alison. "The Marines crossed from the railway to an embankment of the canal which was lined by the enemy, but the Marines fixed bayonets and dashed at them with a rush. . . . . . Nothing could have been finer than the charge of the Marines, and no troops could have stood a determined attack of this kind." About the same time Major Phillips, with 200 of the corps, made a raid on Mex, from which they speedily dislodged the enemy. At Mahuta the Royal Marine Artillery did admirable service with the loss of only one man, and on the following day 400 of them were with Graham in his advanced position at Kassassin Lock, a battalion of the infantry remaining at Mahsameh. In the action of the 28th of August the Marine Artillery were posted on the southern bank, where they encountered many attacks; which, however, were "always hurled back by that noble corps." In General Graham's dispatch he refers in high terms to the conduct of Captain Tucker: "Near the right of our position a Krupp gun, taken from the enemy at Mahsameh, had been mounted on a railway truck, and was being worked by a gun detachment of the Royal Marine Artillery under Captain Tucker. This gun was admirably served, and did great execution amongst the enemy. As the other guns had to cease firing for want of ammunition, Captain Tucker's gun became a target for the enemy's artillery, and I counted salvoes of four guns opening on him at once with shot and shrapnel; but although everything around and in the line was hit, not a man of the detachment was touched, and this gun continued to fire to the end, expending ninety-three rounds." Nor were the infantry behind their brethren of the artillery that day. They it was who led—about the same time that Drury Lowe made his memorable cavalry charge—the advance against the enemy, who melted away before them, "only one attempt being made at a stand, which broke at the first volley from the Royal Marines." In the second engagement at Kassassin the Royal Marines may almost claim to have been the heroes of the day. They were stationed between the King's Royal Rifles and the 84th, and two of the three guns taken from the enemy were captured by the Royal Marines. At Tel-el-Kebir they were in Graham's Brigade under Colonel Howard Jones.

"While the Brigade, of which they formed part, deployed into line, a continuous fire of shot and shell was poured into it. As soon as the brigade formation was complete, Colonel Jones formed the Marines for "attack" by sending forward three companies in fighting line, with three in support, and two in reserve, and as the first of these in extended order approached the position they found themselves destitute of all cover, while under a fire that every moment increased in fury and intensity.

"Yet the marines pressed forward up the slope of the glacis, reserving their fire, as ordered, until within about one hundred and fifty yards of the first ditch, when, fixing bayonets, the fighting line being reinforced by its supports and by the reserves under Lieutenant-Colonel Graham, the whole worked their way by a succession of impetuous rushes, in spite of a terrific fire of cannon and musketry, to the summit of the works and, with loud cheers, threw themselves into the ditch, and dashing up the slope of the nine-foot parapet, met the foe in a close hand-to-hand fight with but and bayonet. This lasted but a short time, as the Egyptians in that quarter broke and fled in all directions. The Marines 'followed them up for a distance of about four miles, until they came to Arabi's head-quarter camp at Tel-el-Kebir. This they found standing, but evacuated, it having evidently been left in haste, as everything appeared in disorder. Here they were ordered to halt and occupy some of the deserted tents.' The casualties among the Marines were very severe; amongst them 'Major Strong, who was shot through the heart while most gallantly leading his fighting line up the glacis, within twenty yards of the enemy; Captain Wardell, one of the most valuable and efficient officers in the battalion, was also killed, being shot through the head close in front of the parapet while cheering on his men.'"

The official records of their casualties that day put them at "two officers and three non-commissioned officers and men killed; one officer and fifty-three non-commissioned officers and men wounded." Captain Luke of the corps splendidly avenged the death of Captain Wardell. He noted the Egyptian who had shot him, and watching his opportunity, singled him out, and "by one stroke severed his head from his body."

When war again broke out they were again employed, and at El Teb were in the Second Brigade, being on the left of the advance. At Tamai the whole shock of the fierce rush fell upon the Marines and the 65th; at Abu Klea they were on the right face of the square; they were with the force in front of Metemneh when Stewart fell. At Abu Uru they shared with the Guards the honour of holding the front face; at Metemneh, on the 21st of January, Major Poe of the R.M. Light Infantry was amongst the wounded. At Hasheen the Marines (with whom were the Berkshire Regiment) were first dispatched against the enemy; they were the first to reach the eminence, and "by a well-directed fire on the enemy, covered the advance of their companions." "The Marines," we read, "elicited loud applause from the Cavalry for the splendid manner in which they attacked the enemy, acting with independent judgment, yet under the control of the most perfect discipline." In the attack on M'Neill's Zeriba, on the 23rd March, 1885, they were again conspicuous for their courage and calmness, and received ungrudging praise for their conduct in this, the last of the military operations which come under our notice. As is well known, our force was completely taken by surprise; before our men knew that an enemy was near they were yelling and shouting in their midst. A correspondent's letter gives a vivid picture of the part taken in that wild hour by the Marines. "I was just on the edge of the Marines' square and was caught in the storm—a hissing, yelling, roaring, and fantastic-looking sea of black forms; the furious enemy in overwhelming force. Then came that frightful stampede of horses, camels, mules, in one struggling, screeching, helpless and confused mass. Regaining my feet, I found myself in the Marines' square. Panic, even in those few moments, seemed to have disappeared, and the brave fellows were firing steadily and well." Some sixty Arabs managed, in the first fierce rush, to get within the Marines' square, but—not one of them got out again. Calmly, as those who were masters even of that terrible position, did the Marines receive the hideous charge. There was no panic, no hurry. Each man knew his duty and did it. Eight marines were killed and twelve wounded in this untoward but brilliant encounter, which closes for the present the long list of the gallant services of the Royal Marines.

A short glance should be given to one or two of the most important of the "Departments" connected with the army.

ARMY CHAPLAINS* may be said to date officially from 1662, though previous to that

---

* Chaplains wear a black single-breasted frock-coat with standing collar, with the badges of their rank on the collar; a forage cap of black cloth, with black patent leather drooping peak, ornamented with black embroidery; black leather gloves.

date the spiritual needs of the Royal Forces were more or less recognised, and with most of the armies which have made our country what it is were to be found

> "Pious men, whom duty brought
> To dubious verge of battle fought,
> To shrive the dying, bless the dead."

Clode remarks upon the remarkable omission from the Prayer-book of any service or office for the army, pointing out that in this respect the navy is better provided for. His explanation is as follows: "Looking at the feeling of all classes of the people towards the army at the period of the last revision of the Liturgy, it need not be a matter of surprise that the clergy did not see fit to recognise the military forces of the Crown as the chief visible strength of the kingdom." The Articles of War of 1662—3, however, rendered it incumbent upon every chaplain to read the Common Prayers to the soldiers under his charge, "and to preach to them as often as with convenience shall be thought fit." From the year 1662 to 1796 every regiment had a chaplain appointed by the Sovereign's commission, and, indeed, a chaplain may be said to have "formed as much part of the establishment as a field officer." Stringent regulations, moreover, were from time to time made with a view to preventing, either by the chaplain or those committed to his cure, the neglect of the prescribed religious observances. During Marlborough's wars frequent mention is made of the presence of chaplains with the troops, and on more than one occasion their services are referred to in terms of praise. The laxity, however, which characterized the Church in the eighteenth century seems to have extended to the army chaplains; a commission on military matters which sat early in the present century reported that the appointment had gradually become "apparently a sinecure," that the duties were sublet, and when in 1793 "an army was sent from this kingdom to Flanders, there was only one regimental chaplain present with his corps; the army was, however, accompanied by four or five other clergymen who acted as deputies to their respective employers." In the expedition destined for the West Indies under Sir R. Abercromby no chaplain put in an appearance, despite the General's orders requiring the personal attendance of the chaplains of all the regiments under his command. This extraordinary omission was due, it is said, to an implied understanding that they were to be exempt from personal service. The first Chaplain-General, the Rev. John Gamble, was appointed in 1796, when a determined effort was made to correct the abuses which had crept into the department; regimental chaplains were discontinued, and arrangements made for utilising the services of the parochial clergy for troops in barracks. Still matters were not satisfactory; in 1806 the Duke of York "noticed with much concern that . . . . Sir James Craig embarked in command of a corps of about 4,000 men with one chaplain; Lord Cathcart embarked with a corps of 14,000 men with one chaplain; and it appears that Sir David Baird's corps, consisting of nearly 4,600 men, was actually unattended by any clerical officer of any description." Later on there was an entire absence of the clerical element in the armies under Generals Auchmuty and Crawford, and in those under General Fraser, General Beresford, and Sir John Moore; while Lord Cathcart's expedition against Zealand had but one chaplain for the 14,000 men of which it was composed. For a time matters mended; the termination of the long war with France once more brought the soldier within the purview of the parochial clergy, and in 1829 the office of Chaplain-General was abolished; to be revived, however, seventeen years later. From that date to the present the Army Chaplain Department has been the object of increased attention; the system adopted has worked well, and there are not a few instances recorded where, in the exercise of their spiritual functions, army chaplains have displayed heroism and courage which has received and deserved the most honourable recognition. One at least—the Rev. J. W. Adams—is amongst the wearers of the Victoria Cross, while another, the Rev. R. Collins, R.C. Chaplain with the forces in Egypt, should, many think, be also included in that "golden book" of honour.

The exploits of Mr. Adams are thus described in "The Victoria Cross in Afghanistan":—

"In the midst of the turmoil and confusion around, Sir Frederick Roberts remained cool, and momentarily gave rapid orders to stem the living torrent that was rushing towards him. Now he witnessed that which caused him afterwards to make a special report of the circumstance. A man in black close-fitting coat, having on his head a helmet, yet with a white band around his throat, was near him—not a fighting soldier it was evident. He was a clergyman, a chaplain attached to the British force. He was the Rev. J. W. Adams. This Christian gentleman threw himself from his horse to help a wounded man of the 9th Lancers, whom he saw staggering towards him. The horse, alarmed at the struggling around him, started back, broke away, and was lost. The courageous clergyman helped forward the wounded man to further assistance, then made his way back on foot. He reached a deep nullah or water-course. He perceived at its bottom that which called for instant action; there lay two horses on their backs, with their riders underneath in the water drowning. The horses were struggling and lashing out to get free, rolling upon the men under them at every movement. Down to the bottom and up to the waist in water rushed the gallant chaplain. He seized the reins of the nearest animal, and with Herculean strength pulled him off his prostrate rider, who, half stunned and suffocated, yet managed to gain the bank. Again the clergyman turned and repeated his deed for the remaining trooper. Both men were assisted not a moment too soon, for numbers of Afghans running up barely gave the brave chaplain time to get away. He had saved the lives of two men and prevented their being cut to pieces by the advancing enemy. This, too, at the imminent peril of his own life. The rules for granting the Victoria Cross were altered in his favour, and he was recently gazetted to his, indeed, well-merited reward." *

Another instance of gallant Christian work amidst the stress of battle is afforded by the account of Mr. Gordon's behaviour during the sortie from Kandahar; though, alas, in his case the record has to state that "a brave man was killed while in the performance of his self-imposed duties during the sortie from Kandahar on the 15th of August, 1879, at the moment, indeed, in which he was performing an act of noble devotion. This man's name was the Rev. G. M. Gordon, of the Church Missionary Society, who was mortally wounded whilst attending to the men under a heavy fire. Here is what was said of this excellent man by General Primrose in the dry details of military dispatches: —'I take this opportunity of paying my small tribute of admiration to a man who, by his kindness and gentleness, had endeared himself to the whole force, and who, in the end, died administering to their wants.'"

Amongst the numerous other instances which might be quoted, we will take the one before referred to from the last Egyptian War:—

"Conspicuous in one of the improvised squares—at Hasheen—were the figures of the Rev. Reginald Collins (Roman Catholic chaplain) and Major Alston fighting back to back, 'the reverend combatant having seized the nearest available weapon, a revolver, which he wielded as if to the manner born.' At this time one of the native regiments became somewhat unsteady and wild in their firing, to the peril of the little square under Major Alston. On this the Rev. Mr. Collins gallantly offered to cross the bullet-swept ground that intervened, and convey the Major's orders to cease firing. Stepping forward, calm and collected in demeanour, the chaplain walked, his life in his hands, across to the Indians, to whom he gave the necessary orders, and then returned as calmly to the little square which he had just left. His reception must have been some com-

* A short reference to this incident is made in Vol. I. p. 75.

pensation for the dreadful risk he had run. The men, struck with his heroism, raised cheer after cheer, and placing their helmets on their bayonets, waved them frantically in their enthusiasm."

THE ARMY MEDICAL DEPARTMENT * has a very ancient lineage. Surgeon-Major Gore in his interesting work says, "The earliest notice of army surgeons occurs in the year 1223, the commencement of the reign of Henry III., shortly before he led his army to France to attempt the reconquest of Normandy. It was in the form of a recommendation from the Chief Justice to the Bishop of Chichester of 'one Master Thomas, an army surgeon, who knew how to cure wounds, a science particularly useful in the siege of castles;' but it was not till two reigns afterwards, *tempus* 15 Edward II., A.D. 1322, that paid medical officers to attend on the army are mentioned in the wardrobe accounts of that monarch." "So early as the reign of Edward II.," says another writer, "we find a chirurgeon for every 1,900 men. His pay was fourpence per diem. Henry V. had one surgeon and twelve assistants with his army, and they rank thus in his military code: 'Soldiers, shoemakers, taylors, barbers, physicians, and washerwomen.'"

From that time to the present every British army has been attended, with more or less sufficiency, by trained medical men, the service receiving considerable impetus and encouragement from the ill-fated Charles I. It is beyond our province to follow in any detail the development of the service, interesting though the review of the history would be. "The present Army Medical Department," says Archer, "must be traced from the reign of Charles II., when the nucleus of a standing army was established." Very curious are some of the *notabilia* gathered together by Gore; amongst others may be instanced the following prescription—somewhat reminding us of the "treatment" adopted in one of Hawley Smart's novels, by the cheery doctor to the hipped and mount-less young officer—sent to General de Ginkle by Sir Patrick Dun. "Chester ale, claret, potted chicken, and geese. This is the physic I advise you to take. I hope it will not be nauseous or disagreeable to the stomach. A little to be taken on a march."

During the War of Independence Dr. Jackson (Frazer's Highlanders) greatly distinguished himself, remaining with the wounded; in default of dressings for them he

* The special regimental badge of the Medical Staff Corps is the Geneva Cross. The uniform is blue with black facings and scarlet shoulder knots. The medical officers attached to the Household Cavalry or Foot Guards wear the uniform of the corresponding rank of combatant officers, substituting cocked hat for helmet or bearskin.

disrobed himself of his only shirt and tore it into bandages, his noble conduct so greatly pleasing the American General that when the British wounded could be exchanged he was sent back with them, no parole being required nor exchange demanded. During the Peninsular War Lord Wellington referred in terms of the warmest praise to the courage and devotion of the Medical Staff, and that such praise was fairly earned may be gathered from the following fact recorded by Napier: "During the ten months from the siege of Burgos to the Battle of Vittoria inclusive, the total number of sick and wounded which passed through the hospitals was 95,348. By the unremitting attention of Sir James McGregor, and the medical staff under his orders, the army took the field preparatory to the battle with a sick list under 5,000." During the Crimean War the principal medical officer was Sir John Hall, of whom Lord Raglan writes (after the Alma): "Dr. Hall was in the field the whole time and merits my approbation for his exertion in discharging his onerous duties." The action of Surgeon Wilson of the 9th Hussars in organizing the rescue party which saved the life of the Duke of Cambridge has been before noticed; Surgeons Mowat, Sylvester, and Hales gained the Victoria Cross; Surgeon O'Callaghan of the 62nd was amongst the foremost and bravest at the Redan. During the Mutiny five medical officers earned the Victoria Cross—Surgeon Reade, Surgeon M'Master, Surgeon Gee, Surgeon A. D. Home, and Surgeon Bradshaw; Hartley, McCrea, Douglas, and Reynolds are also amongst those who have earned the same incomparable distinction; but the names of all of the Medical Staff who have gained fame for themselves by acts of courage and humanity would make too long a list to permit of their insertion. We may, however, mention Surgeons Temple and Manley, who, in the New Zealand War, so pre-eminently distinguished themselves. At the Pah of Rangiriri, where Captain Mercer was so desperately wounded, " Assistant-Surgeon William Temple, Royal Artillery, seeing his friend rolling on the ground in agony, was anxious to take assistance to him and the numerous wounded. It was a service of the utmost peril, entailing almost certain death. The spot where Mercer and his wounded comrades lay was close to the Pah, and the defenders of the latter had concentrated a cross fire on the place in order to forbid approach. First one soldier, then another, advanced on the errand of mercy; but one after another was shot down as he drew near. Then, heedless of his own life, sprang forward William Temple. His progress was watched with breathless anxiety. It seemed impossible that he could escape. When he reached the spot which had proved so fatal to his predecessors, the enemy's fire was redoubled, and the gallant surgeon was enveloped in smoke. Many must have thought that it was his winding sheet; but no, when the thick white cloud cleared away Temple was seen, apparently unhurt, leaning over Mercer and assiduously busied in the attempt to soothe his agony. Fortune favours the brave, it is said, and it certainly did so on this occasion. Instinctively he had stooped when the Maories had fired, and their bullets had whistled harmlessly over his head. When once by Mercer's side he was perhaps too close to the Pah to be hit. At all events, throughout that afternoon spent in tending not only Mercer, but the other wounded men who lay in clusters almost, as it were, under the muzzles of the enemy's muskets, he was untouched.

"Dr. Manley was present at the assault and capture of four Pahs, but it was on the occasion of a serious disaster that he won the Victoria Cross. The Maories had constructed a strong stockaded work at Tauranga, called the 'Gate Pah.' It was situated on a narrow strip of land connecting a peninsula with the mainland, and on each side of the Pah was a swamp extending to the sea. It was thought only possible to attack it in front.

"Commander Hay was one of the first to fall, mortally wounded. Samuel Mitchell, captain of the foretop of H.M.S. *Harrier*, casting aside all thoughts of personal safety, raised Commander Hay in his arms, and, under a heavy fire, carried him out of the Pah. There he met Dr. Manley, who had volunteered to accompany the storming party, and who, notwithstanding the panic, confusion, and terror which prevailed on every side, calmly dressed Commander Hay's wound, and then entered the Pah to see if there were any more wounded whom he could succour. It is said that he was one of the last officers to leave the Pah. Throughout that sad evening his efforts were to alleviate suffering where necessary, and Sir William Wiseman, commanding the Naval Brigade, reported that he 'ministered to the wants of the wounded and dying amid the bullets of the enemy with as much *sang froid* as if he had been performing an operation in St. George's Hospital.' He subsequently nobly justified his right to the Victoria Cross. Before leaving New Zealand he happened to be present during the disembarkation of some artillery in the Waitotara River. As he was quitting the steamer a gunner fell overboard. The man was in imminent danger of being drowned, but Dr. Manley promptly sprang into the water and rescued him. For this feat he was awarded the bronze medal of the Royal Humane Society." Nor must Lance-Corporal John Farmer be forgotten, who, during the engagement with the Boers at the Majuba Mountain on the 25th February, 1881, "showed a spirit of self-abnegation and an example of cool courage which cannot be too highly recommended. While the Boers closed with the British troops near the wells Corporal Farmer held a white flag over the wounded, and when the arm holding the flag was shot through he called out that he had 'another.' He then raised the flag with the other arm, and continued to do so until that also was pierced with a bullet."

Regimental surgeons have recently ceased to exist, a medical staff being attached to every expedition. Very considerable feeling was excited at the change, into the merits or demerits of which we do not propose to enter. "Although," says Archer, "no longer attached to regiments as formerly, when they proved a very valuable element in promoting harmony, and tempering when absolutely necessary—a privilege never abused—the severity of discipline in cases where their peculiar position enabled them to do so with advantage to the service—the medical officers are everywhere popular."

THE ARMY SERVICE CORPS* is the present representative of organizations known as the Land Transport Corps, the Military Train, the Control Department, and the Commissariat and Transport Department. These again at various times had subdivisions, and it is beyond the scope of the present work to trace minutely the various devolutions and absorptions which from time to time have taken place, inasmuch as to do so would demand considerable space, without—except to those peculiarly interested—any counterbalancing degree of interest. The regulation of many of the matters now falling within the province of the Army Service Corps was originally in the hands of civilians appointed by the Treasury, but in 1858 the "Commissariat" became endowed with a military character. In 1861 the control of the Military Stores was in a like manner transferred from the civil to the military management, and the ORDNANCE STORE DEPARTMENT† of to-day is the representative of the former Military Store Department. During the Peninsular War there was a Waggon Corps which was subsequently disbanded, and in 1854 was formed the Land Transport Corps, which three years later was named the Military Train. This body rendered sterling service during the Crimea, the Mutiny, and the war in China, and was entitled to the distinctions "Lucknow," "Taku Forts," "Pekin."

"During the India Mutiny," says a writer, "the Military Train were employed as

* The Army Service Corps have a blue uniform with white facings and white shoulder cords; white and blue band on cap.

† The uniform of the Ordnance Store Department is blue, with facings and edgings of scarlet, buff and scarlet (for officers, gold), lace band on cap and the letters O. S. C. in brass on the shoulder straps.

cavalry, and in that capacity did excellent service on the 15th April, 1858, during the pursuit of Koer Singh's army from Azimghur. After the enemy had been driven from their position on that day, a squadron of the 3rd Sikh Cavalry, a squadron of the Military Train, and two horse-artillery guns were sent across in pursuit. They soon came up with the rebels, who, driven to desperation and in superior numbers, fought desperately. Lieutenant Hamilton, commanding the Sikhs, was almost immediately wounded, unhorsed, and surrounded by rebels cutting at him as he lay on the ground. Two brave fellows, Michael Murphy and Samuel Morley, of the Military Train, hastened to his assistance. Murphy cut down several of his opponents, but, though wounded himself, he stuck to Hamilton's side. He was aided by Morley. That man's horse had just been killed under him, but he hastened on foot to Murphy's side, cut down a Sepoy, and fought over Hamilton's body till other men came to his aid. Both obtained the Victoria Cross."

In 1870 the Military Train was abolished and a "Control Department" was formed, which included a "Purveyor's Department," "Commissariat Department," "Commissariat Staff Corps," "Military Store Department," and "Military Store Staff Corps," which were all grouped together under the "Supply and Transport Sub-Department." Four years later this Sub-Department was re-named the Army Transport Corps. Subsequent changes have since been made, but the title of the "Army Service Corps" is that given in the Army List.

There are besides, the ORDNANCE STORE CORPS, taking the place of the "Department" similarly named, and the ARMY PAY DEPARTMENT, the latter taking the duties of the Pay Sub-Department formed in 1876. There are also the ARMY SCHOOLS DEPARTMENT* and MILITARY PRISONS DEPARTMENT,* which do not call for any detailed notice.

We now come to a regiment which may be described as the first of the Auxiliary Forces of the Crown, the HONOURABLE ARTILLERY COMPANY OF LONDON.† It is scarcely possible to name a military body whose history, from its lineage and traditions, appeals with greater force and fascination to all subjects of the British Crown. We might indeed, without incurring any grave charge of undue hyperbole, go further and say that

---

* Uniform blue with scarlet facings.

† The uniform for the Cavalry is a blue hussar uniform; for the Artillery blue with scarlet facings; for the Infantry, scarlet with blue facings and bearskin cap—the chief distinction from the Grenadier Guards being silver lace instead of gold. The mottoes are *Arma pacis pulchra* and *Dieu et mon Droit*. The crest is an elaborate one, the "supporters" being a pikeman and musketeer.

the interest attaching to the Honourable Artillery Company exceeds the limits of merely national feeling, and becomes European if not universal in its stretch. For there is little doubt that, to use the words of its most recent chronicler,* "the antiquity of the Honourable Artillery Company is unequalled by any other military body throughout the world." In the days of the Red King, when

> "The ways were filled with rapine,"

and the struggling, yet even then important, commerce of the empire city of London was threatened by free lances, or, less euphoniously, by robbers and freebooters, an "armed company" of citizens was formed to protect lives and property. Previous to this these prototypes of the military "nation of shopkeepers" had given stern proof that they could wield other weapons than yard measures or weaver's bats. Under Ethelred, son-in-law of Alfred the Great, they had stormed the Danes in their castle of Benfleet; in the following reign they again and again hurled back the same fierce adversaries from their walls. During the last reign of Edmund Ironside they thrice drove back the forces of the conquering Canute. Even the great Conqueror himself, when the arrow at Sanguelac had seemed to place England at his mercy, hesitated to enter London till intrigue had disarmed its sturdy populace.

As at present constituted the Honourable Artillery Company date from the reign of Henry VIII.† The bluff monarch was fully conscious of the value of the citizens of London as fighting material. In those days invasion by a foe was by no means deemed unlikely, and he set himself to establish such a force as should hold London free from danger. An Act was therefore passed, the preamble of which will explain its object.

"The Kyng our Sovereign Lord, callyng to his most noble and gracious remembrance that by the feate and exercise of the subjecttes of this his realme in shotying in long bowes, there hath contynually growen and been within the same grete nombre and multittude of good archers, which hath not oonly defended this realme and the subjecttes thereof against the cruell malice and danger of their owteward enemys in tyme heretofore passed, but also with litell nombre and puyssance in regarde have done many notable actes and discomfetures of warre against the infidelis and other. And furthermore subdued and reduced dyverse and many regyons and countrees to their due obeysaunce to the grete honour, fame, and suertie of this realme, and subject and to the terrible drede

---

* Captain Woolmer Williams. † 1537.

and fere of all strange nacions any thyng to attempte or do to the hurte or damage of theyme or any of them."

"At the time," says Major Raikes, "of the passing of this Act, the old Artillery Ground of London, upon which the City Butts were erected, stood on the site of the present Devonshire Square, and of Duke Street and streets adjacent thereto. To encourage the practice of the citizens, a Charter was granted on the 25th August, 1537, to the Master of the Ordnance and two others (gentlemen of the Privy Chamber) for the purpose of constituting a Fraternity, consisting of four masters or rulers, and such brethren as they should admit, for promoting the science of artillery, viz., for long-bows, cross-bows, and hand-guns. A Civic Guild or Company, with the ordinary government pertaining to such societies, was thus created, and out of this society, and subordinate to it, has sprung a military organization now known as the Honourable Artillery Company of London. These two bodies, so closely associated together, must not be mistaken for each other."

The Charter referred to commences, "To all Judges, Justices, Maires, Sheriffs, Bailiffs, Constables, and other o^r Officers, Ministres, and Subgietts We latt you with that of o^r grace especiall certain science and mere mocion we Have graunted and licensed And by this Pnts Doo graunt and licence for us and o^r heyres to our trusty and well-beloved S'vnnts & Subgietts Sr Cristofer Morres, Knight, Master of o^r Ordennes, Anthony Knevett and Peter Mewtes, Gentlemen of o^r Preve Chambre, Overseers of the Fraternittè or Guylde of Saint George;" and goes on to grant certain privileges, amongst which are—

1. To choose and admit their own members.

2. To choose and elect amongst themselves every year, four Under-Masters and Rulers to oversee and govern the Fraternity.

3. They were empowered to use a common seal and to make laws and regulations for the good government of the Fraternity.

4. They were granted licence to use and shoot with the long-bows, cross-bows, and hand-guns, both in London and the suburbs, and all other parts of the Realme of England, Ireland, Calais, and Wales.

5. No other Fraternity or Guild could be formed in any part of the Realm unless licenced by the Masters and Rulers of this Fraternity.

6. The Masters and Rulers and their successors were especially exempted from being empanelled on any Quest or Jury throughout the Realm.

The Royal Charter had its due effect; the citizens of London gave good heed, not only to the practice of archery but to military matters generally; so much so, indeed, that in the time of Henry's heroic daughter there were some complaints of the number of the many military bodies in training. But there was good excuse for enthusiasm in military matters.

"The time was one of great excitement, the Spanish Armada was then hanging like a vast cloud over the political horizon, and all men's minds were earnestly discussing how they might best avert the danger. Among the merchants there were many able soldiers who had served abroad; these seem to have led the way in the formation of an association of citizens of similar rank, who submitted themselves voluntarily to continual exercise and study of the theory and practice of war, with the view of being able to train and command on emergencies large bodies of their fellow-citizens. Within the first two years they numbered above three hundred members, 'very sufficient and skilful to train and teach common soldiers the managing of their pieces, pikes, and halberts, to march, countermarch, and ring.' A pleasant evidence of the spirit in which they congregated is given by their custom of letting every man serve by turns every office, from the corporal's up to the captain's. And as the Armada grew more and more a reality, every month bringing fresh news of its advancing state, plenty of work was found for these merchants of the Artillery Company. The City furnished no less than 10,000 men for the public defence, who were officered chiefly by the civic authorities and the captains of the Artillery Garden; and the Government exhibited its appreciation of this force in a marked manner: while 1,000 men were sent to the great camp at Tilbury, the other 9,000 were kept by the Queen around herself as a part of the army appointed for her protection, and which was commanded by Lord Hunsdon."

In recognition, says Captain Williams, of the very important services rendered by the Company at this critical period, the members were honoured by being appointed, by an Order in Council of Her Majesty, to the rank of officers in the various trained bands throughout the country. In the reign of James I. the Hon. Artillery Company obtained the lease of their present ground in Finsbury, and early in the following reign the ill-fated Charles I. became a member. Shortly afterwards some disagreement arose between the Company and the City authorities, in which the Privy Council sided with the City, but the King with the Hon. Artillery Company. Charles addressed to the Company the following letter, quoted in Major Raikes' History, and it is easy to be credited that the Privy Council were much displeased at His Majesty's action in the matter. But the act was a right royal one, and it may well be imagined that in after years, when the

White King's blood had been shed at Whitehall, the members of the Honourable Company regarded with something of self-reproach and more of regret the kindly and courteous letter signed "Charles R.," addressed to his "trustie and well-beloved" subjects of the "Artillery Garden."

"Charles R.

"Trustie and well-beloved we greet you well. Whereas we are informed that the worthie and commendable institution of yor voluntary Company of the Artillerie Garden, hath been soe well pursued by yor industrious and forward endeavours that you are not only become ready and skilfull in the knowledge and use of Armes and military discipline, but that from thence, as from a fruitfull Nursery, all the trayned bands of our Cittie of London, and divers of the Companyes of the counties adjoyning have beene supplied wth fitt and able Leaders and Officers, whereby our Service hath received much Advantage, and the kingdome in generall a very great benifitt. And being unwilling that a Societie of soe good use to the publique, and of soe much safetie and honor to our renowned Citie of London should be dissolved or discontinued, as we are given to understand it is in great danger through some distractions which you have lately suffered about the Election of your Captaine. We have thought fitt hereby to will you not be hastie to disband, but if ye find that ye are molested needlessly or unjustly by any then have recourse to us and you shall find such due encouragement as soe commendable a Societie deserves. Given att our Court at Newmarkett, the Eight day of March, in the Seaventh yeare of our Raigne.

"To our trustie and well-beloved Humfrie Smith, Ald^r president of the Company exercisinge Armes in the Artillerie Garden, London, and to the Rest of the Companie."

At the Restoration it may be assumed that the Company took part in the Grand Military Procession described by Nichols.

"First marched a gallant troop of gentlemen in cloth of silver, brandishing their swords, and led by Major-General Brown; then another troop of two hundred in velvet coats, with footmen attending them in purple liveries; a third, led by Alderman Robinson, in buff coats, with cloth of silver sleeves, and very rich green scarves; a troop of about two hundred, with blue liveries laid with silver, with six trumpeters and several footmen in sea-green and silver; and several hundred others; and last of all five regiments of Horse belonging to the Army, with back, breast, and head-pieces, which 'diversified the show with delight and terror.'"

The sentiments of the Company at this period seem to have been strongly monarchical. Charles II. had scarcely ascended the throne when the Duke of York was elected Commander, and from an account given of a feast to which the Duke was invited, it is evident that the Hon. Artillery Company of London were strong adherents of the Court party.

"Amongst the healths, they drank one to the happy Succession in the Right Line, and it is reported that they drank so many that one of the grave City Sirs lost his beaver hat and gold hatband, and left the greater company to sport with the footboys; and that the Duke promised to defend the Religion established by law, of the Church of England."

The above account, it may be needless to observe, came from an "Opposition organ."

On Lord Mayor's Day, 29th October, 1683, the members of the Company were to the fore, and were very gallantly and richly habited; many of the musketeers in buff, with head-pieces of massive silver, all with red feathers, and most of the pikemen, as well as the officers, wore very rich embroidered belts; they also had the six new colours lately presented by the colonels of the six regiments of the Trained Bands.

At the time of the Great Plague the company were threatened with corporate as well as individual danger. So grievous was the cry against overcrowded burial-places, that an attempt was made to appropriate the Artillery Gardens as a cemetery! Sir John Robinson, the new president, opposed this tooth and nail, fortunately with success; and to this day in recognition of his services his name may be seen, written in letters of gold, in the famous Vellum Book of the Company. Despite the loyal toasts above mentioned, and the royal favour that they enjoyed during the reign of James II.,* it does not appear that the Company, as a whole, was other than favourable to the Revolution; William III. by Royal warrant confirmed "all their former rights and privileges," and a few years later, by another warrant, recommended to the care of the Company, "that all the commissioned officers of all Trained Bands of our City of London may list themselves members of the said Society, that so, by the frequent practice of arms, according to their rules, they may be the better qualified to perform their trust in their respective commands." No occurrence of interest occurred during that or the following reign. On the accession of George I. the right of the Company to take part in the royal procession was urged and

* The title "Honourable" seems to date from the commencement of James's reign.

granted, and the Prince of Wales was appointed Captain-General. At a review held in 1722 the officers of the Company wore, for the first time, scarlet uniforms, and shortly afterwards the King presented them with a sum of £500, which was employed as the nucleus of a fund wherewith the New Armoury House was built.

The old Armoury, which the present one replaces, had been completed in 1622, and the following verses were composed by the Marshal, and, as has been said, considering the age in which they appeared, show more than ordinary merit. They are, moreover, worth quoting for the information they convey.

LINES COMPOSED BY THE MARSHAL ON THE COMPLETION OF THE ARMOURY IN 1622.

LONDON'S HONOUR, AND HER CITIZEN'S APPROVED LOVE, EXERCISING ARMS IN THE ARTILLERY GARDEN, LONDON.

The Fabrick.	This Architecture, Phœnix of our Age, (All Europe cannot shew her Eqipage) Is Mars his Mistress, which retains the Store Of Mars his Arms, being Mars his Paramore. This Fabrick was by Mars his soldiers framed, And Mars his Armouries this Building named.
The Soldiers' Honour.	It holds five hundred Arms, to furnish those That love their Sovereign, and will daunt his Foes, They spend their time, and do not care for Cost; To learn the use of Arms, there's nothing lost. Both time and Coin, to do their Country good, They'll spend it freely, and will lose their blood.
The Aldermen's Love.	Our City London is a Royal Thing; For it is called the Chamber of our King, Whose worthy Senate we must not forget, Their grant and our Request together met. They cherish us, and we do honour them; Where Soldiers find true Love, they'll love again.
The Ground.	The Ground wheron this Building now doth stand, The Teasel Ground hath heretofore been nam'd.
The Donor of the Ground.	And William Prior of the Hospital Then of our blessed Lady, which we call Saint Mary Spittle without Bishopgate, Did pass it by Indenture, bearing date January's third day in Henry's Time, Th' Eight of that name; the Convent did conjoin.
The Use.	Unto the Guild of all Artillery, Cross-bows, Hand-Guns, and of Archery.
The Term of Years.	For full three hundred years, excepting three; The Time remaining we shall never see.

The Council's Confirmation.	Now have the noble Council of the King Confirm'd the same, and under Charles his Wing We now do exercise, and of that little Teasel of Ground, we inlarge St. Mary Spittle. Trees we cut down, and Gardens added to it; Thanks to the Lords, that gave us leave to do it.
A Loyal Subject's Desire.	Long may this Work endure, and ne'er decay, But be supported till the latest day, All loyal subjects to the King and State, Will say Amen, maugre all Spleen and Hate.

MARISCHALLUS PETOWE,
Composuit.

No incident of interest occurred for some years, but in 1780, at the time of the Gordon Riots, the Hon. Artillery Company proved that they were no mere carpet knights. Well it was for the city and the kingdom, that men such as they were to the fore at a crisis of so terrible a nature. In truth "men's hearts were failing them for fear;" far and wide were buildings in flames; in every thoroughfare bands of maddened miscreants were rioting and pillaging; everywhere in the streets of the good City of London women and children were flying for their lives. From the nature of their constitution the Hon. Artillery Company have had but few occasions when the arms they carried could be used for grimmer purposes than pageants and reviews, and the circumstances attending the Gordon riots were of so memorable a nature that it can scarcely be out of place here to quote the description of them given by Walpole.

"I came myself yesterday and found a horrible scene. Lord Mansfield's house was just burnt down, and at night there were shocking disorders. London and Southwark were on fire in six places, but the regular troops quelled the sedition by daybreak, and everything now is quiet. A camp of ten thousand men is formed in Hyde Park, and regiments of horse and foot arrive every hour.

"I was at Gloucester House between nine and ten. The servants announced a great fire; the Duchess, her daughters, and I went to the top of the house, and beheld not only one but two vast fires, which we took for the King's Bench and Lambeth; but the latter was the New Prison, and the former at least was burning at midnight. Colonel Heywood came in and acquainted His Royal Highness that nine houses in Great Queen Street had been gutted and the furniture burnt, and he had seen a great Catholic distiller's at Holborn Bridge broken open and all the casks staved; and since, the house has been set on fire.

"At ten I went to Lord Hertford's, and found him and his sons charging muskets.

Lord Rockingham has two hundred soldiers in his house, and is determined to defend it. Thence I went to General Conway's, and in a moment a servant came in and said there was a great fire just by. We went to the street door and thought it was St. Martin's Lane in flames, but it is either Fleet Prison or the distiller's. I forgot that in the court of Gloucester House I met Colonel Jennings, who told me there had been an engagement at the Royal Exchange to defend the Bank, and that the Guards had shot sixty of the mob; I have since heard seventy, for I forgot to tell your Ladyship that at a great council, held this evening at the Queen's house, at which Lord Rockingham and the Duke of Portland were present, military execution was ordered, for, in truth, the justices dare not act.

"After supper I returned to Lady Hertford, finding Charing Cross, and the Haymarket, and Piccadilly, illuminated from fear, though all this end of the town is hitherto perfectly quiet, lines being drawn across the Strand and Holborn to prevent the mob coming westward.

"I do not know whether to call the horrors of the night greater or less than I thought. My printer, who has been out all night and on the spots of action, says, not above a dozen were killed at the Royal Exchange, some few elsewhere; at the King's Bench he does not know how many, but in other respects the calamities are dreadful. He saw many houses set on fire, women and children screaming, running out of doors with what they could save, and knocking one another down with their loads in the confusion. Barnard's Inn is burnt, and some houses, mistaken for Catholic. Kirgate says most of the rioters are apprentices, and plunder and drink have been their chief objects, and both women and men are still lying dead drunk about the streets. Brandy is preferable to enthusiasm. I trust many more troops will arrive to-day. What families ruined! What wretched wives and mothers! What public disgrace!—ay! and where and when and how will all this confusion end, and what shall we be when it is concluded? I remember the Excise and the Gin Act, and the rebels at Derby, and Wilkes's interlude, and the French at Plymouth, or I should have a very bad memory, but I never till last night saw London and Southwark in flames!"

"There is a well-known engraving," quotes Major Raikes, who gives a reproduction of it in his work, "of the Gordon Riots in Broad Street on Wednesday, the 7th of June, 1780, in which the Artillery Company and the London Association are represented firing on the mob, who are sacking a house in the foreground. The command to fire is being given by the Major, who is standing with his hat off to mark the solemnity of the occasion. A prominent figure in the group is the Surgeon, Sir William Blizard, lifting up a wounded man; a ruffian is aiming a blow at him but is checked by another man who recognises the errand of mercy on which the officer is engaged."

It was after the Gordon Riots that the only honorary member ever elected by the Company was admitted in the person of Captain Barnard Turner, who had been in command of the London Military Association during the whole of the disturbances. About this time, too, occurred a circumstance which brings into clear relief the sturdy independence and jealousy of outside interference which the Company has always exhibited. By permission of the Company some bodies of regular troops had been quartered on their ground. When all danger of a renewal of disturbances had passed away the Company wrote to Lord Amhurst suggesting that they had been put to very considerable expense, and requesting that the troops might be removed. Lord Amhurst seems to have been under the impression that the Lord Mayor had the right of granting the user, for his reply was to the effect that he had understood from the Lord Mayor that no difficulty would be raised and that he should have to consult him. The Lord Mayor wrote as follow :—

"SIR,—I have been informed that a Court of Assistants of the Artillery Company is summoned for this afternoon, to receive an answer from Lord Amhurst to the letter sent by last Court. I should be glad (before any answer is given) to have a copy of the said letter to lay before the Court of Lieutenancy, which I shall order to be held for that purpose on Thursday next.

"BRACKLEY KENNETT, Mayor.
"To Peter Longes, Clerk to the Artillery Company."

But if the writer was Lord Mayor of London, the recipients were the Hon. Artillery Company, and were not disposed to allow a mere civilian's interference. The following letter is in its way a masterpiece :—

"MY LORD,—I am desired by the Court to acquaint you, that the letter received from Lord Amhurst concerns the Members of the Artillery Company, and them only; nor does it require any answer.

"I am, &c.,
"PETER LONGES, Clerk."

The Lord Mayor laid this correspondence before the Court of Lieutenancy, but after some discussion they simply passed a vote of thanks to his Lordship for writing to the Company. The result was that the Company gained their point, and the ground was not occupied by the troops.

But the question remained for a long time one of debate, and in October, 1796, the Militia were advised to make overt display of their claim. Accordingly the Honourable Artillery Company having assembled under arms, the gates were locked, and one company posted at each entrance to the ground, the other divisions remaining as a reserve with the field officers in front of the Armoury House, the artillery division being stationed at the angle with the field-pieces. Between twelve and one o'clock the Militia, with bayonets fixed and drums beating, arrived at the east entrance, headed by Captain Jennings, of the East Regiment, who demanded admission for the purpose of exercising the London Militia, or "Trained Bands," a similar demand being made by Captain Porter, of the West Regiment. The demands were, as might be expected, "peremptorily refused;" the Militia marched back again, litigation followed, and eventually a satisfactory compromise was arrived at.

The Gordon Riots have been by no means the only occasion on which the Honourable Artillery Company have been called on to uphold authority. Their historian rightly observes that "during the last and for a considerable portion of the present century, they constituted almost the only military force on which the civil authorities could rely for assistance in case of sudden emergency or disturbance." They were on duty several times during the disturbances of 1794; six years later, when the Bread Mob endangered the peace of the city, they were again under arms. "Although it was past eight o'clock on the evening of the 15th of September when the Lord Mayor requested the Colonel to call out the Company, yet by twelve o'clock over a hundred men were under arms." The Colonel at this eventful period—eventful, not only for the Honourable Artillery Company, but for the nation at large, who were in constant anticipation of the threatened invasion by Bonaparte—was Colonel Le Mesurier, who devoted himself untiringly to rendering the Company thoroughly effective in every detail.

The Government having requested that the Company should be in constant readiness, an order was issued in the following terms: "This Court being deeply impressed with a sense of the duty incumbent on every loyal man to be ready to defend his King and his country at all times, and more particularly at this juncture, when the United Kingdom is threatened with invasion, do require of every member of the Honourable Artillery Company to keep himself in perfect readiness to be under arms on the first order." Members who were likely to be absent were to leave their addresses with the commanding officer of his division. When the conclusion of peace relaxed this state of tension the Company gave to Colonel Le Mesurier a splendid token of their recognition of his services. There were presented to him at a general Court a silver cup and cover, holding five quarts and weighing nearly nineteen pounds, a sword and sword-belt mounted with gold, and a silver tea-tray weighing close upon seventeen pounds. On several occasions the Honourable Artillery Company have furnished the guard for the Bank of England when, at election times or from other causes, the Guards have been withdrawn.

We must pass over much that is interesting in the history of the corps, and content ourselves with indicating the more important events, premising that the existing histories will well repay perusal. In 1803 a Yager or Rifle Company was formed, the numbers being limited to 100, and the uniform being dark green, with "Yeoman Crown" beaver cap. They were abolished in 1854, the members being absorbed into the Infantry companies. Early in the reign of George IV. formal permission was granted for the Armorial bearings of the Company to be registered at the Heralds' College, and at the commencement of the following reign, as a special mark of the Royal favour, "the King directed that henceforth the uniform of the Company should be similar to that worn by the Grenadier Guards, substituting silver for gold." The blue uniform for the Artillery was adopted in 1851 and the bear-skin caps in 1853. On the occasion of the State Visit paid by Her present Majesty to the City, it was the Hon. Artillery Company who furnished the Guard of Honour in the Guildhall Yard, and on the day of her coronation they were alligned between the 1st and 3rd battalions of the Grenadier Guards. One of the most important events connected with the Company which have occurred during the present reign has been the resumption by the sovereign of the appointment of the officers, the custom for some time previously having been that the Company should themselves elect their company and subaltern officers. Very considerable searchings of heart occurred on this occasion. The Royal Warrant ran as follows:—

"Victoria R.

"Trusty and Wellbeloved, We Greet you Well! We being well satisfied of the Loyalty and good affection of Our Artillery Company, and being therefore willing to promote the welfare and preservation of it in its ancient good Order and Discipline, have thought fit to authorise and empower you frequently to exercise Our said Company in Arms, as well in the Ground commonly called the Artillery Ground, near Moorfields, as in other places where they have formerly exercised.

"And We do hereby likewise give you full power and Authority to hold Courts free and public for the annual choice of Officers, except as hereinafter mentioned, and on such other occasions as may be necessary and requisite for the better Government of the said Company, according to the ancient rules and practice thereof (except in so far as such rules or practice may be inconsistent with this Our Royal Warrant), in such place and places, and at such time and times, as hath been usual. But We reserve to Ourselves the Appointment from time to time of the Field Officers and the Adjutant of Our said Company as heretofore.

"And as a mark of Our Royal favour, and of Our interest and Concern in the welfare of Our said Company, We further reserve to Ourselves the appointment from time to time of all other Commissioned Officers of Our said Company.

"And We hereby declare it to be Our Royal Will and Pleasure, that the appointment of all Commissioned Officers of Our said Company (other than Field Officers and the Adjutant) shall endure for the period of five years and no longer, and that the persons appointed shall be selected by Us from the Members of Our said Artillery Company, provided that as often as any Vacancy or Vacancies shall occur amongst the Officers so appointed and selected, the same shall be supplied by Us in the manner aforesaid.

"And We do hereby will and direct that the Regimental Sergeant-Major of Our said Company shall be appointed from time to time by the Captain-General and Colonel of Our said Company, and that all other Non-commissioned Officers of Our said Company shall be appointed from time to time by the Lieutenant-Colonel, and shall be selected by him from the Members of Our said Company, provided that as often as any Vacancy or Vacancies shall occur amongst the said Non-commissioned Officers the same shall be supplied by the said Lieutenant-Colonel of Our said Company.

"And We likewise recommend unto your care that all the Commissioned Officers of Our Trained Bands of Our City of London may list themselves Members of the said Society, that so by the frequent practice of Arms according to their rules they may be the better qualified to perform their Trust in their respective Commands, And for your so doing this shall be your Warrant.

"And for your further encouragement We do think fit to confirm and continue Our most dearly beloved Consort Albert Augustus Charles Emmanuel, Duke of Saxony, Prince of Saxe-Coburg and Gotha, Knight of Our Most Noble Order of the Garter, and Field Marshal of Our Army, Captain-General and Colonel of your Company, and shall testify Our good Will towards you on all occasions proper for Us to express it in.

"And we do hereby annul Our Royal Warrant bearing date the fourteenth day of September, in the year of Our Lord One thousand eight hundred and Forty-three, and all such rules and practice of Our said Artillery Company as may be inconsistent with this present Warrant.

" And so We bid you heartily farewell.

"Given at Our Court at St. James's, the Tenth day of October, 1849, in the Thirteenth year of Our Reign.

"By Her Majesty's Command,

"G. GREY.

" To Our Trusty and Well-beloved the President, Treasurer, and Court of Assistants of Our Artillery Company of London."

Contrary to what was expected, this gave rise to a great deal of discontent among a certain number of members, who, instead of regarding it as a high honour that all officers should hold their commissions direct from the Sovereign, looked upon it as the withdrawal of one of the Company's greatest privileges, and at the General Court in October, after the new Royal Warrant had been read, the Rules were proposed to be altered so that no officer who held rank "under other authority" than that of election by ballot, should be allowed to sit on the Court, and the proposal was unfortunately carried by a majority of four, and the Article referring to military offences was also altered, again giving the Court exclusive power in such cases instead of the Military Committee.

The new Court elected at the General Meeting, comprising a majority of opponents of the new Warrant, resulted in a petition to the Queen being subsequently adopted, praying Her Majesty to restore the ancient privilege of electing the officers, which was duly presented to the Home Secretary.

The Company now became completely divided into two contending parties, the malcontents numbering 126, of whom 27 subsequently recanted, and the Loyalists, or those in favour of the new warrant, numbering 190. Both parties now drew up an address to H.R.H. Prince Albert, the one expressing their gratification at the honour conferred by the new warrant, and the other petitioning for a reversion to the former system, and stating that, "Had Her Majesty been advised to preserve to the Company its ancient elective privilege, many modifications in the present system would have been willingly agreed to." Prince Albert, in reply to this, expressed his regret and surprise at the tone of the whole address, and stated that "It would become a matter for the consideration of Her Majesty's Government how far they would permit the existence in the heart of London of an armed body entirely free from the established rules of discipline, or power of enforcing it, and without which—as embodied in the Mutiny Act—the constitution of this country does not sanction the maintenance of an armed force even by the Sovereign."—(*Woolmer Williams*.)

The election of a new Court in 1850 put an end to the *impasse*, fifteen of the opponents of the Royal Warrant being replaced by an equal number "pledged to give a loyal support to the military authorities."

A troop of Horse Artillery was formed in 1860, and the Light Cavalry in 1863; the former, however, was discontinued in 1869. It had, however, attained a high degree of excellence, as the following account of the Easter Review held in 1863 shows.

"All eyes were immediately directed with intense eagerness towards the course, and the first notes of a most lively air had scarcely died away before the horse troop of artillery, belonging to the Honourable Artillery Company, headed by Captain Jay, came up at a dashing pace. The men were well mounted, and in an evident cue to follow their leader at whatever pace he liked to take them. Each of their guns was drawn by four horses, which are kept specially, and used only for 'gun-work,' and better horses for the purpose were never chosen or employed in the service of 'The Royal Horse.' From a gentle canter they gradually increased their pace till it reached a racing gallop, when no little anxiety was manifested for the safety of the amateur corps, from the knowledge that 'drivers' of artillery require long and continuous practice before they can skilfully manage their difficult and dangerous duty. Confidence was, however, soon restored to the over-anxious spectators, and cries of 'Bravo, bravo, Honourable Artillery Company!' reiterated on all sides as they witnessed the 'gallop past,' not only unattended with any kind of mishap whatever, but proving itself a triumph of volunteer skill in the science of horse artillery, and an earnest testimony to the pluck of English gentlemen in the art of driving and riding, even though that driving be the very hazardous experiment to amateurs, of a heavy gun-carriage, with its ponderous accompaniment. The efficiency of Captain Jay's horse troop has been repeatedly tested at reviews, but on no occasion more successfully than on Easter Monday. The idea of such a troop first originated with the late Prince Consort, and in its progress and development His Royal Highness took a deep and sincere interest. The formation of it was entrusted to Captain Jay; and to his indefatigable perseverance in keeping the members punctual to their drill, and obedient to the able tuition of Mr. Reed, the riding master attached to the 2nd Regiment of Life Guards, and a picked sergeant of the Royal Artillery, is their present high character as volunteer horse artillery essentially due. The 9th Lancers followed them, but at a pace which was comparatively slow when contrasted with that at which the Honourable Artillery Company had led the way."

Several efforts have—as has before been said—from time to time been made by other military bodies, both regular and auxiliary, to obtain the right of user in the ground belonging to the Honourable Artillery Company, and in 1873 the most recent of these efforts culminated in the endeavour made by the City of London Volunteer Regiments, claiming as the representatives of the London Trained Bands, to obtain the joint use of the parade ground known as the Honourable Artillery Ground, to the enjoyment of which the Volunteers are undoubtedly entitled.

The Hon. Artillery Company declined to receive the letter of claim, despite the subsequent assurances of the Volunteers that they "did not intend to convey anything offensive," and the latter petitioned the Corporation of London for their assistance.* The Hon. Artillery Company then took the opinion of eminent counsel,† and submitted to them two questions, which, with the answers, are subjoined.

1. "Whether, having reference to the leases granted to the Company, the Volunteers have any right whatever to use the Artillery Ground?"

Answer.—"We are of opinion that the Volunteers have no such right."

2. "Whether the Artillery Company are entitled to the exclusive use of the ground, subject only to the rights of the Commissioners of Lieutenancy and Militia?"

Answer.—"We think that the Artillery Company are entitled to the exclusive use of the ground, subject only to the rights mentioned in the question."

From time to time questions had arisen as to the precedence of the Regiment; and at the Review held at Brighton in 1883 the Yeomanry claimed the right, as representing

---

* The Lord Mayor, Aldermen, Recorder, and Sheriffs are reminded in the petition that they are honorary members of the Court of Assistants of the Hon. Artillery Company.

† J. D. Coleridge and Charles Bowen.

a senior branch of the service, to march past before the Light Cavalry of the Company. The Duke of Cambridge decided the question *pro tem.* in favour of the Company, and in the following June the matter was set finally at rest by the promulgation of the following General Order:—" Her Majesty has been pleased to command that the Honourable Artillery Company shall, in consideration of its antiquity, take precedence after the Regular Forces."

One could wish that it were possible to close this notice of so ancient and distinguished a corps by the statement that in its government it is now as it has been for the best part of two hundred and fifty years. Unfortunately, however, circumstances of a comparatively recent date have in one important particular caused a break in the continuity of one distinguishing custom. Since 1660 till a few months ago the Company had been " commanded in an unbroken line by the Sovereign or the Heir-apparent;" now the space in the Army List which was formerly occupied by the name of H.R.H. the Prince of Wales as Captain-General is vacant. We do not propose to enter into the causes which led to so unfortunate a result; we would conclude in the words of its historian that, " A Regiment that can boast of having held the foremost rank as a Military Body in the reign of Henry VIII., of having had its members appointed by Queen Elizabeth to high commands over the forces at Tilbury, destined to repel the invasion of the Spanish, had they attempted a landing, indeed presents an existence of the very greatest possible interest, and no Society can show a Muster Roll of so many distinguished Noblemen, Men of Letters, and eminent Citizens, contemporaneous with its earlier existence, than the Honourable Artillery Company."

One of the foremost and most remarkable of the many privileges which the Honourable Artillery Company enjoys over and above all other military bodies in the empire is that of its being the only "military" body outside the control of Parliament, being entirely self-supporting, and existing only under the direct control of the Crown; and being thereby the only force that could be called out by the Sovereign without the consent of Parliament. In this way it may be more properly considered as a "body guard" to the Sovereign.

Though not coming within the limits assigned by the title Her Majesty's Army, it may not be out of place to refer very shortly to the fact that the Honourable Artillery Company has a daughter Association in the Ancient and Honourable Artillery Company of Massachusetts. In 1636 one Robert Keayne, a member of the Honourable Artillery Company of London, emigrated to America, and immediately organized an Artillery

Company on the lines of his old corps. This was joined by many who like himself could lay claim to the "Artillery Garden in Finsburie" as their *alma mater* in arms, and in 1638 the Company received a charter from the Governor. The late Prince Consort and H.R.H. the Prince of Wales are the only special Honorary Members ever constituted by the Ancient and Honourable Artillery Company.

The next branch of Her Majesty's Military Forces which calls for notice is the MILITIA—"the constitutional force for the defence of the realm."

"All to whom traditionary usage is dear—and the number is not limited, happily, in this country—must have an interest in maintaining the Militia as an important element in our scheme of national armaments. The Militia is the oldest of our military institutions. The obligation to take up arms to preserve the peace of the shire, or defend the realm against strange enemies, has from time immemorial been part of the statute law of the land. These forces were raised and marshalled by the deputies of the Crown—the lord-lieutenants of the counties—through whom all internal arrangements for the defence of the country were made. After the Restoration, the laws were revised, and the Militia established on a constitutional basis."

This epitome, gleamed from the work of a thoughtful writer on military matters,* gives in few words the definition of the force we are now dealing with.

From the nature of their constitution and the conditions of their service, it is evident that a description of the origin, growth, and organization of the Militia, though eminently interesting, must lack those incidents which lend fascination to the history of the regular army.

Far back in the record of the kingdom must the origin of this national force be looked for; in the forces arrayed against Danes and Northmen, in the army which fought stubbornly on the peaceful Sussex coast against the victorious conqueror, in the levies which in later days English kings summoned to their standards to guard against invasion—

> "That pale, that white-faced shore
> Whose foot spurns back the ocean's roaring tides,
> *   *   *   *   *   *
> That water-walled bulwark, still secure
> And confident from foreign purposes"—

fought, and fought right valiantly and Englishly, the predecessors of our Militia of to-day. Numerous statutes—commencing perhaps with one passed in the thirteenth

* Major Griffiths.

year of the first Edward—regulated and limited the liability of all able-bodied subjects to bear arms in defence of the kingdom. A glance at some of these will be of interest as showing, not only the growth of the Militia as a body, but as proving the unvarying recognition by the *people* of the advantage to the realm of keeping intact, within its constitutional limits, the Personal Prerogative of the Sovereign. The statute of Winchester (13 Edward I. c. 6), provided that every man should keep in his house "harness for to keep the peace after the antient assize"—the last two words indicating not obscurely the existence of a prior, though doubtless ruder, organization; it assigned a property qualification regulating the degree of defensive preparations required; and provided for a system of supervision to see that the enactment was duly complied with. In the first year of Edward III. another Act was passed limiting the service of the Militia to their own shires or counties, and, while disclaiming on the part of the king the right to compel any one to "bind themselves by writing to come to the king with force and arms whenever they should be sent for," asserted "that every man is bound to do to the king, as his liege lord, all that pertaineth to him without any manner of writing." The next important statutes were passed in the reign of Edward VI., and provided for the appointment of lord-lieutenants of counties, and imposed upon the inhabitants the duty on the occasion of "any commotion, rebellion, or unlawful assembly to give attendance upon the said lieutenant to suppress the same." This statute was in force during the reign of Elizabeth, and under its provisions the lord-lieutenants took order for the defence of the realm against the Spanish Armada; the defeat of which, be it remarked in passing, was, according to Clode, "the first service that called forth the gratitude of the country towards its soldiers."

When Charles II. was restored to his throne, Parliament, anxious, by consolidating the military power in the hands of the Sovereign, to avert the possibility of another rebellion, passed an Act under which the employment of the Militia was regulated for nearly a hundred years. This Act laid down what Clode rightly describes as "the great constitutional doctrine" embodied in the following words: "Forasmuch as within all His Majesty's realms and dominions, the sole, supreme government, command, and disposition of the MILITIA, and of all forces by sea and land, and of all forts and places of strength, is, and by the laws of England ever was, the undoubted right of His Majesty." By this Act the Militia of each county was placed under the command of a lieutenant, to be appointed by the Crown, and the composition of the force was recognised as including cavalry. During the reign of Charles II. the Whig party, as they would have been called in a later day, seem to have looked to the Militia as "a counterpoise to the standing army and a national security," and the Royal veto was called into exercise to prevent the proposed embodiment of the force as a warning to, and safeguard against, the then universally feared hobgoblin of "Popish practices."

This probably may account for the fact that the Militia were not at all times a *universally* popular force. Dryden was doubtless fickle enough in his political affections, but "glorious John" was as unlikely to embrace a cause which had not a fair following of supporters as he was himself to play the rôle of the—

"One still strong man in a blatant land."

His description of the Militia, though spiteful and undoubtedly inaccurate, may be taken as representing that of at least a section of the community:—

"And raw in fields the rude Militia swarms:
Mouths without hands, maintained at vast expense;
In peace a charge, in war a weak defence:
Stout once a month they march, a blustering band,
And ever, but in times of need, at hand."

A more accurate estimate is that given by Clode: "The value of the services of the Militia in times of national emergency cannot fairly be questioned. In the apprehension of greater dangers than those which hitherto have happened, and from which it is said that a standing army alone can protect the country, it must not be overlooked that during the last century two hostile descents were successfully made upon the coasts of Great Britain; but attended with very different results. In Scotland, where no National Militia then existed, the Pretender landed with a hundred men, and spread desolation into the centre of both kingdoms. In England, where the Militia and Volunteers had been organized, the French forces that attacked the coasts of Devon and Cornwall were the one routed and the other captured by the English local forces."

After the Revolution the Militia were frequently called out, as they were during the alarms of "the '15 and '45," and twelve years after the incursion of Prince Charles Edward their organization was fixed on the basis on which, to all intents and purposes, it now rests, a Bill, which had for its object the reducing of the Royal authority over the force, having in the meantime been brought in and defeated. "The Act of 1757," to take the epitome given by Perry, "abolished the liability of individuals to provide men in favour of a liability on the part of the county or parish. The men (between 18 and 50) were chosen by lot under the superintendence of lieutenants of counties, and had to serve three years or to provide a substitute." By this Act, "the Crown," writes Clode, "had given to it a more direct authority over the appointment of officers, as the names of the deputy-lieutenants were to be approved, and of the officers to be submitted for a twenty days' 'veto,' previously to their appointment. In addition, the Crown had the appointment of the adjutant and sergeants." The officers, except the adjutant, had to have a property qualification; the pay of the men when drawn out and embodied was to be the same as for soldiers of the line; the Crown had the power, under certain conditions, of embodying the Militia "in case of actual invasion, or upon imminent danger thereof, or in case of rebellion," in which case they were to be placed under general officers of the regular army. In the year 1786 the Militia Laws were consolidated by the Act 26 Geo. III., c. 107, which contained in its preamble these emphatic words—again to quote Clode : " A respectable military force, under the command of officers possessing landed property within Great Britain, is *essential* to the constitution of this realm, and the Militia, now by law established, has been found capable of fulfilling the purposes of its institution ; and through its constant readiness on short notice for effectual service has been of the utmost importance to the national defence of this Kingdom of Great Britain." In 1802 non-Protestants were rendered eligible, and subsequent enactments enable the "whole Militia force of the three kingdoms to be concentrated upon any point in one kingdom which the enemy may select for his attack." The Militia establishment for Ireland dates from 1715, and that for Scotland from 1797.

From time to time, as policy directed, the Militia were encouraged to volunteer in certain fixed proportions for the regular army, but this was at first jealously regulated. During the period of the Peninsular War, however, Mr. Pitt made the Militia the recruiting ground for the standing army, and subsequent enactments provided for a constant flow of militiamen into the ranks of the regulars. At the close of the long Peninsular War the Militia were disembodied, and from that time till 1852 may be said to have existed in a state of suspended animation, only the permanent staff remaining to preserve its existence. In 1852 the political sky, which had been clear since the stupendous thunder-clap of Waterloo, began to be overcast, and the Government of the day proceeded to reorganize the Militia. The distinguishing features of the new enactment were the enlarged power given to the Crown, the reduction of the property qualifications for officers, and the "greater encouragement for line officers on half-pay to serve in the Militia, and preference given to voluntary enlistment, with the right of exercising the ballot in case of necessity." "The establishment, or organization, government, and direction of the Militia formed the subject of inquiry by Royal Commissioners appointed in July, 1858, and their report was presented to Parliament early in the session of 1859. Such of their recommendations as were adopted by the Government, and needed statutory authority, were carried out by the 22 and 23 Vic., c. 38, and the 23 and 24 Vic., c. 94. The Militia also came under the notice of the Royal Commissioners appointed in May, 1866, to inquire into recruiting the Regular Army. Their report was made in October of the same year, and presented to Parliament in the session of 1867. After showing that the sources of supply from the Army would form but a small reserve force, their report proceeds thus:—'We are of opinion that it is to our Militia we must look for the solid and constitutional reserve of the country, and we would earnestly recommend that more attention should be given to its organization; that its numbers should be maintained up to the full legal quota; and that, so far as is possible, the period for drilling the recruits should be more extended.'"

In 1870 the command of the Militia was transferred to the Crown from the lieutenants of counties, and the Militia as a body form an integral part of the Infantry Brigades. They still remain only liable to home service, but the Militia Reserve—composed of men who volunteer for this service—may be required to serve abroad in case of war. The age at which recruits are accepted is from seventeen to thirty-five and the term of service is six years. The age for those who re-enlist is up till forty-five.

The foregoing pages will have shown the *general* history of the Militia Force; there are not wanting, however, more detailed histories of individual regiments to which we shall shortly refer.

The embodied services of the Militia, since its establishment in 1757, are thus summarised by the author before quoted: "The first occasion was immediately after its formation when, during the Seven Years' War, it was embodied against invasion. The second instance was during the American War, when, in 1778, France entered into treaty with America; this was also against invasion, and the force remained embodied till 3rd March, 1783. The third time was for the suppression of insurrection and rebellion, succeeded by the threat of invasion. The proclamation of embodiment was issued in December, 1792, and of disembodiment in April, 1803. The fourth occasion was in 1803, upon the apprehension of a descent upon the coast by the Emperor Napoleon. The fifth time was in 1815, under the authority of the 55 Geo. III.,

c. 77. The sixth instance was during the Crimean War, under the authority of 17 Vic., c. 13. The last instance was during the Indian Mutiny, under the sanction of the 20 and 21 Vic., c. 82."

To these may perhaps be added the subsequent occasions when it has become necessary, in the interests of peace, to be prepared for war, and when, though not embodied, many of the Militia regiments volunteered for foreign service.

The Artillery Militia dates from 1853,* but many of the brigades had before that date been in existence as infantry.

The Artillery Militia consists of thirty-nine brigades attached to the artillery divisions. The *precedence* of Artillery Militia Brigades is now regulated by the Divisional system, previously to which the order was settled by ballot. The dates and figures following are taken from the compilations made by Major Raikes and Mr. Perry.

Attached to the Eastern Division are:—
    The Kent Artillery Militia, 1798 (18).†
    The Prince of Wales's Own Norfolk Artillery Militia, 1798 (22).
    The Suffolk Artillery Militia, 1759 (25).
    The Royal Sussex Artillery Militia, 1798 (26).

To the Southern Division:—
    The Antrim Artillery Militia, 1854 (1).
    The Haddington Artillery Militia, 1855 (3).
    The West Cork Artillery Militia, 1854 (4).
    The Royal Cork City Artillery Militia, 1793 (5).
    The Donegal Artillery Militia, 1854 (8).
    The Dublin City Artillery Militia, 1854 (9).
    The Duke of Edinburgh's Own Edinburgh Artillery Militia, 1854 (11).
    The Fife Artillery Militia, 1798 (12).
    The Forfar and Kincardine Artillery Militia, 1798 (13).
    The Hampshire Artillery Militia, 1853 (16).
    The Duke of Connaught's Own Isle of Wight Artillery Militia, 1778 (17).
    The Royal Lancashire Artillery Militia, 1853 (19).

---

* "Cumberland and Fife had been represented in 1808 by small artillery corps."—*Perry.*

† The first Brigade is always composed of Royal Artillery. The Militia Brigades rank after in the order given. The dates are those of their respective formations, and the figures in parentheses indicate the precedence each brigade formerly held.

The Limerick City Artillery Militia, 1793 (20).

The Mid-Ulster Artillery Militia, 1854 (21).

The 1st or Tipperary Artillery Militia 1793 (27).

The Waterford Artillery Militia, 1793 (29).

The Argyll and Bute Artillery Militia, 1798 (30).

The Wicklow Artillery Militia, 1793 (33).

The Duke of Connaught's Own Sligo Artillery Militia, 1793 (34).

The Londonderry Artillery Militia, 1793 (21).

The Clare Artillery Militia, 1793.*

To the Western Division :—

The Royal Cornwall and Devon Miners' Artillery Militia, 1798 (6).

The Devon Artillery Militia, 1759 (7).

The Durham Artillery Militia, 1853 (10).

The Royal Glamorgan Artillery Militia, 1854 (15).

The Northumberland Artillery Militia, 1798 (23).

The Royal Carmarthen Artillery Militia, 1759 (24).

The Royal Pembroke Artillery Militia, 1759 (24).

The Yorkshire Artillery Militia, 1860 (31).

The Royal Cardigan Artillery Militia, 1854 (32).

Each of the Channel Islands has a regiment of Artillery.

It will be impossible in the space at our disposal to do more than glance briefly at some of the more interesting features connected with a few of the regiments of Militia. Regarded as a *whole*, the history of the auxiliary forces of the Crown is one replete with interest to all, but the history of individual regiments has of necessity, except in one or two instances, nothing which appeals to the general reader. It must not, therefore, be thought that the non-mention of a regiment implies that it is of less worth than another, but merely that its records, though eloquent, in the vast majority of cases, of steady work and praiseworthy zeal, are not of sufficient general interest to call for notice. Even in the case of regiments which have "seen service," so far as the expression is applicable to the Force, there is necessarily but a sameness of incident, which—were the writer to narrate in full—would provoke the deserved reminder *ab uno disce omnes*.

* Infantry till 1881.

The KENT ARTILLERY MILITIA, formed as above stated in 1798, were embodied in 1803, and were employed "in the capacity of gunners," two companies being detached to Forts Moncrieff and Sutherland, near Hythe, while the remainder were stationed at Dungeness. The time was one of intense excitement, "the English Ambassador had been insulted in the Tuileries, and English blood—plebeian or patrician—boiled at the insult. Against the expected invasion, the gallant East Kent were arrayed as auxiliaries to the Royal Artillery, and as such received commendations." They were inspected by Sir John Moore, who in the general orders issued to officers commanding forts, gave them some advice, needful for amateurs, but which certainly would not have been given had not the gallant general known that the men he was addressing were of "the stuff from which the finest soldiers in the world are made." They were cautioned against careless firing, and reminded that it is at close quarters their fire would have the greatest effect, and that it is only then that a brave enemy will be defeated. "The officers and men of the East Kent," goes on Sir John Moore, "will I trust recollect this, and not think of abandoning their guns, or of retiring until absolutely forced."

The regiment continued embodied till the termination of the war, and their next embodiment of importance was during the Crimean War, when they served on garrison duty at Malta. It is added in the records of the regiment that such was their good conduct and high state of discipline, that the commandant at Woolwich, where they had been stationed previously to their embarkation, "specially requested that the East Kent Militia might be again stationed there on their return from Malta."

To take almost at haphazard another regiment of artillery—this time from the Southern Division—we find that as early as June, 1685, "our Sovereign Lord, with the consent of his estate of Parliament, directed that the Militia Rendezvous for the counties of Haddington, Berwick, Linlithgow, and Peebles," should be discharged. The Militia regiment for the "shire of Haddington" was reassembled four years later, but this date must not be taken as the earliest record of the force now known as the HADDINGTON ARTILLERY MILITIA. As its present commanding officer * well observes, to decide with any definitiveness on the early history of any military force in this country involves a more than slight acquaintance with the history and methods of the several nationalities which have combined to create England: the Roman system, the Saxon system, and the Feudal system—each renders its quota to the composition of Her Majesty's army of to-day; and, accordingly, the origin of the Haddington Militia, like

* Colonel Dawson.

that of most similar regiments, must probably be sought for at a far earlier date than that for which strict evidence can be found. Colonel Dawson's is a valuable suggestion towards the classification of the Militia. He thinks that to the Roman system we are indebted for many of the characteristics of the Force as now established; the Saxon system supplied the *fencible* element, which is so essential a part of it; while to the Feudal system we owe the Territorial influence which, less perhaps in the Militia than in the Yeomanry and some disbanded forces of volunteers, was as good and valuable as its existence was apparent.

To resume, however, our sketch of the Haddington Artillery, we find, passing over the intervening years, that in 1802, in accordance with an order to that effect, the Militia force to be contributed by the four localities above mentioned was to be named the Berwickshire, or 1st Regiment of British Militia, and the Earl of Home was appointed Colonel. The following year the regiment was embodied, and mustered seven companies, shortly afterwards increased to eight. Colours were presented in August of the same year, and, after serving in various quarters, and contributing largely to the regular army, the regiment was disbanded at Coldstream in the summer of 1814, being re-embodied the following year for a few months. In 1854 a Royal Warrant was issued constituting the regiment Artillery, and the following year, in consequence of the Crimean War, it was embodied under the title of the Haddington Artillery Regiment of Militia. It was disembodied in 1856, was augmented by two additional batteries in 1874, and in 1882 became the 2nd Brigade (Scottish Division) Royal Artillery. In 1885 the brigade proceeded to Portsmouth, where it arrived *forty-seven hours after the first roll-call had been made;* and it is satisfactory to state that the highest praise was credited to it for its "highly satisfactory training, and for the particularly smart way the brigade disembarked and embarked at Portsmouth."

In September of the present year the brigade was designated the Haddington Artillery of the Southern Division Royal Artillery.

Raised in 1853 by Colonel Sir Duncan McDougall, formerly in command of the 93rd Highlanders, the Royal Lancashire Artillery Militia held its first annual training in October, 1853. The war with Russia led to its being embodied in January, 1855, when the headquarters were stationed at the North Fort, Liverpool, with detachments at Chester, Carlisle, and Tynemouth. On the outbreak of the Indian Mutiny, the duty devolved upon the Royal Lancashire Artillery Militia of garrisoning the forts on the south-east coast from Dover to Portsmouth, replacing those batteries of the Royal

Artillery which had been ordered to India. The regiment was afterwards ordered to Kinsale, Ireland, and returned to Liverpool in June, 1860, to be disembodied.

Another typical regiment of Artillery Militia is the Royal Pembroke Artillery, belonging to the Western Division; another is the Limerick City Artillery, also belonging to the Southern Division. The following extract from "Distinguished Regiments of Militia" gives an accurate account of the services rendered by this latter regiment, whose career, subsequent to the close of the Crimean War, presents no features of sufficient interest to merit particular mention here:—

"LIMERICK CITY ARTILLERY.—This regiment distinguished itself in 1798. A body of French troops under General Humbert landed at Killala Bay, where they were joined by a large number of rebels, and marched on Castlebar, where he put to flight a superior force of the king's troops, and the battle was called in derision, 'The Races of Castlebar.' General Humbert then pushed on to Sligo with upwards of 5,000 men; the town was garrisoned by the Limerick City Militia, commanded by the second Viscount Gort, then Colonel Vereker, and a troop of Dragoons. The Colonel marched out at the first alarm with 400 of his men and about thirty Dragoons, and took up his position in a defile at Coloony, about five miles from the town, where the French were repulsed and afterwards fell into the hands of Marquis Cornwallis. The Limerick Militia lost about twenty-seven killed and forty wounded, and the French and rebels about twice that number. The engagement took place on the 5th September, 1798, and lasted four hours; the colonel, one captain, and one lieutenant, were wounded, and one lieutenant and one ensign killed. The regiment received the thanks of Parliament; the colonel got an honourable augmentation to his arms, with the motto 'Coloony'; and medals were struck and presented by the Corporation of Limerick to those engaged. Volunteered for foreign service 9th April, 1855."

The SLIGO ARTILLERY, South Division, was formerly known as the Sligo Rifles, Duke of Connaught's Own, and the date of its formation is given as 1793. Like many other Militia regiments, however, there are traces more or less distinct of a much earlier existence. It would appear that it was originally known as the 22nd Light Infantry, and an old painting, now in the possession of Colonel Wood Martin * of the regiment,

---

* It is interesting to note, as evidencing the traditional connection of local families with the Militia, that the portrait in question, date *circa* 1756, is that of an ancestor of Colonel Wood Martin, to whom the writer is indebted for much interesting information respecting the regiment.

shows the uniform as having been red, with yellow facings, white lappets to coat, and the three-cornered hat familiar to us from old-world prints. "The Sligoes," as they were then called, were embodied during the Peninsular War, and acquitted themselves with marked courage at the battle of Vinegar Hill, Colonel King and two officers besides several rank and file, being wounded and others killed. It is somewhat strange that a regiment which had given such undeniable proofs of courage as had "the Sligoes," should have regarded with so much distaste service with the regular army, but that this was so may presumably be gathered from a report of a court-martial of the period, by which the punishment awarded to the culprit was that he should "join the regular army." During the Crimean War "the regiment suddenly appears" as the 124th Regiment, or Sligo Rifles, and some years later was "compulsorily transformed" into an Artillery Brigade, and known as the 8th Brigade (Duke of Connaught's Own) North Irish Division, Royal Artillery.

The CORNWALL AND DEVON MINERS ARTILLERY has a long record of steady service, though the details do not present any features of particular interest. It is recorded that "on the inspection of the regiment at Portsmouth by Major-General Whitewicke in 1800, he found that the accoutrements differed from those of all other regiments, the men wearing no cross-belts but waist-belts instead."

The work above quoted gives the following sketch of the ROYAL PEMBROKE ARTILLERY:—"This regiment was first embodied on the 2nd January, 1793. They volunteered for service in Ireland, and embarked on the 6th April, 1799; they also volunteered in 1808 to be attached to the 43rd Foot, to serve in the Peninsula under General Moore, for which they received the thanks of the King (George III.). On the 30th March, 1810, they were made a Light Infantry regiment, and, on the 17th July, 1811, a Rifle regiment; on the 8th September following they embarked for Ireland, where they had volunteered to serve. They last volunteered for foreign service at the time of the Indian Mutiny, on the 19th July, 1858."

Two regiments of Artillery Militia—the EDINBURGH and the ISLE OF WIGHT—have, as honorary colonels, princes of the blood, the Duke of Edinburgh commanding the former and the Duke of Connaught the latter. The CHANNEL ISLANDS ARTILLERY have a natural claim to the credit embodied in the distinction "Jersey," commemorative of the abortive French invasion in 1781. Amongst the regiments which volunteered for foreign service on the occasion of the Crimean War and the Indian Mutiny may be mentioned the 1st or SOUTH TIPPERARY ARTILLERY, while they, as well as the ROYAL PEMBROKE ARTILLERY, the LANCASHIRE ARTILLERY, the LONDON ARTILLERY, and the DONEGAL ARTILLERY, also volunteered for foreign service during the latter.

The Engineer Militia consist of the ROYAL ANGLESEA and the ROYAL MONMOUTHSHIRE, the latter county having the precedence. This corps constitutes the Fortress Forces of the Royal Engineers, having their headquarters at Beaumaris and Monmouth respectively. The Royal Anglesea includes the Carnarvon and Merioneth subdivisions, and the Royal Monmouthshire the Glamorgan and Brecon counties.

Another very important branch of Engineering is that of the Submarine Miners, of which there are six Militia divisions—the Portsmouth, the Plymouth, the Thames and Medway, the Harwich, the Milford Haven, and South Wales and Severn. The Anglesea and Monmouth corps date from 1775 and 1760 respectively, and were transformed into Engineer Militia in 1877; the Portsmouth Division dates from 1878 and the others from 1886. The uniform of the Engineer Militia resembles that of the regular force, with the exception of the shoulder straps, which are blue, edged with yellow, and have metal letters M.R.E.

We now come to the great bulk of the Militia force—the Infantry. In England and Wales there are 101 Militia battalions, in Scotland 13, and in Ireland 26. The distinctive titles of the Militia regiments—many of which, as has been before noticed, have a lineage reaching back into the earliest periods of the history of the country—have, since the adoption of the Territorial system, been lost, and they are now known as the 3rd, 4th, &c., battalions of the Territorial regiments to which they are affiliated. It would be an interesting, though perhaps a somewhat monotonous task, to take each Militia battalion *seriatim* and give in full all the details of dates, embodiments, trainings, and changes of command which have occurred since its establishment on its present basis. But for these details, which would be valued by those professionally interested we must refer to other sources. The scope of the present work will only permit of a very short summary being given, except in one or two cases, of the history of the regiment. We shall take them in the order of the Territorial regiments to which they belong.

The 3rd Battalion of the Royal Scots Lothian Regiment consists of the Edinburgh or Queen's Regiment of Light Infantry Militia, whose order of precedence under the ballot before referred to was 126.

The EDINBURGH or QUEEN'S REGIMENT of LIGHT INFANTRY MILITIA, now the 3rd Battalion of the Royal Scots, originated in the 10th or Edinburgh North British Regiment of Militia raised in 1798, though the regimental historian, Major Dudgeon, traces the probable lineage to a much earlier date. They were disbanded in 1802 after a service which had gained them the warmest praise from the authorities. The next period of embodiment was from 1803 to 1815, during which time they performed with the same *éclat* the various duties—guarding of prisoners, suppression of smuggling, and the like—which fell to their lot, and contributed to the regular army 833 men. The Crimean War brought another occasion for the calling out of the Militia, and in 1856, on the occasion of the visit of Her Majesty to Holyrood, the regiment received the title of the Queen's Regiment of Light Infantry Militia.

The badges worn on the forage cap and glengarries, as well as the star on the helmet plate of the Territorial Regiment, are derived from the Edinburgh Light Infantry.

The 2nd ROYAL SURREY MILITIA, the 3rd Battalion of the "Queen's," dates from 1759. Their history presents an unbroken record of steady work, which from time to time has been duly acknowledged by those in command. In 1803, on the occasion of the review by the Duke of York, then commander-in-chief, held at Ashford, the 2nd Royal Surrey Militia received the gratifying praise of being declared in a "higher state of efficiency than any other regiment inspected by his Royal Highness on that occasion," and the badge of a star, similar to that worn by the Coldstream Guards, was granted in recognition thereof.

The EAST KENT MILITIA, now the 3rd Battalion of the "Buffs," dates from 1778, and ranked 49th in precedence. They are one of the regiments which, at the time of the Crimean War, were employed on Mediterranean stations and bear the distinction "Mediterranean" on their colours. They bore the 'White Horse,' and the mottos *Invicta* and *Nec aspera terrent*, the former of which has been adopted by the Territorial regiments.

The 1st ROYAL LANCASHIRE MILITIA, now constituting the 3rd and 4th Battalions of the King's Own (Royal Lancaster Regiment), date from 1760 and 45th in precedence. In 1804 they volunteered for service in Ireland and were granted the badges of the Harp and Crown in recognition of their patriotism. The Territorial regiment owes the rose borne on their accoutrements to the Militia battalions. The 1st Royal Lancashire Battalion are also amongst the regiments entitled to bear "Mediterranean" on their colours for their services during the Crimean War.

The Lancashire Militia may be considered a typical representative regiment, and the painstaking researches by Colonel Lawson Whalley into its history enable us to give somewhat fuller details. We find an honourable incident connected with it so early as 1642, when King Charles I. summoned to his headquarters at York Colonel and Captain Ffarington, both officers of the regiment. The latter subsequently took an active part in the defence of Lathom House, and " was named by Charles II. 'Knight of the Royal Oak.'" It does not appear what part the regiment took in the Revolution, but in 1690 we find them actively employed under King William III. in his Irish campaign, fighting at Carrickfergus, the Boyne, and Athlone. At the time of the Jacobite rising of 1715 the Lancashire Militia fought at Preston, losing no fewer than eleven officers and a hundred and five rank and file. They were again actively employed in "the '45," when the Lancaster Company, as part of the regiment of volunteers called the Liverpool Blues, had several engagements with the enemy, and were present at the capitulation of Carlisle.

In the year 1759 they were again embodied, and two years later, having formed a guard of honour to receive the Princess Charlotte, received from the King new colours, his Majesty also directing that "the regiment for the future should be termed 'His Majesty's Royal Regiment of Lancashire Militia,' and that the Colonel's Company should be called the 'King's Company.'" The regiment was again embodied from 1778 to 1783; and in 1794, on the occasion of a Brighton review, supplied, by special order, the body-guard to the King. After service in various parts of England, the Lancashire Militia, in 1798, volunteered for Ireland, and the following year were remarkable for the great number that volunteered into the line, Captain Williamson, two officers, and the whole of his company joining the 36th Foot. Later on, in the same year, they were ordered to be called the 1st Royal Lancashire Militia. They were again embodied in 1803, and received the order to wear the Red Rose of Lancaster on their colours. In 1811 they were employed in the suppression of the Luddite Riots at Nottingham, and in 1814 volunteered for Ireland, where they remained till March, 1816. In 1831 the title of the regiment was altered to "The Duke of Lancaster's Own," and for many years—not, indeed, till 1852—they were not called out. At the time of the Crimean War they volunteered for foreign service, and were quartered at Fano, Paxe, Santa Maura, and neighbouring places, in recognition whereof they bear the above-named distinction on their colours. They again volunteered to serve abroad in 1876—7, when the relations with Russia assumed a threatening aspect; an offer which was again made during the Egyptian complications of 1882, and which obtained for the commanding officer well-merited compliments for the promptitude displayed.

THE NORTHUMBERLAND MILITIA,* the 3rd Battalion of the Northumberland Fusiliers, is fortunate in having not merely a long and honourable career, but powerful patronage and a capable historian.† Far back in old feudal times we come across mention of the progenitors of the Northumberland Militia of to-day. Alnwick, their present headquarters, held its own bravely amongst the princedoms of the realm, boasting an army of over 3,000 men, and the old song of Percy told as well the doings of those noble chiefs as of the—

"Knyghts and squyers and chosen yeomanry,
And archers fine withouten raskaldry,"

who fought with them. They harried the Scots, grieved sore when on Shrewsbury Plain the terrible tidings spread apace, "Young Harry Percy's spur is cold;" were amongst the warriors who fought so well yet fruitlessly at Hedgeley Moor, when Ralph Percy—he whose dying vaunt, "I have kept the bird in my bosom," rings yet in the hearts and ears of gentlemen whether noble or simple; and held their own through all the wild times that lingered later in Northumberland than perhaps in any other part of England.

The present regiment was raised in 1759, when the Earl of Northumberland held the rank of Brigadier-General, the uniform being scarlet with buff facings, and the Colonel, Sir Edward Blackett. The first few years of their existence were passed in the usual duties devolving upon militia regiments. They were disembodied, served their annual trainings, and took part in many loyal and political feastings and rejoicings. In 1778, when war with France seemed imminent, the regiment was embodied under Lord Algernon Percy as Colonel, and in 1780, were ordered to London. Their services during the Gordon Riots are historical, their principal stations being in Lincoln's Inn and the Temple, after which they went to Dorking. The papers of the period referred on several occasions to the invaluable services of Lord Algernon Percy and the Northumberland Militia, who "behaved in such a manner as to gain the applause of all." The inhabitants of the localities which their courage and promptitude saved from destruction were not backward in giving substantial proof of their gratitude—with one exception, as extraordinary as reprehensible. "The great fears and apprehensions which the inhabitants suffered were owing to the office of the Sheriff of Middlesex being situate in Took's Court, which office was violently threatened by the rioters; yet it is wonderful that neither the

* The Northumberland Militia (3rd Battalion Northumberland Fusiliers) used to bear the badge of a Castle with the motto *Libertas et navale solum*.
† Major Adamson, late 3rd Battalion Northumberland Fusiliers.

Sheriff, Under-Sheriff, or his Deputy subscribed a single shilling for the benefit of the poor soldiers, who, after a very harassing and fatiguing march,* were immediately employed to protect this office and the neighbouring inhabitants from danger."—(*Morning Chronicle and London Advertiser*, 19th June, 1780, quoted by Major Adamson.) After sojourning at Southampton and Chatham, they were disembodied in 1782, being re-embodied two years later. They were stationed at various places in England, and when at Hornsea Camp, in Yorkshire, were noticeable as being collectively and individually the biggest regiment present, numbering about 1,300 men, occupying more room when drawn up in line, and the individuals requiring more cloth for their uniforms "than for almost any other regiment of equal number." In 1799, 266 privates joined the regular army, and, three years later, the regiment was disembodied after more than nine years' actual service.

They were again embodied in 1803, and in 1805 we hear of them passing over Blackfriars Bridge, with advance and rear guards, and attended by an excellent band of music. "They were in high spirits and seemed about 1,000 strong, and a finer regiment cannot be conceived." On several occasions the regiment had expressed their willingness to serve in Ireland, and in 1811 the offer was accepted, and, as a mark of distinction, they were made Light Infantry. They remained two years in Ireland, and on their return to Newcastle received a veritable ovation from the townsmen. In 1814, after eleven years' service, they were disembodied, having during the term received more praise and commendation than often falls to the lot of any regiment, however distinguished, and having during the fifteen years between 1799 and 1814 contributed no fewer than 1,532 volunteers to the regular army. In 1855 they were again embodied, and during the Crimean War contributed 400 officers and men to Sebastopol. They were disembodied in May, 1856, and since that date, beyond keeping up their well-known efficiency during the annual training, no event of note has occurred to the Northumberland Militia, who in 1882 became the 3rd Battalion of the Northumberland Fusiliers.

The 1st and 2nd WARWICK MILITIA, now respectively the 3rd and 4th Battalions Royal Warwickshire Regiment, date from 1759, and ranked 36th and 53rd in precedence. From its Militia battalions the Territorial regiment derives the cognisance of the Bear and Ragged Staff.

The ROYAL WESTMINSTER MILITIA, the 3rd Battalion of the Royal Fusiliers, City of

---

* They had marched the day of their arrival nearly forty miles, and were *instantly* despatched to the scene of danger.

London Regiment, date from 1797, and ranked 5th in precedence. They bear the distinction "Mediterranean" on their colours, having been one of the regiments employed there during the Crimean War.

The Warwick Militia was raised before the peace of 1763. During the mutiny at the Nore, 1797, a portion of the regiment did duty on board the *Standard* man-of-war, and was one of the first of the English Militia to volunteer for duty in Ireland during the rebellion of 1798. Four hundred of them formed part of the army under Lord Cornwallis which marched against the French. The following letter bears gratifying testimony to their conduct on that occasion.

"Dublin Castle, 17th December, 1798.

"My Lord,

"I have received, through the Duke of Portland, the King's most Gracious Commands to signify to you the high sense which his Majesty will always entertain of the meritorious and distinguished services of the Officers and Men of the Warwickshire Regiment of Militia under your Lordship's command, and that it is His Royal Pleasure that you do take the earliest opportunity of acquainting them that His Majesty will ever retain the most grateful remembrance of the Zeal and Liberality with which they have sacrificed their domestic comforts for the protection of their fellow-subjects and the General Interests of the Empire.

"I have the honour to be, My Lord,

"Your Lordship's Most Obedient, Humble Servant,

"Colonel, (Signed) "Cornwallis.

"The Marquis of Hertford, &c., &c.

"Warwick Militia."

In September, 1811, the Warwick Militia again served in Ireland, where they remained till the beginning of 1813.

In 1852, when the ballot was suspended and the raising of the Militia by voluntary enlistment was enacted, the regiment was designated the 1st Regiment of Warwickshire Militia, as a second regiment was raised in that year and named the 2nd Regiment of Warwickshire Militia, to which this corps gave upwards of 300 volunteers.

For their service during embodiment at the time of the Crimean War, the regiment was voted the thanks of Parliament.

The ROYAL LONDON MILITIA, the 4th Battalion of the Royal Fusiliers, date from 1796, and ranked 106th in precedence. To their 4th Battalion the Royal Fusiliers owe their second or complementary title of the City of London Regiment. The name of the regiment in itself well-nigh supplies a history; one of these regiments claiming descent from the Trained Bands of the city, the Royal London Militia can boast of a long lineage and a fair fame. Local histories, and, incidentally, the history of the Honourable Artillery Company of London, before referred to, give in considerable, though scattered detail, the narrative of this typical "constitutional force."

The ROYAL SOUTH MIDDLESEX MILITIA, the 5th Battalion of the Royal Fusiliers, date from 1797, and ranked 128th in precedence. Like the linked battalion just referred to, their history embodies some of the most interesting epochs in the chronicles of London.

The 2nd ROYAL LANCASHIRE MILITIA, now constituting the 3rd and 4th Battalions of the King's (Liverpool Regiment), date from 1797. Their number of precedence was 113th. In common with all the Lancashire Militia, they have had considerable service from time to time in support of the Civil Power, and have received marked encomiums for the manner in which they have performed the duties—often ungrateful—which have come in their way.

The 1st and 2nd NORFOLK MILITIA, now respectively the 3rd and 4th Battalions of the Norfolk Regiment, date from 1759, and ranked 39th and 40th in order of precedence. From them the Territorial regiment derives the Castle in their badges.

The ROYAL NORTH LINCOLN MILITIA, 3rd Battalion Lincolnshire Regiment, date from 1759, and ranked 8th in precedence; the ROYAL SOUTH LINCOLN MILITIA, the 4th battalion, being raised at the same date and ranking 28th. The latter regiment was first embodied at Boston, served in the North of England during the Seven Years' War, and during the troublous times from 1790 to 1803 performed most useful duty—chiefly that of garrison—in Ireland, Scotland, and the Eastern Counties. From 1813 to 1816, Ireland was again their principal quarters, as it was subsequently during the Crimean War. The regiment "has always been one of the first to volunteer to be embodied in time of war," and South Lincolnshire—in which it is exclusively recruited, has every reason to be proud of the 4th battalion of its Territorial Regiment, to whose badges, by the way, the Militia battalions contribute the Star.

The 2nd and 1st DEVON MILITIA constitute respectively the 3rd and 4th Battalions of the Devonshire Regiment, and date from 1759. The former, which ranked 25th in precedence, used to have as a badge a Lion Rampant, which was lost on the recent change.

The 1st or 4th Battalion ranked 41st in precedence, and supplied the "Castle of Exeter" to the badges of the Territorial Regiment.

The WEST SUFFOLK MILITIA and the CAMBRIDGE MILITIA now form the 3rd and 4th Battalions of the Suffolk Regiment. They date from 1795 and 1778 respectively, and ranked 10th and 68th.

The 1st and 2nd SOMERSET MILITIA, constituting the 3rd and 4th Battalions of the Prince Albert's (Somersetshire Light Infantry), date from 1759, and ranked 16th and 47th respectively. Previous to the absorption into the Territorial Regiment, the 1st Somerset Militia used to bear as a badge the Crest of Monmouth, with the Motto *Defendimur*.

The 2nd and 4th WEST YORK MILITIA, forming the 3rd and 4th Battalions of the Prince of Wales's Own (Yorkshire Regiment), date from 1759 and 1798 respectively, and were numbered 21st and 133rd. Of the former it is recorded that during the Gordon Riots in 1780 they were stationed at the British Museum, to protect it from the rioters. In 1797 they manned the batteries at Sheerness during the mutiny of the fleet, and a detachment of the regiment brought Richard Parker a prisoner from the *Sandwich*. They served in Ireland at the time of the riots in 1798—9, and again in 1814, 1815, and 1816, and volunteered for foreign service on the 19th January, 1855, and were sent to the Mediterranean, the name of which they bear as a distinction.

The order for the formation of the 4th West York Militia was received at Leeds on 5th April, 1853, the establishment to be as follows, under the command of Lieutenant-Colonel Lord Beaumont, viz., ten companies, consisting of 81 officers, sergeants, and drummers, 1,070 rank and file.

The regiment was embodied in January, 1855, under Lieutenant-Colonel the Hon. N. H. Massey, and did duty at Bradford and Hull until May, 1856, when it was disembodied at the headquarters, Leeds.

In 1875 H.R.H. the Duke of Edinburgh visited Leeds for the purpose of opening an exhibition of art, &c., on which occasion the regiment took part in the proceedings and was highly commended for its steadiness and soldier-like appearance. In 1882 the regiment trained in barracks at York under its new Territorial title of the 4th Battalion of the Prince of Wales's Own (West Yorkshire) Regiment, and five years later His Royal Highness the Duke of Cambridge, at a review of the York Garrison, expressed himself in eulogistic terms with regard to the appearance and efficiency of the regiment.

The EAST YORKSHIRE MILITIA—one of the eight Yorkshire Regiments—is now the 3rd Battalion of the East Yorkshire Regiment, to which it gives the name. Dated from 1760 the East York ranked 12th in precedence, and had as badge the White Rose.

The BEDFORD MILITIA is the 3rd Battalion of the Bedfordshire Regiment and dates from 1763, its former rank being 18th. An exhaustive account of the regiment has been written by the late Sir J. M. Burgoyne, and will be valued by those to whom the detailed history of the regiment is of interest. On the recent change the regiment lost the distinctive Light Infantry Bugle which it used to have as badge.

The HERTFORD MILITIA, dating from 1759, is the 4th Battalion of the Bedfordshire Regiment, and formerly ranked 30th in precedence. The post of Honorary Colonel is now occupied by the present Prime Minister.

The LEICESTERSHIRE MILITIA, the 3rd Battalion of the Leicestershire Regiment, date from 1760 and ranked 26th. On various occasions they rendered good service, and were granted the Harp and Crown in memory of their courage and discipline during the Irish troubles of 1798. They were among the regiments which volunteered for foreign service at the time of the Indian Mutiny.

The WEXFORD MILITIA, NORTH TIPPERARY MILITIA, and KILKENNY MILITIA, supply respectively the 3rd, 4th, and 5th Battalions of the Royal Irish Regiment. Of these the last named is the oldest, dating from 1793, while the Wexford, and North Tipperary, as at present constituted, were formed in 1855. The Irish Militia Regiments have been foremost in rendering such services as fall to the lot of the Force, and the Kilkenny Fusiliers took their part in the stirring events which, during the latter part of the last and early in the present century, crowded together in such quick succession in the Sister Isle.

The 5th YORK MILITIA and the NORTH YORK MILITIA supply in their turn the 3rd and 4th Battalions of the Princess of Wales's Own (Yorkshire Regiment). They date from 1853 and 1759 respectively, and had the numbers of precedence 4 and 22. The latter used to be a 'rifle' regiment, and the present is the third recorded uniform—the first being red with black facings, and the second assimilated to that of the Rifle Brigade. The 3rd battalion, it may be remarked, formerly had buff facings.

The 7th ROYAL LANCASHIRE MILITIA, now the 3rd Battalion of the Lancashire Fusiliers, was raised in 1855: the number of precedence being 130.

The ROYAL AYR and WIGTOWN MILITIA, now the 3rd Battalion Royal Scots Fusiliers, date from 1802, when they were formed "from the disembodied non-commissioned officers and men of the then Ayr and Renfrew, or 7th North British Militia, commanded by the

Earl of Glasgow." The first colonel was Archibald, Lord Montgomerie, who had formerly served in the Black Watch, and who held the command of the Ayrshire Militia—as the 3rd Battalion Royal Scots Fusiliers was then called—for five years. The facings of the regiment were buff, and colours were presented, on the year following their enrolment, by Lady Montgomerie. The Militia being called out in 1803, the Ayrshire were busily engaged on garrison duty, at Dundee, Edinburgh—where they kept guard over some French prisoners of war—Colchester, Chelmsford, Portsmouth and other places. In 1807 and the following years a considerable number 'extended their services' to the line, about eleven officers and seven hundred men joining the regular army between that date and the battle of Waterloo. The regiment returned to Scotland in the summer of 1809 and continued to be employed in garrison and guard duties. In 1813—following closely upon the recognition of their 'uniform zeal and good conduct' by the Commander-in-Chief and Lord Lieutenant, the regiment received the intimation that "His Royal Highness the Prince Regent was pleased to approve the Ayrshire Militia being styled His Royal Highness the Prince Regent's Royal Regiment of Ayrshire Militia, and to have blue facings."

Early in 1814 the regiment were ordered to Ireland, where their familiar task of garrison duty was diversified by a little excitement in the suppression of smuggling and illicit stills and in keeping the peace. They returned to Scotland in 1816, and in March of the same year were disembodied.

In 1854 the word "Rifles" was substituted for "Militia" in the title of the regiment, which was generally designated the Royal Ayrshire Rifles. In 1855 they were again embodied till the termination of the Crimean War, and remained in garrison at Ayr. In 1860 the Wigtownshire quota of the Galloway Rifles were amalgamated with the Royal Ayrshire Rifles, and in August of the same year the title of the regiment was again altered to the Royal Ayrshire Regiment of Militia Rifles, and the distinctive badge of the Thistle granted. Six years later another change was made: they became the Prince Regent's Royal Regiment of Ayr and Wigtown Militia, and the uniform was fixed at red with blue facings. In 1881 they became annexed to their present Territorial regiment, of which at first, however, they were the 4th battalion, the 3rd being the Scottish Borderers' Militia, since transferred to the King's Own Scottish Borderers. In July, 1889, new colours were presented to the regiment by the Countess of Stair.*

* For most of the information given above the author is indebted to the "Records of the Ayrshire Militia," which have been kindly placed at his disposal by their compiler, the Hon. Hew Dalrymple.

The 1st and 2nd ROYAL CHESHIRE MILITIA form the 3rd and 4th Battalions of the Cheshire Regiment and date from 1759 and 1797 respectively, their relative numbers of precedence being 6 and 103. To the former the Cheshire regiment of to-day owes the Prince of Wales's Plumes borne amongst their badges.

The DENBIGH AND MERIONETH and the CARNARVON MILITIA form the 3rd and 4th Battalions of one of the most famous of Her Majesty's army, the Royal Welsh Fusiliers. Raised in 1760 and 1778 respectively, we find the former, when as yet unidentified with its redoubtable line battalions, bearing as insignia the Red Dragon of Wales, while the latter bore, as the Carnarvon Rifles, the Bugle of all Rifle corps.

The ROYAL SOUTH WALES BORDERERS MILITIA and the ROYAL MONTGOMERY MILITIA form the 3rd and 4th Battalions of the South Wales Borderers. The former is composed of the Militia of the counties of Brecknockshire and Radnorshire, which were raised in 1760 and 1778 respectively; the latter, the Montgomery Militia, was raised in 1778, the order of precedence being 50th and 57th respectively.

The SCOTTISH BORDERERS MILITIA, now the 3rd Battalion of the King's Own Scottish Borderers, may be looked upon as a type of the famous Scotch Militia regiments, the doings of whose forerunners ring through the romantic history of the northern Kingdom. The regiment was raised in 1797 from recruits drawn from the localities of Dumfries, Kircudbright, Roxburgh, and Selkirk, and ranked 81st in order of precedence, and was amongst the regiments which volunteered for foreign service at the times of the Crimean War and Indian Mutiny.

The SECOND ROYAL LANARK MILITIA furnish the 3rd Battalion of the Cameronians (Scottish Rifles), and date from 1854.

The FERMANAGH MILITIA, the ROYAL TYRONE MILITIA, and the DONEGAL MILITIA constitute the 3rd, 4th, and 5th Battalions of the Royal Inniskilling Fusiliers. They all date from 1793, but the 4th Battalion, the Royal Tyrone Fusiliers, claim to be the oldest Fusilier Regiment of Militia in the United Kingdom, and the first regiment that mounted guard on Dublin Castle carrying the Union Jack. They have a special badge consisting of the Star of St. Patrick within a Union Wreath with a Crown over. They used, moreover, to boast the motto *Ut prodie*, which, however, was lost on the introduction of the Territorial system.

The Royal Tyrone Regiment of Fusiliers present some special features of interest. Their first embodiment dates from 1783, when they were granted the badge and motto still retained by them alone of all other regiments, whether regular or auxiliary. The former was the Star and Cross of St. Patrick with, in the centre, "Quis separabit" and "MDCCLXXXIII." Ten years later, on the second embodiment, the regiment received the title of "Royal" and the numerical precedence of the 2nd Tyrone Regiment of Militia, and in the Irish Rebellion of 1798 gained for themselves great distinction, fighting at Vinegar Hill, Naas, Kildare, Arklow, and numerous other places, and being frequently commended for their efficiency and steadiness in action. During the Peninsular War a large number of men volunteered into the line, and at Waterloo, where the 28th and 32nd Regiments fought so stubbornly and well, amongst their ranks might have been seen three hundred or more of the gallant Royal Tyrone men, who had had no time to exchange their Militia uniform for that of their new regiments.

During the Crimean War, no fewer than four hundred volunteered into the line, and it was during the continuance of that war that the regiment was named "Fusiliers," which title, as well as the prefix "Royal," they gave to the Territorial regiment on their amalgamation with the 27th and 108th Regiments of the line.

The list of commanding officers is a strong one, commencing with the Marquis of Abercorn, who held that position for fifteen years when the regiment was first raised. The present commander is Colonel Lewis Mansergh Buchanan, late Connaught Rangers, from whom we may quote the following interesting data:—

"The 4th Battalion of the Royal Inniskilling Fusiliers is the only regiment possessing a corps of Irish bagpipes, and is also singular among Militia regiments as having always worn the busby in full-dress. The present average height of the men is 5 feet $7\frac{4}{10}$ inches. In 1883 it attained the highest points in rifle practice yet reached by a Militia regiment."

The ROYAL SOUTH GLOUCESTER MILITIA, and the ROYAL NORTH GLOUCESTER MILITIA, constitute the 3rd and 4th Battalions of the Gloucestershire Regiment, and date from 1750 and 1761 respectively, being ranked as the 23rd and 69th in Militia precedence. The Royal South Gloucestershire were a Light Infantry regiment and bore the characteristic Bugle; the 4th Battalion, the Royal North Gloucestershire, were entitled to bear as badge the Royal Crest.

From the little that can be learnt of the history of the latter regiment prior to 1759 it would seem that at the time of the rebellion they sided with the Parliament, while at the Revolution their sympathies were loyal to King James. The introduction of the Militia Acts of 1759 was by no means popular in Gloucestershire, and some rioting took place, but the dissatisfaction was short-lived, and in 1761 "the North Gloucester Regiment of Militia was embodied as a Battalion of Fusiliers, and consisted of seven companies. The facings were blue, the lace gold, and remained so until 1805, when the lace was changed to silver." Their first duty seems to have been as guard over the French prisoners of war at Bideford, and during the period of embodiment from 1778 to 1782 they were engaged in garrison duty at various places. In 1793 they obtained the prefix of "Royal;" the King, who had had opportunities of noticing both the Gloucestershire regiments during his stay in Weymouth, having expressed himself as highly pleased with their soldier efficiency. In 1798 the regiment, which had ceased to be Fusiliers two years previously, volunteered for duty in Ireland, where, however, "they were not called upon for any active service in the field." But the service they did— that of garrisoning towns and keeping in awe the disaffected—was of sterling value, and amply merited the general praise which the regiment had received. In 1801 they were stationed at Dover. An invasion was hourly expected, and detachments were ordered to patrol the beach. While engaged in this duty one of the officers records that he could distinctly observe what was passing at Boulogne. "I could see the smoke of Nelson's bombardment, and hear the booming of the cannon." The regiment was disembodied in 1802, but the following year was re-embodied, and during their stay at Portsmouth were under the command of General Whitelock, whose name, four years later, became a by-word for his mismanagement at Buenos Ayres. During the Peninsular War they volunteered largely into the regular army, the favourite regiment, apparently, being the 9th. In 1811 the regiment was again in Ireland, and in 1813 two complete companies, officers and all, were supplied by the Royal North Gloucester to the line. The following year they were disbanded, and on the Royal North Gloucester, as on all Militia regiments, fell a deep sleep, from which they were only awakened in 1852. During the Crimean War they again supplied volunteers for the line, and in 1857—8 passed some months in Ireland. From that date to the present no incident has occurred which calls for notice.

The following is of interest as regards both battalions. A writer in the *Gentleman's Magazine*, speaking of the Norfolk Militia and quoting from a paper of the time, says that:—

"Their uniforms were very handsome and *genteel*, and it was *surprising* how soon they made themselves master of the exercise, and there was the greatest emulation among the men who should be most forward in their duty.

"July, 1759, the Norfolk Militia were reviewed at Kensington, where Mr. Woodhouse, a gentleman of the family of Lord Woodhouse, marched as a private militiaman, when they highly pleased thirty thousand spectators in Hyde Park. His Majesty seemed highly pleased with them, and the Guards received them with drums beating and colours flying. His Royal Highness the Prince of Wales, who was present at this review, fell in at Richmond with divisions of both battalions, and ordered each a bank note of £50. His Majesty condescended to pull off his hat to every officer."

The WORCESTER MILITIA, which supply the 3rd and 4th Battalions of the Worcestershire Regiment, date from 1778, and give to the badges of the regiment the cognisance of Worcester Castle.

The 5th ROYAL LANCASHIRE MILITIA form the 3rd Battalion of the East Lancashire Regiment, and, bearing in mind the numerous regiments of Militia furnished by the county, it may not be out of place to give a somewhat fuller sketch of its history.

The 5th Royal Lancashire Militia, now the 3rd Battalion East Lancashire Regiment, date from 1853. There had, however, been another regiment bearing the same designation, which was embodied in May, 1798. This first regiment was not a success: it was numerically weak, and this defect was remedied by admitting to its ranks a detachment of a hundred and twenty-three men from another regiment, who had declined to extend their service to Ireland. "Very few of them had hats, and ye whole had been plundered by their comrades in revenge for their refusal to embark for Ireland." The regiment altogether was a sore trial to its commander, Colonel Patten, who commented bitterly on "the very discreditable appearance of these men," adding, "out of 600 men, 136 were from ye —— Regiment, *having refused to go to Ireland*, and I did not expect much from them." This regiment was disbanded the following year. In 1853 the present regiment was formed, and was embodied during the Crimean War, receiving on its termination very high praise from the commanding officer of the division for their "excellent conduct" and "ready cheerfulness." The Brigade Order, indeed, was yet more emphatic. The Brigadier "does not think any regiment could have evinced a greater zeal, a stronger desire to improve, or a more willing obedience." From December, 1855, to May, 1856, the regiment was quartered in Ireland, and on its return home was disembodied in June of the latter year. Four years later, the 5th Royal Lancashire Militia were granted, as distinctive badges, the " Red Rose and Laurel Leaf on their appointments, and the Red Rose in gold on the forage cap." In 1881 the regiment received its present designation, and white and gold supplanted blue and silver in the facings and lace.

The 1st and 3rd ROYAL SURREY MILITIA form the 3rd and 4th Battalions respectively of the East Surrey Regiment. Raised in 1759 and 1798 respectively, the former contributes to the badges of the Territorial regiment the arms of Guildford, and the latter the Star.

The ROYAL CORNWALL RANGERS MILITIA.—The Royal Cornwall Rangers, the 3rd Battalion of the Duke of Cornwall's Light Infantry, date from 1760, and are one of the Militia regiments which give the title to the Territorial regiment with which they are linked. There does not seem a time when the regiment was not "Royal"; in 1799 the Army List referred to them as the Royal Cornwall Militia, and though the prefix appears for a time to have fallen into disuse it was resumed by authority in 1874. During the anxious years intervening between 1806—1811, the Royal Cornwall Militia were employed in the north of England and other places, earning the hearty commendation of the authorities. They were, too, the first Militia regiment which volunteered to extend their service to Ireland, receiving in recognition of their soldierly zeal the title of the Royal Cornwall Light Infantry. Two years they remained in Ireland, and on returning to England were disembodied in 1814. In 1831, on the request of Colonel Lord Valletort, King William constituted them a Rifle regiment, with the title of "The Duke of Cornwall's Rangers." Passing over the intervening years, during which their history was much the same as that of other Militia regiments, we come to 1875, when the present Hon. Colonel, H.R.H. the Prince of Wales, was appointed, and the regiment officially designated "The Royal Cornwall Rangers, Duke of Cornwall's Own." The distinctive character of a Rifle regiment was lost on the introduction of the Territorial system, and the Royal Cornwall Rangers became the 3rd Battalion of the Duke of Cornwall's Light Infantry. In 1884, while the fame won by the line battalions in Egypt was still fresh in the minds of all, the Royal Cornwall Rangers were presented with new colours at the hands of Lady Elizabeth St. Aubyn.

The 6th WEST YORK MILITIA, the 3rd Battalion of the Duke of Wellington's West Riding Regiment, were raised in 1853. In common with all the Yorkshire Militia regiments, the 6th West York used to bear the cognisance of the White Rose as a badge. The present applicability of the first title of the Territorial regiment is evidenced by the fact of the Duke of Wellington being the Hon. Colonel of its Militia battalions.

The ROYAL CUMBERLAND MILITIA and the ROYAL WESTMORELAND MILITIA furnish the 3rd and 4th Battalions of the Border Regiment; the former were raised in 1760, and the latter—the Westmoreland Light Infantry—raised in 1759, were amongst the Militia regiments which provided their quota to the Provisional battalion which, under Wellington, shared with the regular troops the campaign of 1814 in the south of France.

The ROYAL SUSSEX MILITIA, the 3rd Battalion of the Royal Sussex Regiment, date from 1778, and used to be known as the Royal Sussex Light Infantry. To them does the Territorial regiment owe the Garter and Cross of St. George among its badges.

The HAMPSHIRE MILITIA are now the 3rd Battalion of the Hampshire Regiment. They were raised in 1759.

The Hampshire Militia when raised was formed into two independent corps, the North Hants, with black facings, and the South Hants with yellow facings, and these regiments maintained a separate existence for nearly a century. The North Hants were on being raised commanded by the Duke of Bolton, and the South Hants, which included the Isle of Wight, by Sir Thomas Worsley, of Appledurcombe, in that island. Both regiments were immediately embodied, and so remained for more than three years, till the autumn of 1762. The North Hants were again, it is believed, embodied and moved to London, with other Militia regiments, in 1779, in consequence of the Lord George Gordon riots, and were subsequently embodied during all the wars which took place between that time and 1815. Early in this century they were stationed both in Scotland and Ireland." In 1852, on the revival of the Militia force, both regiments came out for training, the North Hants under the Marquis of Winchester at Winchester; the South Hants, which sometime previously had been made Light Infantry, under Sir John Pollen, at Southampton, but in the December of that year, the two corps were amalgamated into one regiment and called the Hampshire Militia. They had then black facings and were under the command of the Marquis of Winchester. From the Militia of Hampshire, as originally constituted, both the Hampshire Artillery Militia, and the Isle of Wight Artillery derive their origin.

It may be here mentioned that one of the first officers appointed to the South Hants when it was first raised was the historian Gibbon, and the following reference from his autobiography shows the value he attached to the position:—

"The discipline and evolutions of a modern battalion gave me a clearer notion of the Phalanx and the Legion, and the Captain of Hampshire Grenadiers has not been useless to the Historian of the Roman Empire."

By a somewhat strange coincidence Gibbon was succeeded in the command of the regiment by another historian, Wm. Mitford, who, besides his History of Greece, wrote a treatise upon the military force, and particularly the Militia of England.

After the amalgamation in 1853, the Hampshire Militia was embodied and kept together, serving at Portsmouth, Aldershot, and Winchester, during which time it gave many officers and men to the regular army. In 1872 Lord Winchester was appointed Hon. Colonel, being succeeded in the command of the regiment by Lieutenant-Colonel Briggs, who had served with the King's Dragoon Guards in the Crimea. In 1881 the title of the regiment was changed to that of the 3rd Battalion of the Hampshire Regiment, and the facings were changed from black to white. In 1885 Colonel Briggs resigned, and was succeeded by the present commanding officer, Sir Nelson Rycroft, Bart.

The 1st King's Own Stafford Militia form the 3rd and 4th Battalions of the South Staffordshire Regiment. Raised in 1778, their career has been a useful and honourable one, as is evidenced by the fact that King William IV. gave them, in recognition of fourteen years' "Royal duty" performed by the regiment at Windsor Castle, the right to wear the Castle as a badge, and it is still so borne on the waist-plates of the Territorial regiment. The Royal South Staffordshire are amongst the Militia regiments entitled to bear "Mediterranean" as a distinction.

The Dorset Militia, the 3rd Battalion of the Dorsetshire Regiment, "were raised in 1757, and was commanded by the Hon. George Pitt, afterwards Lord Rivers. The regiment, being the first regiment equipped at the time, bear 'No. 1' on their buttons. In 1798 the regiment went to Ireland and landed at Waterford. The following year the town of Carrick-on-Suir presented the Colonel (the Earl of Dorchester) with a valuable sword, and the officers with some plate for their mess, as a token of their appreciation of their services whilst quartered there." Their subsequent career has been comparatively uneventful. Before the amalgamation they used to have as a badge the crest and coronet of Lord Rivers, the founder of the regiment.

The 4th Royal Lancashire Militia are now known as the 3rd Battalion of the Prince of Wales's Volunteers (South Lancashire Regiment). They were raised in 1797, and were a Light Infantry regiment. Their precedence number was 84.

The Royal Glamorgan Militia, the 3rd Battalion of the Welsh regiment, date from 1761, and were formerly known as the Royal Glamorgan Light Infantry.

The Royal Perth Militia, the 3rd Battalion of the famous Black Watch, were raised in 1798, and were formerly the Perth Rifles and as such wore the uniform and characteristic badges of Rifle corps. They are one of the regiments of Militia honoured by having a royal prince to command them, their honorary colonel being H.R.H. the Duke of Edinburgh.

The ROYAL BUCKS MILITIA and the OXFORD MILITIA form the 3rd and 4th Battalions of the Oxfordshire Light Infantry, and, as becomes regiments connected with so famous a corps, have a record of their own which places them high up on the honour scale of Militia regiments. The Royal Bucks Militia has, moreover, the advantage of having in its late Commander, Colonel Caulfield Pratt, an historian to whom the records of the regiment are a study of enthusiastic affection, and the *esprit de corps* which has ever characterized the Royal Bucks flourishes still as strongly as ever. From the "Short Accounts of Famous Militia Regiments" the doings of the regiment may be epitomised as follows:—

In 1794, the regiment being encamped at Weymouth, where the King was at that time staying, formed his personal guard; for which service His Majesty was pleased to confer the above title on them. In June, 1798, they volunteered for service in Ireland, and embarked at Liverpool for Dublin, where they arrived on the 2nd July, and were the first English regiment to land. In the spring of 1799 they returned to England, and in the same year sent four hundred officers and men into the 4th Foot (King's Own). In 1813, provisional battalions of Militia were formed. The 1st Battalion, which was mainly composed of this regiment, and was commanded by the Duke of Buckingham and Chandos, embarked the same year for Bordeaux, and served in France during the war.

A fuller history, however, may be extracted from the reports of the ceremony of the presentation of new colours to the regiment in 1869 by the Duchess of Buckingham. Amongst those present were "the Rt. Hon. B. Disraeli and Viscountess Beaconsfield," while the ceremony of consecration was performed by another now "vanished hand," that of the late Bishop of Oxford.

"The regiment was raised in the reign of Charles II., and obtained its title, 'The Royal Bucks, King's Own Militia,' on the occasion of being selected when encamped near Weymouth, in the year 1794, to form the personal guard of His Majesty King George III., when he visited that place. In June, 1798, the regiment volunteered, with its Colonel Marquis of Buckingham, to serve in Ireland, that country being then in even a worst state than it is at present, and in open rebellion. The reception accorded to the regiment, which was the first Militia regiment that volunteered to go to Ireland,

and the first that landed in the country, by the authorities, upon their landing at Dublin from Liverpool, was exceedingly complimentary and enthusiastic. When the regiment returned to England next year, four hundred of the men volunteered into the line, and with sergeants, corporals, and privates, and with the due and regulated proportion of officers, joined the 4th or King's Own Regiment of Infantry. Besides this the regiment continued to furnish year by year its full quota of men to the line (principally to the 14th or Buckinghamshire Regiment of Foot) during the continuance of the French war. In the year 1808, the regiment, with their noble Colonel Earl Temple, volunteered to serve in Spain during the period of the invasion of that country by the French army. The Ministry did not avail themselves of the offer, but the Commander-in-Chief, the Duke of York, expressed his high sense of the gallantry which inspired the offer. In 1813, the regiment again served in Ireland, our friends in the sister isle being again in rebellion to obtain 'justice.' In the same year, the first provisional battalion of Militia for foreign service was formed by the Royal Bucks King's Own Regiment, and embarked for Bordeaux, under the command of the Duke of Buckingham and Chandos, and they served in France, under his Grace the Duke of Wellington, during the time the allied armies were in possession of that country. On leaving, each officer of the regiment was presented with the *Fleur de Lis*, by Louis XVIII.

"On the 7th April, 1855, the regiment was quartered at Canterbury, and was selected, as being the most efficient corps in the district, to receive the Emperor of the French upon his landing at Dover with the Empress, and remained there during the Imperial visit, forming a guard of honour again upon the departure of the Emperor and Empress from this country on the 14th April. On the 24th April of the same year, two companies of the regiment marched from Canterbury to Woolwich, followed by the remaining companies and headquarters on the 9th May, under the command of Lieutenant Colonel Pratt. During their stay at Woolwich, the regiment performed garrison duty, and upon leaving for the Tower of London, a highly complimentary garrison order was issued by Major-General Whinyates, C.B.K.H., in which the following expressions occur: 'I cannot permit the Royal Bucks King's Own Militia to leave the garrison without expressing my great satisfaction at the steady discipline and conduct I have observed during the six months it has been under my orders. The military deportment and appearance of the regiment at all times, its steadiness under arms and in battalion, and in precision in movements, attest the careful attention devoted to its instructions and interior economy by the officer in command, and the officers of the corps.'

"During the period of its embodiment the regiment was called upon to give volunteers to the line, for service in the Crimean War. This was readily taken up, and, as in 1799, four hundred men again volunteered for foreign service."

It is a proud boast for the Colonel of a Militia regiment to be able to assert, as did Colonel Caulfield Pratt: "This regiment has left the country on three occasions. Twice it went to Ireland, when that country was in a state of rebellion, and again, from the year 1813 it served under the great Duke of Wellington, until peace was proclaimed."

When, in 1878, the Reserves were mobilised to give emphasis to the warnings of Her Majesty's Government, the Royal Bucks were quartered at Aldershot, and at the inspection proved that they still made good their claim to be a *corps d'élite* amongst Militia regiments. It bears no slight testimony to the valuable services rendered to the regiment by Colonel Caulfield Pratt, that on his resignation of the post of Colonel, he was made Hon. Colonel.

The OXFORD MILITIA, formed in 1778, has also a long record of meritorious service, and bears the distinction of "Mediterranean."

The ESSEX (RIFLES) MILITIA and the WEST ESSEX MILITIA, the 3rd and 4th Battalions of the Essex Regiment, date from 1759. The former used to bear an oak-leaf on their accoutrements which, according to Archer, was commemorative of the hiding of King Charles II. in an oak-tree in the forest of Hainault. To the same battalion the Territorial Regiment is indebted for its badge of the "Arms of Essex."

The 2nd DERBY MILITIA, the ROYAL SHERWOOD FORESTERS MILITIA, and the 1st DERBY MILITIA form the 3rd, 4th, and 5th Battalions of the Sherwood Foresters (Derbyshire Regiment). They date respectively from 1855, 1778, and 1778, the 4th and 5th battalions being considerably senior in point of age to the 3rd. The Militia battalions of the Sherwood Foresters are favoured in the possession of very distinguished honorary colonels, the Marquis of Hartington, the Duke of Portland, and Sir F. Roberts, V.C., commanding the 3rd, 4th, and 5th battalions respectively.

The romance that hangs about the very name of Sherwood Foresters induces us to glance for a moment at the earliest history of the fighting men of Nottinghamshire.* In 1298 at Falkirk, where

> "Spears shook and falchions flashed amain,
> Fell England's arrow flight like rain,"

* A task rendered easy by the very interesting *resumé* of the Sherwood Foresters kindly forwarded to the author by Captain Napier Pearse.

the splendid Nottinghamshire archers bent their trusty bows to a good purpose; at Nevill's Cross, Cressy, and Poictiers the Nottinghamshire men were foremost amongst the English yeomen; at Shrewsbury, where

> "——the double reign
> Of Harry Percy and the Prince of Wales"

came to an end when the noble Percy was slain, Sir John Clifton and Sir Hugh Shirley and other brave knights and gentlemen of Nottinghamshire fell fighting at the head of their men. "At Agincourt, in 1415, the Nottinghamshire Archers again played a prominent part, and there, for the first time on record, they fought as 'Sherwood Foresters,' their banner being thus quaintly described by Drayton :—

> 'Old Nottingham, and archer clad in green,
> Under a tree, with his drawn bow that stood,
> Which in a chequered flag far off was seen ;
> It was the picture of bold Robin Hood.'"

But we must reluctantly pass from "those old times of sport" and glance briefly at the modern history of the regiment. In 1759 the reorganized regiment of Militia became known as the 42nd, or Nottinghamshire, and during the French wars of the last century and the beginning of the present, the 45th Regiment was formed and from time to time replenished from the Nottinghamshire Militia. " Few regiments," says Captain Pearse, "have seen more arduous service than the 45th, and none have earned for themselves a higher renown. Should any be disposed to sneer at the bloodless record of a Militia regiment, let them look at the honours upon the tattered colours of the gallant 45th, and remember that it was by Nottinghamshire Militiamen that those honours were won." With those words, eloquent of an enthusiasm for the regiment not, perhaps, too common amongst Militia officers, we might well close our notice of the Sherwood Foresters Militia. Their traditional skill in shooting still clung to them, and gained them the sobriquet of the "Nottinghamshire Marksmen," followed shortly afterwards by that of the "Saucy Notts." The whole regiment volunteered for service in Spain. When they were called on to volunteer for service in Ireland, 886 out of a total of 900 enthusiastically welcomed the opportunity. In October, 1812, the "memorable order" was issued by which the Nottinghamshire Militia were directed to take over the duties usually performed by the Foot Guards at the Tower of London; not only this, but for nearly a month did this famous Militia regiment do duty at St. James's Palace, the Treasury, the Bank of England, and other places usually guarded by Household Troops, with the result that, before the year was out, at the suggestion, it is believed, of the Prince Regent himself, the regiment became the Royal Sherwood Foresters.

The regiment was embodied at the time of the Crimea and Indian Mutiny, and in 1858 "stood at the head of the whole British Army in shooting, having done better than any other regiment in Her Majesty's service." Since that time the regiment has not been embodied.

The 3rd ROYAL LANCASHIRE MILITIA, now supplying the 3rd and 4th Battalions of the Loyal South Lancashire Regiment, date from 1797. They are one of the Militia regiments that bear the distinction of "Mediterranean."

The NORTHAMPTON AND RUTLAND MILITIA give the 3rd and 4th Battalions to the Northamptonshire regiment. They both date from 1761, and the former has proved its efficiency on several occasions, bearing, like the regiment last mentioned, the "Mediterranean" distinction.

The Northampton and Rutland Militia give the Horseshoe and St. George's Cross to the Regimental badges.

The WEST KENT MILITIA, the 3rd Battalion of the Queen's Own (Royal West Kent Regiment), date from 1759, and were formerly known as the West Kent Light Infantry. The Hon. Colonel is H.R.H. the Duke of Connaught.

A very ancient lineage can be boasted by the West Kent Militia. There have been few struggles on English ground in which the men of Kent have not borne their part right manfully, and sovereigns and chieftains were fain to reckon upon them as a very potent factor in their disputes. At the time of the Armada we find them under command of Sir J. Norris and others—worthy types of "the gallant squires of Kent"—garrisoning Tilbury and guarding the threatened coast. Fifty years later the Kentish Militia formed part of the expedition, under the Marquis of Hamilton, against the Covenanters, after which they joined the army of the king at Berwick. Passing over the painful scenes of the next few years, we next hear of the men of Kent rendering great service at the time of the Great Fire of London, and the following year being gathered in readiness to repel the expected Dutch raid. At the time of the Jacobite rising of 1745 they were again embodied, and a few years later, namely, in 1759, the West Kent Militia was established on a new footing. They were embodied during the Seven Years' War, and again during the revolt of the American Colonies, and it was during this latter period that, "on the occasion of the visit of George III. to the camp at Winchester, the West Kent Militia, as the senior regiment in camp, furnished a guard of honour. At a levée after the review the king knighted the captain of the guard as being the commander of the first Militia guard of honour ever mounted on the person of the King of England."

The regiment gained great credit for its conduct during the mutiny at Spithead, when it was stationed at Portsmouth, and also for its services in Ireland, for which it volunteered in 1798. In 1803 the West Kent were again embodied, and remained so for over eleven years, during which period they were stationed at various places in England; in the embodiment of the Waterloo year they served in Ireland.* During the Peninsular War, as well as in the Crimean War, a very large number, both officers and men, joined the regular army. In 1853 they were made a Light Infantry regiment, and in 1876 divided into two battalions, which, five years later, became the 3rd and 4th Battalions of the Queen's Own Royal West Kent Regiment, and changed the grey facings and silver lace for the blue and gold of a Royal Regiment.

The 1st WEST YORK MILITIA, the 3rd Battalion of the King's Own Yorkshire Light Infantry, also date from 1759, and were formerly a Rifle regiment. They have shared with the other regiments of Yorkshire Militia the not infrequent services which the Force has from time to time rendered in aid of the Civil Power.

The SHROPSHIRE MILITIA and the HEREFORD MILITIA consitute the 3rd and 4th Battalions of the King's Shropshire Light Infantry. Both regiments date from 1778, though there was a regiment of Shropshire Militia raised in 1762.

"In 1795 a Company of Artillery was added to the Regiment. In 1797 they marched to Scotland, and were the first regiment sent there. In 1813, they were sent to Cork, and did duty in Ireland till 1815, when they returned to Shrewsbury."

The ROYAL ELTHORNE MILITIA and the ROYAL EAST MIDDLESEX MILITIA form the 3rd and 4th Battalions of the Duke of Cambridge's Own Middlesex Regiment. The former were raised in 1853 as the 5th Middlesex Light Infantry, and the latter in 1778. The 3rd battalion volunteered for foreign service on the occasions of the Crimean War and Indian Mutiny.

The HUNTINGDON MILITIA, the ROYAL 2nd MIDDLESEX MILITIA, the CARLOW MILITIA, and the NORTH CORK MILITIA, furnish the 5th, 7th, 8th, and 9th Battalions to the famous King's Royal Rifle Corps—the "60th" of former days. The 1st, the Huntingdon, date from 1759, the 2nd Middlesex Rifles (the Edmonton) from 1778, the Carlow from 1793,

---

* During the fifty-seven years between 1759 and 1816 the regiment had been embodied for over thirty.

and the North Cork also from 1793. The 9th Battalion volunteered for foreign service at the time of the Crimean War and Indian Mutiny.

The ROYAL WILTSHIRE MILITIA, the 3rd Battalion of the Duke of Edinburgh's Wiltshire Regiment, dates from 1759, and bears the "Mediterranean" distinction.

The 6th ROYAL LANCASHIRE MILITIA, constituting the 3rd and 4th Battalions of the Manchester Regiment, dates from 1855.

The 2nd and 3rd KING'S OWN STAFFORD MILITIA, forming the 3rd and 4th Battalions of the Prince of Wales's North Staffordshire Regiment, date from 1797 and 1798 respectively, the former having been a Light Infantry and the latter a Rifle regiment.

The 3rd WEST YORK MILITIA forms the 3rd Battalion of the York and Lancaster Regiment. We find records of this Regiment in the reign of James I., and in that of William and Mary, and the present Yorkshire regiments of Militia may be said to have been reorganized on a basis of considerable antiquity in 1757. The history of the regiment by Lieut.-Col. Raikes gives a quantity of most interesting details, for which, however, we must be contented to refer our readers to the work itself. The regiment has, during its various periods of embodiment, seen a considerable amount of hard work: suppressing the riots at York and Hull, volunteering for service in Ireland, contributing a quota to the provisional battalion in the Peninsula, and on more than one occasion volunteering to join the regular army *en bloc*. The 3rd West York obtained the first place in the ballot for precedence amongst Militia regiments, and may, accordingly, boast the distinction of being the First Regiment of Militia. In 1811 a Royal Warrant was issued granting to the regiment the White Rose as a badge, and in 1853 it was constituted Light Infantry.

The 1st and 2nd DURHAM MILITIA are now the 3rd and 4th Battalions of the Durham Light Infantry. The former, the Durham Fusiliers, date from 1760; the latter, the North Durham, from 1853.

The 1st ROYAL LANARK MILITIA, the 3rd and 4th Battalions of the Highland Light Infantry, date from 1798; and the HIGHLAND RIFLE MILITIA, the 3rd Battalion of the Seaforth Highlanders (Ross-shire Buffs, The Duke of Albany's), from 1798, when they were raised from the districts of Ross, Caithness, Sutherland and Cromarty.

The latter regiment was raised in April, 1798, and then known as the Ross or 2nd NORTH BRITISH MILITIA. The first embodiment lasted for four years, and the second and third covered the greater part of the Napoleonic Wars. In 1808 the regiment volunteered bodily for foreign service, and though the offer was not accepted, the patriotic spirit which prompted it was duly acknowledged. The regiment, then known as the 96th Ross-SHIRE MILITIA, was embodied during the Crimean War, and in 1877 when war seemed a question of hours, the gallant Ross-SHIRE, then designated the HIGHLAND RIFLE MILITIA again volunteered *en bloc* for foreign service. It will not be out of place here to state that, "as regards shooting, the Ross-shire Militia has always been 'a crack corps.' Since the commencement of the Army Inter-Regimental Rifle Matches, the battalion has almost invariably been first in the Militia team match, which was won solely by the battalion in 1882, 1883, 1885, 1886; it was second in 1887, and first in 1888."

The regiment has experienced almost as many changes in uniform as in name, and it seems a pity—considering that it is probably the most Highland of all Highland regiments *—that the often-expressed wish of officers and men for the substitution of the kilt for the trews is not adopted. Between 1862 and 1871 the kilt was worn, and it will be remembered that the affiliated line battalions are amongst the kilt-wearing regiments.

The ROYAL ABERDEEN MILITIA, the 3rd Battalion of the Gordon Highlanders, date from 1797. The Hon. Colonel is H.R.H. the Prince of Wales, and the regiment has ever borne a high character for efficiency.

The HIGHLAND LIGHT INFANTRY MILITIA, the 2nd Battalion of the Queen's Own Cameron Highlanders, date from 1803, when they were raised from Inverness, Banff, Moray, and Nairn. They are the only Militia regiment which forms the 2nd battalion of a Territorial regiment.

The ROYAL NORTH DOWN MILITIA, the ROYAL ANTRIM MILITIA, the ROYAL SOUTH DOWN MILITIA, and the LOUTH MILITIA form the 3rd, 4th, 5th, and 6th Battalions of the Royal Irish Rifles, and all date from 1793. The 4th Battalion, the Antrim Militia, volunteered for foreign service at the time of the Crimea and Mutiny.

The ARMAGH MILITIA, the CAVAN MILITIA, and the MONAGHAN MILITIA form respectively the 3rd, 4th, and 5th Battalions of the Princess Victoria's (Royal Irish Fusiliers), and date from 1793. The 4th Battalion, the Cavan Militia, present some features of interest. They were first embodied under the command of Colonel, the Earl of Bellamont,

---

* All the men are Gaelic speaking Highlanders, and, as showing the universal preference for the kilt, a vote taken at a recent annual training had only five dissentients—and they were not Highlanders—from the proposal in favour of its adoption.

with Lieutenant-Colonel Sir Robert Hodson second in command. Lord Bellamont resigned in 1797, and was succeeded by Colonel John Maxwell, afterwards Lord Farnham.

"In June, 1798, the regiment was engaged at the battle of Arklow, and lost six men killed and had nine seriously wounded. It was engaged a few days later at Vinegar Hill, and General Needham, who commanded on both occasions, referred in his dispatch to Lord Cornwallis to its 'steady, soldier-like, and gallant conduct in action.' With two short intervals the regiment remained embodied for twenty-five years, namely, till March, 1816. On the death of Lord Farnham, in 1838, Colonel Alexander Saunderson was appointed Colonel. In December, 1854, the Earl of Bective, now Marquis of Headford, was appointed Lieutenant-Colonel, and on the 8th of January, 1855, the regiment was embodied. The colours were presented on 18th December, 1855, by the Countess of Bective; and in December of the same year the regiment moved to Aldershot Camp, then but lately formed, and there remained till May, 1856, when it returned to Ireland. During the Crimean War a large number of men and several officers went to join the line regiments, and then and later on, in 1858, volunteered for any service. In July, 1874, Lord Headford retired from the command, and was succeeded by Lieutenant-Colonel Hardress Saunderson, who died in June, 1881, and the present commander, Lieutenant-Colonel Dease, was appointed in his place. On the 21st July, 1881, the regiment became the 4th Battalion of the Princess Victoria's Royal Irish Fusiliers. Under their new title they received, on the 10th of June, 1887, from Lady Audrey Butler, the colours of the Territorial regiment."

The SOUTH AND NORTH MAYO MILITIA constitute the 3rd Battalion, the GALWAY MILITIA the 4th, and the ROSCOMMON MILITIA the 5th, of the Connaught Rangers, all the regiments having been raised in 1793. Previous to the Territorial system the 3rd Battalion, which was raised by the Marquis of Sligo, used to bear his crest as a badge in addition to the Harp and Crown common to all Militia regiments. The 6th Battalion, the Roscommon Militia, was amongst the regiments that volunteered at the time of the Mutiny and Crimean War.

The HIGHLAND BORDERERS MILITIA and the ROYAL RENFREW MILITIA date from 1803 and 1798, the former being recruited from the districts of Stirling and Dumbarton, Clackmannan and Kinross. The Royal Renfrew Militia were embodied in 1803, and served for some time in England, being amongst the troops commanded by Sir John Moore in anticipation of a French invasion. After serving in Ireland the regiment was disbanded in 1816, from which date till its next embodiment in 1855 it "appears to have only trained once." From 1859, however, the training has been annual. The regiment claims that it "has invariably been kept up to its establishment and has given a great many officers and men to the regular army, notably during the Peninsular and Crimean Wars."

The KING'S COUNTY MILITIA, the QUEEN'S COUNTY MILITIA, and the ROYAL MEATH MILITIA constitute respectively, the 3rd, 4th, and 5th Battalions of the Prince of Wales's Leinster Regiment Royal Canadians. All three regiments of Militia date from 1793, and the first-named fought at Vinegar Hill under Colonel L'Estrange, and were subsequently represented by a wing at the heroic defence of Newton Barry. They have also served in Guernsey and in England, and previously to their absorption into the Leinster Regiment were, as was the 2nd Battalion, a Rifle Regiment. The 5th Battalion, as the Royal Meath Militia, used to wear a "Tara Brooch" as a badge.

The SOUTH CORK MILITIA, the KELLY MILITIA, and the ROYAL LIMERICK COUNTY MILITIA, form respectively the 3rd, 4th, and 5th Battalions of the Royal Munster Fusiliers, and all date from 1793. The 3rd Battalion was amongst the regiments of Militia that served at Vinegar Hill.

The KILDARE MILITIA, the ROYAL DUBLIN CITY MILITIA, and the DUBLIN COUNTY MILITIA—dating the former from 1794, and the two latter from 1793—form the 3rd, 4th, and 5th Battalions of the Royal Dublin Fusiliers.

The QUEEN'S OWN ROYAL TOWER HAMLETS MILITIA, the ROYAL LONGFORD MILITIA, the KING'S OWN ROYAL TOWER HAMLETS MILITIA, and the WEST MEATH MILITIA form the 5th, 6th, 7th, and 9th Battalions of the Rifle Brigade, Prince Consort's Own. The 5th and 7th Battalions used to have as badge "Tower of London;" the 6th Battalion, which earned honourable distinction in the fighting at Castlebar in August, 1798, and throughout all the rebellion, used to have the Prince of Wales's plume and motto, and the 9th bore the "Irish Cross and Shamrock Wreath."

The CHANNEL ISLANDS MILITIA, divided into the Jersey Command, and the Guernsey and Alderney Command, call for notice, as being amongst the few Militia regiments which have had the fortune to be engaged in actual warfare. The Militia of these islands have a very considerable antiquity. As Captain Perry well observes, "almost every war we have had with France has witnessed an attack on Jersey." The island ran a considerable chance of being captured in 1779, when a powerful squadron, under the Duke of Nassau, threatened it. On this occasion the Militia were ready, and would doubtless have given the invader a warm reception, had not the English fleet under Sir James Wallis completely routed the would-be invader. In 1781, a more serious attack was made, which for a time threatened to wrest the old Norman possession from the Crown of England. The French commander, the Baron de Rullecour, succeeded in surprising the Governor and extorting submission from him and the leading inhabitants. Fortunately, however, Major Pierson, of the 78th, rallied the Militia and the small body of Regulars, and inflicted on the jubilant French a complete and unexpected defeat. The French commander was killed, but so, unfortunately, was the gallant Pierson, who found death and honourable fame at an age at which many have not yet begun to consider life seriously.* In recognition of this achievement the Jersey Infantry Regiments bear the distinction "Jersey, 1781."

The Jersey Command consists of the 1st, 2nd, and 3rd Regiments of the Royal Jersey Light Infantry Militia, who bear as badges "A bugle surmounted by the Royal Crest; a sprig of laurel on each side on Glengarry; three Lions Leopardés on a shield placed on a Saltire Cross on the collar."

The Guernsey and Alderney Command, which includes the small islands of Herm and Jethou, consists of the 1st, 2nd, and 3rd Regiments of the Royal Guernsey Light Infantry; they bear as badges the Bugle on the Glengarry, and on the collar one "Lion Leopardé." "On the helmet plate are three Lions Leopardés, on a shield surmounted by a sprig of laurel, below the shield is a bugle with strings." The uniform is scarlet, with blue facings, and the mottoes are *Pro aris et focis* and *Dieu aie*.

Alderney and Sark have Artillery, but no localized Infantry.

The next branch of the Auxiliary Forces which we have to consider is the YEOMANRY. Though a popular and essentially national force, considerable difficulty exists in tracing, with any accuracy and detail, the history of the various regiments which go to compose it. Lieut.-Col. Raikes, to whom intricacy of research is seldom an obstacle, writes that "The Yeomanry is by far the most difficult branch of the Army or Auxiliary Forces of which to trace the history, owing to their having been almost inseparably connected with both the Militia and Volunteers at the earliest periods of their existence. Towards the close of the seventeenth century (during the reign of Charles II.), and in the Acts passed at that time, the Militia is spoken of as both horse and foot. A century later they appear as the 'Hunter Volunteers,' being armed by

* He was not twenty-five when he died.

order of George III." This, however, applies principally to the early history. In many cases the more recent chronicles have been carefully compiled, and such corps possess regimental records equal in accuracy, if not in general interest, to those of the regular cavalry. The general history of the force subsequent to their "Hunter Volunteer" phase, is briefly as follows:—The various corps of Fencibles and Volunteers raised towards the middle of the eighteenth century included troops of horse which were called Volunteer or Fencible Cavalry, and later Volunteer Yeomanry Cavalry. "All the mounted corps were disbanded in 1800, but a number of independent troops were maintained during the following ten years by voluntary effort, and in 1813 were again regimented under county titles" (*Perry*). Another crisis in the history of the force occurred in 1827, when the Government grants thitherto made were in many cases withdrawn. As a result some of the old regiments were disbanded, but four years later were, in a good number of cases, re-formed. "In 1793 and 1794 a large force of Yeomanry was raised, or, as they were called, 'Gentlemen and Yeomanry.' An addition of 20,000 men was made in 1796, under the name of 'Provisional Cavalry.' One of the principal duties of the Yeomanry has always been the unpopular service of quelling riots and disturbances. The Yeomanry were at first raised mostly in independent troops, which were subsequently formed into regiments. Some corps date their formation from the time their first troop was raised, others from the time they were incorporated as a regiment. Many troops in almost every regiment having been disbanded at different periods, and new troops having been subsequently added, it becomes very difficult to decide the actual period from which a regiment dates its formation; even two Parliamentary returns compiled at the War Office on the subject, and issued within a few years of each other, do not agree in most instances in the date of formation of the various regiments. Previous to the year 1828 there were 124 corps in Great Britain, containing 500 troops and upwards of 24,000 men. In 1828 they were reduced to 38 corps, or 210 troops and 10,000 men, of which number about half served gratuitously. Within the next few years several corps were added, but in March, 1838, they were again reduced from 325 troops, with 18,074 men, to 244 troops and 13,204 men."

In the year 1843 the Yeomanry were increased by 6 troops being transferred from the unpaid to the paid establishment. In the year 1870 they were again reduced; all corps under 4 troops being disbanded unless they could raise that number, and corps of 10 and 12 troops being reduced to 8. Ireland formerly had a very large force of Yeomanry and Volunteers, and the former took an active and conspicuous part in the suppression of the Rebellion of 1798. In the year 1817 the non-commissioned officers and men of the Yeomanry and Volunteers in Ireland numbered upwards of 40,000 men; in 1829 there were 35,000. The whole of the Irish Yeomanry were finally disbanded by the 31st March, 1834.

There are thirty-nine regiments of Yeomanry Cavalry, representing nearly 14,000 men. The order of precedence was settled in 1885, and in the following notices is indicated by the figures in brackets. Yeomanry Cavalry, it may here be mentioned, carry no standards.

The AYRSHIRE YEOMANRY (7) date from 1803. The uniform is blue with scarlet facings and gold plume, and helmet without plume. The regimental badge is "St. Andrew and the Cross."

The BERKS (HUNGERFORD) YEOMANRY (26), raised in 1831, have a scarlet uniform with blue facings, with helmet and white plume. The badge is a Crescent with blazing Star, the arms of the ancient borough of Hungerford.

The BUCKINGHAMSHIRE—THE ROYAL BUCKS HUSSARS (21) date from 1800. They were on duty as the cavalry escort at Windsor Castle, when the formidable nature of the Chartist Riots necessitated the removal to the scene of danger of the Life Guards. The uniform is green, with scarlet facings and busby bag, and red and white plume. They have no regimental badge.*

The CHESHIRE (The Earl of Chester's) HUSSARS (8) date from 1794. The uniform is blue, with scarlet facings and white busby bag. The badge is the Prince of Wales's Feathers.

The DENBIGHSHIRE HUSSARS (16) date from 1830. The uniform is blue, with scarlet facings and busby bag and white plume. The badge is the Prince of Wales's Feathers.

The DERBYSHIRE YEOMANRY (22) date from 1830. Their uniform is blue, with scarlet facings and gold lace, and helmet with scarlet and white plume. The badge is the Red Rose and Crown.

The ROYAL FIRST DEVON HUSSARS (28) date from 1831. The uniform is scarlet with blue facings, scarlet busby bag, and white plume. The badge is the Castle of Exeter.

The ROYAL NORTH DEVON HUSSARS (30) date from 1831. The uniform is blue

---

* Lieut.-Col. Raikes has written a full and interesting account of this Regiment.—Vide *Buckingham Express*, October and November, 1888.

with facings of scarlet, scarlet busby bag, and scarlet and white plume. They bear as badge "Y.C." in a band, with the Crown above resting on two swords crossed and points upwards.

The DORSETSHIRE HUSSARS, the Queen's Own (23) date from 1830. Their uniform also is blue with scarlet facings, red busby bag and white plume. The badge is the Royal Cypher in the Crown with, below, a crossed sword and carbine.

The GLOUCESTERSHIRE, ROYAL GLOUCESTERSHIRE HUSSARS (24), date from 1830. The uniform is blue with yellow facings, gold lace, scarlet busby bag, and scarlet and white plume. They bear no badge.

The HAMPSHIRE CARABINEERS (20) date from 1830. The uniform is blue, with white braid or lace facings on collar and sleeves, and helmet without plume. The badge is the Hampshire Rose with the Crown above on two carbines crossed.

The HERTS YEOMANRY (25) date from 1830. The uniform is scarlet with white facings, and helmet with black plume. The badge is the Hart.

The ROYAL EAST KENT YEOMANRY, the Duke of Connaught's Own (19), date from 1830. They wear a green uniform with red facings, and a helmet with green and red plume. The badge is the White Horse of Kent with the Crown. The Duke of Connaught is the Hon. Colonel.

The WEST KENT HUSSARS, the Queen's Own (32), date from 1831. The uniform is blue with scarlet facings, and busby bag and white plume, the badge being the Kentish White Horse.

The LANCASHIRE YEOMANRY (13) date from 1819. The uniform is blue with facings of scarlet and gold lace, and helmet without plume. The badge is the double-headed Spread Eagle.

The LANARKSHIRE (Queen's Own Royal Glasgow and Lower Ward of Lanarkshire (38) date from 1848. The uniform is blue with scarlet facings, gold lace, and helmet with black plume. The badge is the Crest of Scotland (the Red Lion crowned, with sword and sceptre) with two sprigs of Thistle.

The DUKE OF LANCASTER'S OWN (12) date from 1819. The uniform is scarlet with facings of blue, gold lace, and helmet with white plume. The badge is the Arms of Lancaster.

The LANCASHIRE HUSSARS (39) were raised in 1848. The uniform is blue with blue facings, crimson busby bag, crimson and white plume, and they bear as a badge the Red Rose of Lancaster.

The LEICESTERSHIRE HUSSARS, Prince Albert's Own (10), date from 1803. The uniform is blue with scarlet facings, scarlet busby bag, scarlet and white plume. They bear no badge.

The LOTHIANS AND BERWICKSHIRE YEOMANRY (37) date from 1846. Till recently they were known as the East Lothian Yeomanry. The uniform is scarlet with blue facings, gold lace, and helmet with red and white plume. The badge is "a Wheatsheaf in a circular band with a Crown above."

The MIDDLESEX, DUKE OF CAMBRIDGE'S HUSSARS (27) date from 1831. Their uniform is green with black facings, gold lace, green busby bag, green and red plume. The badge is the Royal Cypher in a Star, over which is a Crown.

The MONTGOMERYSHIRE YEOMANRY (35) date from 1831. They are a survival of the large Montgomery Volunteer Legion, consisting of 20 companies of infantry and 3 troops of cavalry originally raised. During the years 1837-8-9 they rendered frequent and signal service to the civil power on the occurrence of riots, and gained particular praise for their conduct during the last part of the Chartist outbreak. Their uniform is scarlet, with black facings, and helmet without a plume. The badge is the Red Dragon of Wales.

The NORTHUMBERLAND HUSSARS (14) date from 1819, and represent in a great degree the Percy Tenantry Cavalry, raised by the Duke of Northumberland at the end of the last century. The uniform is blue, with scarlet busby bag, and scarlet and white plume, and the badge is Alnwick Castle.

The SOUTH NOTTINGHAMSHIRE HUSSARS (15) date from 1826, being the only Yeomanry corps raised in that year. The uniform is scarlet, with blue facings, gold lace, scarlet busby bag, and scarlet and white plume. The badge is S.N.Y.C. on two crossed swords surmounted by the Crown.

The NOTTINGHAMSHIRE SHERWOOD RANGERS HUSSARS (4) date from 1794. They have frequently been employed in aid of the civil power. The uniform is green, with green facings, gold lace, crimson busby bag, and green and white plume. The badge is a Bugle in a Crown, and the motto adopted by the regiment when raised was, "Loyal unto death."

The QUEEN'S OWN OXFORDSHIRE HUSSARS (34) date from 1831. Their uniform is blue, with crimson facings and busby bag, and crimson and white plume. There is no badge.

The PEMBROKE (CASTLEMARTIN) HUSSARS (18) date from 1830. They were, however, actually raised in 1793, as the Castlemartin Yeomanry Cavalry, by Lord

THE QUEEN'S OWN ROYAL REGIMENT.

STAFFORDSHIRE YEOMANRY.

Cawdor. Four years later they were "instrumental in causing the surrender of an invading French force" of some 1,400 men which landed at Fishguard. Twenty-four years later the regiment was again employed at Fishguard in quelling a corn riot, and during the subsequent years the Pembroke Yeomanry rendered sterling service in the Rebecca riots, which are remembered with terror by many still surviving. The uniform is blue, with facings of white, white busby bag, and red and white plume, and they bear as badge the Prince of Wales's feathers.

The SHROPSHIRE YEOMANRY (6) date from 1795. The uniform is blue, with scarlet facings, gold lace, helmet, and red and white plume. As a badge they bear a Leopard's Face (from the Arms of Shrewsbury).

The NORTH SOMERSET YEOMANRY (11) date from 1803. They wear a blue uniform with blue facings, and helmet with white plume. The badge is the Royal Cypher in a Crown on an unpointed star.

The WEST SOMERSET HUSSARS (33) date from 1831. Their uniform is blue with scarlet facings, red busby bag and white plume. The Royal Cypher on a Maltese Cross in a Crown is the badge.

The STAFFORDSHIRE YEOMANRY, QUEEN'S OWN ROYAL REGIMENT (5) date from 1794. The uniform is blue with scarlet facings, and helmet with white plume. For a badge they bear the Staffordshire Knot in a laurel wreath.

The LOYAL SUFFOLK HUSSARS (29) dating from 1831, have a green uniform with scarlet facings and gold lace, and busby bag with white plume. The badge is L.S.H. and two Crossed Swords.

The WARWICKSHIRE HUSSARS (2) date from 1794. Their uniform is blue with white facings, and busby bag, and plume. The badge is the Bear and Ragged Staff.

The WESTMORELAND AND CUMBERLAND HUSSARS (17) date from 1830, and their amalgamation into one regiment took place in 1843. The uniform is scarlet with white facings and busby bag, and red and white plume.

The ROYAL WILTSHIRE HUSSARS, The Prince of Wales's Own Royal Regiment (1) date from 1794. They received the title Royal for the services rendered during the riots of 1830. The uniform is blue, with facings, busby bag, and plume scarlet. They bear the Prince of Wales's Feathers as a badge.

The QUEEN'S OWN WORCESTERSHIRE HUSSARS (31) date from 1831. The uniform closely resembles the last-mentioned regiment, being blue with scarlet facings, busby bag, and plume. They bear, however, no badge.

The PRINCESS OF WALES'S OWN YORKSHIRE HUSSARS (3) date from 1794, being raised as the Yorkshire West Riding Yeomanry, and have a blue uniform, with blue facings, scarlet busby bag, and black plume. The White Rose of York supplies the badge.

The YORKSHIRE DRAGOONS (9), till lately the 1st West York Yeomanry, date from 1803. They were actively employed for the first years of their career, and "received the thanks of the House of Lords for their readiness and useful services during the war which terminated in 1814." Again in 1820 and 1842 they received the "special thanks of the Sovereign" for their efficient services. The uniform is blue, without facings, helmet and white plume. The badge is the White Rose.

The PRINCE OF WALES'S OWN 2ND WEST HUSSARS (36) date from 1843. The uniform is blue with white facings, gold lace, helmet and white plume. The badge is composed of the Prince of Wales's Feathers and the White Rose.*

The Volunteer Force suggests by its mere name one of the most remarkable—perhaps the most remarkable—Institutions of this or any other nation, of the present or any preceding age. It is almost needless to say that the present splendid army of citizen soldiers is by no means the first assemblage of Volunteers which the country has known, but it is the first which has ever attained to the same excellence, whether of organisation, discipline, or military capability. Adequately to attempt a description of the inception, growth, and characteristics of the Volunteer Force would require a volume; the task has been, we are aware, essayed, and not unsuccessfully; but we venture to think that there is still room for a comprehensive account of the Volunteers, which, if the treatment be but worthy of the theme, should rank as well amongst the most important histories, as amongst the most fascinating works of popular literature.

To a very great extent, Volunteer service preceded, even after the earliest ages, fixed or professional service. It needed no feudal tenure or obligation, still less did it need hire or reward, to make men fight for hearth and home, for wife and children. The sturdy defenders of coast, and marches, and borderland of centuries ago were the predecessors of the—

"Loyal people shouting a battle cry"—

whom the world of to-day has seen—and seen with amazement and awe and envying admiration—formed, self-impelled, into an army whose very existence has, as confessed by friends and foes alike, rendered their country absolutely impregnable and mightier and more imperial than ever of yore. There were Volunteers enrolled in considerable force

* In the above classification of dates, badges, etc., Captain Perry's list has been largely adopted.

during the American War of Independence; when, drunk with the blood of princes and nobles, the French Republic, arising, maddened from the devilish orgies of the Terror, spurned God and threatened man, the splendid British armies which saved Europe had their place at home supplied by three hundred thousand Volunteers; at other times of public need Volunteers have sprung to the front. But such embodiments were, so to speak, solely *ad hoc*. When the danger passed away, the Volunteers vanished into thin air, like the saintly or celestial warriors of song and fable, who after serving their country in emergency, disappear.

The present Volunteer Force dates from 1859. For years previously to that date Volunteering had been "in the air;" in 1847 the letter from the Duke of Wellington, the hero of Waterloo, who through all his grand career had

"Never sold the truth to serve the hour,
Or paltered with Eternal God for power—"

was made public in which he wrote: "Excepting immediately under the guns of Dover Castle there is not a spot on the coast on which infantry might not be thrown at any time of tide, with any wind, and in any weather," and prayed, in words to which the personality of the writer lent an indescribable force and pathos, that "the Almighty may protect me from being a witness to the tragedy which I cannot persuade my contemporaries to take measures to avert." Yet even this earnest appeal was disregarded, thanks, as an able writer puts it, "to the timorous agitation, kept alive by the so-called 'peace' party, led on by its eloquent shepherds who chanted Arcadian lays, and hurled denunciations against all proposals for increased armament." Five years later, however, the county—in one sense, perhaps, the most Arcadian of all—Devonshire, formed a regiment of rifle volunteers; the following year, 1853, the Victoria Rifles, the direct representatives of the "Duke of Cumberland's Sharpshooters" of the last century, sprang again into existence. In 1859, when, to quote the words of the then Mr. Disraeli, "our pacific relations with France were not a question of days or weeks, but of hours," Lord Derby's Ministry issued the famous circular authorising the enrolment of Volunteer Corps. Before many months had passed a Volunteer army of a hundred and fifty thousand men had been created, one of the conditions of whose existence was, that they should "provide their own arms and equipments and defray all expenses attending the corps, except in the event of its being assembled for actual service," a contingency which would arise in the event of "actual or apprehended invasion."

For a period there was unbounded enthusiasm; then came the phase of ridicule.

Military men—some of whom have since become the warmest advocates of the Force—were at no pains to conceal their contempt; superior persons derided it in season and out; facetious ones found in it an inexhaustible fund for cheap wit. In *Punch* "the Volunteer" was a stock jest, rivalling in laughter-making attributes Mr. Briggs, the ladies' crinolines or Mary Jane's escapades in the kitchen. Doubtless the movement, or rather the accidents of the movement, had a comical side. One remembers what Walter Scott—himself an enthusiastic Volunteer officer—wrote in "The Antiquary" of the movement in his time.

"I called to consult my lawyer, he was clothed in a dragoon's dress, belted and casqued, and about to mount a charger, which his writing clerk (habited as a sharpshooter) walked to and fro before his door. I went to scold my agent for having sent me to advise with a madman; he had stuck into his head the plume which in more sober days he wielded between his fingers, and figured as an artillery officer. My mercer had his spontoon in his hand, as if he measured his cloth by that implement, instead of a legitimate yard. The banker's clerk, who was directed to sum my cash account, blundered it three times, being disordered by the recollection of his military *tellings off* at the morning drill. I was ill, and sent for a surgeon—

> 'He came,—but valour so had fired his eye,
> And such a falchion glittered on his thigh,
> That, by the gods, with such a load of steel,
> I thought he came to murder—not to heal.'

I had recourse to a physician, but he also was practising a more wholesome mode of slaughter than that which his profession had been supposed at all times to open to him."

The same causes led to the somewhat similar criticism made by a reviewer of the infant Volunteer Force now in its full vigour.

"There were no such special incentives in 1859 as on former occasions, yet the excitement and enthusiasm were far more widespread and continuous. England became one great drill-ground. Every full-grown adult, rich or poor, married or single, was seized with the contagion, and according to his means, contributed his aid. Local magnates, peers and their heirs-apparent, merchant princes, the great employers of labour, either raised corps, or assisted with handsome subscriptions. At all places where men congregated—at the Inns of Court, at Lloyd's, the Baltic, the great centres of learning—bodies of Volunteers were promptly organized. Other professions were not behind-hand; artists exchanged their mahl-sticks for rifles, doctors freely offered their services as regimental surgeons, the Church furnished its quota of honorary chaplains. On every side amateur soldiering was the favourite relaxation; hard-worked men of business and clerks, who were tied all daylight to their office stools, gladly surrendered their hours of leisure to be taught the goose step and the manual and platoon. A terminology, unknown hitherto beyond the barrack-yard, was in everybody's mouth. Men in a hurry 'doubled,' they did not run; if they went round a corner they ' wheeled ' to the right or left, or 'changed their flanks.' Friend meeting friend in the streets exchanged a military salute. All alike were anxious to assume the military air; the most sensible were satisfied with holding up their heads and maintaining an upright carriage, but great numbers insisted upon parading themselves in uniform about the streets."

The sentiment of the gutter found expression in the scarcely veiled and terrible taunt "Who killed the dog?" Sapient quidnunc-lings shook vacant foreheads as they muttered something about "playing at soldiers;" professed well-wishers could find nothing stronger in praise than a guarded tribute to the good moral effect of drill exercise for young men. All this was but thirty years ago. Now Volunteer officers bear Her Majesty's Commission; the same military salutes are accorded to them as to officers of the regular army; armed parties of Volunteers are saluted by the Guards, and military authorities of the highest rank seem to take every opportunity by frank praise and cordial recognition to make amends for past coldness. Not long ago the present Adjutant-General thus referred to the Volunteer movement!—"It is a great and real element of strength, and should the country ever be invaded, it will be a sword of might in the hands of those who know how to use it. Its existence alters greatly the conditions under which we shall henceforth engage in any European conflict, for, thanks to it, we could now send every regular soldier out of England, entrusting the home defence to that Force. To it the army owes a debt of gratitude for many reforms in drill, brought about through the persistent advocacy of its members, who have specially devoted themselves to that particular subject."

This grand result—that Great Britain presents now to the world at large the spectacle imaged by the poet of " a noble and puissant nation rousing herself like a strong man after sleep " is due to the selfless zeal, to the unquenchable enthusiasm, the open-handed *esprit de corps* of the Volunteers.

But the Volunteer movement survived ridicule, survived, too, the yet more incredible coldness of the authorities. The one feature of their organization which seemed indelibly to impress itself upon every government was its *voluntary* character. It was thought essential that this should be emphasized, and consequently to the most moderate requests the Volunteers received for reply a firm and conscientious " non possumus."*

The constant drills and exercises which have rendered them so effective a force represent, be it always remembered, so many hours taken from the limited spare time at their command; the encampments, which are productive of so much good, mean a positive expenditure in money, and a curtailment in many cases of the annual holiday; efficiency in marksmanship is fostered and encouraged by prizes from funds provided by the officers. The holding of a commission involves, indeed, a recognised annual expenditure of no trifling amount; Volunteer officers are splendidly jealous of the appearance and well-being of their corps, and it requires no very vivid imagination to suggest a thousand calls upon their purse.

A valuable paper in the *Nineteenth Century*, contributed by a well-known and zealous Volunteer officer,† thus sums up the actual work of Volunteers:—" When first joining they give up nearly all their leisure time to learn the rudiments of drill. Night after night you will see the men coming at the appointed hour, *straight from their work*, to join the squad to which they have been attached, striving hard to master the dry and uninteresting details which the sergeant instructor is doing his best to instil into them; some are sharp and pick them up quickly, others dull or careless; these last make the work much harder to those who are quick and willing, for as the pace of a squadron must be measured by the capacity of the slowest horse in it, so is the progress of a squad retarded by those who are difficult to teach. The work of volunteers is nearly always done in the evenings, as, of course, they cannot afford to sacrifice a day's pay or less for the purpose of undergoing their self-appointed labours. Shooting must be done by daylight, and going to the ranges usually takes a whole day; for this, they must have the sanction of their employer, who perhaps is not always willing to grant it, and in very many cases they sacrifice a day's pay. Some cannot get through their classes in one day, and have to try again; others go several times for the purpose of making themselves skilled shots, not satisfied to comply merely with the requirements of the authorities. When

---

* On a comparatively recent occasion one of the most distinguished Volunteer regiments, acting on the advice of a general officer of high standing, wished to develop their transport service. They applied for the *loan* of some waggons, of which a large quantity were lying unemployed at a Government yard. *They were refused.* On enquiring in the House of Commons into the circumstances, the minister questioned admitted the fact, and gave as a reason that there was no precedent for such a loan being made!

† Colonel Routledge, 2nd Volunteer Battalion Royal Fusiliers.

spring comes round, and open-air drill is possible, they sacrifice their well-earned Saturday half-holiday, don their uniform, and attend the parade of their battalion, either for a drill of two hours or more, or a long march through the streets, or on country roads. When Easter arrives, with its possible four days' holiday, some thousands of them sacrifice this to join the marching column in course of formation. They not only surrender their holidays, and in some cases sacrifice their wages, but spend money for the privilege of doing so."

It must not, however, be supposed that no pecuniary grant is made by the State. For every Volunteer certified by the Adjutant as efficient an allowance of thirty-five shillings is made to the regiment (assuming that the proper quota was present at the last official inspection); for each proficient officer and sergeant there is an additional grant of fifty shillings, while a special grant of thirty shillings is made in respect of officers who produce a certificate that they have passed in tactics or signalling—branches of military knowledge, be it observed, to which many officers enthusiastically devote themselves. On the occasions of "encampments" an allowance of two shillings, with travelling allowance of two and sixpence if more than five miles from headquarters, is made to each individual, and a similar sum is paid for the period, not exceeding four days, during which a Volunteer corps is joined to a "marching column." * "A moderate amount of camp equipment is also lent by Government," but complaints have been known that the official view of permissible "wear and tear" is so stringent as in some cases to induce dispensing *in toto* with the 'assistance.' It is, moreover, the exception rather than the rule when the encampment or march is limited to the six or four days above mentioned, so that the Government contribution falls far short of the actual expenses.

It may perhaps give an idea of the inestimable value of the Volunteer force when we consider that in numbers—taking these at 257,834—it exceeds the Regular Army by four-fifths, the Militia by three-fourths, is four times as strong as the Army Reserve, and eighteen times as strong as the Yeomanry, while its cost is not one twenty-second part of the whole appropriations for effective services! Every Volunteer corps has a permanent staff, which consists of an adjutant and two or three sergeants from the regular branch. The uniform is in the great majority of cases the same as that of the Line battalions of the same territorial regiment. The lace is, however, silver instead of gold, and no sash is worn by the officers.

* It is more when they are joined with Regulars or Militia battalions.

There are now two hundred and ten Volunteer Battalions attached to the Territorial Regiments of the army. Previous to 1881 there were a very much larger number of distinct corps, amounting at times—including Cavalry, Artillery, and Engineer Volunteers—to something like a thousand.

In the ensuing pages we shall treat of each Volunteer battalion in the order of the precedence observed in the "Army List." Full histories of each corps have yet to be written, nor would a full account be in many cases of general interest. Many of the Volunteer regiments, however, have a record which will well repay perusal, and of such we shall give as full a sketch as circumstances permit.

To group the Volunteers under the heading of the arms of the service to which they belong, we find that—

Of CAVALRY there are three regiments:—

>   The Fifeshire Light Horse Volunteers.
>   The Forfarshire Light Horse Volunteers.
>   The Roxburgh Mounted Rifles.

Of ARTILLERY Corps there are sixty-two, divided amongst

>   The Northern Division.
>   The Lancashire Division.
>   The Eastern Division.
>   The Cinque Ports Division.
>   The London Division.
>   The Southern Division.
>   The Western Division.
>   The Scottish Division.
>   The Welsh Division.

Of ENGINEER Volunteers there are:—

>   Fortress and Railway Forces Royal Engineers (20 corps).
>   Submarine Miners (9 corps).
>   Engineer and Railway Transport Volunteers.

Of Infantry Volunteer Regiments there are, as has been before observed, TWO HUNDRED AND TEN BATTALIONS contributed by NINETY-FOUR LOCALITIES.

Volunteer Cavalry are represented by three Scottish Corps—The FIFESHIRE LIGHT HORSE VOLUNTEERS, the FORFARSHIRE LIGHT HORSE VOLUNTEERS, and the ROXBURGH MOUNTED RIFLE VOLUNTEERS. From time to time some wonder is expressed that more bodies of this arm of the service have not been enrolled from amongst the volunteering portion of the community. The necessary cost would naturally prevent the formation of cavalry corps in any number, but the fact that, of necessity, each corps would be recruited entirely from the higher classes of the community would, one might think, of itself suffice to suggest the incorporation of a few corps, every member of which would claim and enjoy the social position accorded in years gone by to the "Gentlemen Troopers" of certain Regiments of Horse. The Fifeshire Light Horse Volunteers date from June, 1860, when they were raised from the districts of Cupar, St. Andrew's, and Kirkcaldy, and formed into a regiment under the command of the late Earl of Rosslyn. Their appearance at the Edinburgh Review of 1860 excited general admiration. Additional troops were raised and added in 1877 and 1883, and the Forfarshire Light Horse Volunteers were raised in 1886.* The uniform is scarlet with facings of blue. The 1st Roxburgh (Border Mounted Rifles) owe their existence to the efforts of Sir George Douglas and Viscount Melgund. They have on several occasions distinguished themselves as marksmen, winning on two occasions the "Lloyd Lindsay" prize at Wimbledon, and gaining deserved reputation for their efficiency in reconnoitring and signal work. The uniform is grey with facings of black.

The TYNEMOUTH ARTILLERY VOLUNTEERS can claim to be the senior Artillery corps in the Kingdom, and date from the 2nd of August, 1859. Had, indeed, the original intention been carried out, the date would have been earlier by some four months. This intention was that the Tynemouth Volunteers should form a corps like the Hon. Artillery Company of London, having both infantry and artillery. The idea, however, did not commend itself to the authorities, and accordingly the two arms were incorporated as distinct forces, the artillery becoming, as has been observed, the senior corps in the country. The strength of the 1st Northumberland Volunteer Artillery, as they were then called, was at the outset some eighty-three of all ranks, and their first exercise took place in the November following their incorporation. The uniform was grey with black facings and appointments, and artillery busby. The year following another corps of artillery—afterwards the 3rd Northumberland—sprang from the Tynemouth Volunteers, which, from

* A very interesting sketch of the Scotch Volunteer Regiments is given in the "Scottish Military Directory," published by D. Douglas, Edinburgh, and compiled by Lieutenant Cavaye, of the Cameron Highlanders.

that time to the present, may be said to present an unbroken record of success. It would indeed occupy too much space to enumerate the achievements, in the way of prize winings, sham fights and reviews, in which the corps has from time to time distinguished itself. It should be mentioned that in 1879 the 3rd Northumberland and the 1st Durham Artillery Volunteers were for a time amalgamated with, and known as, the 1st Northumberland. When the connection was dissolved considerable indignation was caused by the fact that in the shifting the Tynemouth had somehow lost their precedence of the *First* Artillery Volunteers and were relegated to the third place. This, however, has subsequently been remedied, and they have resumed their original position, and now boast a strength of nine batteries. It is an interesting coincidence that not only is the corps the Senior Volunteer Artillery Corps, but the commanding officer, Colonel Pilter, is the oldest volunteer officer now serving.

The 1st NORTHUMBERLAND ARTILLERY VOLUNTEERS date from 1859, when the two batteries of which they at first consisted were amalgamated with the Tynemouth. Towards the latter part of 1860, however, the strength having augmented to six batteries, they became an independent brigade under Colonel Trotter. For a time they were known as the 3rd Northumberland, their colleagues of Tynemouth retaining the numerical distinction of 1st. In 1879, however, they became a distinct regiment under the style of the 1st Northumberland and Sunderland Artillery Volunteers. As will be seen, the "Sunderland" became in its turn separate, and the regiment now under notice became the 1st Northumberland, having as its Hon. Colonel, the Duke of Northumberland. Amongst the prizes gained by the corps may be mentioned, the first prize for the shell competition at Shoeburyness in 1871, which was won by Battery Sergeant-Major Page's detachment, and the City of London Challenge Cup of 1878, which fell to the capital shooting of the detachment under Battery Sergeant-Major Patrick.

The 2nd NORTHUMBERLAND ARTILLERY VOLUNTEERS—the "Percy"—date from March, 1860, though there had been "Percy Artillery Volunteers" enrolled many years previously, before the thunders of Waterloo had secured to the country an immunity from invasion. The first year of their existence was a busy one; their first appearance in uniform was on the anniversary of the Queen's birthday, and the following August they took part in the Royal review at Edinburgh, and were especially noticed by Her Majesty. The following year the Duke of Northumberland presented to the corps a battery which he had had erected at a considerable expense. Three years later, when the strength had increased to six batteries, the same nobleman, who in 1865 became Hon. Colonel, defrayed the whole of the cost of clothing the brigade on its augmentation. In 1866 a battery of horse artillery was added, which, however, in accordance with the decisions of Government, was disbanded in 1870. In 1881 the corps again won Royal and general praise on the occasion of the review at Edinburgh in August of that year, and in 1882 occurred the "crowning glory" "when the Queen's prize, the City of London Gold Cup, the Canadian Prize and others, were brought home from the National Artillery competitions at Shoeburyness by Sergeant-Majors E. B. Gibson and Thomas Watson." Very numerous have been, on other occasions, the prizes won by the Percy Artillery, who may justly claim to be in the first rank amongst the eminent regiments of the kingdom.*

Attached to the 2nd Northumberland Artillery are the 1st BERWICK-ON-TWEED ARTILLERY, which date from February, 1860. Despite the smallness of the corps, which consists of only two batteries, the 1st Berwick-upon-Tweed can show a record of triumphs in the shooting contests which may make many another regiment envious. The corps are distinctly jealous of their individuality. There is a traditional brotherhood between them and the 2nd Northumberland. They would almost vie with the latter in loyalty to both their Hon. Colonel and commanding officer, but for all that, they have no wish to become amalgamated, or to cease to be the 1st Berwick-on-Tweed Artillery Volunteers, with their special buttons† and shoulder-strap, their own Captain Commandant,‡ and their separate orders from headquarters.

The 1st EAST RIDING OF YORKSHIRE ARTILLERY VOLUNTEERS date from December, 1859, when they were enrolled at Burlington, Flamborough, and Filey. The two first-named places supplied No. 1 Battery under Captain Haworth, and the volunteers from Filey constituted No. 2 Battery under Captain Cortis. Before long, Whitby, Scarborough, and York contributed their quota, and the corps, which numbers some 360 members, now boasts eight batteries.

The 2nd EAST RIDING OF YORKSHIRE ARTILLERY VOLUNTEERS date from 1860, Colonel Martin Samuelson being their first commanding officer, and the subordinate ranks being fully and ably supplied. The present Lieutenant-Colonel Commandant was gazetted a Second Lieutenant early in the same year.

The 1st NORTH RIDING OF YORK ARTILLERY VOLUNTEERS date from 1860, when they

* The Duke of Northumberland is Hon. Colonel, and Earl Percy the Lieutenant-Colonel of the corps which bears their name.
† A bear chained to a tree—the arms of Berwick.
‡ Major Caverhill.

were enrolled under the late Admiral Chaloner as commanding officer. Their present strength is nine batteries, and amongst the prizes gained by the corps at Shoeburyness are included the following:—1874, H.M. the Queen's Prize, won by the detachment under Battery Sergeant-Major Nicholson; 1876, the Prince of Wales's Prize, won by detachment under Battery Sergeant-Major Crowe; 1888, the Scotland Cup, won by detachment under Sergeant Johnson; 1889, the National Artillery Association Prize (nine cups), won by detachment under Sergeant Jenkins; and in the same year the 3rd Middlesex Artillery Prize, and the prize given by the Secretary of State for War, won by detachment under Sergeant-Major J. Hall. The corps is honoured by having as its Lieutenant-Colonel the present Lord-Lieutenant of Ireland, the Earl of Zetland.

The 1st CUMBERLAND ARTILLERY VOLUNTEERS date from 1860, and represent several corps now amalgamated under this title. They are one of the most favoured corps in the matter of spiritual and physical supervision, boasting no fewer than five chaplains and six surgeons.

THE 1st DURHAM ARTILLERY VOLUNTEERS were raised in 1859, and the two batteries which formed the nucleus of the present strength of six batteries, were placed under Capt. William Young, who was succeeded as commanding officer by the present Hon. Colonel Sir Hedworth Williamson. In 1880 the corps was—much to their surprise, and not a little to their annoyance—amalgamated with the 1st Northumberland Artillery Volunteers, the composite corps bearing the title of the 1st Northumberland and Sunderland Artillery Volunteers. Within the last few months, however, this has been altered, and the title and position are now as stated.

The 2nd DURHAM ARTILLERY VOLUNTEERS also date from 1859, when they were raised at Seaham, and owe their existence, as well as their boast of being not only one of the most efficient, but also one of the largest contingents in the Artillery branch of our citizen army, to the energy and enthusiasm of the late Marchioness of Londonderry. At the Hyde Park Review of 1860, the 'Seahams' were the only regiment present from the district, and won golden opinions.* The corps now numbers twelve batteries, boasts a splendid band, and has won so many prizes that enumeration is out of the question, but amongst them have been the National Artillery Prize, the Challenge Cup of Scotland, the Prince of Wales's Prize, the Prize of the Dominion of Canada, and *two* Queen's Prizes. The late Marquis of Londonderry, Colonel Commander of the regiment, was president of

* Capt. Ogilvie states that the Seahams were the only volunteer regiment present from the district north of Manchester, and that the whole cost of the undertaking was defrayed by the Marchioness.

the National Artillery Association, which has done so much to improve the "big gun" shooting of the country. The terrible colliery accidents in 1871 and 1880 wrought sad havoc in the ranks of the Seahams, and amongst those hurt were, by a strange coincidence, "the No. 1's of both the winning detachments of the Queen's Prizes."

The 3rd DURHAM ARTILLERY VOLUNTEERS, now attached to the 1st Newcastle-on-Tyne Artillery Volunteers, date from 1860. In 1859 an infantry corps had been formed, but before very long was amalgamated with due official sanction. In 1867 the "South Shields" Artillery were the champion shots for the year; in 1873 they "began to rush into the front rank of Artillerists," wining prize after prize. Since then there has been to some extent a disposition to rest upon their laurels, but great hopes are entertained that, under Major Dawson, the 3rd Durham will reassert their position as a leading corps amongst Volunteer Gunners.

The 4th DURHAM ARTILLERY VOLUNTEERS were raised in 1859, at West Hartlepool The writer before quoted (Captain Ogilvie) in his mention of the corps refers to the undoubted fact that the Hartlepool Volunteers of to-day might—were there no break in the succession—claim an antiquity equal to that of the Hon. Artillery Company of London, inasmuch as in the reign of Henry VIII., in which period the charter of the latter company was granted, the men of Hartlepool had their organization complete, and contributed not a little to the military security of the realm. In 1872 the 4th Durham Artillery absorbed the 19th Durham Rifle Corps, then disbanded, the present commanding officer* was appointed, and the strength of the corps raised to eight batteries. Few regiments can show a better record in the way of prizes, and it will be a matter of gratification to all its members and friends that when the Russo-Turkish war seemed to threaten the peace of the Empire, the 4th Durham volunteered for foreign service.

The 1st WEST RIDING, the 2nd WEST RIDING, and the 4th WEST RIDING ARTILLERY VOLUNTEERS, complete the contribution of Yorkshire to this branch of the auxiliary service.

The 2nd WEST RIDING YORK ARTILLERY VOLUNTEERS were raised in 1871 through the exertions of Major Holroyde, and were first known as the 8th West York Artillery Volunteers, forming part of the 1st West York Administrative Brigade. In 1880 the 8th West York Artillery Volunteers, with the other corps forming this Administrative Brigade, were formed into the 2nd West York Artillery Volunteers under Lieutenant

* Colonel Cameron.

Colonel Sir C. Frith, with Major Holroyde as second in command. In the year 1877 the corps became Position Artillery, and is now one of the most efficient regiments in the auxiliary service.

Taking the 4th WEST RIDING ARTILLERY VOLUNTEERS as another representative corps we find that they were raised at Sheffield in 1861 under the command of their present Lieutenant-Colonel, Colonel Creswick. Beginning with the comparatively small number of 192, the strength at the time of writing is 442, of whom 439 are returned as efficient. When the corps became a Brigade of Position Artillery it was divided into four batteries, previous to which time the corps could boast of having won no fewer than twenty-six prizes in various competitions, including the Montreal Challenge Cup in Canada, 1884. The Queen's Prize during the same competition was won by an amalgamated detachment commanded by Captain Allan of the 4th West Riding Artillery Volunteers, and containing two other members of the same corps. The Hon. Colonel of the corps is the Duke of Norfolk.

The NEWCASTLE-ON-TYNE ARTILLERY VOLUNTEERS may be said to be the direct representatives of the ARMED ASSOCIATION which, towards the close of the last century, enrolled themselves as a body of Loyal Volunteers, and practised amongst other military exercises big gun firing, with special regard to the defence of the Tyne. The present corps dates from May 1860, when it was incorporated with a strength of two batteries, increased within a few years to six. In 1872 the present quota of eight batteries was made up, and two years later the South Shields Artillery Volunteers, the 3rd Durham, were attached. For some time the corps was purely "Garrison" Artillery, but owing in great measure to the energy and generosity of its first Commanding Officer, the late Colonel Alhusen, who supplied at his own expense "a battery of beautiful six-pounder field-pieces," they were able to extend their duties. They were, moreover, the first of the Artillery Volunteers to be entrusted with breech-loader guns by Government, which were issued on trial in 1870, "after a great deal of unnecessary correspondence and frivolous excuses, enough, in fact, to have made any man throw up the movement in disgust." The "trial" was, however, so satisfactory, and the Newcastle-on-Tyne Volunteers showed themselves such adepts with the guns, that they retained possession of them till 1888, when the corps was selected as one of Position Artillery entirely. From the commencement the corps have been a notable example of the ungrudging enthusiasm of volunteer officers, "the whole of the draught horses, as well as much of the harness and appointments, being the private property of firms with which the various officers are connected and are lent gratuitously."*

The nine corps of Lancashire Artillery Volunteers date from 1860, and have their headquarters as follows :—the 1st, 2nd, 4th, 6th, and 8th at Liverpool; the 3rd at Blackburn; the 5th at Preston; the 7th (the Manchester Artillery) at Manchester; and the 9th at Bolton. As we propose to glance at some length at the volunteer movement as it affected Lancashire when treating of some of the Infantry Battalions, we will only mention here that the Artillery Brigades have, from the dates of their incorporation, shown a steady enthusiasm and devotion that well merit and account for the high position they occupy.

The 1st CHESHIRE AND CARNARVONSHIRE and the 1st SHROPSHIRE AND STAFFORDSHIRE ARTILLERY VOLUNTEERS complete the Lancashire division. The former represents a considerable number of independent corps raised in the neighbourhood, and which were grouped together into an Administrative Brigade. Both corps have done good work and gained considerable commendation on various occasions.†

The Eastern Division Royal Artillery has three Volunteer Brigades attached to it.

The 1st VOLUNTEER (NORFOLK) BRIGADE used formerly to be known as the 1st Norfolk and Suffolk; the 2nd VOLUNTEER (ESSEX) BRIGADE was formerly the 1st Essex, and has attached to it the Harwich Cadet Corps; the 3rd VOLUNTEER (LINCOLNSHIRE) BRIGADE was formerly the 1st Lincolnshire. The headquarters of the Brigades are respectively Great Yarmouth, Stratford, and Grimsby. The Norfolk Brigade is another instance showing the absorption of several smaller corps, by the fact of its possessing six surgeons and as many chaplains.

The Cinque Ports Division will, to the minds of many, seem at first sight the most important of the artillery commands; and though it may be open to doubt whether an invading enemy would now choose that part of the coast for an attack, it is impossible to forget that not so very many years ago the probability of this being done seemed imminent.

The 1st VOLUNTEERS (SUSSEX) BRIGADE of the Division has been for long more familiarly known as the 1st Sussex Artillery Volunteers, and as such has earned

---

* "The Newcastle-on-Tyne Artillery Volunteers have always been celebrated for their magnificent repository detachments."

† The 1st Cheshire and Carnarvonshire boast no fewer than eight surgeons.

honourable distinction for effectiveness, as beseems a brigade whose headquarters are at London-super-Mare.

The 2nd SUSSEX, now the 2nd Volunteer Brigade of the Division, have as their Hon. Colonel the Marquis of Hartington, whose family connections with Eastbourne—the headquarters of the Brigade—render the choice a natural one.

The 1st KENT, now the 3rd Volunteer Brigade of the Division, are recruited from the neighbourhood of Gravesend, and may thus claim to have under their care one of the most, perhaps the most, important of the positions in the country. Kent showed early a distinct zeal for the artillery service. The Gravesend Corps, raised in 1860, soon numbered two companies; in quick succession to these, corps were raised at Faversham, Sheerness, Blackheath, Greenwich, Plumstead, Woolwich Arsenal, Sandgate, Gillingham, Sheerness, and Woolwich Dockyard. The Gravesend corps was commanded by Lieut.-Colonel Gladdish, and had as captain a gentleman of local popularity in the person of Captain Rosher.

The CINQUE PORTS, now the Cinque Ports Brigade of the Division, has its headquarters at Dover, and represents several smaller corps, which at the commencement of the volunteer movement sprang into being. These were raised at Dover, Folkestone, Ramsgate, Sandwich, Walmer, Hastings, and Hythe, in the early part of 1860, and with the formation were associated the names of Captain Worlaston, Captain Commandant of the Dover corps; Captain Kennicott, R.N.; Captain Cutler; Major Thomson, K.D.G.; Captain Harvey, and Captain G. W. V. Vernon Harcourt. The Cinque Ports Artillery Volunteers are justly proud of the position they hold in the force, and their efficiency and successes reflect no small credit on the corps as a whole.*

The 2nd KENT ARTILLERY VOLUNTEERS belong to the London Division of the Royal Artillery, and have their headquarters at Plumstead.

The 3rd KENT ARTILLERY VOLUNTEERS—the "Woolwich Arsenal" Brigade—are a brigade of Position Artillery, and their headquarters, as indicated, at Woolwich. The Hon. Colonel is Sir J. M. Adye, G.C.B., and the brigade occupies a very high position in the Auxiliary Artillery. The Woolwich Arsenal Artillery Volunteers stepped directly into a very front rank. Their Colonel Commandant was Colonel Tulloch, of the Royal Artillery, and very few months elapsed before they were able to number seven batteries. The Dockyard Artillery Volunteers were not far behind,

---

* The Cinque Ports Artillery Volunteers have ten surgeons, one veterinary surgeon, six acting and two honorary chaplains.

numbering as they soon did five batteries, and having as commanding officer, Major Thornton.

The 2nd MIDDLESEX ARTILLERY VOLUNTEERS have, like their brethren of the 3rd Kent, the honour of having as their Hon. Colonel another distinguished artillery officer, in the person of Lieut.-General Sir E. B. Hamley, K.C.B. The brigade has always had a reputation for steady and effective work, and has elicited no small praise for its capable and soldierlike performances.

The 3rd MIDDLESEX ARTILLERY VOLUNTEERS are commanded by Lord Truro, one of the aides-de-camp to the Queen, and constitute what may be called the West End contribution to the Artillery Volunteers of the London Division, having their headquarters in the familiar locality of Charing Cross.

The 1st (CITY OF LONDON) ARTILLERY VOLUNTEERS in their turn spring from the heart of the City proper, having their headquarters in Whitecross Street. The Hon. Colonel is the Duke of Teck, and the Lieutenant-Colonel Commandant, Lieut.-Colonel W. Hope, one of the Volunteer officers who can boast the proud honour of a " V.C." after their names, gained in that fruitful field of glory, the Crimea.

The Southern Division Royal Artillery has three Volunteer brigades:—The 1st HAMPSHIRE, now the 1st Volunteer (Hampshire) Brigade of the Division, have their headquarters at Southsea, and, with the 3rd VOLUNTEER (HAMPSHIRE) BRIGADE stationed at Southampton, boast precedence of second amongst the Artillery Volunteers. The 1st Dorsetshire Artillery Volunteers now form the 2nd VOLUNTEER (DORSETSHIRE) BRIGADE of the SOUTHERN DIVISION, and have their headquarters at Weymouth.

Two corps were raised in Hampshire in the early days of the movement, one at Bitterne, and one at Southsea. The latter made rapid strides towards efficiency, under its first captain commandant, Captain Hall, of the 73rd Regiment, soon boasting two batteries, an excellent drill ground, and being in a position to dispense with any entrance fee. They, moreover, speedily acquired a capital band. The uniform when the corps was first raised was blue with scarlet facings, and brown leather belt.

The three following Brigades form the Volunteer contingent of the Western Division Royal Artillery. The 1st Devonshire, now the 1ST VOLUNTEER (DEVONSHIRE) BRIGADE of the Division, has its headquarters at Exeter.

The 1st and 2nd Devonshire rank third in precedence.

No fewer than eleven Artillery Corps were raised in Devonshire; the following localities contributing companies in the order given:—Woodbury, Sidmouth, Teignmouth, Torquay, Exeter, Dartmouth, Exmouth, Woodbury, Paignton, Salombe, and Brixham. The first commander of the Exeter Company was Captain Kingdon, while many representative names, such as Vivian, Tonkin, Brent, English, Pullin, Blake, and Tracey, are to be found amongst the first officers.

The 2nd Devonshire, now the 2ND VOLUNTEER (DEVONSHIRE) BRIGADE of the Division, whose headquarters are at Devonport, has attached to it the Cadet Corps of Mannamead School, Plymouth.

The Duke of Cornwall's, late the 1st Cornwall, and now the 3rd VOLUNTEER (DUKE OF CORNWALL'S) BRIGADE of the Division, has its headquarters at Falmouth. In this as, unfortunately, in many similar cases, we can only find space to record the fact that the Duke of Cornwall's Artillery Volunteers has since its inauguration won golden opinions for its strength and efficiency.

Ten corps represented the sturdy enthusiasm of Cornwall for the Artillery Volunteer movement. Padstow, Looe, Fowey, Charlestown, Par, Par Harbour, Polruan, Hayle, and Buryan, were the localities represented; while the brawny workers in the Fowey Consols Mine furnished a corps from their own number. The commander of the Brigade Staff was Lieut.-Colonel Gilbert of the Royal Artillery.

The Scottish Division Royal Artillery has no fewer than fifteen Volunteer Brigades.

The CITY OF EDINBURGH ARTILLERY VOLUNTEERS date from July, 1859, when they were raised "as a Volunteer Artillery Artists' Corps, composed of artists and amateurs, among whom may be mentioned such well-known names as the following: Gourley Steele, W. J. Orchardson, J. M'Whirter, G. Pettie, W. F. Vallance, Noel Paton, and Geo. Aikman." Noel Paton was appointed Captain in October, 1859. The following year the corps were represented at the Review of 1860, and since that date its strength has materially increased. It now numbers about six hundred of all ranks, with two field and seven garrison batteries, and at most of the important prize meetings has done remarkably well.

The headquarters of the Brigade are in Edinburgh, and attached to it are the 1st Berwickshire Artillery Volunteers.

The 1ST EDINBURGH CITY ARTILLERY VOLUNTEER CORPS were the first Artillery Volunteers to be raised in Scotland, and the fifth in the United Kingdom. Before they had been three years in existence they numbered nine batteries, and were considered, with justice, one of the most important corps in the Kingdom.

The 1ST MIDLOTHIAN ARTILLERY VOLUNTEERS, to which is attached for capitation purposes the 1st Haddington Artillery Volunteer Corps, raised in October, 1859, were also amongst the first Artillery Volunteers whose services were accepted, their first commanding officer being gazetted in December, 1859. Before many months had elapsed they attained their present strength of eight batteries. They were known as the "Midlothian Coast" Artillery Brigade, and have always kept up a high standard of efficiency.

The BANFF ARTILLERY VOLUNTEERS, the Aberdeen, Banff, and Elgin of a former nomenclature, also date from 1859. The present Hon. Colonel is the Duke of Fife, and the brigade is a strong and efficient one, and claims precedence as the third Volunteer corps in Scotland.

The FORFARSHIRE ARTILLERY VOLUNTEERS were also amongst the earlier formed brigades. Their headquarters are at Dundee, and the strength of the brigade has warranted its having a Lieutenant-Colonel Commandant. The 1st Forfarshire possesses no fewer than fourteen batteries, seven of which are at Dundee, and the numerical strength is not far short of twelve hundred. The corps can show, too, a satisfactory record in the matter of prize winning.

The RENFREW AND DUMBARTON ARTILLERY VOLUNTEERS were raised in 1859, and have their headquarters at the busy port of Greenock. There are seven batteries, stationed at Greenock, Port Glasgow, Helensburgh, and Dumbarton.

The FIFESHIRE ARTILLERY VOLUNTEERS, formerly the "Fife and Stirling," date from the same year, and in contrast with the brigade last mentioned, have their local habitation amongst the "studious shades" of the university city of St. Andrews. It is a strong brigade, numbering, we believe, some thirteen batteries.

The 1st LANARKSHIRE ARTILLERY VOLUNTEERS may claim to owe their origination to a remark made by the late Prince Consort. The occasion was the opening by Her Majesty of the Loch Katrine Waterworks, and Captain—afterwards Colonel—Dreghorn of the 3rd Lanark Rifles, was introduced to the Prince, who, in the course of conversation, expressed the anxiety felt by the military authorities as to the sufficiency of gunners. Captain Dreghorn spoke to some friends on the subject, and with such good effect that during the following month three companies had been enrolled, which before the end of the year had increased to eight. These were formed into a brigade, which by the time of the Royal Review in August, 1860, numbered eleven companies. By the middle of 1868 the full complement of seventeen companies was attained, and at the time of writing the 1st Lanarkshire Artillery Volunteers may claim to be one of the most efficient, as they are one of the strongest, brigades in the auxiliary service. They are fortunate in having a splendid range, well-appointed batteries, and able and enthusiastic officers. The present commander, Colonel Kidston, can claim the honour of being the senior Volunteer in Lanarkshire at present on active duty. It is—or rather, used to be—so often urged that Volunteer duties are as free from danger as from serious work, that it may be well to recall an occurrence only too intimately connected with the 1st Lanarkshire Artillery Volunteers, which proves that such immunity is by no means absolute. In 1880, when several officers of the regiment were engaged at shell practice, an explosion occurred, whereby some—including Major Matheson, Captains Reid and Shaw, Lieutenant Brown, and the Adjutants, Captain Wilson, R.A., and Captain Marsh, R.A.—were more or less severely wounded, and the deservedly popular commander, Lieutenant-Colonel West Watson, received his death blow. The corps has been fortunate in numbering amongst its adjutants some whose names are familiar for gallant service and valuable teaching,* while the past and present chaplains† are as valued by the corps for their good services as by the world at large for their "Good Words."

The AYRSHIRE and GALLOWAY VOLUNTEERS date from November, 1859, and are recruited from the neighbourhoods of Ayr, Wigton, and Kirkcudbright. Like the Lanarkshire they are a strong and efficient corps, and previously to 1880 were known as the 1st Administrative Brigade, Ayr.

The ARGYLL AND BUTE ARTILLERY VOLUNTEERS date from 1860, and under the command of Colonel Campbell, have maintained a high position amongst the Scottish Brigades. Their headquarters are at the picturesque town of Rothesay.

The CAITHNESS ARTILLERY VOLUNTEERS, better known as the Caithness and Sutherland Artillery, date from 1860, the Caithness contingent having the priority in point of date. The present strength is eight batteries, of which six are in Caithness and two in Sutherlandshire; the latter being the successors of the 1st Sutherland Artillery Volunteers, raised by the Duke of Sutherland.

The ABERDEENSHIRE ARTILLERY VOLUNTEERS (Aberdeen and Kincardine) date from 1859, though some of the batteries were raised at a later date. Four batteries at Aberdeen, four in Kincardine, and two at Peterhead and Fraserburgh were in 1861

* Captain Nott, R.M.A., who had served in India and China; Captain, now Colonel Wilson, R.A., of Bhotan, Jowaki, and Afghan fame; Major Hine, R.A., F.S.S., the well-known authority on tactics and other military matters.

† The first chaplain was the late Dr. Norman Macleod, who was succeeded by his son, Dr. Donald Macleod.

constituted the 1st Aberdeenshire Administrative Brigade. Others have subsequently been added. The corps is a strong and efficient one, and is fortunate also in possessing exceptionally fine drill halls.

The BERWICKSHIRE ARTILLERY VOLUNTEERS are, as has been before stated, attached to the 1st Edinburgh Artillery Volunteer Corps.

The INVERNESS-SHIRE (or the HIGHLAND) ARTILLERY VOLUNTEERS (Inverness, Cromarty, Nairn, Ross, and Elgin) dating from November, 1859, are, as might be expected, a strong corps, numbering twelve batteries, and have achieved satisfactory successes in the various artillery competitions.

The last of the Volunteer brigades of the Scottish Division are the ORKNEY ARTILLERY VOLUNTEERS, raised in 1859, and amalgamated with the Caithness Artillery Volunteers. Small though the county is which they represent, it has seen plenty of rough fighting in bygone days, but it is doubtful whether the Fane of St. Magnus, or the hoary palaces whose ruins abut on to it, ever saw a finer set of men than the Kirkwall Volunteers of to-day. The quarrels of the rebellion have still their favourable outcome for the Kirkwall Artillery, who find "Cromwell's Fort" a valuable rendezvous for practice.

The Welsh Division Royal Artillery has three volunteer contingents—Glamorganshire, Gloucestershire, and Worcester.

The 1st GLAMORGANSHIRE ARTILLERY VOLUNTEERS date from 1859, and have their headquarters at Cardiff.

The 1ST GLOUCESTERSHIRE ARTILLERY VOLUNTEERS (Gloucester and Somerset) were also among the earlier formed of Volunteer Artillery corps. The first companies raised were at Bristol, Newnham, Gloucester, Clevedon, and Weston-super-Mare. The headquarters are at Bristol, and the strength of the corps is well maintained.

The WORCESTER ARTILLERY VOLUNTEERS (Worcester and Monmouth) date from a somewhat later period. The headquarters are at Worcester, and attached to the brigade is the cadet corps of Malvern College.

The Engineer Volunteers date as a rule from 1859; the Submarine Miners, however, consisting of nine divisions, were only formed as recently as 1886. The Engineering Branch of the auxiliary service has from the first enlisted public sympathy and appreciation, nor is it easy to measure accurately the importance of the movement. The annals of the various Divisions of necessity present a sameness, and we should not, therefore, feel justified in repeating dates and statistics which would be in many cases identical. The first of the Divisions in order of precedence is the 1st Middlesex; then follow the Lanarkshire, the Edinburgh City, the Lancashire, the Newcastle-on-Tyne, the Yorkshire (W. Riding,) the Gloucestershire, the Cheshire, the Denbigh, the Tower Hamlets, the Cumberland, the Surrey, the Hampshire, the Glamorgan, the Essex, the Devon, the London, the Flint, the Northamptonshire, the Durham, the Somerset, and the Aberdeenshire—in the order named. Of these the Northamptonshire is attached to the Tower Hamlets and the Flint to the 1st Lancashire, while the Gloucestershire have two cadet corps, the Cheltenham College and the Clifton College, and the Tower Hamlets one cadet corps—the Bedford Grammar School—attached to them.

The history of the 1st NEWCASTLE-ON-TYNE ENGINEER VOLUNTEERS, with whom were associated till quite recently the 1st Durham Engineer Volunteers, will be as typical an example as can be selected of the history and achievements of this branch of the auxiliary service.

In 1860 it was determined to form a company of Engineers in connection with the Volunteer movement in Newcastle. The material was ready to hand. The world-famed factories of Lord Armstrong at Elswick included amongst the staff employed as well able theorists and mathematicians as skilled workmen, and accordingly a company was formed under the command of Captain Westmacott. In 1868 the Newcastle Company were attached to the Durham Engineers, who had their headquarters at Jarrow, and in 1880 a complete consolidation was accomplished, the regiment being known as the Newcastle-on-Tyne and Durham Engineer Volunteers. This connection was, however, dissolved in the early part of last year (1889), when the respective designations were fixed as they now stand. The Newcastle Regiment have the honour of having inaugurated amongst the Volunteers of the North the Ambulance Corps. The idea originated in 1875, with Surgeon Cook, who found an energetic supporter in the then Adjutant, Major Trimble, and the latter lost no time in organizing the newly formed detachment according to the regulations in force in the regular army. "To prove that the members of the Newcastle and Durham Engineers did not intend to play at soldiers, but that if occasion required they were ready to take their place beside their brothers of the regular service," we may mention that in the Egyptian Campaigns of 1882 and 1885, detachments from the regiment (the majority being from the Newcastle wing) volunteered —*and were accepted*—for active service, on the understanding that when the war ended they would be granted a free discharge. The Volunteers of 1885 were fortunate enough to take active part in the campaign under Sir Gerald Graham, and were presented with the Egyptian Medal and the Khedive Star on their return, " in the presence of such a gathering of representative Volunteers as had never before assembled under one roof." *

Both regiments devote themselves to their work with enthusiasm, and the military authorities speak of their progress in the highest terms. Practical evidence of their proficiency was given on the occasion of the Newcastle Exhibition in 1887, when " there was on view in the grounds a siege battery for guns with magazines complete; across the lakes were constructed a trestle bridge 60 feet long, a bridge of casks 130 feet, and a treble stiffened sling bridge 100 feet long, all constructed by the 1st Newcastle, under Colonel A. S. Palmer, during the months of March and April, in the evenings after the men had finished their hard day's work in factory, shop, or office."

Such is the history of the 1st Newcastle and the 1st Durham Engineer Volunteers, and similar to it, *mutatis mutandis*, may be said to be in essentials the history of the other corps of the same arm of the service. Not, perhaps, that the same opportunities have occurred or have been utilised in the same manner, but the same enthusiasm for work, the same carelessness of personal comfort, the same intelligent aptitude for performing heavy labours and for mastering scientific details, the same marked progress towards valuable efficiency, may be credited in measure that but slightly varies to all the corps of Engineer Volunteers.†

The Submarine Mining Corps of the Engineer Volunteers dates from 1886. Previously to that date, however, the advisability of such an institution had been pointed out by Lieutenant-General Sir A. Clarke; and Colonel Palmer, of the 1st Durham Engineer Volunteers, immediately set himself to work to prove the feasibility of the suggestion. He applied (towards the end of 1883) to the War Office for authority to form "a submarine mining company for the defence of the Tyne." At first the Government did not seem to appreciate this prompt response to the suggestion of their Inspector-General of Fortifications, but after some delay the requisite permission was granted, subject to the condition " that Captain Palmer would find the necessary craft, &c., at his own expense, and that the men should undergo a course of training on the River Tyne;" then "if found qualified for this service his application would be

---

* The Volunteers of 1882 had arrived at Chatham ready for embarkation, when the fall of Tel-el-Kebir satisfied the authorities that no further troops need be sent.

† The uniform of the Engineer Volunteers is scarlet, with blue facings, white cords and shoulder cords, and white band and button on forage caps. The Submarine Mining Company wear S.M. on the shoulder straps, and the efficient non-commissioned officers and sappers a silver grenade on the right arm.

granted." Colonel Palmer accepted the condition, and provided not only the "necessary craft, &c.," but a considerable part of the cost of the experiments, which were forthwith made at Clifford's Fort, the men of the Durham Engineer Volunteers working with a company of Royal Engineers, with the result that the Durham men were reported "highly qualified for carrying out this important duty."

It may therefore, with justice, be claimed by the Tyne regiment that they "inaugurated a movement from which emanated the further extension of submarine mining by Volunteers throughout the United Kingdom."

Quick to follow the example of their brethren in the North, the Bristol Engineer Volunteer Corps formed a company for the protection of the Severn; then followed the 1st Lanarkshire for the defence of Greenock, and the 1st Lancashire for that of the vast commercial interests concentrated in Liverpool. The Tees and the Forth, the Tay and the Humber, are now each protected by a corps of Submarine Miners of the Engineer Volunteers, while the division at Falmouth keeps watch and ward over the Cornish harbour.

We now come to the Infantry Volunteers, who form the great bulk of that portion of the Auxiliary Forces. Invaluable as the Artillery and Engineers are, useful and popular as would undoubtedly be a Cavalry contingent, there is no doubt that to the world in general, the Infantry are the force conjured up by the employment of the word "Volunteers." They it was who seemed particularly summoned by the Laureate's clarion call:—

"Riflemen, riflemen, riflemen, form!"

They it was who, alike in print and picture, in eulogy and satire, seemed the visible exponents of the national strength, which the country had evoked to guard against possible danger from one who might perhaps be

"——— a faithful ally,
But only the devil knows what he means."

As has been before observed, we propose to take the Infantry Volunteer Battalions in the order of the Territorial Regiments to which they now belong; the actual order of precedence will be, except in a few cases, of but little interest to the general reader, who will find the same date claimed as that of the foundation of many of the regiments. We must go to poetry for an adequate description of what the year 1859 saw in this

Island Empire. When Roderick Dhu disclosed himself to the chivalrous Knight of Snowdon, we read :—

> "Instant, through copse and heath arose
> Bonnets and spears and bended bows;
> On right, on left, above, below,
> Sprung up at once the lurking foe;
> * * * * * * *
> As if the yawning hill to Heaven
> A subterranean host had given."

So, when our country bade another possible foe pause and take heed, there sprang up, as if by magic, to enforce the stern warning—from "town and tower and hamlet," from pastoral valleys and teeming factories, from crowded docks and cavernous mine, from the desk and the Exchange, from the form and from the University—an army unknown and undreamed of, and which from that day to this has waxed ever mightier in strength and skill.

As a thoughtful writer has expressed it : "From the day of their general enrolment, England took a still higher place in the scale of nations. Of threats and fumings there have been plenty, but Europe has always known where to draw the line when diplomatically dealing with the great nation of the West. When the kinglets of semi-barbarism have revolted, English volunteers have promised military aid; when ancient nations like the Soudanese have massed in unknown numbers to embarrass Britain's authority, the English volunteer has again come forward with his 'I am ready!' The chivalrous aristocrat, the merchant, and the manufacturer have associated in a common bond of sympathy with the plebeian, to prepare, should the need be, for all the vicissitudes and hardships of men of valour and honour. The great powers of Europe have learned that we are something more than a 'nation of shopkeepers,' and have treated us with far more consideration and civility since 1857 than before that period."

The QUEEN'S RIFLE VOLUNTEER BRIGADE—the uniform is grey with facings of the same colour—which forms the first volunteer battalion of the Royal Scots (Lothian Regiment, Regimental District, No. 1) has a history and pedigree which claims for it a notice at some length.* It would be interesting did space permit to glance at the military history of Edinburgh in bye-gone days, to sketch the achievements of the old volunteer forces—the volunteers of the '15 and '45, the Royal Edinburgh

---

* An interesting history of the brigade has been compiled by Lieutenant Stephen, from which many of the incidents noted have been gleaned.

Volunteer Regiment, the Edinburgh Defensive Band of 1781, and the Royal Edinburgh Volunteer Regiment—the Old Blues—organized in 1794—but we must take up the history with the commencement of the present movement. Amongst the earliest promoters of the Queen's Rifle Volunteer Brigade were the late Hugh Miller, Mr. Henry (the inventor of the rifle bearing his name), Mr. Macrae, and one of the present hon. colonels, then Major Davidson. So early as 1853 Hugh Miller had attracted public attention by his article "Our Best Ramparts," in which occur the passage, "Of all the monarchs in whose cause Scotchmen have spent their blood or treasure, never was there a monarch constitutionally representative of half the amount of solid good represented by the reigning sovereign, or yet possessed personally of half the solid worth." Men of light and leading threw themselves into the project with enthusiasm; a 'Citizens' Company' was formed, "the earliest members of which may safely be referred to as the first enrolled Volunteers in Scotland;" while to the legal profession "belongs the honour of having the first properly organized and trained company of Volunteers in Scotland," (*Stephen*). In August of 1859, ten companies had been formed, and these were constituted into a regiment styled "The City of Edinburgh Rifle Volunteer Corps," and ranking eleventh in order of priority. The following month another company was formed, for which is claimed the credit of being "the first formed in the kingdom in connection with the Civil Service of the Crown." When the regiment was only two months old they had the opportunity of mustering before Her Majesty, who was pleased to express her high appreciation of "their appearance and fine soldierly bearing," and who gave emphasis to her approval by conferring knighthood on the then Hon. Colonel, Sir John Melville. The historian of the regiment states that this was the first occasion upon which Her Majesty saw any body of Volunteers under arms in the country; other regiments, however, make a like claim. Additional companies continued to be formed, each company receiving its designation from the civil calling of its members. These were the "Advocates," the "Citizens," the "Writers," the "Accountants," the "Solicitors," the "Bankers," the "Freemasons," the "Merchants," the "High Constables," the "Highlanders," the "Artisans,"—many of these descriptions applying to two or three companies. It would be but tedious repetition to describe the appearance and comportment of the brigade at the various reviews and similar pageants in which they took part. Often they were placed in positions which compelled the onlookers to compare them with some of the finest regiments in the regular army. Authorities and public alike saw them emerge triumphantly from the ordeal; "those who came to laugh at muddles, used their breath to cheer successes." Regimental bands were formed, which soon attained a high degree of proficiency; fresh companies of Highlanders continued to be enrolled; and in 1865 the regiment received the "distinguished honour" of its present title—"The Queen's City of Edinburgh Rifle Volunteer Brigade." Up till 1879, the Highland companies had worn the distinctive dress, and some annoyance was felt at the War Office Order which had the effect of changing this. The regiment has from its earliest days given particular attention to shooting, and many are the prizes—including amongst others the coveted "Queen's Prize," the Prince of Wales's, the Duke of Cambridge's, the St. George's Challenge Vase—which have fallen to their skill.

Amongst the members of the regiment are to be found not a few whose names are familiar to a far larger circle than can be formed by the kindly Land o' Cakes. We have mentioned Hugh Miller and Mr. Henry; both the Artisans' and Merchants' Companies numbered at different times amongst their Captains R. M. Ballantyne, the novelist, loved wherever English-speaking boys are to be found; the Advocates' Company included Privates J. B. Balfour, now Solicitor-General for Scotland; W. Watson, now Lord Watson of the Court of Appeal; and David Wedderburn, who as Sir David Wedderburn is known in connection with a *soi-disant* "national movement" in India;[*] the late James Grant (novelist), Sir J. Noel Paton, John Ballantyne, R.S.A., and Keeley Halswelle, R.A., have all been in the ranks of the Queen's Brigade. The regiment has no fewer than four Hon. Colonels—the Lord Provost of Edinburgh for the time being, Lord Moncrieff, Colonel Davidson, C.B.—both of whom have been connected with the Queen's Rifle Volunteer Brigade from its earliest times—and General Viscount Wolseley, who has on several occasions manifested his interest in the regiment. There is a cadet corps connected with the brigade, its ranks being supported by some of the well-known "scholastic establishments" of the modern Athens.

Such a brigade as the Queen's Rifle Volunteer Brigade would naturally aim at completeness, and we find that they have thoroughly equipped services of cyclists, signallers, transport waggons, and ambulance. Another contingent must in no way be lost sight of, namely, the Mounted Infantry, who form a compact squadron some thirty strong, under the command of Captain Wardrop, their originator. Subjoined is a some-

[*] The Advocates' Company and the Writers to the Signet Company have both ceased to exist. It was somewhat wittily suggested that the former should have as uniform "red tape facings with blue bags," and as motto, "Retained for the defence."

what fuller, though by no means an exhaustive list of some of the greater successes of the Brigade.

In 1875 Private Fraser won the 1st stage in the Alexandra, a similar success falling to Private Simpson in 1881. In 1871 Ensign Logan won the Association Cup (Snider), and in 1873 Private Clark brought home the same trophy. In 1869 Private Fraser won the Duke of Cambridge's Prize. In 1882 Corporal Lunan won the Glen Albyn Prize. In 1873 Private Clark gained for Scotland the International Irish Challenge Trophy. Ensign Gow, in 1867, won the Martin's Challenge Cup. Private Macpherson, in 1884, won the Olympic Prize. In 1862 Sergeant Smith won the Prince of Wales's Prize. In 1873 Sergeant Menzies won the Queen's Prize. In 1871 Private Clark won the St. George's Challenge Vase. In 1869 Private Fraser tied for the Secretary of State for War's Prize, which coveted trophy was gained in 1874 and 1886 by Captain Murray and Private Adamson respectively, while in 1885 Private Yates secured for the Brigade the Wimbledon Cup.

The 4th VOLUNTEER BATTALION OF THE ROYAL SCOTS,* formerly the 3rd, and more recently the 2nd E. R. V., dates from 1867, when it was raised by the present Hon. Colonel, Colonel Hope, then a captain in the 16th company of the Queen's Rifle Volunteer Brigade. Nearly all the officers and sergeants of that company followed their captain, with the result that the 3rd Edinburgh was from the first most ably officered. This battalion has also a cadet corps attached to it.

The 5th VOLUNTEER BATTALION ROYAL SCOTS was formerly known as the 1st MIDLOTHIAN and dates from 1859, having been 32nd in precedence. It was raised at Leith, and by 1861 numbered eight companies, a strength which was, two years later, increased by the amalgamation into their ranks of the 4th Midlothian Rifle Volunteers. The uniform is scarlet with facings of black. Amongst other shooting triumphs may be mentioned that of Sergeant Henderson, who in 1865 won the second stage of the Albert.

The 6th VOLUNTEER BATTALION ROYAL SCOTS is composed of the old 2nd MIDLOTHIAN, dating from the same year. The uniform is practically the same as that of the 5th battalion. The regiment has a fair shooting record, Captain Thorburn winning the Wimbledon Cup in 1884, and the Curtis and Harvey Prize in 1888.

The 7th and 8th VOLUNTEER BATTALIONS ROYAL SCOTS consist of the late 1st HADDINGTON and 1st LINLITHGOWSHIRE Volunteers, whose numbers of precedence were

---

* The uniform is scarlet with facings of blue.

57 and 82 respectively. The title by which the present 7th Volunteer Battalion Royal Scots was first known to contemporary history was "the 1st Administrative Battalion 57th Haddingtonshire Rifle Volunteers," a somewhat cumbrous appellation, compared with which the present is simplicity itself. The strength was seven companies—subsequently reduced to six, and the uniform grey. This, however, was changed some time back for the present uniform—green with facings of scarlet. In 1877 the regiment gained the Curtis and Harvey Prize, Lieutenant Blackwood being the winner.

The 8th Battalion—the 1st Linlithgow—originally consisted of four companies raised in 1858 and 1861, in Linlithgow, which were formed into one battalion in 1862. The uniform is similar to that of the 7th Volunteer Battalion. The Hon. Colonel of the latter regiment is the Earl of Rosebery, whose uncle, the Hon. Captain Bouverie Primrose, was instrumental in founding the Civil Service Company of the 1st E.R.V. In 1880 Private Bennie won the aggregate for the Martini-Henry shooting. In 1881 Private Scott won the Martin's Challenge Cup. In 1886 Corporal Greig won the aggregate for all comers.

The Queen's (Royal West Surrey Regiment, Regimental District, No. 2) has four Volunteer battalions, composed of the 2nd SURREY, the 4th SURREY, the 6th SURREY, and the 8th SURREY RIFLE VOLUNTEERS, dating respectively from 1860, 1859, 1860, and 1860. The first-named regiment has attached to it the Cadet corps of Whitgift's School at Croydon; the 4th Surrey has the Cadets from the famous Charterhouse School; Bermondsey supplies a Cadet corps to the 6th; while the 8th Surrey has two similar corps attached, those of Mayall College, Herne Hill,* and Southwark. The 2nd West Surrey, now the 1st Volunteer Battalion of the Queen's, date from March, 1860, when they were raised at Croydon, the first commander being Colonel Campbell, who had seen considerable service in the Bengal Artillery. It was not long before other corps were attached, followed in due course by the Cadet corps from Whitgift's School. The 4th Surrey, now the 2nd Volunteer Battalion of the Queen's, deserves mention for the valuable impetus it has given to the marksmanship of the Volunteers. The original style of the regiment was the 5th, or Reigate Rifle Volunteers. To them were attached the corps from Dorking, Guildford, Farnham, Godstone, and elsewhere, and after passing through the intermediate Administrative Battalion stage, the Reigate Company became the 2nd Volunteer Battalion of the famous Queen's. The present Hon. Colonel of

* The Mayall College Cadet Corps has a green uniform with scarlet facings.

the regiment * is an example of a most efficient officer who, entering the corps as a private, raised himself by sheer force of merit to the command, during which the 4th Surrey attained to the high position it still holds. Charterhouse School provides a Cadet corps. In 1868 Private Kingsmiddle won the 2nd stage of the Alexandra, in 1883 Sergeant Peate won the 1st stage, and in 1882 Quartermaster Larmer won the Alfred Prize. The 6th Surrey, which now forms the 3rd battalion of the Queen's Royal West Surrey Regiment, was originally known as the Bermondsey Rifle Corps, which ranked 10th amongst the County Volunteer Corps. In 1868 the 10th formed with the 23rd the 4th Administrative Battalion, which twelve years later became known as the 6th Surrey. The most recent change has been that to its present designation. To the present Lieutenant-Colonel the 6th Surrey owes a great deal. It was, we believe, at his instance, that the regiment adopted the Queen's scarlet for their uniform, and it is to his free gift that they are indebted for the spacious headquarters and drill-hall, the possession of which makes them the object of envy to less-favoured regiments.† The regiment has made its mark in the shooting record, Colonel Gall and Sergeant Smith having been distinguished at Wimbledon. The Cadet corps was raised in 1885 by Captain (now Major) Johnston, and has been a valued and popular contingent. In 1884 Captain Foster won one of the Association Cups at Wimbledon. In 1870 Private Humphries won the Queen's Prize. In 1888 Sergeant Smith won the Prince of Wales's Prize, and in 1882 won the Association Silver Medal for the 1st stage of the Queen's Prize. The uniform of the 1st and 2nd battalions is green with facings of scarlet, that of the 3rd and 4th is that of the Territorial regiment—scarlet with facings of blue.

The Buffs (East Kent Regiment, Regimental District No. 3) have two Volunteer battalions, late the 2nd KENT and the 5th KENT RIFLE VOLUNTEERS, dating from 1859. By June, 1860, Kent numbered its corps up to thirty-nine, of which the earliest enrolled were those from Maidstone, Lee, Woolwich, Canterbury (two), Kidbrook, Sydenham, Chatham, Greenwich, and Tunbridge. The uniform of the former is green with facings of scarlet, that of the latter green and facings of the same colour.

The King's Own Royal Lancaster Regiment—Regimental District, No. 4—has one Volunteer battalion, the 10th LANCASHIRE, also dating from 1859, to which is attached

---

* Colonel Searle.

† The site of the premises had been in Colonel Bevington's family for years. It is stated that it was formerly the residence of the "prophetess," Joanna Southcote, whose frenzied declamations were delivered where the officers and staff of the 3rd Volunteer Battalion Queen's now assemble.

the Cadet Corps of Rossall School.* The uniform is scarlet with facings of blue, that first chosen being grey with facings of scarlet.

The Northumberland Fusiliers—Regimental District, No. 5—have three Volunteer battalions.

The 1st Volunteer Battalion Northumberland Fusiliers were formerly known as the 1st NORTHUMBERLAND AND BERWICK-ON-TWEED RIFLE VOLUNTEER CORPS, and dates from 1859, that is to say, that its component parts, the Volunteer Companies formed at Hexham, Morpeth, Belford, Alnwick, Bellingham, Allendale, and Lowick, then sprang into existence. Later on these corps were formed into an "Administrative Battalion" under the title of the First Administrative Battalion of Northumberland Rifle Volunteers, the command being given to the Earl of Tankerville, who still holds the position of Hon. Colonel. In 1880 the "Administrative Battalion" was constituted a Regiment with the style of the 1st Northumberland and Berwick-on-Tweed Rifle Volunteer Corps, and in 1883 received its present Territorial designation. "It is noted as a first-class shooting regiment, many of its members having distinguished themselves at Wimbledon." The uniform is grey with facings of scarlet.

The 2nd NORTHUMBERLAND, who now form the 2nd Volunteer Battalion of the Northumberland Fusiliers, were originated in December, 1859, and—as at first they consisted only of two companies—were attached to the three rifle companies at North Shields, under the command of Major Potter. But the two companies, drawn from the artisans of the iron and alkali works at Walker-on-the-Tyne, have grown into the strong battalion of to-day, while the three companies to which they were attached in their youthful weakness have disappeared. In 1862 the present Hon. Colonel took the command, and the regiment began to give earnest of its shooting prowess in various competitions. The uniform is scarlet with facings of green.

The 1st NEWCASTLE-ON-TYNE RIFLES, which constitute the 3rd Volunteer Battalion of the Northumberland Fusiliers, owe their origin to the Newcastle Rifle Club formed in the early part of 1859. Before the close of 1860 they numbered thirteen companies. One of the companies, it is interesting to note, is stated to have worn the kilt, while another, called the "Guards" company, was composed of men not less than six feet in height. There was also at that time a cadet corps. Owing to the death and retirement of some of the officers the strength of companies was in 1869 reduced to eight, but

* The uniform of the Cadet Corps is grey with facings of scarlet.

the numbers have been well kept up. In 1873 the grey, which had hitherto been the colour of the uniform, was abandoned in favour of scarlet. Captain Ogilvie remarks in his sketch of the regiment that "St. George's Day is religiously observed as a festival by the officers and members of the regiment, when it is no uncommon thing to see all ranks donning the rose in their hats in honour of the occasion, while the officers in addition usually meet round the festive board. The uniform is scarlet with facings of white.

The Royal Warwickshire Regiment—Regimental District, No. 6—has two Volunteer battalions.

The 1st WARWICKSHIRE, which forms the first, dates from November, 1859, when it was raised at Birmingham. The 1st Warwick rank amongst the foremost of the shooting regiments. In 1879 Private Osborne tied for the Alfred Prize; in 1872 Corporal Bates won the Curtis and Harvey Prize; in 1864 Lieutenant Birt won the *Daily Telegraph* Prize, and won the Dudley Prize the same year; in 1863 Sergeant Kirkwood won the Duke of Cambridge's Prize, which was also gained by Private Osborne in 1881; in 1879 Corporal Bates tied for the Glen Albyn; in 1884 Private Osborne again distinguished himself by winning the St. George's Challenge Vase, and the same year won the Secretary of State for War's Prize; in 1872 Corporal Bates tied for the Windmill Prize. The uniform is green with facings of scarlet.

The 2nd WARWICKSHIRE dates from the same time, the uniform being the same as that of the territorial regiment, scarlet with facings of blue. Attached are two cadet corps, those of Rugby School, and the King's Grammar School, Warwick.

There is yet another battalion of the Royal Warwickshire Regiment which deserves notice, viz:—The 1st CADET BATTALION, ROYAL WARWICKSHIRE REGIMENT. Cadet *Corps* had been previously known, but it was reserved for the present commanding officer, Major Fordyce, to initiate and bring to a practical issue the idea of a cadet *Battalion*. In 1884 he commenced his correspondence with the Government, and after endless difficulties and delays had the satisfaction of seeing issued the Army Circular of 1886 authorising cadet battalions as a recognised part of the Volunteer force. The " Establishment" consists of 17 officers, 7 staff sergeants, 18 sergeants, and 360 rank and file. The officers and staff are naturally adults; the remainder " is composed of thoroughly respectable youths aged 14 to 18, who pay a sum of ten shillings towards their outfit. Amongst these may be found artisans, apprentices, clerks, shop assistants, telegraph messengers, public school lads, and sons of ministers, manufacturers and tradesmen." The battalion resembles in nearly every particular of management battalions of adult Volunteers; the drill is the same, the eight days' training under canvas is enforced, and the uniform is assimilated to that of the line battalions of the Royal Warwickshire. Since the battalion has been started it has received high praise from those high in authority. General Dormer, who inspected it shortly after its formation, declared that "he had nothing but praise for it"; the Duke of Cambridge wrote commending its efficiency; in 1887, when the first enthusiasm had had time to cool were it of the ephemeral nature, Lord Wolseley wrote to Major Fordyce congratulating him "with all his heart" upon the success achieved with the Cadet Battalion, and adding—"From a military point of view I cannot say too much in favour of your scheme." That this last opinion is justified may be gathered from the fact that since the foundation—only three years and a-half ago—something like *eighty* members of the battalion have joined the regular army. It is to be regretted that so little pecuniary support has been given by Government to so valuable an enterprise. No capitation fee is allowed, and the suggestion made by the First Lord of the Treasury that £5 should be given for every recruit who joined the army after two years' service in the battalion was not adopted, with the result that a very considerable sum of money has had to be found by Major Fordyce, the founder of this pioneer of Cadet Volunteer Battalions.

The Royal Fusiliers (City of London Regiment, Regimental District, No. 7) have two Volunteer Battalions.

The 1st Volunteer Battalion, late 10th MIDDLESEX, date from 1861, and have maintained a high position. The Hon. Colonel is General Sir D. Lysons. Amongst other shooting successes may be mentioned that of Corporal Elkington, who won the Windmill Prize in 1888. The uniform is scarlet with facings of dark blue.

The 2nd Volunteer Battalion is composed of the 23rd MIDDLESEX, which owed its origin to the exertions of the late Sir J. Villiers Shelley, M.P. for Westminster. The regiment was formed to all intents and purposes in 1860, but through some misunderstanding the formal acceptance of its services was not notified till March in the following year, when it was known as the 46th Middlesex. The present commanding officer, Colonel Routledge, took an active part in the formation of the regiment, which, in 1867, numbered eight companies.

Volunteer corps, like most other personalities, individual or corporate, have their periods of depression, and such a period was experienced by the 46th Middlesex from

1867 to 1872. In the latter year, however, things looked brighter; in 1876, Colonel Routledge was appointed to the command, and the regiment was able to boast as its Hon. Colonel the late Sir Charles Russell, V.C., whose Crimean prowess was still fresh in the minds of all. The number of companies was restored to the original strength, and, as against a numerical strength of 509 in 1876, within ten years the numbers reached over eight hundred. The original colour of the uniform was grey, but in 1875 this was changed for scarlet, and within the last few months permission has been received for the regiment to wear the Fusilier busby. The composition of the regiment—which, as being a typical one, we have noticed at some length—is that the rank and file are nearly entirely drawn from the respectable working classes, while the officers are men of good social position. The standard of discipline is very high, and the shooting record good. The Hon. Colonel is Lord Wolseley, whose interest in the regiment has been frequently evidenced, and whose remarks on the occasion of his annual inspections have come to be looked for as not improbably shadowing the military views of the Government at the time.

The King's Liverpool Regiment—Regimental District, No. 8—has seven Volunteer battalions. Lancashire did well in the way of raising Volunteer corps; before the close of 1860, she could boast no fewer than seventy-six. The battalions attached to the King's Liverpool Regiment are supplied by the 1st LANCASHIRE, dating from December, 1859; the 5th LANCASHIRE, junior only by a couple of days to the 1st; the 13th LANCASHIRE, dating from the same month; the 15th LANCASHIRE, the Liverpool Rifle Volunteer Brigade, dating from January, 1860; the 18th—the "Irish"—also dating from January, 1860; and the 19th LANCASHIRE, to which is attached the 1st ISLE OF MAN, dating from nearly the same period. The uniform of the 1st Lancashire is green with black facings, that of the 5th and 18th green with scarlet facings, and that of the 13th, 15th, 19th, and 1st Isle of Man scarlet with facings of blue. Amongst the successes at the butts scored by the Volunteer Battalions may be mentioned the following: In 1871 Private Way of the 1st Lancashire tied for the Windmill, and three years later took the Wimbledon Cup; in 1881 the regiment won the Mullen's Competition; in 1871 and 1872 taking the Belgian Challenge Cup. In 1873 Private Sprott was the winner in the 2nd stage of the Albert Prize. In 1866 Private Formby, of the Liverpool Rifle Brigade, won the Wimbledon Cup; in 1888 Private Wattleworth won the Olympic Prize, and in 1879 Sergeant Houton the Martin's Challenge Cup; in 1888 Major Davidson won the Martini-Henry Association Cup, and in 1883 Private Thornton won the prize in the

Snider Aggregate. In 1867 Private Formby tied for the 1st stage of the Alexandra, and in 1864 Mr. Ashton, an honorary member of the corps, won one of the Association Cups. In 1877 Private Jameson, of the 15th Lancashire, won the Queen's Prize; in 1888 the regiment was successful in winning the Mullen's Competition.

The Norfolk Regiment—Regimental District, No. 9—has four Volunteer battalions, formerly the 1st NORFOLK, the 2nd NORFOLK, the 3rd NORFOLK, and the 4th NORFOLK respectively, which represent sixteen corps which sprang into existence between July, 1859, and the same month in the following year. The 1st Norfolk dates from August, 1859, when it was raised with influential supporters at Norwich. In 1870 Corporal Sexton, of the 1st Norfolk, won the Snider Association Cup, and in 1882 the Aggregate Martini-Henry Prize at Wimbledon; in 1887 Sergeant Ringer won the Alfred Prize; and in 1877 Corporal Buts won the Silver Medal in the first stage of the Queen's Prize.

Twelve years or so have passed since from the 2nd NORFOLK VOLUNTEER Corps and part of the 3rd Administrative Battalion of the Suffolk Rifle Volunteers was formed the 1st Administrative Battalion Norfolk Regiment. Three years later the 2nd Norfolk Volunteer Corps was renamed the 2nd Norfolk Volunteer Battalion, and three years later again it assumed its present designation.

With a very similar history to that of the preceding, the 3rd and 4th Norfolk Volunteers present few data of interest except to those locally or personally interested. The Norfolk County School at North Elmham supplies a Cadet corps to the former. The uniform of all the Volunteer battalions is scarlet with facings of white.

The Lincolnshire Regiment—Regimental District, No. 10—has two Volunteer battalions, the 1st and 2nd LINCOLN. No fewer than twenty Volunteer corps were formed early in the movement, and of these the 1st Lincoln was the first, dating from October, 1859. The 2nd Lincoln was not far behind, and the two regiments have maintained a steady degree of excellence. In 1868 Sergeant Lowe won the Martini Challenge Cup, and the Prince of Wales's Prize and the St. George's Challenge Vase the following year; in 1873 Corporal Willows won the Silver Medal in the Queen's Prize, and in the same year tied for the Grand Aggregate; in 1884 the Martini Challenge Cup was again credited to the Lincoln men, this time by the shooting of Corporal Dickinson, of the 2nd Lincoln; in 1873 Sergeant Hall tied for the Prince of Wales's Prize; in 1885 Sergeant Bulmer, of the 2nd Lincoln, and in 1886 Private Jackson, of the 1st Lincoln, won the Queen's Prize. The uniform of the 1st Lincoln is scarlet with facings of white; that of the 2nd Lincoln, scarlet with facings of blue.

To Devonshire, as has been stated, belongs the honour of supplying the *first* Volunteer regiment under the present organization. A meeting was called in Exeter early in 1852 and passed resolutions in favour of raising a volunteer corps, and, in the Memorial, recalled to the recollection of the authorities that the Devonshire village of Torbay was chosen as his landing place by the Prince whom the last Revolution in England placed upon the Throne. Their services were accepted in March of the same year, and the Exeter and South Devon Volunteers forthwith began their career.* The Devonshire Territorial Regiment—Regimental District, No. 11—has five Volunteer battalions, formed respectively by the 1st, 2nd, 3rd, 4th and 5th DEVONSHIRE RIFLES. The 1st or veteran regiment has before been referred to; the uniform is green with facings of black. The Devon corps have done well at the butts. In 1861 Sergeant Rowe won the Dudley Prize; in 1874 Corporal Brooks, of the 1st Devon, tied for the Curtis and Harvey Prize; in 1878 Private Gratwicke won the St. George's Challenge Vase; and in 1880 the Secretary of State for War's Prize. The 2nd Devonshire, uniform green with scarlet facings, dates from December, 1859, and the 3rd from 1860. Taking the last named as a typical West Country corps, we find that when first formed it was styled the 1st Administrative Battalion of Devonshire, and was recruited from several places, including Tiverton, Ottery St. Mary, Colyton, Collumpton and Bampton, while the 1st and 3rd Devon Mounted Volunteer Corps were also attached. The uniforms were various, with the result that at reviews their appearance was probably more artistic than military. In 1880, the Administrative Battalion became the 3rd Devonshire Rifle Volunteers.

The regiment has always shown considerable enthusiasm and has gained a high place amongst shooting regiments. As early as 1868, the Company raised at Bampton, then commanded by the present Lieutenant-Colonel of the regiment, set the example to the county of going under canvas, and since then the camping out has become a regular part of the year's routine. Amongst other triumphs at the butts may be mentioned that of Private Beck, who in 1881 gained the Queen's Prize at Wimbledon. The uniform is grey with facings of green. The 4th Devonshire dates from February, 1860, and like the last-named regiment represents a number of separate corps. In 1875 Major Pearse won the Martini Challenge Cup and the Queen's Prize; in 1885 the same officer won the Secretary of State for War's Prize; Private Ward, of the 4th Devon, won the first stage of the Alexandra Prize in 1887, and the following year won the Aggregate Prize

* An animated correspondence appeared in 1860 in the *Volunteer Gazette* as to the relative seniority of the 1st Devon and the Victorias.

for all comers; while in the earlier stages of the Wimbledon meeting, Captain Madden (in 1869) tied for the Windmill Prize. The uniform is scarlet, with facings of white.

The 5th Devonshire, the "3rd (Haytor) Volunteer Battalion," dates from March in the same year, and also represents several small corps, some of which had before their amalgamation gained an honourable name for themselves as marksmen. The uniform is scarlet with facings of green.

The Suffolk Regiment—Regimental District, No. 12—has four Volunteer battalions, representing some sixteen corps which were raised in the county in the early days of the movement, as well as those raised in Cambridgeshire. The 1st SUFFOLK dates from October, 1859, and has attached to it the Cadet corps of Queen Elizabeth's School at Ipswich. Amongst the prizes won by members of the regiment may be mentioned the Silver Medal in the Queen's Prize Competition, carried off by Corporal Hayward in 1864. The uniform is green with facings of black. The 6th SUFFOLK, which constitutes the 2nd Volunteer battalion, dates from 1860; the uniform is grey with facings of scarlet. The 1st CAMBRIDGESHIRE, the 3rd Volunteer battalion, dates from the same year, and is the only one of the Volunteer battalions which has adopted the red uniform with blue facings. The CAMBRIDGE UNIVERSITY VOLUNTEERS, formerly the 2nd Cambridgeshire, which form the 4th Volunteer battalion, date from the same period. The 2nd Cambridge, now the 4th (Cambridge University) Battalion of the Suffolk Regiment, has been one of the foremost of the shooting regiments. Distinguished in having as Hon. Colonel H.R.H. the Prince of Wales, the Cambridge University corps has sent to the butts at Wimbledon such well-known shots as Lord Waldegrave, Colonel Humphry, and Privates Ross, St. John Clerke, Piggott, Lattey, McKenell, and Richardson. The uniform is grey with facings of the same colour.

The Prince Albert's (Somersetshire Regiment)—Regimental District, No. 13—has three Volunteer battalions. The county formed as many as 23 corps, most of which have been absorbed into the three following regiments:—The 1st SOMERSET, dating from October, 1859, the 2nd SOMERSET, dating from the same month, and the 3rd SOMERSET, dating from February, 1860. The Somerset regiments can show a good record of shooting successes. Amongst others, Sergeant Danger in 1870 tied for the first stage of the Alexandra, and Ensign Green in the same year won the *Daily Telegraph* Prize; in 1868 the county gained the China Challenge Cup; in 1875 Private Welch secured the Curtis and Harvey Prize; Private Mather in 1879 tied for the Glen Albyn; in 1871 Private Kennington won the Martini Challenge Cup; in 1865 Private Poole won the Prince of

Wales's Prize; in 1868 Lieutenant Carslake won the Queen's Prize; in 1887 Lieutenant Hole won the St. George's Challenge Vase; in 1872 Private Hawkins tied for the Windmill. The uniform of the 1st Somerset is that of the Territorial regiment, scarlet with blue facings; that of the 2nd and 3rd is grey with facings of black.

The Prince of Wales's West Yorkshire Regiment—Regimental District, No. 14—has as Volunteer battalions, the 1st WEST RIDING OF YORKSHIRE VOLUNTEERS, the 3rd WEST RIDING, and the 7th WEST RIDING. The two former date from September, and the latter from November, 1859. The three regiments, with the others that have been incorporated with them, soon gave evidence of their value, and were particularly fortunate in their officers, the commander of the Administrative Battalions and the captain commandant of the York—the first corps—having both been majors in the King's Dragoon Guards. The uniform of the 1st West Riding is scarlet with facings of blue; that of the 3rd, or Bradford Regiment, scarlet with facings of white; and that of the 7th, whose headquarters are at Leeds, grey with facings of the same colour. The Western division of the county has produced some good shots. In 1865 Private Sharman won the Queen's Prize, and the same year the Prize given by the Secretary of State for War fell to Ensign Cockerham; the following year Lieutenant Chapman won the St. George's Challenge Vase; in 1869 Sergeant Kirk—a Silver Medal man—won the Irish Challenge Trophy; in 1870 Captain Eddison won the 2nd stage of the Alexandra, and in 1873 the Olympic Prize; in 1865 Sergeant Marriott won the Henry Peek Prize; in 1867 and 1868 the *Daily Telegraph* Prize was won by Sergeant-Major Cooke and Corporal Wilkinson respectively, and in 1867 the China Challenge Cup fell to the West York marksmen.

The East Yorkshire Regiment—Regimental District, No. 15—has two Volunteer battalions, formerly known respectively as the 1st and 2nd East Riding of Yorkshire Volunteers. The 1st EAST RIDING dates from November, 1859, when it was raised at Hull, Major Walker Pease being the first commanding officer. It is of course needless to say that the corps, raised at Howden, Bridlington, Driffield, Market Weighton, have been amalgamated with both the Volunteer battalions of the East Yorkshire Regiment. The uniform of the 1st East Riding is scarlet with facings of white.

The 2nd EAST YORKSHIRE VOLUNTEERS date from 1860, in the February of which year the principal corps was raised at Beverley under Captain Barkworth. Like the 1st East Riding the uniform is assimilated with that of the Territorial regiment. In 1865 Colour-Sergeant Kirk won the Silver Medal, and in 1873 tied for the Grand Aggregate; in 1867 Major Boynton took the Wimbledon Cup. To these must be added the local successes that the East York regiments have achieved.

The Bedfordshire Regiment—Regimental District, No. 86—has three Volunteer battalions, being respectively the 1st and 2nd HERTFORDSHIRE and the 1st BEDFORDSHIRE VOLUNTEERS. Hertfordshire had contributed some ten corps of Volunteers to the national army between October of 1859 and July of 1860, of which the first formed was the nucleus of the present 1st Volunteer Battalion, which was raised at Hertford on the 22nd of November, 1859. The Berkhampstead Corps, at which place the headquarters of the 2nd Hertfordshire still are, was raised in March of the following year, and the two regiments between them have attracted many of the smaller corps, such as those raised at Hemel Hempstead, Bishop Stortford, Ware, and Royston. Watford, St. Albans, and Hertford also raised corps. The uniform of the 1st Hertfordshire—to which is attached the Cadet corps of Haileybury College—is grey with facings of scarlet; that of the 2nd Hertfordshire is grey with facings of grey. In 1868 Corporal Runshall gained the Prince of Wales's Prize; in 1870 and 1874 Corporal Young gained the Silver Medal in the Queen's Prize, and in 1871 tied for the Windmill, Lieutenant Baker in 1874 winning the Curtis and Harvey Prize.

The 1st BEDFORDSHIRE dates from February, 1860. Five corps were raised in the county, most of which have been incorporated. The first commanding officer of the 1st Bedfordshire was Captain Crosbie, of the Rifle Brigade. The uniform is that of the Territorial regiment, scarlet with facings of white. Amongst other triumphs may be mentioned that of Sergeant Tildesley of the 1st Beds, who in 1873 won the St. George's Challenge Vase.

The Leicestershire Regiment—Regimental District, No. 17—has only one Volunteer battalion, the 1st LEICESTERSHIRE. Three companies were raised in Leicester, one at Belvoir, and one at Melton Mowbray, and the first in date gives its name to the present battalion, being raised in August, 1859. The first commanders were Captains Manfield Turner and H. St. John Holford, the latter of whom is now Lieutenant-Colonel Commandant of the regiment. Attached to the 1st Leicestershire is the Cadet corps of Uppingham School. The uniform is scarlet with facings of white. In 1862 Major Halford won in the 2nd stage of the Albert, and in 1871, as Colonel Sir H. Halford, gained one of the Association Cups and the Duke of Cambridge's Prize; in 1867 Private Brooks tied for the Alexandra (1st stage); in 1876 Lieutenant Toller tied for the Grand Aggregate. In 1871 Private Brooks tied for the "Henry Peek," and in 1878 Private Messenger for the Glen Albyn.

The Princess of Wales's Own (Yorkshire Regiment)—Regimental District, No. 19—

has for its Volunteer battalions two regiments formed from some of the eighteen corps raised in the North Riding. The 1st NORTH RIDING VOLUNTEERS date from 1860; the present Hon. Colonel, Earl Cathcart, was one of the first Lieutenant-Colonels. The uniform is scarlet with facings of white.

The 2nd NORTH RIDING OF YORKSHIRE VOLUNTEERS date from the same month; the present Lieutenant-Colonel, Sir W. Cayley Worsley, being gazetted Captain of the Hovingham company. The uniform is scarlet with facings of grass green. Amongst the greater successes of the North Yorkshire may be mentioned that of Private Ross, who won the first Queen's Prize (1860); of Private Styan, who in 1864 tied for the first stage of the Alexandra; and of Sergeant Metcalfe, who in 1872 won the Prince of Wales's Prize.

The Lancashire Fusiliers—Regimental District, No. 20—have three Volunteer battalions, the 8th, the 12th, and the 17th LANCASHIRE VOLUNTEERS.

The 8th LANCASHIRE RIFLE VOLUNTEERS, now forming the 1st Volunteer Battalion of the Lancashire Fusiliers, date from 1859, on the 4th of August in which year Her Majesty accepted the services of the Bury Rifle Corps.* Other companies soon followed; it is but to repeat a familiar truism to say that nowhere was the patriotic enthusiasm greater than it was in Lancashire; whenever the Bury Volunteers appeared on parade or at inspection, they received compliments on their efficiency. An amusing account, throwing no little light on the Volunteers of 1860, is given by Mr. Hayhurst, of the adventures of a representative member of the Bury Volunteers at the Hyde Park Review of 1860.

"The two Shaws of the Bury Volunteers were there; they had an experience unique and rare as well as amusing. Mr. James Shaw and Mr. John Henry Shaw had been selected to represent the 8th at the great metropolitan review, and repaired to London in high glee. Their uniforms were, of course, carried in carpet bags, the journey being effected in the non-identity of civilian clothes. On reaching the chief city of the world, the two worthies with the representation of Bury Volunteering upon their shoulders, proceeded to their hotel to refresh and attire themselves in the famed regimentals of the 8th L.R.V. Passing through the streets, some of the *gamin* made fun at their expense, and rather unpolitely inquired which of them had shot 'the dog?' A sort of hue and cry on the point was raised by the youthful cockneys, to the intense disgust of

---

* An interesting history of the Volunteer movement in Bury and Rossendale has been compiled by W. T. H. Hayhurst.

Shaw, J. H., who returned to his hotel, and resumed the character of a civilian. Shaw, James, however, went heroically onward, but arrived late on the review ground in Hyde Park. With his characteristic urbanity, he approached a mounted officer, who happened to be passing, told him he had travelled from Lancashire, and inquired how he should proceed in order to secure a good view of the march past. 'Come with me, sir,' said the officer, 'and we'll see what accommodation remains.' The pair went on and on, through crowds of civilians and columns of Volunteers, meanwhile engaging in rapid friendly talk, the one about Lancashire, and the other about London and the Volunteers. Presently they arrived at the grand stand, upon which the kindly-disposed officer 'planted' our friend Shaw, as the gentry and officers of the line fell back to accommodate the new-comer. 'Good day, my friend; glad we have met,' said the mounted guide as he galloped off, with a salute to the Bury lad, leaving him standing almost alone and somewhat embarrassed, as he returned the salute without the opportunity of sufficiently acknowledging his obligations. Presently Mr. Shaw heard the first gun of the Royal Salute, and the cheers of the vast crowds proclaimed that the Queen had entered the review ground. Twenty thousand Volunteers stood to attention as Her Majesty, escorted by the Life Guards, passed by the Grand Stand, with the King of the Belgians at her side, and Prince Arthur and Princess Alice sitting opposite to her. On either side rode Prince Albert and the Count of Flanders, the Prince of Wales and Princess Jules of Holstein. Then the march past began, and friend Shaw was puzzled, not to say amazed, to find his friendly guide riding foremost, followed by a brilliant staff of cavalry. The Bury sergeant was still alone—standing there, speaking not, and none daring to speak to one who had been accommodated by His Royal Highness the Duke of Cambridge."

Passing over the earlier years of the corps, during which its popularity increased—to quote a hackneyed saying—"by leaps and bounds," and during which prizes were won at all meetings, and general officers vied with each other in praising the 8th Lancashire Volunteers, we find that in 1873 the original uniform of grey with black facings was discarded in favour of the "Queen's scarlet," and a few years later the strength was raised by authority to eight companies, every man of whom was returned as "efficient." The 8th Lancashire Volunteers have been fortunate, from the very commencement, in heir officers; the present Hon. Colonel* was the first Captain gazetted to the regiment; to the late commanding officer—Colonel Mellor—not the local Volunteers only, but the

* Colonel Hutchinson.

whole service, owe a debt of gratitude.* It may not be out of place in treating of a regiment connected with a locality so rich in historical associations, to add that the present capacious Drill Hall is on the site of the old Bury Castle,

"Where, in old, heroic days,"

old Lancashire warriors, whose very names are lost, fought with or against the "short Roman broadsword," or held their own in fierce foray and wild war. Not only at Wimbledon, but in most places where they compete, have the Bury Volunteers gained credit, Lieutenant Whitehead, Sergeant Hutchinson, and Sergeant Greenhagh being amongst the champion shots. Amongst the prizes won have been the Dudley, the Wimbledon Cup, the Bass, the Windmill, the Guy and Moncrieff, the Curtis and Harvey, the Martinis, Queen's First Stage, besides those at other provincial competitions, whose number precludes even mention. The present uniform is scarlet with facings of white.

The TWELFTH and SEVENTEENTH LANCASHIRE VOLUNTEERS, which constitute the 2nd and 3rd Volunteer Battalions of the regiment, date from 1860. Space will not allow of our saying more than that they well maintain the traditional credit of Lancashire Volunteers. To the 3rd Volunteer Battalion is attached the Cadet corps of Salford. The uniform of both battalions is scarlet with white facings.

The Royal Scots Fusiliers—Regimental District, No. 21—have three Volunteer Battalions composed of the regiments formerly known as the 1st and 2nd Ayrshire, and the Galloway Volunteers.

The 1st AYRSHIRE, now the 1st Volunteer Battalion Royal Scots Fusiliers, date from 1859, and from almost the time of their formation have been distinguished as a "shooting regiment." In the "big things" at Wimbledon they have always secured a good place,† in 1888 standing first in order of merit out of the 212 corps of Rifle Volunteers in accordance with the results of the musketry returns issued from the War Office. It is worthy of note that the present commanding officer‡ has been connected with the regiment from the earliest period of its existence, his name standing No. 1 on the original roll of members. The uniform is that of the Territorial regiment, scarlet with facings of blue.

* Colonel Mellor invented the cooking ranges so universally used in camping grounds, as well as the portable mess-huts which are so vast an improvement on the former accommodation.

† Amongst the champion marksmen of the regiment may be mentioned Major McKerrell, Martin Boyd, and the Lowes.

‡ Colonel J. Dickie.

The 2nd AYRSHIRE is composed of—roughly—so many of the numerous rifle corps (about twenty) raised in Ayrshire as are not included in the 1st Ayrshire. They date from the same time, and have always been a distinguished and efficient regiment. A more detailed but far from complete list of the honours of the Ayrshire corps is as follows: In 1867 Private McKenna won the Albert Prize, and in 1885 Major McKerrell achieved the same distinction; in 1875 Private Boyd tied in the Grand Aggregate (which he won in 1888), Private Lowe gaining the same success in 1882, and the same year being first in the (Snider) Aggregate; in 1877 Private Boyd won the Wimbledon Cup, and in 1885 gained another prize in the shape of the Curtis and Harvey Prize, and also won one of the Association Cups; in 1882 the County were the winners of the China Challenge Cup. In 1885 and 1888 the Dudley Cup was gained by Major McKerrell, and in 1886 by Private Boyd, Major McKerrell gaining the Bass Prize in 1888. Ensign Gray in 1871 won the International Irish Challenge Trophy; in 1877 Sergeant Hyslop won the St. George's Challenge Vase; in 1873 Private McCreath tied for the Secretary of State for War's Prize, having in 1869 tied for the Windmill Prize. The uniform, like that of the 1st Ayrshire, is scarlet with facings of blue.

The GALLOWAY RIFLE VOLUNTEER CORPS, constituting the 3rd Volunteer Battalion of the Territorial regiment, dates from 1860, when it was raised principally in Kirkcudbright and Wigtown, and known as the Kirkcudbright and Wigtown Rifle Volunteers. The uniform is grey with facings of scarlet. In 1884 the Henry Peek Prize was won by Private Bruce.

The Cheshire Regiment—Regimental District, No. 22—has five Volunteer battalions—the 1st, 2nd, 3rd, 4th and 5th CHESHIRE VOLUNTEERS. Thirty Rifle corps were raised in Cheshire in about nine months, and these corps are, with but few exceptions, represented in the five Volunteer battalions of the present Cheshire Regiment. The 1st CHESHIRE dates from 1859, when it was raised at Birkenhead; the 2nd CHESHIRE—the Earl of Chester's Rifles—was raised in the following November; Knutsford—the present headquarters of the 3rd CHESHIRE, and Stockport—the headquarters of the 4th CHESHIRE, both raised companies in March, 1860; while Congleton, where the 5th battalion is stationed, raised a corps in September, 1859. It will easily be understood that the various changes which have taken place in the nomenclature and disposition of the various original corps cause, in many cases, a corresponding alteration in the apparent precedence. Cheshire has undoubtedly a good shooting record. For the Alexandra Prize Private Woolley tied in 1870, and Lieutenant Tobin in 1871. Private

Woolley won the St. George's Challenge Vase in 1876, and again tied for the Grand Aggregate in 1879; the Wimbledon Cup was won by Private Ward in 1873, and the Snider Association Cup in 1875; the China Challenge Cup fell to the County in 1879; for the Curtis and Harvey Prize Private Williamson tied in 1878, and in the same year the Martini Challenge Cup was won by Private Stokes, and ten years later by Captain Timmins; the first stage of the Queen's Prize, carrying with it the Silver Medal, was won in 1867 by Captain Wright, and in 1880 by Corporal Scott; Captain Turner gained the (Martini-Henry) Wimbledon Cup in 1881, and for the Windmill Prize Privates Dutton and Bratherton tied in 1876. In 1886 the St. George's Challenge Vase fell to Private Marr. The uniform of the 1st and 5th Cheshire is grey with facings of scarlet; that of the 2nd, scarlet with facings of buff; and that of the 3rd and 4th, scarlet with facings of white.

The famous Royal Welsh Fusiliers—Regimental District, No. 23—have two Volunteer battalions, the 1st DENBIGHSHIRE and the 1st FLINT AND CARNARVON. Both regiments date from the early period of the movement, include many corps raised in the neighbouring districts, and boast a record of steady progress of which any regiment might be proud. Amongst other successes may be instanced that of the Alfred Prize, won by Lieutenant Ward in 1878. The uniform is that of the Territorial regiment—scarlet with facings of blue.

The South Wales Borderers—Regimental District, No. 24—have four Volunteer battalions—the 1st BRECKNOCKSHIRE, and the 1st, 2nd, and 3rd MONMOUTHSHIRE. They all date from about the same period. The uniform of the 1st, 3rd, and 4th battalions is that of the Territorial regiment, scarlet with white facings; that of the 2nd battalion is green with black facings.

The King's Own Scottish Borderers—Regimental District, No. 25—have three Volunteer battalions—the Roxburgh and Selkirk, the Berwickshire, and the Dumfries Volunteers.

The ROXBURGH AND SELKIRK were early formed, and were for some time known as the Border Rifle Volunteers. The uniform is grey with facings of the same colour, and attached to the corps are the Roxburgh Mounted Rifle Volunteers.

The BERWICKSHIRE RIFLES date from 1859, when they were raised as the 53rd (Berwickshire) Volunteers. Four years later, we gather from the "Scottish Military Directory," the strength had so increased as to warrant the regiment becoming an Administrative Battalion, on which occasion, the title was changed to the 1st Battalion

County of Berwick. The next and last change was that which transformed it into the 2nd Volunteer Battalion of the "K. O. B.'s," whose uniform, scarlet with blue facings, it wears.

The 1st DUMFRIES RIFLE VOLUNTEERS, which constitute the 3rd Volunteer Battalion, were also raised in 1859. The regiment was always a strong one, and was speedily formed into an Administrative Battalion. In 1880 this battalion, the 1st Administrative Battalion Dumfriesshire Rifle Volunteers, became the 1st Dumfries Rifle Volunteers, a title which it retained till the comparatively recent adoption of the Territorial nomenclature. The uniform is scarlet with facings of blue. The Volunteer Battalions of the K.O.B's are not without their distinctions as marksmen. Private McVittie (1st Dumfries) tied in 1874 and in 1882 for the Grand Aggregate; in 1878 he took the Olympic, and in 1881 the Olympic again, as well as the Bass Prize; in 1882 the Belgian Challenge Cup fell to the 1st Roxburgh, and in 1885 the China Challenge Cup to the Dumfries; in 1880 Corporal Milroy won the Martini Challenge Cup. The St. George's Challenge Cup was won by Ensign Grieve of the Roxburgh in 1868, and in 1874 by the redoubtable McVittie of the Dumfries, the former marksman gaining the Windmill Prize, second stage, in 1866 and 1867, and the latter winning in 1882 the prize given by the Secretary of State for War. Corporal Forest followed Ensign Grieve by gaining the same Windmill Prize in 1868.

The Cameronians (Scottish Rifles)—Regimental District, No. 26—have attached to them five Volunteer battalions. These are the 1st, 2nd, 3rd, 4th, and 7th Lanarkshire.

The 1st LANARKSHIRE date from July, 1859, when they were raised as the Glasgow 1st Western Rifle Volunteers. Undoubtedly the initiator of the movement was Mr. Archibald K. Murray, who in the early part of May in the same year had, *ex proprio motu*, inserted in a local paper an advertisement requesting "gentlemen favouring the formation of Volunteer Rifle Corps for Glasgow" to place themselves in communication with him. The day following he had received sufficient answers to warrant him in convening a public meeting, resolutions to form Rifle Corps passed, and the following month saw a vast quantity of companies. It will easily be understood that in a town like Glasgow, which from the earliest days had been foremost in responding to the call to arms, this latest *avatar* of the volunteering spirit should be welcomed with boundless enthusiasm. There had been volunteers of Glasgow in the army which bade the hapless Mary abandon all hope of reigning over her northern heritage; volunteers from the same sturdy city had supported the reigning dynasty in the troubles of 1715; again in the '45 they fought with no small loss and equal honour; the Glasgow Volunteers which were raised at the time of the American rebellion were incorporated into the regular army; during the time of the Peninsular War foremost amongst the many volunteer regiments raised throughout the length and breadth of the land were the Glasgow Volunteers, the Glasgow Volunteer Light Horse, and the Armed Association of Glasgow. Fragments of these various bodies remained, amongst them being the "Sharpshooters," which assumed a corporate form some four years after the battle of Waterloo, and Lieutenant Cavaye, in the "Military Directory" before quoted, asserts that "when the movement of 1859 was set on foot, a meeting of the surviving officers, non-commissioned officers, and privates of the Glasgow Light Horse of 1796, of the Volunteers of 1803, and of the Sharpshooters of 1819 was held, and these formed themselves into a corps which was called 'The Old Guards of Glasgow.'" In 1860 the various companies known as the 1st, 2nd, 9th, 11th, 15th, 17th, 18th, 33rd, 39th, 53rd, 63rd, 72nd, 76th, 77th, and 79th were consolidated into the 1st Lanarkshire Rifle Volunteer Corps, the original uniform being grey with black accoutrements. From that date the regiment has pursued an onward career, taking part in most of the important functions held in the northern kingdom, and adopting with praiseworthy zeal the annual camps which have done so much for the force. The uniform now is grey with facings of blue.

The 2nd LANARKSHIRE, dating also from 1859, was subsequently known as the 1st Administrative Battalion Lanarkshire Rifle Volunteers, and included the 16th, 42nd, 44th, 52nd, 56th, and 57th Companies, to which were subsequently added the 102 and 103rd. In 1873 the title of the regiment was changed to that of the 16th Lanarkshire Rifle Volunteers, the original 16th Company having been raised at Hamilton under Captain Austin; the next change was to the 2nd Lanarkshire Rifle Volunteers, which obtained till the most recent alteration, by which the regiment became the 2nd Volunteer Battalion of the Scottish Rifles. The uniform is scarlet with facings of blue.

The 3rd LANARKSHIRE also date from 1859, and have always preserved a tradition that they should be placed first in order of priority. Captain Orr, in his history of the 7th Lanarkshire Rifles, quotes a letter from Major Mactear of the 3rd, in which the writer brings forward some strong reasons for his contention. The question was authoritatively settled in favour of the 1st Lanarkshire—the Western, but Major Mactear contends that the latter were sworn with the wrong oath, namely, that for members of Parliament and Justices of the Peace, and even then nearly three weeks later than were the 3rd—or Southern—Regiment. He claims moreover that along with the 2nd, the 4th and the

5th of the three numbered companies, they "had the high honour (on the occasion of the opening by Her Majesty of Loch Katrine water works) of being the first Volunteers ever seen by the Queen, Prince Albert, and Royal Family." The first commander was Colonel Dreghorn, and the regiment has always held a very high standard of proficiency. The uniform is scarlet with facings of blue.

The 4th LANARKSHIRE, formerly known as the Northern Rifle Company, had their offer of service accepted in October, 1859, the first commander being Colonel Tennant. Eight other companies were subsequently added, and in 1861 the corps became the 4th Lanarkshire Rifle Volunteers. The uniform is scarlet with facings of green.

The 7th LANARKSHIRE form the 5th Volunteer Battalion, and were formerly known as the 4th Administrative Battalion, then as the 29th Lanarkshire, and later again as the 7th Lanarkshire Rifle Volunteers. The localities from which they were raised were Coatbridge, Summerlee, Gartsherrie, Airdrie, and Baillieston, and in 1862—when these were formed into the Administrative Battalion—the command was given to Major Hozier. The uniform adopted was modelled on that of the Cape Mounted Rifles, in which distinguished corps the first adjutant, Captain Mainwaring, had served, and the historian of the corps records that "on many occasions inspecting officers highly complimented the regiment on its excellent dress and equipment." In 1870 the uniform was changed for the following: Black serge Norfolk jacket, dark green facings, Gordon tartan trowsers, sealskin busby, and black and green plume; and in 1873 the style of the regiment became the 29th Lanarkshire Rifle Volunteers. In 1879 the scarlet uniform with yellow facings, which is the present uniform of the regiment, was adopted, and the style of the corps became the "7th Lanarkshire Rifle Volunteers." From the earliest date the regiment have been indefatigable in acquiring a good position as a shooting corps, and the numerous prizes given for battalion competition have materially advanced this result. The marksmanship, indeed, of all the Volunteer battalions of the Scottish Rifles has always been of a very high order, as may be seen by the fact that the Alexandra, the Grand Aggregate, the Martini-Henry Aggregate, the Aggregate Snider Competition, the Belgian Challenge Cup, the *Daily Telegraph* Prize, the Irish Challenge Trophy, the Martini Challenge Cup, the Olympic, the Silver Medal, the St. George's Challenge Vase, the Secretary of State for War's Prize, and the Windmill Prize, have been won by McNabb, Gilmour, Paton, Ingram, Somerville, Lawson, Armstrong, Cowan, Whitelaw, Taylor, McOnie, Brown, and Paton respectively.

The Gloucestershire Regiment—Regimental District, No. 28—has two Volunteer battalions. The 1st (CITY OF BRISTOL) VOLUNTEERS date from September, 1859, when they were raised, the then Mayor of Bristol being the Hon. Colonel, a post his successors have held ever since. The first commanding officer was Colonel Bush, who, as well as his second in command, Major Payne, had borne commissions in the regular army. The movement was supported with the greatest enthusiasm, the ranks were quickly filled, and wealthy residents gave satisfactory financial support. The progress made was marked, and in 1867 the Queen's Prize fell to a marksman of the Bristol Rifles. It may be mentioned that the present Major (Hon. Lieutenant-Colonel) Morcom Harwood was one of the first to receive his Ensign's commission. The uniform is green with facings of red.

The 2nd GLOUCESTER represent the two corps which were raised on the same day in Gloucester, the 2nd company being known as the "Gloucester Dock Company." In addition to the companies raised in Bristol and Gloucester, Stroud, Cheltenham, Tewkesbury, and Dursley raised Rifle corps. To the 2nd Gloucester, as now constituted, is attached the Cadet corps of the Gloucester County School. The uniform is green with facings of red. Subjoined are a few of the more notable trophies of the Bristol and Gloucester Volunteers: The Queen's Prize, the Alexandra, the Martini-Henry Cup, the "Any Rifle" Association Prize, the Duke of Cambridge's Prize, the China Challenge Cup, the *Daily Telegraph* Prize, the Duke of Cambridge's Prize, the Albert Prize, the Henry Peek Prize, the Silver Medal, the Olympic Prize, the Secretary of State for War's Prize, and the Windmill Prize, which have been gained by Lane, Roberts, Baker, Pottinger, Gibbs, Peek, Hutchinson, Gouldsmith, and Tothill respectively.

The Worcestershire Regiment—Regimental District, No. 29—has two Volunteer battalions—the 1st and 2nd WORCESTERSHIRE. The 1st Worcestershire, which dates from 1859, when a company was raised at Wolverley, represents various corps raised at Tenbury, Kidderminster, Bewdley, Halesowen, Dudley, Stourport and Stourbridge, the corps at the last-named place, now the headquarters of the battalion, being commanded by Captain J. Foster, late 1st Dragoon Guards.

The 2nd WORCESTERSHIRE RIFLE VOLUNTEERS, which now constitute the 2nd Volunteer Battalion of the Worcestershire Regiment, though not actually formed till 1860, date from 1859, a Rifle club, which was the nucleus of the present regiment, being then in existence. The originator of the 2nd Volunteer Battalion of the Worcestershire Regiment was the present Quartermaster, Captain F. Simms, whose letter to a local paper in November, 1859, roused the enthusiasm of the "Faithful City."

Two city companies were then formed, and in the following August, companies which had been raised at Pershore, Malvern, Evesham, Ombersley, Redditch, Droitwitch, Upton and Bromsgrove, were formed with them into the 2nd Administrative Battalion of Worcestershire Rifle Volunteers under the command of Colonel Scobell. The following year, the 2nd Worcestershire had many opportunities of taking part in reviews and inspections, and on every occasion elicited high praise from the authorities present, and before many years had passed received a specially high compliment from Colonel Cartwright, who, after inspecting some manœuvres, observed that "he had inspected some forty or fifty of the metropolitan corps within the past two years: there were certainly many excellent regiments among those corps, but he could say with truthfulness that the 2nd Worcestershire Battalion was equal to any of them." In 1874 the facings of the uniform, which, till then, had been crimson, were changed to those at present borne. The regiment steadily progressed in every way, the exceptionally handsome prizes offered by the county as well as by their own officers contributing not a little to their triumphs as marksmen; and in 1876, the inspecting officer reaffirmed, 'with advantages,' the encomium passed by his predecessor ten years before, saying that "he could state, with perfect truth, that the 2nd Worcestershire Rifle Volunteers were one of the most efficient corps in England." In January, 1880, the title of the battalion was changed to the 10th Worcestershire Rifle Volunteer corps, but the following October it assumed the more familiar sound of the 2nd Worcestershire Rifle Volunteers; in 1883 the present designation was adopted.* In 1886 the regiment, determined not to be behindhand, adopted the suggestions which had been made, and at the annual camp appeared an ambulance detachment properly equipped. It is needless to say that by such a regiment the Jubilee year was duly observed—Worcestershire, it may be remarked, being, we believe, the only county which assembled *all* its territorial forces at one place and time. The best score for the Alexandra Prize at Wimbledon has been twice made by Worcester men: in 1870 by Lieutenant Purchas of the old 14th, and in 1877 by Lieutenant Danks of the old 8th.

The uniform of both volunteer battalions is green with facings of the same colour.

The East Lancashire Regiment—Regimental District, No. 30—has two Volunteer battalions, the 2nd and 3rd Lancashire Volunteers.

* Captain Simms, to whose interesting sketch of the history of the regiment, kindly placed at his disposal, the writer is much indebted, records a fact which it is to be hoped is not of frequent occurrence. During the annual camp in July, 1883, the thermometer (under cover) frequently only registered 40°, and on one morning ice was actually picked up in the camp!

The 2nd LANCASHIRE VOLUNTEERS, which claims to be the oldest—save one—Volunteer corps in the county, date from June, 1859, the present commanding officer receiving his Ensign's commission in the following October.* The first strength was two companies; by 1860 it had increased to four companies, and in process of time the two companies raised at Clitheroe, and formerly known as the 62nd Lancashire, were added. The strength then was represented by ten companies, with a numerical establishment of 1,007 of all ranks. This "maximum strength has been maintained for many years, the percentage of non-efficients not exceeding one per thousand on the average." It is a matter of regret with the corps that they do not possess a good practice range, but the figure of merit for class firing is a high one. We may note that on the occasion of the first competition for the Queen's Prize at Wimbledon, a representative of the 2nd Lancashire was only six points behind the winning score. The uniform is scarlet with white facings.

The 3rd LANCASHIRE, which form the 2nd Volunteer Battalion of the East Lancashire Regiment, also date from 1859, and have amalgamated several smaller corps. The regiment is a strong and popular one. The uniform is scarlet with facings of black.

The East Surrey Regiment—Regimental District, No. 31—has four Volunteer battalions, the 1st, 3rd, 5th, and 7th SURREY. The 1st Surrey, claiming to be the first of what may be called the Metropolitan Volunteer corps whose services were accepted by Her Majesty,† date from June, 1859, but a glance at the history of the corps will suffice to show that the real date of origin must be sought for at an earlier period. It may not be out of place, in dealing with a corps so eminently representative as the 1st Surrey, to take the opportunity of tracing shortly the history of the Volunteer movement in this typical "Home" county.

An Armed Association was formed in Christ Church, Surrey, early in 1798; similar associations were formed at Bermondsey, Rotherhithe, and Newington, and before long amalgamated with the Christ Church Association, the combined corps being then styled the 1st Regiment of Surrey Volunteers, and taking part as such in the review held in Hyde Park in 1803. The year before Waterloo, the stalwart and picturesque men of Surrey with their uniform of "blue with scarlet facings, helmet cap crested with a black plume, pantaloons and gaiters" ceased to exist. It is true they had not actually fought, but there was a time when the probability of their doing so seemed one of hours. An army had actually been formed for invasion. Exaggerated

---

* Colonel Robinson was enrolled on the 3rd of June, and is the oldest member now serving in the corps.
† Due exception must, of course, be made in favour of the Victorias.

statements were promulgated through the length and breadth of France pointing out the fabulous wealth of England, and the absolute ease with which it could be appropriated. General Roche, commander of the Army of Invasion, issued a sort of General Order in the following terms: "Courage, citizens, England is the richest country in the world, and we will give it up to you to be plundered. You shall march to the capital of that haughty nation. You shall plunder that national bank of its immense heaps of gold. You shall seize upon all private property, upon their warehouses, their magazines, their stately mansions, their gilded palaces; and you shall return to your own country loaded with the spoils of the enemy. Once landed you will soon find your way to London."

It is easy enough to us, English, and of to-day, to sneer with genuine contempt at the tawdry magniloquence and 'Ancient Pistol'-like brag of this precious piece of highfalutin rubbish, but be it remembered France was then a power to be reckoned with, and the threat about marching to London did not sound so utterly ridiculous. And so it was not far-off, improbable, visionary danger that the 1st Surrey of those days, with the rest of their gallant comrades, made them ready to meet. From these men the 1st Surrey of to-day claim a well-nigh direct descent. Dormant for something over thirty years, in 1849 the old military spirit found visible expression in a sort of athletic club formed by Mr. Boucher at Hanover Park. In 1852 this had developed into the "East Surrey or Hanover Park Rifles," and but for a change of ministry would probably then have been gazetted. As it was, when the famous circular of 1859 authorized the formation of Volunteer corps to face a danger well-nigh as grave as that which menaced us in the days of the first Napoleon, the 1st Surrey sprang, Pallas-like, into complete and armed existence, and claim the honour of being, with the exception before mentioned, the first Metropolitan corps whose services were accepted by Her Majesty. Before long there were nine companies, subsequently, however, reduced to six. A squadron of Mounted Riflemen was in early days in contemplation, whose uniform was to be "a green tunic with scarlet facings, a light helmet resembling a hunting cap, with plumes for occasions of parade only, pantaloons, and Napoleon boots." At the time of the Fenian alarm the 1st Surrey was well to the fore, the whole regiment in 1868 being sworn in as special constables. "As a shooting corps," says a Service newspaper, "the 1st Surrey has always worthily held its own, both by its battalion team and by its individual shooting," and a glance at the *personnel* of the regiment shows unmistakably enough that the present officers, like their predecessors of old days, are resolved that no effort on their part shall be wanting to enable "this distinguished regiment" to hold unchallenged its traditional pride of place. Attached to the 1st Surrey is a Cadet corps of Dulwich College. The uniform is green with facings of scarlet.

The 3rd, 5th, and 7th SURREY, representing some of the many corps which, following the example of the pioneer regiment, were formed in the districts of Richmond, Wimbledon, and Lambeth, have also worthily upheld the county fame. Amongst the triumphs won by the East Surrey men at the National Association Meeting may be mentioned the Belgian Cup, won (7th Surrey) in 1867; the Mappin Prize, won by the 1st Surrey in 1878, 1879, and 1886; while in 1879 Quartermaster Larmer (5th Surrey) tied for the "Alfred," and in 1878 Sergeant Watkins (1st Surrey) tied for the Curtis and Harvey.

The Duke of Cornwall's Light Infantry—Regimental District, No. 32—have two Volunteer battalions.

The 1st CORNWALL, which constitutes the 1st Volunteer Battalion, dates from 1859, when it was raised at Falmouth and neighbouring localities. The uniform is grey with facings of scarlet.

The 2nd CORNWALL, dating from about the same period, soon proved itself a highly popular corps, and achieved speedy proficiency in the various details. The uniform is scarlet with facings of white, being the uniform of the territorial regiment. To instance one or two of the Cornish triumphs, we may state that in 1869 Lieutenant Pollard tied in the 1st stage of the Alexandra; in 1874 Private Burns tied for the Grand Aggregate; in 1884 Lieutenant Hambly won the Alfred Prize.

The Duke of Wellington's West Riding Regiment—Regimental District, No. 33—has three Volunteer battalions, being respectively the 4th, 6th, and 9th WEST RIDING OF YORKSHIRE RIFLE VOLUNTEERS.

The HALIFAX RIFLE CORPS, late the 4th West Riding of Yorkshire Volunteers, and now the 1st Volunteer Battalion of the Duke of Wellington's West Riding Regiment, date from 1859, when two companies were formed at Halifax, and known as the 7th West York Rifle Volunteers. Before long six more companies were raised and the regiment became the 4th West York Rifle Volunteers. The original uniform adopted was that of the Rifle Brigade; in 1874—when the strength of the regiment was reduced to six companies—scarlet with blue facings and busby were substituted, the helmet replacing the busby in 1880, and white facings and the badge of the line regiments replacing, in 1887, the blue facings and local emblems theretofore used. On the occasion of the review at Windsor in 1881 the 4th West York were the only Yorkshire regiment present, and have on many occasions been fortunate enough to supply guards of honour to members of the royal family. We cannot linger long enough to allow us to give in any fulness the various triumphs the regiment has won at the shooting butts; both in Yorkshire and at Wimbledon its prowess is well known, Private Sharman, Private Marriott, and Ensign Cockerham having obtained the Queen's Prize, the Alexandra Prize, the Henry Peek Prize, and the Secretary for War's Prize. In every way the Halifax Rifles make good their claims to be a corps d'élite. They have a complete ambulance equipment, an efficient signalling detachment, a cyclist section, two bands—brass and drum and fife—and are fortunate besides in possessing excellent range and headquarters. It is also worthy of note that the two senior officers * are respectively the nephew and son of two of the earliest officers of the regiment.

The 6th WEST RIDING and the 9th WEST RIDING, forming respectively the 2nd and 3rd Volunteer Battalions of the Duke of Wellington's, date from early in the history of the movement, and are both popular and efficient corps. The uniform of the 6th is scarlet with white facings, that of the 9th being scarlet with buff facings.

The Border Regiment—Regimental District, No. 34—has two Volunteer battalions, the 1st CUMBERLAND and the 1st WESTMORELAND. The 1st Cumberland dates from February, 1860, and represents the corps raised at Carlisle, Whitehaven, Keswick, Brampton, Penrith, Alston, and other places, all of which have since been amalgamated. No fewer, indeed, than ten corps sprang into being within as many weeks. Since the date of their formation the 1st Cumberland have made steady progress, and have on many occasions distinguished themselves at the butts. The uniform is scarlet with facings of white.

The 1st Westmoreland, which now forms the 2nd Volunteer Battalion of the Border Regiment, dates from February, 1860, when a company was raised at Kendal. Almost simultaneously companies were raised at Langdale, Windermere, Ambleside, and Grasmere. The uniform is scarlet with facings of white. Not to mention local successes we may mention that at Wimbledon in 1872 Private Palmer (1st Cumberland) tied for the Alexandra Prize, which was won ten years later by Sergeant Black of the same regiment; in 1877 Lieutenant Moser (Westmoreland) won the Albert (2nd stage); in 1880 Lieutenant Mitchell (1st Cumberland) tied for the Grand Aggregate, and won the Snider Aggregate; in 1881 and 1886 the 1st Westmoreland gained the Belgian Challenge Cup;

---

* Lieut.-Colonel Champney, whose uncle, Colonel Ackroyd, was the first colonel; and Major Kirk, whose father, Major Kirk, was "one of the regiment's earliest and most eminent officers."

in 1887 Private Gardner (1st Cumberland) won the Bronze Medal in the "Queen's" Competition; in 1879 Sergeant Riley (Westmoreland) tied for the Windmill Prize.

The Royal Sussex Regiment—Regimental District, No. 35—has three Volunteer battalions.

The 1st SUSSEX, which forms the 1st Volunteer battalion, dates from 1859, in December of which year a corps was formed at Cuckfield. There were at least nineteen various corps raised in Sussex—Brighton, Lewes, East Grinstead, Petworth, Horsham, Arundel, Chichester, Worthing, Bognor, and Eastbourne, being amongst the places most familiar to us of to-day. The present commanding officer of the 1st Sussex was, we believe, one of the earliest officers gazetted, he having been appointed corporal early in 1860. The uniform is scarlet with facings of blue.

The 2nd SUSSEX RIFLE VOLUNTEERS dates from 1859, and is composed of *two* Administrative Battalions, which coalesced in 1874, and six years later became the 2nd Sussex, which title they retained till the most recent regulation transformed them into the 2nd Volunteer Battalion of the Royal Sussex Regiment. The present Hon. Colonel, who had served for some time in the Royal Dragoons, was appointed to the command of the 2nd battalion, the officer in command, Sir. H. Fletcher, being we believe the fourth chief of the 1st battalion, and having, like the Hon. Colonel, served in the regular army. The original uniform of the corps was grey, which in 1874 was changed to scarlet with blue facings. Attached to the regiment is the Cadet corps of St. John's, Hurstpierpoint. The headquarters of the 1st Administrative Battalion were first at Chichester, but since 1866 they have been at Worthing, where are the headquarters of the regiment as now constituted. The headquarters of the 2nd Administrative Battalion were first at Petworth, then at Horsham. Since the amalgamation they have, of course, been at Worthing. On several occasions the 2nd Sussex have done well at Wimbledon, gaining the first and other high places in the competitions for the Queen's, the Alfred, Wimbledon Cup, Henry Peek Prize, the Bass Prize, and others.

The 1st CINQUE PORTS VOLUNTEERS, which occupy the position of the 3rd Volunteer Battalion of the Royal Sussex Regiment, though without discontinuing their distinctive appellation, date from December, 1859, when a rifle corps was raised at Hastings under Captain the Hon. G. Waldegrave. Ramsgate, Rye, Hythe, Folkestone, Deal, Margate, and Dover soon followed, and in due course of time were amalgamated, through various stages, into the regiment as it now stands. The Hon. Colonel is the Lord Warden of the Cinque Ports, the mention of whose office recalls vividly the days when volunteers and regulars alike kept anxious outlook from the old Sussex sea towns, where rumour had it the first descent of the enemy would be made. The uniform is grey with facings of blue.

The 1st HANTS RIFLE VOLUNTEERS, which now form the 1st Volunteer Battalion of the Hampshire Regiment, date from 1859, when several bodies of volunteers were formed into an Administrative Battalion under the command of Colonel Faunce. In 1863 the present commanding officer was appointed, and three years later the regiment began to make giant strides towards efficiency. Two years later, viz. in 1868, two new corps were added, and authorities began to have their attention called to the excellence of the 1st Hants Rifle Volunteers. Though to another regiment of Volunteers* belongs the credit of first adopting as a distinctive element in their training the system of annual camps, the 1st Hants utilised it to such effect that in 1869 the Deputy Inspector of the Reserved Forces induced Lord Northbrook, then the Under Secretary of State for War, to come and see for himself the results. Not long after—*post hoc*, and presumably *propter hoc*—an order was promulgated allowing the now familiar Government grant towards the expenses of the Volunteer encampments. In 1871 the 1st Hants attended the Aldershot manœuvres for sixteen days, and it is claimed for them that they are "the only Volunteer regiment which has been embodied for so long a period at a stretch." In 1877 the grey uniform, which had been the original colour adopted, was discarded in favour of the royal scarlet, with the best results to the regiment. They were the first corps to make the "transport" experiment in its fulness, and the accounts of the first appearance of the transport contingent were most laudatory. One of the leading daily papers commenting on the camping-out of the regiment in 1885, remarks, "How far it is possible for the Volunteers to organize a transport service for themselves was demonstrated in the open-air training of the 1st Hants Rifle Corps a short time ago. As was seen from the interesting reports we published, these Volunteers managed everything for themselves exactly as if they had been an army corps in the field."

As reflecting, not only on the 1st Hants, but on the 2nd and 3rd Volunteer battalions of the same territorial regiment, we may be permitted to cull a few of the eulogistic phrases which appear in the reports in the Daily Press of the Jubilee Review in 1887. "No brigade passed more triumphantly critical examination than the 10th, under Colonel Sir W. Humphrey, Bart. It consisted of the 1st, 2nd, and 3rd Volunteer Battalions of the Hampshire Regiment, and was generally pronounced the best Volunteer brigade in the field, though even here the palm must be given to the 3rd or Portsmouth

* The Berkshire Volunteers.

Dockyard men." "The 4th Division, his first brigade, under Sir William Humphrey, being perhaps the best all-round lot on the ground, composed of the 1st, 2nd, and 3rd Hants Battalions, 2,000 as fine fellows in scarlet as one could wish to see." "The two most formidable-looking brigades on the ground were the Royal Marines and the Hampshire Volunteers, but it would be difficult to say which marched better." "The three scarlet corps of Sir William Humphrey's brigade were an honour to Hampshire, and were largely voted the best brigade of Volunteers on the ground."

Attached to the 1st Hampshire is the Cadet corps of Winchester College.

The 2nd HAMPSHIRE date from February, 1860, and the 3rd HAMPSHIRE from the same month, Southampton and Portsmouth being the nucleus corps of the regiments, and the first commanders—Captain Grimes and Captain Villancy respectively—having both seen service in the Madras army. The 4th HAMPSHIRE, the Bournemouth company, was raised at Christ Church in March of 1860, the Earl of Malmesbury being the first commander; the 5th HAMPSHIRE, the Isle of Wight Regiment, dates from January, 1860, and represent eight corps raised at Ryde, Newport, Ventnor, Sandown, Cowes, Freshwater and elsewhere. The whole was under the command of Colonel Dunsmere, formerly of the "Black Watch," and the Newport corps was commanded by Sir J. Simeon, Bart. As is well known, the Hon. Colonel of the regiment is Prince Henry of Battenberg, and the regiment itself has the somewhat rare distinction for a Volunteer corps of being styled "The Princess Beatrice's Own."

As specimens—and specimens only—of the successes won by the men of Hampshire it may be mentioned that in 1871 Lieutenant Newman won the Alexandra first stage; in 1888 Captain Arnell won the Hop Bitters Trophy; in 1883 Sergeant Noble won the Alfred Prize; and in the same year Private Hyde carried off the Windmill Prize.

The South Staffordshire Regiment—Regimental District, No. 38—has three Volunteer battalions—the 1st, 3rd and 4th Staffordshire Volunteers. No fewer than thirty-six corps of Volunteers were raised in Staffordshire, of which those belonging to the Southern Division are represented by the three regiments above mentioned.

The 1st STAFFORD, the Handsworth corps, date from August, 1859, the first commander being Captain Elwell. The uniform is scarlet with facings of white.

The 3rd STAFFORD, which constitute the 2nd Volunteer Battalion, date from November, 1859, when two companies were raised at Walsall, the first commanding officer being Captain Darwell. In 1888 Colour-Sergeant Ford won the Challenge Vase at Wimbledon. The uniform is scarlet with facings of white.

The 4th STAFFORD, forming the 3rd battalion, claims, according to some accounts, "to be the first Volunteer company in the county under the 1859 dispensation." There appears to have been a Rifle club already established and in full working order at Wolverhampton, when the famous circular of General Peel, the summoning spell of the Volunteer force, was issued. Colonel Gough and Colonel Vernon, afterwards Lieutenant-Colonel of the Administrative Battalion, when discussing the circular conceived the idea of making that Rifle club the first Volunteer company in the kingdom. A third company was raised at Wolverhampton, and the present Hon. Colonel, Colonel Levinge, appointed to the command. "As a shooting corps," writes a service journal,* "the 3rd South Staffordshire has more than held its own in the county, having won the Dartmouth Shield in about half the competitions that have taken place for it . . . . . Numbers of this corps have also won fame at Wimbledon, notably Sergeant Garnett, who carried off the Prince of Wales's Prize in 1865."

The Dorsetshire Regiment has one Volunteer battalion, the 1st DORSETSHIRE. The earliest in date of the twelve corps which were formed by the middle of July, 1860, seems to have been the Wareham corps, the date of which is given as the 28th of January, 1860. The present Hon. Colonel became commander of the Administrative Battalion which was shortly formed from these various corps. Amongst the earliest supporters of the Dorchester corps was the Prince of Wales, on whose property their range was situated. In 1864 Sergeant Aldridge of the old Dorset Rifles won the Snider Association Cup, and in 1882 Corporal Lodder won the Martini Challenge Cup. Attached to the 1st Dorsetshire is the Cadet corps of Sherborne College. The uniform is grey with facings of scarlet.

The Prince of Wales's Volunteers (South Lancashire Regiment) has two Volunteer battalions, the 9th LANCASHIRE and the 21st LANCASHIRE. The 9th Lancashire dates from the 1st of October, 1859, when it was raised at Warrington, the first commanding officer being the same gentleman as the one that now holds the position. The uniform was green with black facings at the commencement of the career of the Warrington corps, with which in the course of time other of the many Lancashire corps became amalgamated. The present uniform is scarlet with green facings.

The 21st LANCASHIRE, forming the 2nd Volunteer Battalion of the Prince of Wales's Volunteers, dates from February, 1860. The 47th LANCASHIRE RIFLE VOLUNTEERS, as they used to be called, date from the latter end of 1859, and their formal acceptance

* *The Volunteer Record.*

of service from early in 1860. In March of that year the regiment numbered five companies, which shortly after expanded into eight. The present Hon. Colonel was gazetted to the Lieutenant-Colonelcy in July, 1860, in which month we may note that Colonel Pilkington, the present commanding officer, obtained his company. The St. Helens corps has always been a strong and efficient one, and the 21st Lancashire, as it came to be called, has on many occasions made its mark as a shooting regiment, securing some of the most valued prizes in the various competitions in which it has taken part, the present Colonel, Sergeant West, Ensign Parr, and Corporal Taylor—the latter the winner of the Queen's Prize in 1877—being amongst the representative marksmen. The uniform is green with facings of scarlet.

The Welsh Regiment—Regimental District, No. 41—has four Volunteer battalions, which are supplied by the 1st Pembrokeshire, the 1st Glamorganshire, the 2nd Glamorganshire, and the 3rd Glamorgan or Swansea Rifles, which last preserves its earlier name and style.

The 1st PEMBROKESHIRE dates from the earliest days of the Volunteer movement, ranking fifth in order of precedence. The first commanding officer was the Hon. R. F. S. Greville, who was captain of the corps raised at Milford. The uniform is scarlet with facings of dark blue.

The 1st GLAMORGANSHIRE, which forms the 2nd Volunteer battalion, also dates from 1859, when it was raised at Margam, the late Hon. Colonel * being the first commanding officer. The uniform is scarlet with facings of blue.

The 2nd GLAMORGANSHIRE, forming the 3rd Volunteer battalion, dates from the same time. There were five corps raised in 1859 in Glamorganshire, and others subsequently, and the 2nd Glamorganshire is the present representative of several of these. The uniform is scarlet with facings of white.

The 3rd GLAMORGAN is another representative of the original corps raised in the county, all of which, it may be noted, rank twenty-seventh in precedence. The first commanding officer was Captain L. Dillwyn, M.P., and the corps presents another of the welcome instances which show, in the Army List of to-day, the owner of the same name occupying the same high position. The regiment is honoured by having as its Hon. Colonel the Prince of Wales, who is fitly associated with one of the most distinguished Volunteer regiments in his own Principality. The uniform is scarlet with facings of green.

* C. R. M. Talbot, M.P., the "father" of the House of Commons. It is sad, on the eve of publication, to have to say of so honoured and representative a gentleman that "his place knows him no more."

The Black Watch (Royal Highlanders) has no fewer than six Volunteer battalions raised in Forfarshire, Perthshire, and Fifeshire.

The 1st FORFARSHIRE dates from 1859, before the close of which year their services were accepted. "Sir John Ogilvy, the present Hon. Colonel, was the first colonel of the regiment, and the present commanding officer, Colonel Mitchell, has been in the regiment since its formation." The uniform is scarlet with facings of blue.

The 2nd FORFARSHIRE, which is now called the 2nd (Angus) Volunteer Battalion, also dates from 1859 and represents several corps raised in the neighbourhood. In due process these corps became, in 1874, the 1st Administrative Battalion of Forfarshire Rifle Volunteers, and a few years later were again metamorphosed into the 2nd Forfar or Angus Rifles.

The 3rd (DUNDEE HIGHLAND) VOLUNTEER BATTALION was first known as the 10th Forfarshire Rifles, and as such have gained a very foremost place amongst the shooting regiments. In 1878, Private McKenzie tried for the Glen Albyn Prize at Wimbledon, and in 1880 won it, and in 1879, Quarter-Master MacDonald gained the silver medal of the N.R.A. in the first stage for the Queen's Prize. In 1883 Forfarshire won the China Challenge Cup. When first raised, the 10th Forfarshire wore the kilt, but for some years this has given place to the trews. The uniform is scarlet with facings of blue.

The 1st PERTHSHIRE forms the 4th Volunteer battalion of the Black Watch, and dates from 1861. "It was formerly," states the *Military Directory*, "a Rifle Regiment clothed in green, but adopted the uniform of the Royal Highlanders in 1883." The 1st Perthshire has always held a high position for marksmanship. The uniform is scarlet with blue facings. Attached is the Cadet corps from Glenalmond College, whose uniform is grey with black facings.

The 2nd PERTHSHIRE, now called the 5th (Perthshire Highland) Volunteer Battalion, was formerly known as the 3rd (or Breadalbane) Perth Rifles. It was raised in 1860, and in 1880 became the 2nd Perthshire. The Prince of Wales's Prize, the Duke of Cambridge's Prize, the St. George's Challenge Vase, the Secretary for War's Prize, and the *Daily Telegraph* Prize, have been gained by Captain Robertson, Private Fergusson, Private Farquharson, and Sergeant McCowan. The uniform is dark grey with facings of red.

The 1st FIFESHIRE, now the 6th Volunteer battalion, represents several smaller corps raised in 1859 and the earlier part of 1860. The Fife Rifles are amongst the "shooting" regiments, being able to count many successes at the butts. The uniform is that of the Territorial Regiment—scarlet with blue facings.

The Oxfordshire Light Infantry—Regimental District, No 43—have four Volunteer battalions.

The 1st OXFORD UNIVERSITY BATTALION dates from December, 1859, when it was raised under the Colonelcy of the Prince of Wales, who still holds the position. The first commanding officer was Colonel the Hon. R. Spencer, who had for many years served in the Royal Artillery. Amongst other prizes won by the regiment may be mentioned that given by the Secretary of State for War, which was gained by Captain Barnett in 1888. The uniform is scarlet with facings of dark blue. The Oxford Military College furnishes a Cadet corps.

The 2nd OXFORDSHIRE, the Oxford City Rifles, also date from December, 1859, when they were raised under Captain Bowyer, formerly of the 14th Dragoons. The corps has always been an efficient one, Private Harris gaining for the regiment in 1871 the Prince of Wales's Prize at Wimbledon, and Corporal Webb tying for the Windmill Prize in 1873. The uniform is scarlet with facings of white.

The 1st BUCKS RIFLE VOLUNTEERS, which retain, without the addition of "Volunteer Battalion," their original designation, date from 1860. Their career has been an exceptionally prosperous one; at every review and public function in which they have participated praise has been awarded generally and unstintingly; such authorities as Lord Wolseley and Sir Evelyn Wood have spoken strongly in their eulogy, and the local popularity of the regiment speaks highly for its excellent *morale*. The shooting moreover, fostered as its exercise is by the great interest taken in the county, is above the average; as one instance out of many of which may be mentioned the winning of the Curtis and Harvey Prize by Lieutenant Freemantle in 1887. The uniform is grey with facings of scarlet. The present Hon. Colonel, Lord Barrington, was the first gazetted commander of the "Buckingham" Rifles, and the present commanding officer, Colonel Wethered, was gazetted at the same time as an ensign in the Great Marlow corps.

The 2nd BUCKS is formed by the Eton College Volunteers, till quite lately the only *battalion* of the Cadet calibre. The doings of the "Eton Boys" at the butts are matters of common knowledge, and their uniform of grey with facings of light blue is as familiar as it is popular. Amongst the champions of the regiment may be mentioned Captain Godsall, who has won the Wimbledon Cup, the Dudley Prize, the Secretary for War's Prize, and the Bass Prize.

The Essex Regiment—Regimental District, No. 44—has four Volunteer battalions. Sixteen corps were raised in the latter part of 1859 and the first six months of 1860.

The 1st ESSEX dates from August of the former year, when a corps was raised at Ilford under the command of Captain Davis. The uniform was the same as that now worn, green with facings of black. Attached to the 1st Essex are the Cadet corps of Ongar Grammar School and the Forest School at Walthamstow.

The 2nd ESSEX also dates from 1859, the present Lieutenant-Colonel being appointed to the command of the Chelmsford corps. The 2nd Essex has been for a considerable time highly thought of as a shooting regiment, on eight occasions having won the county shield presented by Colonel Coope, and, amongst other achievements, the Silver Medal and the Bronze Medal, won by Corporal Wisker and Private Rippon at Wimbledon. For many years the regiment has availed itself of the annual "camp," and amongst its means and appliances to proficiency may be mentioned a Gardner gun, the efficient working of which has on more than one occasion elicited most favourable comments. A Cadet corps from Falstead is attached to the regiment, whose uniform is green with green facings. The 2nd Essex is distinguished in possessing as its Hon. Colonel so renowned a soldier as Sir Evelyn Wood, V.C.

The 3rd ESSEX dates from January, 1860, when a corps was raised at Plaistow, the present commanding officer being one of the first captains. The Hon. Colonel of the regiment is Baron von Pawel Rammingen. The uniform is green with green facings.

The 4th ESSEX was raised at Silvertown in February, 1860, the present Lieutenant-Colonel being captain commandant. The uniform is, like that of the 2nd and 3rd battalions, green with green facings.

The Sherwood Foresters (Derbyshire Regiment)—Regimental District, No. 45—has four Volunteer battalions. Fifteen corps were raised in Derbyshire, which are now represented by the 1st and 2nd Volunteer battalions of the Territorial regiment.

The 1st DERBYSHIRE dates from July, 1859, when the first corps was raised at Derby. The same city provided three more corps, ranking as the 4th, 5th, and 15th DERBYSHIRE RIFLES respectively, and the localities of Chesterfield, Buxton, Sadbury, and Chapel-en-le-Frith followed suit. There are two Cadet corps attached to the regiment, those of Derby and Trent College respectively. The uniform is scarlet with white facings.

Early in May, 1859, the ROBIN HOOD RIFLES were formed, and by the close of the year their number reached the respectable figure of 600, which for many years now has increased to over a thousand, "all efficient." True to the traditions enshrined in their name, the "Robin Hoods" have always been a first-rate shooting corps, a fact which was recognised when, in 1862, "A" Company, being the best shooting company in the

Volunteer force, was selected to shoot against the Australian team, and emphasized thirteen years later when Sergeant Loach won the Grand Aggregate Prize at Wimbledon. And it is not only in shooting, but in all the qualifications that go to make a first-rate regiment, that the Robin Hoods hold a high position, and both commanding officer * and adjutant † have reason to be proud of the estimation in which their corps is held. We will quote the remarks of two inspecting officers. In 1887 Colonel Kingsley, addressing the regiment after the inspection, said, "Your turn-out, camp, and drill are as good as I have ever seen in any line regiment;" and in 1889, Sir H. Wilmot, V.C., assured the Colonel that "he had nothing but praise to give," adding "I have no hesitation in saying that I have never seen a Volunteer battalion so smart and so efficient as are the Robin Hoods: your drill in the field and your conduct in quarters would be a credit to any regiment under the sun."

The uniform of the Riding Hoods is the traditional " Lincoln Green," and there has always been a strong feeling against in any way losing their own identity by adopting the uniform or designation of the Territorial regiment.

The 2nd NOTTINGHAMSHIRE form the 4th Volunteer battalion of the Sherwood Foresters. Eight rifle corps were raised in Nottinghamshire in March and April of 1860, and in the course of time the 1st Administrative Battalion was formed, to the colonelcy of which the present commanding officer was appointed in 1865; when the "administrative" gave place to the "consolidated" system, the 1st Administrative Battalion became the 2nd Nottinghamshire. The uniform was originally grey, but was changed to scarlet in 1875.

Such a regiment as the Sherwood Foresters deserves some notice of its shooting triumphs, the Alexandra, the Grand Aggregate, the Army Rifle Association Cup, the Belgian Challenge Cup, the *Daily Telegraph* Prize, and the Silver Medal being amongst the trophies won by Taylor, Milner, Loach, Edge, Toplis, and Mayfield. The uniform is scarlet with facings of Lincoln green.

The Loyal North Lancashire Regiment—Regimental District, No. 47—has two Volunteer battalions, the 11th and 14th LANCASHIRE, dating from October, 1859, and February, 1860, respectively. The headquarters are at Preston and Bolton respectively, and the regiment has several successes at the butts. The uniform is scarlet with facings of white.

* Colonel Seely.
† Captain Dalbiac, 45th Regiment, to whose kindly supplied notes respecting the Robin Hood Rifles the writer is much indebted.

The Northamptonshire Regiment—Regimental District, No. 48—has only one Volunteer battalion, the 1st NORTHAMPTONSHIRE. Five corps were raised altogether, the first in date being the Althorpe company, which dates from August, 1859, when it was established with Earl Spencer as the captain. The present senior Major, Hon. Lieutenant-Colonel Hollis, was appointed to a lieutenancy in the 4th company raised at Northampton. In 1869 the Belgian Prize was won by the county. The uniform is grey with scarlet facings.

The Princess Charlotte of Wales's (Royal Berkshire Regiment)—Regimental District, No. 49—has also only one Volunteer battalion, the 1st BERKSHIRE. Dating from 1860, the 1st Berkshire represents seven corps which were raised at Reading, Windsor, Newbury, Abingdon, Maidenhead, Wokingham, and Sandhurst. The present Lieutenant-Colonel Commandant, Lord Wantage, V.C., was, as Colonel Lloyd Lindsay, the first commanding officer. The uniform is scarlet with facings of blue. Attached to the 1st Berkshire are the Cadet corps of Wellington College—grey, with facings of dark blue—and Bradfield College, whose uniform is that of the Territorial regiment. In 1868, 1875, 1878, and 1885 the 1st Berks gained the Belgian Challenge Cup; in 1876 Corporal Witherington won the first stage of the Alexandra; in 1871 Sergeant Soper won the Curtis and Harvey Prize; from 1883 to 1887 the regiment brought away the Mullens Prize.

The Queen's Own (Royal West Kent Regiment)—Regimental District, No. 50—has three Volunteer battalions. Between August, 1859, and June, 1860, no fewer than thirty-nine corps had been raised in "the Garden of England."

The 1st KENT, which constitutes the first Volunteer battalion of the Queen's Own, dates from the 29th of August, 1859, Viscount Hardinge being the junior Lieutenant-Colonel. The uniform of the Maidstone corps, the first in order of date, was described as "Rifle green with black braid. Badge, a silver horse; motto, *Invicta*." The present uniform is green with facings of the same colour.

The 3rd KENT, which forms the 2nd Volunteer battalion, dates from November, 1859, when corps were formed at Lee and Greenwich, Kidbrook following in December. We believe we are right in saying that the present Lieutenant-Colonel Commandant and Lieutenant-Colonel date their commissions as lieutenants in the Greenwich and Lee companies respectively from the former month. In 1882 Sergeant Morgan won the Olympic Prize at Wimbledon, and in 1885 Sergeant Oliver won the Association Cup (Martini-Henry). The uniform is green with facings of black.

The 4th KENT, forming the 3rd Volunteer battalion, is the famous Woolwich

Arsenal corps, which soon after its formation had eight companies, second to none in the force. The date given as its formal starting-point is March, 1860. The first Colonel Commandant was Colonel Tulloch of the Artillery, and the present commanding officer was, we understand, a lieutenant in No. 7 company. The senior captain (hon. Major) Denton, was in command of No. 8 company. The uniform is scarlet with green facings.

The King's Own (Yorkshire Light Infantry)—Regimental District, No. 51—has only one Volunteer battalion, the 5th WEST RIDING, dating from November, 1859. The Wakefield company soon had other corps attached, and in due course the Administrative Battalion was formed, and the regiment gave proof of its great popularity. For efficiency and marksmanship the 5th Yorkshire has always stood high. The uniform is scarlet with facings of blue.

The King's (Shropshire Light Infantry)—Regimental District, No. 53—has three Volunteer battalions. Sixteen corps were raised at the time of the great movement, and of these the first was the Wellington corps, which dates from October, 1859, the first gazetted officer, we believe, being Captain Eyson. Very marked have been the successes of the Shropshire regiments in shooting competitions, the Queen's Prize, the Windmill Prize, the Wimbledon Cup, the Irish Challenge Trophy, the Alfred Prize, the Association Cup (Snider), the China Challenge Cup, the *Daily Telegraph* Prize, and the Martini Challenge Cup, having been won by such marksmen as Roberts, Rae, Wyatt, Davies, Pichen, Owen, and Lyndon. The uniform of the 1st SHROPSHIRE, which forms the 1st Volunteer battalion, is scarlet with facings of white; that of the 2nd SHROPSHIRE, constituting the 2nd Volunteer battalion, grey with facings of black.

The 1st HEREFORDSHIRE, the Hereford and Radnor Rifles, hold the position of 3rd Volunteer battalion to the Shropshire regiment. Seven corps were raised in Herefordshire, and were speedily associated with "their brothers of Radnorshire," the men of Presteign, Knighton. In 1864 Sergeant Dodd brought away the Prince of Wales's Prize, and in 1883 the 1st Herefordshire were the winners in the competition for the Belgian Challenge Cup. The uniform of the 1st Herefordshire is scarlet with facings of black.

The Duke of Cambridge's Own (Middlesex Regiment)—Regimental District, No. 57—has four Volunteer battalions. It may not be out of place here, in treating of those belonging to the regiment which has the territorial designation of "Middlesex," to glance at the general history of the Volunteer movement as it affected the metropolitan county. Strangely picturesque are the glimpses we get of the old Volunteer regiments, which did so well in the days of our fathers, gaining, too, not a little in that picturesqueness from the scenery of the pictures, showing the parks and streets and squares familiar by name to us of to-day, but scarcely recognisable in their quaint, old-world guise. Wits and beaux jostled footpads and bullies as they elbowed their way through streets so foul and narrow that nowadays they would be incontinently condemned. Peaceful citizens who would cross London after dark prudently waited till they mustered numbers enough to brave the passage perilous of Great Turnstile or Marylebone Lane; on Blackfriars Bridge a pitched battle took place, only two years before the Gordon riots, between a band of smugglers and some soldiers, in which the soldiers "were only partially successful"; at the corners of streets exposed gibbets groaned with their ghastly burdens; offal, garbage, and sewage blocked up the filthy gutters, washed away sometimes by a torrent of blood from a fetid slaughter-house. Undoubtedly there are shadows in the pictures, nor is the darkness always cleanly or wholesome. But in the midst of it all—the riot and dirt and insecurity—what *men* they were, even the rank and file, and how strong and masterful, for themselves and their country, were the leaders—Warriors, Statesmen, Scientists, and Lords of the domain of letters. Streets might be foul and unsafe, corruptions rife, sanitation and cleanliness unknown, but the country held her own haughtily amongst the Powers of Europe, while she forced the Princes of India to transfer to her Imperial sway their fabulous wealth and ancient heritage. And it is amongst the men who lived in these stirring times, in that "crowded hour of glorious life" in the country's history, that we must look for the forefathers of the Middlesex and London Volunteers of to-day.

Matters were serious enough at the end of the last century. The fleet of flat-bottomed boats was ready; the passage was one of a few hours; other nations were powerless to help us. It was not only a question of a hostile force landing on British coasts; that would be bad enough, but—what then could be done to save the wealthiest city in the world? London would lie open to the invading troops maddened with visions of her wealth.

"If they once may win the bridge, what hope to save the town?"

wrote a later poet in his matchless description of the danger that once threatened imperial Rome. Once the coast is gained, what chance of saving London? asked the anxious and cautious at the time of Napoleon's threat. Hurried meetings of military authorities sketched out plans: amongst other precautions lines of earthworks were to be erected reaching from the Lea at Tottenham to the Thames at Hammersmith. But the descendants of the stubborn old Middle-sexe, who in days gone by had done such brave ruthless deeds against Briton and Dane, had yet another answer to the vital question—the enrolment of the Volunteers. Hogarth and Rowlandson give us sketches of the military element of the then society, but it is often but the humorous, sometimes the ridiculous, side, which is portrayed. The Volunteers of '98, the "Loyal Bands," "Volunteer Guards," present to us, as we *read* of them, bodies of men in whose ranks we are proud to think our fathers may have borne arms. But when we see *pictures* of them, this right and natural sentiment somewhat fades. We forget the deeds in gazing at the counterfeit presentment of the doers. The costume itself seems quaint to a degree, and loses nothing of the quaintness in its treatment by the artists.

We know—we keep repeating to ourselves—that they were in their way heroes; that but for their united action and bold front we might be now a satrapy of France, or at any rate have sunk to the place of a second-rate power. But, they don't *look* it, and we fall to murmuring feebly in exculpation of our momentary disloyalty to the memory of men who did so well, the comical apology of the American poet—

> "I know it is a sin
> For me to sit and grin
> At him here;
> But the old three-cornered hat,
> And the breeches, and all that,
> Are so queer!"

After all, the feeling of ridicule is but transient. We laugh with edifying impartiality at some of the pictures of the rifle corps of to-day in the costume they first adopted. What could well be more comical than a London corps dressed in a sort of stage brigand costume, sky blue in colour, with a "Garibaldi" hat and a long drooping feather *à la* the Tyrolese singers? But the corps that started on its military career clad in this fearful and wonderful costume is and always has been one of the most distinguished of all the Volunteer regiments. To return, however, for a moment to the Middlesex * Volunteers of the last century. The names and composition of some of them will be noticed in dealing with their successors; suffice it to say that having ably and effectively done the duty that came in their way they were, with some few exceptions, disbanded.

For many years before 1859 thinking men had had in view the desirability of reorganizing the Volunteer Force. So early, we believe, as 1837, had Mr. Hans Busk, of

---

* In the expression "Middlesex" are included in this connection the "London" regiments.

the regiment now known as the "Victorias," suggested the step to the Government, and from that time he and others who held the same view had on various occasions sought to influence public opinion in its favour. A political accident, as is well known, brought the subject to the front with a rush. Since the Crimean War the reciprocal feelings between France and England had become somewhat estranged; to the feverish and excited vision of the French populace the carelessly strong attitude of this country became more and more irritating. An attempt was made on the life of the Emperor. There was but little doubt that the miscreant had for some time sheltered in England, and not improbably had here hatched his diabolical scheme. This fact acted as a torch to combustible fuel. Hysteric shrieks for vengeance were howled forth by pseudo-patriots and demagogues; Government officials caught the infection; fire-eating colonels besought "our faithful ally" for leave to march against perfidious Albion; there were not wanting circumstantial proposals of the *modus operandi* of crushing the Island Empire's pride and power. To say that there was a "scare," scarcely does justice to the national character. There was no scare, but plenty of serious alarm, and more of patriotic determination. Throughout the land rose up the cry for permission to arm, and in May of 1859 was issued the famous circular so often before referred to. Then the Volunteer movement, as at present constituted, commenced in good earnest.

The 3rd MIDDLESEX is composed of various corps raised at Hampstead, Barnet, Hornsey, Highgate, Tottenham, and Enfield, which at one time were represented by the 2nd and 6th Administrative Battalions. In 1862, however, they were amalgamated under the present Hon. Colonel as commanding officer. As with most of the Middlesex regiments, we are compelled to pass over the incidents affecting the growth and progress of the successors of the old Hampstead Volunteers, and content ourselves with glancing briefly at some of their gains at the butts. In 1883 Sergeant Downes won the *Daily Telegraph* Prize at Wimbledon, and on other occasions the 3rd Middlesex have returned victors from county and local competitions. The uniform is grey with facings of scarlet.

The 8th MIDDLESEX, the 2nd Volunteer Battalion of the Middlesex Regiment, dates from early in the movement, and like its companions, represents the amalgamation of many other local corps. The present Hon. Colonel, was, we believe, gazetted early in 1860 as Commander of the Hounslow Company. In 1884, Private Gallant won the Queen's Prize at Wimbledon, and other trophies have from time to time been credited to the regiment. The uniform is grey with grey facings.

The 11th MIDDLESEX, the Railway Rifles, the 3rd Battalion of the Territorial Regiment, date from about the same period as the corps before mentioned. A popular and meritorious regiment, whose Hon. Colonel is the Duke of Sutherland, and commanding officer Sir W. Charley, the modern 11th Middlesex has earned for itself golden opinions for efficiency and smartness. The uniform is grey with facings of scarlet.

The 17th MIDDLESEX—the North Middlesex Rifles—comprise several of the old companies, and when first raised had their headquarters at Islington. The uniform is green with facings of black.

The famous KING'S ROYAL RIFLE CORPS has no fewer than ten Volunteer battalions. Of these the first are the "VICTORIAS" of old renown.

Incidentally, we have more than once mentioned the Victoria Rifles. Before the close of the eighteenth century they were in existence, and when other of the loyal and patriotic Volunteer associations then formed were disbanded, the Duke of Cumberland's Sharpshooters, as they were then called, were allowed—not without much trouble and the exertions of friends in high places—to retain their corporate existence as a rifle club. Years passed on, till, when the country became naturally attracted to the personality of the future sovereign, and men's thoughts and anticipations turned to the quiet Palace of Kensington where dwelt in maiden seclusion the Heiress of Alfred and the Confessor, of Normans and Plantagenets, of Tudors and Stuarts, the Sharpshooters solicited and obtained permission to be called "The Royal Victoria Rifle Club." From the earliest commencement of their existence they had been emphatically a *rifle* corps, having been the first of the Volunteers who received the then somewhat novel equipment of Riflemen. The impetus given in 1835 was not in vain; the Royal Victoria Rifle Club made unmistakable progress in efficiency; they secured capital premises and range; amongst their officers was Captain Hans Busk, to whom undoubtedly belongs the honour of initiating and stimulating the Volunteer movement of 1859.

From the time of their renaissance in 1859 the career of the Victorias has been a brilliant one. No regiment is more familiar at reviews and parades than they; few regiments have been more forward in availing themselves of every means of attaining excellence. They were, we believe, the first Volunteer corps which received formal sanction for the formation of "Mounted Infantry," and it would be but to repeat an oft told tale to dwell upon the credit that body has received. And the present Victorias have not let the hand lose its cunning which gained for their predecessors the sobriquet of Sharpshooters. The Queen's Prize has been twice won; the Wimbledon Cup, the Alexandra, the Association Cup, the (Snider) Association Cup, and the Duke of

THE 1st MIDDLESEX (VICTORIA RIFLES)
VOLUNTEERS.

(4TH VOLUNTEER BATTALION KING'S ROYAL RIFLE CORPS.)

Cambridge's Prize have been gained by Pixley, Martin Smith, Thornbury, Dickens, and Bernard. Attached to the Victorias is the Cadet corps of Marlborough Place. The uniform is green with facings of black.

The 2nd SOUTH MIDDLESEX have, like their comrades, the Victorias, a long and interesting history. Some amusement was caused at one of the earliest meetings, January, 1860, of this corps, when one of the speakers announced that a French gentleman had expressed his opinion in a recent conversation with a relative of the speaker's, that the Emperor's legions would be in England in the following May. Their triumphs at the butts have been many and continuous. The first commander was Lord Ranelagh, and the uniform the same in essentials as at present, grey with red facings.

The WEST LONDON and WEST MIDDLESEX—to the latter of which is attached the Harrow Corps—comprise the 3rd and 4th Volunteer battalions of the King's Royal Rifles. Both are distinguished corps, the Hon. Colonel of the former being Lord Chelmsford, and of the latter Gen. Cameron, C.B. Uniform grey with scarlet facings.

The 6th MIDDLESEX, the ST. GEORGE'S RIFLES, date from early in the movement, being the eleventh metropolitan corps formed into a battalion. But there were St. George's Volunteers raised in the neighbourhood of Hanover Square in 1792, which must not be confounded with the St. George's, Hanover Square, Armed Association, which sprang into being in 1798. The colours of the old corps are still preserved by their successors. Attached to the St. George's is the veteran corps of the Victorias, neither regiment being numerically strong, though both are amongst the most distinguished in the Volunteer service. The present Hon. Colonel was the first commanding officer appointed to the regiment. Amongst the marksmen of the regiment who have gained renown are Major Waller, the winner of the Duke of Cambridge's Prize in 1876, Corporal Cutting, who tied for the Curtis and Harvey in 1877, and Private Pouncey, who won the (Snider) Association Cup in 1868. Uniform green with scarlet facings.

Originally known as the 18th Middlesex, the HARROW CORPS, attached to the West Middlesex, soon gave evidence of healthy vitality. It was raised in the latter part of 1859, many of the leading residents in the neighbourhood supporting it both by purse and in person. In 1884 Sergeant-Major Gilder won the Curtis and Harvey Prize, and in 1871 the Dudley Prize, in 1881 the Secretary for War's Prize, and in 1884 the Wimbledon Cup. Attached to the 9th Middlesex is the Cadet corps of Harrow School, which has its own shooting triumphs. Uniform green with green facings.

THE 12th MIDDLESEX—the Civil Service—to which is attached the 25th BANK OF

ENGLAND RIFLES, represent, as may well be imagined, one of the most important features in the movement—the participation of the civil servants of the Crown. Originally known as the 21st Middlesex, they were speedily honoured by the appointment of the Prince of Wales as Hon. Colonel, and few regiments have a more brilliant record of success and achievements. The uniform is grey with facings of blue, that of the Bank of England Rifles, green with facings of the same.

The 13th MIDDLESEX, the popular Queen's Westminsters, form the 8th Volunteer battalion of the King's Royal Rifle corps, and, like so many others of the Middlesex regiments, date their origin from the last century, when they were raised as the Royal Westminster Volunteers. Early in their career the latter received their colours from the King, and these are still in the possession of the Queen's Westminster. The old Royal Westminster Volunteers remained embodied till 1814, when they were disbanded, to be restored to active existence when another Napoleon caused our attention to be directed to the possibility of invasion. The present Hon. Colonel, then Earl Grosvenor, spared no pains to make the Westminster Volunteers of 1860 fully equal to their predecessors. Such they speedily became, and at the Royal Review of June, 1860, were numerically strong enough to be able to stand as a separate battalion. It is stated that a short time previously to this, the regiment had the honour of an impromptu inspection by the Queen in person, on which occasion they claim to have given the "first Royal salute which Her Majesty received from a Volunteer corps." Amongst those who have served in the regiment may be mentioned, in addition to the Duke of Westminster and Colonel Howard Vincent, Lord Thesiger, the Dean of Westminster, Sir Morell Mackenzie, and Mr. Justice Denman. Their triumphs at the butts are matter of notoriety. They have twice won the Alexandra Prize, Private Cameron in 1878 and Sergeant Vicars ten years latter securing it for their regiment; in 1876 Private James won the Silver Medal of the Association, an achievement repeated in 1878 by Private Lowe; while in a trial of strength between the Westminster and the 1st Hants in 1875 the former regiment won a decided victory. The uniform is grey with facings of scarlet.

Like so many other of the Middlesex corps, the FINSBURY RIFLES had predecessors at the close of the last century. When raised in 1859 the Clerkenwell Rifle Corps, as their first appellation was, ranked 39th in county precedence. It was noticed that many of the leading commercial firms were the principal supporters. The 3rd company was officered, and in great part manned, by Messrs. Virtue; another company owed its existence to the employés of Messrs. Pontifex. For some time the regiment was not numerically a strong one, but of late years this has been altered. The regiment became the 21st, its present number, in 1878, in which year Major Young won the Albert Prize, and tied for the Glen Albyn and Grand Aggregate, in 1882 winning the Curtis and Harvey Prize, and the Wimbledon Cup, and in 1884 the Bass Prize, the Duke of Cambridge's Prize, and the Curtis and Harvey Prize; in 1883 Lieutenant Milner won the Dudley Prize. The uniform is green with scarlet facings.

The 22nd MIDDLESEX claim a connection of origin with their predecessors in numerical rank, the Finsbury Rifles, having been originally connected with the 39th Middlesex. On becoming a separate corps it was numbered the 40th, and by another revolution of the whirligig of time, or rather of official progression, has become the 22nd. The first Hon. Colonel was Sir J. Yorke Scarlett, who commanded the famous heavy cavalry division in the Crimea. The change in the list of commanding officers has been somewhat trying in its frequent recurrence, the present popular chief being the seventh. The uniform is green with facings of scarlet.

The 25th, the Bank of England Volunteers, are, as before mentioned, attached to the 12th Middlesex. There are not wanting advocates who claim for the Bank Volunteers a very considerable antiquity, and there seems no reason to doubt that from a very early period of the Bank history a company of Volunteers has been in existence. The present corps is manned by the porters and watchmen of the establishment.

The London Volunteers, the 1st—the CITY OF LONDON RIFLE VOLUNTEER BRIGADE*— the 2nd and the 3rd London, complete the tale of the Volunteer battalions of the King's Royal Rifle Corps. We have before glanced at the history of the movement as it affected the metropolis; it only needs to be added here that in the past history of the City, and amongst all the bodies which from time to time have sprung to voluntary armament in its defence, no corps deserve better approval and pride than do the three regiments above mentioned. In the early days it was proposed that the Lord Mayor should be the Hon. Colonel of the City of London Rifle Brigade, but at a public meeting held in the Guildhall his lordship announced that the popular Duke of Cambridge had accepted the position. Fortunate beyond measure, too, are the 2nd London in having as their Hon. Colonel the most popular of British generals; equal fortune had, at the time these pages were originally written, the 3rd London in the chieftainship of the hero of Magdala. "Alas, that 'had,' how sad a passage 'tis."

* The London Rifle Brigade are, we believe, the only Volunteer regiment which still retains the plume on the cap.

The Duke of Edinburgh's Wiltshire Regiment—Regimental District 62—has two Volunteer battalions.

The 1st WILTS consists of various corps, which in 1861 were formed into the 1st Administrative Battalion of Wiltshire Rifle Volunteers. Undoubtedly the regiment has owed a great deal to the present Hon. Colonel, Lieut.-Colonel Everett, appointed to the command in 1866, and to the late Adjutant, Major Gibney, whose sketch of the regimental history will be of value to all interested in the Volunteer movement in Wiltshire.

The 2nd WILTS dates from 1860, when the companies raised at Malmesbury, Chippenham, Devizes, and elsewhere were formed into the 2nd Administrative Battalion of Wiltshire Volunteers under the command of Colonel M. F. Ward (Chippenham Company), late of the 90th Foot. The present commanding officer received his commission as lieutenant in the Malmesbury Company about the same time. Attached is the Cadet Corps of Marlborough College. The uniform is green with black facings.

The Manchester Regiment—Regimental District 63—has six Volunteer Battalions, which might almost claim a volume to themselves. They are respectively the 4th, 6th, 7th, 16th, 20th, and 22nd Lancashire. Of these the 6th, 20th, and 16th were better known as the 1st, 2nd, and 3rd Manchester. The three original Manchester corps were raised in December, 1859, and February, 1860; the Ardwick corps in January, 1860, and the contingents at Ashton-under-Lyne and Oldham in February of the same year. It would be pleasant to dwell upon the connection of the present corps with those originally raised, to trace the process of absorption through the Administrative Battalion stage, and to follow in detail the triumphs of each component factor. But this must not be, and though we might point out how, as exemplified by the 3rd Manchester, the most recent development, that of Mounted Infantry, has been attended by most marked success, and though in all references to the participation of the Manchester Volunteer Battalions we should have perforce to re-echo to the point of weariness the plaudits of "Well done, Manchester!" with which they are always greeted, we must pass on, with the conviction that it needs no written pages to make known the qualities of these distinguished Lancashire regiments. The uniform is scarlet with Lincoln green facings.

The Prince of Wales's North Staffordshire Regiment—Regimental District 64—has two Volunteer battalions, the 2nd and 5th Staffordshire. Dating from an early period in the movement the progress of the 2nd and 5th Staffordshire, as they are now styled, has been continuous and uninterrupted. The present Hon. Colonel and commanding officer of the 2nd Staffordshire were, we believe, amongst the earliest gazetted officers, holding the respective positions of captains of the 16th and 10th Staffordshire corps. The local interest taken may be evidenced by the fact that the commanding officer of the 2nd Staffordshire is Lord Burton, whose name is inseparably connected with the locality of the headquarters. The uniform of the 2nd Staffordshire is scarlet with facings of white; that of the 5th, scarlet with facings of blue.

The York and Lancaster Regiment—Regimental District 65—has two Volunteer battalions. The 1st (Hallamshire), formerly the 2nd West Riding of Yorkshire Volunteers, dates from 1859, in the September of which year some companies were raised at Sheffield, of one of which the present Lieut.-Colonel was Captain. The 8th West Riding dates from April, 1860, when two companies—the 20th and 21st West Yorkshire—were raised at Doncaster. The uniform of both regiments is scarlet with facings of white.

The famous Durham Light Infantry—Regimental District, No. 68—have five Volunteer battalions, being respectively the 1st, 2nd, 3rd, 4th, and 5th DURHAM RIFLE VOLUNTEERS. In June, 1859, the enrolment of a rifle corps for Stockton was decided on, and early in the following year the services of the 1st DURHAM VOLUNTEERS had been accepted by Her Majesty. Once again the old military enthusiasm broke out; valuable prizes, complimentary presentations, poured in on the newly formed corps, and the colours of the old Stockton Volunteers waved over their successors of the movement of our own day. When, in 1861, the adoption of Administrative Battalions came into force, the 1st Durham, the 15th, the 16th, and the 19th, were joined to the 2nd battalion Durham Rifle Volunteers. Later on, the 7th North York company were added, and the amalgamated corps were then known as the 4th Administrative Battalion. After a period of varying fortunes, during which the 7th North York disappeared and the 21st North York was added, the regiment in 1879 became the 1st Durham Rifles. Since that time the movement of the 1st Durham has been one of steady progress. They have gone with enthusiasm into the ambulance question, and on more occasions than can here be mentioned have earned high prizes at competitions and well-deserved encomium from inspecting officers. The uniform is scarlet with facings of white.

The 2nd DURHAM, now forming the 2nd Volunteer Battalion of the Durham Light Infantry, date from 1860, when the first company was formed at Bishop Auckland. Companies were formed at Black Boy, Coundon, Woodland, Butterknowle, Middleton Stanhope, Barnard Castle, and more recently, at Skerrymoor. Since 1881 the regiment has made giant strides, increasing its numbers to double the strength, and in other ways emphasizing its efficiency. The uniform is green with facings of scarlet.

The 3rd DURHAM can boast, like other regiments of the county, a long and interesting career. In 1880 the Sunderland Rifles were attached to the corps, which subsequently became the 5th Durham, but they afterwards became part and parcel of the 3rd Durham. The uniform is scarlet with facings of white.

The 4th DURHAM is described by the historian before quoted as "one of the most popular regiments in the county of Durham," and as rejoicing in the proud sobriquet of the "'Black Watch,' a name by which they are more familiarly known in civilian circles than by their proper designation." Five corps were soon enrolled from amongst "the hardy sons of toil to be found in the district stretching from the banks of the Wear at Durham to those of the Tyne at Felling," and these corps were in due time amalgamated into the 1st Administrative Battalion Durham Rifle Volunteers. In 1880 this 1st Administrative Battalion became the 4th Durham Rifle Volunteers, with a strength of ten companies. The uniform was originally grey, but in 1863 was changed for that at present worn—rifle green with scarlet facings. We may add that of the officers whose names appear in the (1889) Army List, two—the lieutenant-colonel and the hon. chaplain—were amongst the first gazetted on the formation of the regiment.

The 5th DURHAM has had a somewhat complicated history. In 1859 the Gateshead company was formed and known as the 8th Durham; in 1868 the South Shields contingent were enrolled as the 6th Durham; and in 1860 the corps from Blaydon and Winterton were numbered as the 9th Durham, and known as the Tyne and Derwent Rifles. These corps were constituted into the 3rd Durham, then into the 6th, and then, with certain changes not popular with the corps, into the 3rd Durham again. In November of the same year they became the 5th Durham, which title they retained till the recent Territorial nomenclature came into play. The uniform was at first green, but was afterwards changed into scarlet with dark green facings.

The Highland Light Infantry—Regimental District 71—have five Volunteer battalions, the 5th, 6th, 8th, 9th, and 10th LANARKSHIRE.

The 5th LANARK is a two-battalion corps dating, as to each of its constituents, from early in 1860, when the 2nd and 3rd Northern Battalions were raised. Only for a few months did their separate existence continue, and July, 1860, saw the two battalions united. The regiment has taken part with credit in various reviews and similar functions. In 1887 Sergeant Hill won the Silver Medal and the "Hop Bitters" Prize, and in the same year the Belgian Challenge Cup was won by the regiment, and in 1881 Sergeant Murray won the Prince of Wales's Prize.*

The 6th LANARK dates from 1860, when it was known as the 25th Lanarkshire, adopting its present designation in 1880. Numerous other companies are included, drawn chiefly from the "Clyde Artisans," who for some time gave their name to the corps. The present uniform is the third worn, the first having been grey and the second green. The authority before quoted says that the regiment was the first to adopt the new regulation helmet.

Raised in 1859, the 8th LANARKSHIRE had been previously known as the 4th Administrative Battalion and the 31st Lanarkshire (the Blythswood).

The 9th LANARKSHIRE, forming the 4th Volunteer Battalion of the Highland Light Infantry, represent five corps raised in 1860, namely the 37th, the 55th, the 62nd, the 73rd, and the 94th, which in 1863 were consolidated into the 3rd Administrative Battalion of the Lanarkshire Rifle Volunteers. In 1872, soon after the present commanding officer joined, a sixth company, the 107th, was raised at Leadhills, and in 1885 the regiment become the 9th Lanarkshire.

Amongst the public functions in which the regiment has taken part may be instanced the royal reviews at Edinburgh of 1860 and 1881, and the various ceremonies of state connected with the Glasgow Exhibition of 1888. "The shooting of the regiment is very good, and though as yet none of the members have won any of the great prizes at Wimbledon, yet all its efficients have earned the higher grant." There are numerous inter-regimental competitions, and great attention is paid to the "thoroughness" of the annual camping-out, an exercise to which the commanding officer attaches deserved importance. Much of the efficiency of the 9th Lanarkshire is due to the singular good fortune which has attended them in the appointment of adjutants. In 1885, on the retirement of Major Thornton, the first adjutant, Lieutenant-Colonel Andrew Stevenson, of the Black Watch, was appointed, who brought to his task the interesting experience gained in the most recent of our wars, and was succeeded by Captain Towers Clarke. The uniform is scarlet with facings of yellow.†

The 10th LANARK, the Glasgow Highland Volunteers, date from 1868, when a committee of gentlemen, amongst whom were the present Lieutenant-Colonel and senior

* It is recorded in the Directory that in 1879 the corps experienced a severe loss, their drill-hall being blown down during a heavy gale.

† We need not here mention the very numerous prize winners numbered in the Scotch Regiments, and whose names and triumphs are duly recorded in the local record.

Surgeon, was appointed to take steps for the formation of a regiment of Highland Volunteers. The offer of service was made in May, and accepted in July of the same year, permission being granted for the 105th Lanarkshire Rifle Volunteers to assume the additional style of the Glasgow Highland Volunteer Corps, and the tartan of the Black Watch. The present Hon. Colonel, the Marquis of Lorne, was appointed early in 1871, and the regiment has taken part in the reviews of 1876 and 1881. When first founded the 105th was attached to the 2nd Administrative Battalion. The strength has steadily increased; in 1868, out of a maximum of 1,200, but little more than half that number were enrolled, while the present strength is about 1,100. Amongst the shooting successes of the regiment, it may be noted that in 1874 Captain Euston won the Grand Aggregate, and the following year the St. George's Challenge Vase, and in 1885 Private Braithwaite won the Duke of Cambridge's Prize. The uniform of the 1st and 3rd Volunteer battalions and of the 9th Lanarkshire is scarlet with facings of yellow; of the 2nd Volunteer battalion, scarlet with black facings; and of the 5th, scarlet with blue facings.

The SEAFORTH HIGHLANDERS (Ross-shire Buffs) have three Volunteer battalions.

The 1st ROSS-SHIRE, the 1st Ross Highland Volunteer Battalion, of the Seaforth Highlanders, dates from 1860. The uniform when the regiment was first enrolled is stated to have been scarlet with blue trousers and shako with white plumes; this was afterwards changed for the scarlet and yellow facings now worn. In 1865 Captain Ross won the Wimbledon Cup. "There is in connection with the regiment a rifle association, known as the Ross-shire Service Rifle Association."

The SUTHERLAND HIGHLAND VOLUNTEERS, now the 2nd Volunteer battalion of the Seaforth Highlanders, date from early in the history of the movement, and were originally known as the 1st Administrative Battalion Sutherland Rifles, and subsequently as the 1st Sutherland. The regiment has always been a distinguished one, the Prince of Wales becoming Hon. Colonel in 1867, and the post of commanding officer being first held by the Duke of Sutherland, and now by the Marquis of Stafford. In 1867 the present uniform—that of the Sutherland Highlanders—was adopted. In 1883 Sergeant Mackay won the Queen's Prize and the Olympic Prize, and in 1888 Captain Morrison won the *Daily Telegraph* Prize.

The 1st ELGIN, now known as the 3rd (Morayshire) Volunteer Battalion, Seaforth Highlanders, date from 1859. The first companies raised were from the districts of

Forres, Elgin, Rothes, and Carr Bridge, and the strength of the regiment rapidly increased. The uniform is scarlet with facings of yellow.

The Gordon Highlanders—Regimental District 75—have six Volunteer battalions. The 1st Aberdeenshire dates from August, 1859, and by March, 1860, numbered nine companies.

The 2nd Aberdeenshire also dates from an early period, and like the 1st comprises several companies, and is recruited from Aberdeen and the neighbourhood. The 3rd (the Buchan) Volunteer Battalion, formerly the 3rd Aberdeenshire, was originated in 1860 and consisted of seven companies, the first raised of which was numbered the 19th. The 4th Aberdeenshire dates from somewhat later. "There is no record," says the Military Directory, "to show when this battalion was first raised." The present is, we believe, the third commanding officer.

The 5th DEESIDE HIGHLANDERS, formerly the 1st Kincardine and Aberdeen, was for some time known as the 1st Administrative Battalion Kincardine and Aberdeen. The corps, which is a numerically strong one, wears the kilt, and has as Hon. Colonel the Marquis of Huntly.

The 1st BANFFSHIRE dates from 1859, when one company was raised, the last addition being in 1869. The uniform of the 1st, 2nd, and 3rd Volunteer Battalions is scarlet with yellow facings; of the 4th green with scarlet facings; of the 5th green with green facings; and of the 6th grey with black facings.

The Queen's Own Cameron Highlanders—Regimental District 79—have one Volunteer battalion, the 1st INVERNESS-SHIRE HIGHLANDERS, dating from October, 1859. The present strength is ten companies, and the regiment is one of the most popular and best equipped in Scotland. The uniform is scarlet with buff facings.

The PRINCESS LOUISE'S—Argyll and Sutherland Highlanders—have seven Volunteer battalions, the first of which, the 1st Renfrewshire, dates from September, 1859, being the second senior regiment in Scotland. It has taken part in most of the Northern reviews, and has a high character for efficiency.

The 2nd RENFREWSHIRE, also dating from 1859, has a similar record of service, having had many opportunities of supplying guards of honour on the occasion of royal visits.

The 3rd RENFREWSHIRE dates from 1860, and the 4th (STIRLINGSHIRE) from a somewhat earlier date, some of the independent companies being raised in 1859.

The 5th Battalion, forming the 1st ARGYLL, was raised in 1860, and the various corps of which it was composed were formed into an Administrative Battalion, which became in 1880 the 1st Argyll Rifle Volunteers.

The 1st DUMBARTONSHIRE RIFLE VOLUNTEERS, occupying the place of the 6th Volunteer Battalion, date from 1859. It is a strong battalion, possessing a Lieutenant-Colonel Commandant, and numbering something over 1,200 in ranks. The first uniform was grey; this gave place to rifle green, which in due course was abandoned in favour of the present uniform.

The 1st CLACKMANNAN AND KINROSS, which form the 7th Volunteer Battalion, spring from the Alloa Rifles of 1859. These became subsequently the 1st Clackmannanshire, and in 1873 the 1st Kinross was attached. The uniform of the 1st Battalion is grey with facings of scarlet; of the 2nd, 3rd, and 7th, scarlet with facings of blue; of the 4th green with green facings; of the 5th and 1st Dumbartonshire scarlet with yellow facings.

The Rifle Brigade (Prince Consort's Own) has ten Volunteer Battalions. The 7th MIDDLESEX, the well-known London Scottish, date from 1859, their first number being the 15th. The present Hon. Colonel, as Lord Elcho, was the first commanding officer, and the uniform at that time was grey with brown facings. The London Scottish are undoubtedly one of the most "crack" corps in existence, as they are one of the most popular. We have been able before, however, to notice the Volunteer regiments composed of the kindly Scots, and beyond putting on record the fact of their having achieved many shooting triumphs, must reluctantly resist the temptation to dwell longer on their history.

Did space permit it would be more than usually interesting to trace from the beginning of the nation's history the military services rendered by the "men of the Law." This task, however, has been ably and successfully undertaken in a valuable brochure published some three years ago,* and we must content ourselves with the history of the INNS OF COURT RIFLE VOLUNTEERS as it is developed in the present Volunteer movement. We cannot, however, resist referring to the fact, noted by Mr. Norton, that "the first organized body formed by the Inns of Court appears to have been in 1584, when associations were formed by them to assist in the defence of the country from the Spanish Armada," and the Deed of Association under which they were enrolled can still be seen in the Drill Hall of Lincoln's Inn. At the time when the House of Commons first commenced the course of action which forced Charles I. to

* "A Short History of the Military and Naval Services of the Inns of Court," by F. C. Norton, Barrister-at-Law, and Sergeant I.C.R.V.

THE LONDON SCOTTISH
VOLUNTEERS.

(1st Volunteer Battalion Rifle Brigade), 7th Middlesex.

take up arms, the Inns of Court men offered their services to the King, and in answer to enquiries, made it clear to the turbulent Commons that "though they had no intention of interfering with the lawfully constituted authority of Parliament, they did not mean to permit their Sovereign to be insulted by the rabble."* The gentlemen of the Inns of Court formed a Volunteer band in the last century, and it is recorded that at a review in 1803, King George III. conferred upon them the sobriquet they still enjoy of "The Devil's Own." He was enquiring what troops they were, and Erskine, who was in command, replied: "They are all lawyers, sire." "What! what!" exclaimed the King, "all lawyers! all lawyers! Call them the Devil's Own!—call them the Devil's Own!"

In 1859 the Inns of Court petitioned to form a volunteer corps, and the original members were sworn in before Lord Campbell, "thus connecting them with the previous corps, of which he had been a member." First known as the 23rd, they are now formally designated the 14th, but most familiar to all is the old title of the "Inns of Court." In 1878 Private Evans won the Bass Prize, in 1886 Sergeant Simmonds won the silver medal, in 1889 Sergeant Browell won the bronze medal of the Middlesex Rifle Association, in addition to which other prizes have been credited to the corps. The Inns of Court are fortunate in possessing ample accommodation and, as might be expected from such a body, are well to the fore in all the departments of signalling, mounted infantry, ambulance, etc.† The uniform is grey with facings of scarlet.

The 15th MIDDLESEX—the Customs and the Docks—date from 1860, and represent the amalgamation of many corps. The original Custom House Rifles were numbered 26th and commanded by Major Grey. Recent events have impaired their numbers, but few corps can boast a finer material. The uniform is green with scarlet facings.

The 16th MIDDLESEX, the well-known LONDON IRISH RIFLES, which form the 4th Volunteer battalion of the Rifle Brigade, have from their raising, early in 1860, held a very foremost place amongst the Volunteer regiments of the country. In December of 1859, a meeting of "Irishmen residing in London" resolved that a Volunteer Rifle Corps should be organized; this resolution was adopted and supported, not only by the representative men of every class who were present at the meeting, but by

* It will be remembered that one of the finest situations in the play of *Charles the First*, produced by Mr. Irving at the Lyceum, was when, at the instigation of the Queen "the loyal gentlemen of Lincoln's Inn" appear with drawn swords in time to avert the contemplated attack upon the monarch.

† Captain Glen, who has charge of the signalling, has produced a system of transmitting maps or drawings, extending even to likenesses, by signal.

"almost every Peer on the Irish Roll, and every Irishman of distinction." The first Colonel was the Marquis of Donegall, and in the ranks under his command were such men as Lord Palmerston, Lord Francis Conyngham, Lord Otho Fitzgerald, Samuel Lover, Russell—of the *Times*—and Morgan John O'Connell. Before many years had passed, a detachment of the London Irish Rifles followed to his grave Private Lord Palmerston, and on none did the national loss fall more heavily than on the London Irish.

At first the uniform of the London Irish was dark grey with green facings, silver braid, and shako with green plume,* but in 1870 this was discarded in favour of the dark green of the Rifle Brigade.† It will be within the memory of many how at the time of the riots of 1867 and 1887 the London Irish to a man came forward as special constables; it may not, however, be so well known that, when in 1878 war with Russia seemed imminent, Lord Donegall offered the Regiment for active service. The present Hon. Colonel, H.R.H. the Duke of Connaught, succeeded the veteran Lord Gough in 1871, and has always shown the greatest interest in the regiment, heading it at every royal review. As an instance of the genuine *esprit de corps* that animates the regiment we may mention that on the occasion of the Windsor Review in 1881, the present commanding officer sent over to Ireland for shamrock, of which national emblem every officer and man wore a *bunch* in his helmet. The London Irish have a thoroughly equipped ambulance detachment; the transport detachment has, under Major Carroll, become a proverb for efficiency in the service; while the signalling detachment has attained to an extremely high degree of excellence, Colonel Howland Roberts, the second in command, having qualified himself as Officer Instructor. We do not suppose we shall err in describing Colonel Howland Roberts a typical Volunteer officer, as the London Irish are a typical Volunteer regiment. In addition to his thorough mastery of the signalling service, he is a recognized authority in theoretical tactics, and few of the justly valued "war games" are held in London in which he does not take a prominent part. Though the regiment has not won any of the greater Wimbledon prizes, it has always numbered a good proportion of " shooting men," who have taken part in the competition for the Irish Trophy, while Hopkins, Leech, and Despard have been Captains of the Irish Twenty. At the recent Irish Exhibition in London, an incident occurred which gave a crushing retort to some ignorant murmurs as to the loyalty of London Irishmen. The band from Cork refused to play the National Anthem: their place was

* This was subsequently changed to a green ball.

† When the 83rd and 86th Regiments became the "Royal Irish Rifles," and changed their uniform from scarlet to green, " they chose the uniform and facings of the London Irish."

promptly taken by the band of the London Irish, who played it *con amore* amidst the utmost enthusiasm.

The 18th MIDDLESEX represent the Volunteers of Paddington, and boast connection with an older corps. We must be content here with mentioning that it is a very large corps and includes a number of smaller companies. Uniform green with black facings.

The 19th (ST. GILES'S and ST. GEORGE'S, BLOOMSBURY) MIDDLESEX VOLUNTEERS, which occupy the position of the 6th Volunteer battalion of the Rifle Brigade, can trace a practically direct succession from the "Bloomsbury and Inns of Court" Volunteers of the last century. The last-mentioned corps was raised in 1797, and, in common with many other Volunteer regiments then raised, soon boasted both colours and a motto, the latter being "Nolumus Mutari." When the old corps was disbanded about 1814, a considerable sum of money, the balance of the subscriptions, was "deposited in the hands of trustees for the benefit of any future corps which might in later years take their place." And the 37th, now the 19th, in 1877 made good their right to this sum with its accumulations, and also obtained later on from the Foundling Hospital, where they had been preserved, the colours of the old corps.

The 20th MIDDLESEX, the Artists corps, is amongst the best known of the Metropolitan Volunteer corps. Its name conveys the constitution of the regiment: the Hon. Colonel is the President of the Royal Academy, and in its ranks are men who are well known in all branches of "Art and Letters." Uniform grey with grey facings.

The 24th MIDDLESEX—the Post Office Volunteers—have a record of somewhat unusual interest. They date from a more recent period than many of the other regiments, their origin being in 1868, when they were gazetted as the 49th Middlesex. The year previous had been that of the Fenian outbreak, and some 1,500 employés were sworn in as a body as special constables, and soon attained a degree of military efficiency which called forth high praises from the officials. So popular did this public service become that the idea of disbandment was uncongenial to the men, and with the assistance of Colonel du Plat Taylor, they obtained the requisite permission to form a Volunteer regiment. At the review at Dover, of 1869, the 49th gave strong evidence of their value as soldiers, evidence which was emphasized by the part they took in the Egyptian Campaign of 1882, when an Army Postal Corps was raised from their number, and accompanied the army. Their services there were referred to by Lord Wolseley in a dispatch eulogising "the admirable manner in which the Post Office Corps discharged their duties." By the time that they were called on to serve in Egypt the 49th had become the 24th Middlesex, and for many years have maintained an unusually high standard of efficiency.*

The TOWER HAMLETS RIFLE VOLUNTEER BRIGADE date from 1860, when several corps were raised in the locality which are now represented by the 1st and 2nd Tower Hamlets. The uniform of the former is scarlet with blue facings; of the latter, grey with scarlet facings.

We have thus brought to an end our history of Her Majesty's Army. Much—very much—might be added. The "finest soldiers in Europe" is a theme deserving of the fullest and most eloquent treatment. But, too often for the historians, the Army reflects the national trait of reticence. Their brave deeds are here and there blazoned forth in glowing characters. The result of those deeds is a component part of the national history; but many actions which in other nations would be trumpeted far and wide are hidden in official archives, and have to be sought for laboriously in their silent gloom. Nor is this the case with the British army only. There are other armies owning the sway of the Queen-Empress, whose deeds and triumphs yet remain to be recorded. No work that has for its object the making known to Her Majesty's subjects at large the brave things done, the conquests, the patience, the heroism of her soldiers can be useless or void of good. At times, as a traveller in some peaceful woodland may be startled by the malignant hiss of a deadly serpent, we hear from the unsavoury haunts of those who have forsworn loyalty and patriotism, and would fain forswear even their nationality, malevolent outcries against the army, belittling its prowess, and snarling at its cost. A more complete knowledge of the army, of what it has done, of what it is doing and can do, will best silence this shameful clamour, and go far to realise the prayer of the patriot poet—

> "Pray God our greatness may not fail
> Through craven fears of being great."

* For three years the only non-efficient member was the Hon. Chaplain, while in 1882 only one failed to earn the grant. The strength is nearly 1,100.

THE 20th MIDDLESEX (ARTISTS')
VOLUNTEERS.

INDEX.

Abbott, Capt., 14th Hussars, i., 92
Aberdeen Royal Militia, ii., 259
Adams, Rev. J. W., 9th Lancers, i., 75; ii., 201
Albemarle off Dunkirk, i., 10
Albuera, i., 31, 57
Alexander, Private, 90th Regt., ii., 79
Alma, i., 1, 150, 174
Almanza, i., 52, 67, 156
Antrim, Royal Militia, ii., 259
Apperly, Capt., 9th Lancers, i., 75
Arabi Pasha, i., 33
Archdall, Lt.-Col., 12th Lancers, i., 86
Archer, Lieut., 16th Lancers, i., 97
Archers, Royal Co. of, i., 2, 8
Argyll and Sutherland High. (Princess Louise's) i., 71—5
Argyll and Sutherland Highlanders, Vol. Batts., ii., 343
Armagh Militia, ii., 259
Artillery Company, Hon., ii., 207; Charter of, ii., 209; Letter of Charles I. to, ii., 209; Horse Artillery of, ii., 221; Light Cavalry of, ii., 221; Precedence of, ii., 223
Artillery, Royal Horse, i., 114—5, 128
Artillery, Royal, i., 107—131
Artillery, Royal Irish, i., 112
Artillery Volunteers, ii., 275
Ayrshire Yeomanry, ii., 264
Ayr and Wigtown Royal Militia, ii., 243

Baillie, Lieut., 58th Regt., ii., 38
Baker, Russell, Col., i., 25
Balaclava, i., 48, 100, 174
Banks, 7th Hussars, i., 65
Bambrick, Capt., 7th D.G., i., 41
Barrow, Col., 19th Hussars, i., 105
Battle Axe Troop, R.A., i., 130
Beardmore, Sergt., 4th Hussars, i., 56
Beaumont, Major, King's Own Hussars, i., 52
Bedford Militia, ii., 243
Bedfordshire Regt., Vol. Batts., ii., 305
Bell, Capt., 23rd Regt., ii., 133
Bell, Private, 24th Regt., ii., 122
Bennett, Trooper, Blues, i., 21
Beresford, General, i., 83
Berkeley, Capt., 10th Hussars, i., 79
Berks (Hungerford) Yeomanry, ii., 264
Berkshire Regt., Royal, The, Vol. Batts., ii., 329
Berryman, Sergt.-Major, 17th Lanc., i., 101
Bewsey, Sergt., R.A., i., 123—4
Billey, Capt., 7th D.G., i., 42
"Birkenhead," Wreck of, i., 173
"Black Horse," Sobriquet of 7th Huss., i., 65.
Black Watch, ii., 66
"Black Watch," The (Royal Highldrs.), Vol. Batts., ii., 325
Blackwood, Capt., R.A., i., 127
Blair, Col., Scots Guards. i., 165
Blenheim, i., 37, 144, 222
Blood, Capt., R.E., i., 137
Blood, Sergt., 43rd Regt., ii., 47
Blues, The, i., 10, 13, 21
Bonham, Lieut., R.A., i., 123—4
Boosley, Trooper, 19th Hussars, i., 105
Booth, Sergt., 80th Regt., ii., 104
Border Regt., The, Vol. Batts., ii., 319
Borgard, Albert, R.A., i., 110
Borlase, Lieut., Queen's Regt., ii., 116
Bosville, Col., Cold. Guards, i., 158
Bourchier, Lieut., 11th Hussars, i., 82
Bradshaw, Dr., 90th Regt., ii., 80
Brewer, Col., 12th Regt. at Dixmude, ii., 106

Bromhead, 24th Regt., ii., 123
Brown, Lieut., 24th Regt., ii., 124
Brown, Lieut., 101st Regt., ii., 24
Brown, Capt. J. G., 4th Hussars, i., 58, 60
Browning, Trooper, Blues, i., 19
Bruman, Bombardier, R.A., i., 125
Buckinghamshire, The Royal Bucks Huss., ii., 264
Buckle, Capt., R.E., i., 136
Bucks, Royal Militia, ii., 252
Buller, Col., 19th Hussars, i., 106
Burnaby, Col., Death of, i., 152—3
Burn, Murdock, Lieut., R.E., i., 137
Burson, Capt., S. Gould, 9th Lanc., i., 75

Cadogan, Genl., i., 145
Cadwick, Lieut., 17th Lanc., i., 100, 101
Cambridge Militia, ii., 242
Cameronians, The, ii., 77
Cameronians, The, Vol. Batts., ii., 311
Cameron Highlanders, Queen's Own, Vol. Batts., ii., 343
Campbell, Ensign, 43rd Regt., ii., 48
Campbell, Sir Colin, i., 49, 169; ii., 32
Campo, Maj. i., 88
Canadians, Royal, i., 340
Carabineers, Trumpeter of, i., 36
Cardigan, Lord, i., 58, 70, 84, 100
Carlow Militia, ii., 257
Carnarvon Militia, ii., 245
Case, Lieut., R. Fusiliers, ii., 66
Cavalry Volunteers, ii., 275
Cavan Militia, ii., 259
Cetewayo, i., 25
Chamberlain, Private, R.E., i., 135
Channel Islands Militia, ii., 261
Chaplains, Army, ii., 199
Chapman, Lieut., 101st Regt., ii., 26
Chapuis, General, i., 30
Chard, Lieut., R.E., ii., 138
Charteris, Lieut. Hon. A., Cold. Guards, i., 161
"Cheeses," Sobriquet of Life Guards, i., 12
Chelmsford, Lieut., i., 102
"Cherry Pickers," Sobriquet of 11th Huss., i., 83
"Cherubim," Sobriquet of 11th Huss., i., 83
Cheshire Hussars, ii., 264
Cheshire Royal Militia, ii., 245
Chestnut Troop, R.A., i., 115
Chisholm, Scott, 9th Lanc., i., 75
Churchill, Lt.-Col., 15th Hussars, i., 95
Clapham, Capt., 14th Regt., ii., 178
Clarke, Capt., A.K.R. Dragoons, i., 45
Clark, Capt., 93rd Foot, i., 175
Clelland, 9th Lanc., i., 75
Cleveland, Cornet, 17th Lanc., i., 100, 101
Clifford, Col., Royal Dragoons, i., 43
Clowes, Cornet, R.I. Hussars, i., 70, 71
Clutterbuck, Lieut., R.I. Hussars, i., 170
Coghill, Lieut., 24th Regt., ii., 123
Colborne, Col., 52nd Regt., ii., 52
Coldstream Guards, i., 154, 162; Colours of, i., 162
Collins, The Rev. R., ii., 201
Collins, Gunner, R.A., i., 127
Cook, Capt., 11th Hussars, i., 85
Cooper, Private, 24th Regt., ii., 122
Cornwall Rangers, Royal Militia, ii., 249
Cornwall's, Duke of, Light Infantry, Vol. Batts., ii., 318
Copenhagen, i., 115
Corbach, i., 22
Corunna, Retreat from, i., 148
Courtenay, Lieut., Royal Dragoons, i., 43
Coy, Col. J., 5th D.G's., i., 34
Cranford, Major, i., 28

Crawford, Lord, i., 16
Crawford, Trumpet-Major, 4th Hussars, i., 60
Croker, Col., 17th Regt., i., 338
Cruickshank, Major, R.E., i., 137
Cumberland Royal Militia, ii., 249
Cumming, Lt.-Col., 11th Hussars, i., 83
Cunninghame, Sir A., Inniskillings, i., 50
Cureton, Brigadier, 15th Lanc., i., 97
Custance, Col., N. Carabineers, i., 37
Cutts, Lord, Cold. Guards, i., 156

Dalziel, Lt.-Genl., i., 45
Darling, Sergt.-Major, Cold. Guards, i., 158
Darner, Lieut. D., Scots Guards, i., 165
Darrell, Sir H., 7th D.G., i., 41
Davies, Mrs. Christian, Scots Greys, i., 46
"Death's Head or Glory," (17th Lanc.), Origin of, i., 15, 39
De Chair, Midshipman, i., 21
Dewar, Lieut., K.O.G., i., 26
De Salis, Major, R.I. Hussars, i., 70, 71
Denbighshire Hussars, ii., 264
Denbigh and Merioneth Militia, ii., 245
Dennie, Col., 13th Regt., ii., 96
Derby 2nd Militia, ii., 254
Derbyshire Yeomanry, ii., 264
Derbyshire Regt., The, Vol. Batts., ii., 327
Devonshire Regt., Vol. Batts., ii., 302
Devon Hussars, (Royal 1st), ii., 264
Devon Militia, ii., 241
Diamond Rock, H.M.S., ii., 190
"Diehards," The, ii., 3
Dick, Lieut., R.E., i., 133
Dickson, Lieut., 91st Foot, i., 172
Diggens, Lieut., 11th Hussars, i., 82
Dirty Shirts, The (101st), ii., 18
Doakes, Private, 57th Regt., ii., 6
Doctors, Army, and the V.C., ii., 204
Doherty, Capt., 13th Hussars, i., 88, 89
Donellan, Col., 48th Regt., ii., 35
Dorsetshire Regt., Vol. Batt., ii., 323
Dorset Militia, ii., 251
Dorsetshire Hussars, ii., 265
Douglas, Dr., 24th Regt., ii., 122
Dowell, Lieut., R.M.A., ii., 194
Down, Ensign, 57th Regt., ii., 6
Doyle, Col., 14th Regt., ii., 178
Drury Lowe, i., 33, 102
Dryden on the Militia, ii., 226
Dublin City, Royal Militia, ii., 261
Dublin County Militia, ii., 261
Duke of Lancaster's Own, ii., 265
Dundas, Capt., R.E., i., 135, 137
Dunkin, Col., 77th Regt., ii., 9
Dunlop, Lt-Col., 77th Regt., ii., 8
Dupuis, Col., R.A., i., 120
Durham Lt. Infantry, Vol. Batts., ii., 339
Durham Militia, 1st and 2nd, ii., 258
Durnford, Col., R.E., i., 137

"Eagle Troop," R.A., i., 130, Note
Edgell, Capt., Hon. Wyatt, 17th Lancashire, i., 102
Edinburgh or Queen's Regt. of Light Infantry Militia, ii., 236
Edinburgh (Queen's Rifle Vol. Brigade), ii., 291
Edwards, Private, 42nd Regt., ii., 71
Eighteenth Hussars, i., 103
Eighteenth Regiment, i, 264
Eighth Hussars, i., 66, 71
Eighth Regiment, The, i., 345
Eightieth Regiment, i., 193, ii., 102
Eighty-eighth Regiment, i, 193
Eighty-fifth Regiment, ii., 93
Eighty-first Regiment, i., 310
Eighty-fourth Regiment, ii, 155
Eighty-ninth Regiment, i., 263

INDEX.

Eighty-second Regiment, i., 320
Eighty-seventh Regiment, i., 260
Eighty-sixth Regiment, i., 268
Eighty-third Regiment, i., 268
Eleventh Hussars, i., 81—5
Elliott, Col., 15th Hussars, i., 93
Elthorne Royal Militia, ii., 257
Engineer Volunteers, ii., 288—290
Erskine, Major, 15th Hussars, i., 93, 94
Essex Regt., The, Vol. Batts., ii., 326
Essex Militia, ii., 254
Ewart, Sergeant, Scots Greys, i., 48
Eyre, Col., S. Stafford Regt., ii., 101
Eyre, Lieut., 90th Regt., ii., 80

Farrell, Qtr.-Instr., 17th Lanc., i., 101
Fatt, Sergeant, 19th Hussars, i., 105
Feather, Badge of, ii., 117
Feather of Northumberland Fusiliers, ii., 39
Fenton, Sergeant, 19th Hussars, i., 105
Ffrench, Lt., Shropshire Regt., ii., 92
Fifteenth (King's) Hussars, i., 93, 96
Fifteenth Regiment, ii., 172
Fifth (Princess Charlotte of Wales) Irish Dragoon Guards, i., 33, 35
Fifth Regiment, ii., 38; in the Mutiny, ii., 41
Fifth (Royal Irish) Lancers, i., 61, 62
Fifty-eighth Regt., ii., 35; at Laing's Neck, ii., 37
Fifty-first Regiment, ii., 161
Fifty-fourth Regiment, i., 211
Fifty-ninth Regiment, i., 305
Fifty-second Regt., ii., 49; in the Mutiny, ii., 58
Fifty-seventh Regt., The, ii., 1; Old Colours of, ii., 7, *Note*
Fifty-sixth Regiment, i., 230
Fiftieth Regiment, i., 280
Fifty-third Regt., ii., 88
Fighting Brigade, The, ii., 89
First Foot (Royal Scots), i., 166
First Royal Lanark Militia, ii., 258
First (Royal) Dragoons, i., 42—45.
First (King's) Dragoon Guards, i., 21—6
Fitzgerald, Capt., 14th Hussars, i., 91
Fitzgibbon, Viscount, i., 70, 71
Flinn, Thos., 64th Regt., ii., 99
Forty-eighth Regt., ii., 34
Forty-first Regiment, ii., 134
Forty-fourth Regiment, i., 230
Forty-ninth Regiment, i., 177
Forty-second Regt., ii., 66
Forty-seventh Regiment, i., 310
Forty-sixth Regiment, 1, 222
Forty-third Regt., ii., 42
Fourteenth Regt., ii., 176
Fourteenth Hussars, i., 90, 93
Fourth (Queen's Own) Hussars, i., 55, 60
Fourth (Royal Irish) Dragoon Guards, i., 323
Fowle, Lt., 21st Hussars, i., 107
Fowler, Private, 90th Regt., ii., 80
Fraser, Major, i., 65
Frazer, Major, R.E., i., 137
Freeman, Lt., 19th Hussars, i., 105
Freer, Lt., 43rd Regt., ii., 47
French, Capt., 9th Lancashire, i., 74
Frith, Lt., 17th Lancashire, i., 101
Fusiliers, Royal Scots, ii., 73

Gainsford, Lt., Seaforth Highlanders, ii., 83
Gall, Major, 14th Hussars, i., 92
Gambier, Lt.-Col., R.A., i., 122
Gardner, Col.-Sergeant, 57th Regt., ii., 5
Garrick, Capt., i., 28
Gentlemen-at-Arms, i., 2, 3, 5
George II., i., 16
Gethin, Capt., Seaforth Highlanders, ii., 82
Gildea, Col., Royal Scots Fusiliers, ii., 75
Gillespie, Sir R. R., i., 69, 70
Gill, Sergeant, 90th Regt., ii., 80
Glamorgan Royal Militia, ii., 251
Gloucester Militia, ii., 246

Gloucestershire Regt., The, Vol. Batts., ii., 313
Gloucestershire, Royal, Hussars, ii., 265
Goad, Capt., 13th Hussars, i., 90
Godley, Trooper, in Life Guards, i., 18
Gold Stick, i., 12
Gordon, Gen., R.E., i., 134
Gordon Riots, Walpole's account of, ii., 214
Gordon, Sir W., 17th Lanc., i., 100
Gordon Highlanders, Vol. Batts., ii., 343
Graham, Private, 90th Regt., ii., 80
Grant, James, Bandsman 5th Regt., ii., 41
Greathead, Col., 9th Lancashire, i., 74
Green, Capt., R.A., i., 127
"Green Horse," Sobriquet of 5th Dragoon Guards, i., 34; and of 13th Hussars, i., 88
Green, Lt. Andrew, Rifle Brigade, ii., 61
Greenwood, Lt., 10th Hussars, i., 80
Grenadier Guards, i., 140, 154; Colours of, i., 153, 154
Grenfell, Lt., 10th Hussars, i., 80
"Greys," see Scots Greys
Griffiths, Private, 24th Regiment, ii., 122
Guards, Encounter between English and French, at Fontenoy, i., 146
Guards, see Household Troops, etc.
Guise, Major, 90th Regt., ii., 80

Hackett, Major, 4th Hussars, i., 58, 60
Haddington Artillery Militia, ii., 231
Hagart, Col., 7th Hussars, i., 65—6
Hall, Surgeon, Royal Fusiliers, ii., 65
Hampshire Regt., Vol. Batts., ii., 321
Hampshire Carabineers, ii., 265
Hampshire Militia, ii., 250
Hardy, Lt., R.A., i., 126—7
Harford, Lt., 10th Hussars, i., 80
Harrison, Capt., 11th Hussars, i., 85
Harrison, Col., 7th Hussars, i., 65
Hart, Col., R.I. Hussars, i., 68
Hart, Lt. Clare, R.E., i., 137
Hartopp, Lt., 17th Lanc., i., 100
Harward, Lt., 80th Regt., ii., 103
Hassard, Lt.-Col., 57th Regt., ii., 6
Hassel, Private, 5th Regt., ii., 39
Havelock-Allen, Sir H., ii., 98
Havelock, Sir Henry, ii., 97
Hawthorne, Bugler, 52nd Regt., ii., 52
Hay, Col. (93rd), i., 175
Hearsey, Lt., 9th Lanc., i., 75
Heneage, Cornet, R.I. Hussars, i., 70
Henn, Lt., R.E., i., 137
Henry, Sergt., R.A., i., 121
Hertford Militia, ii., 243
Herts., Yeomanry, ii., 265
Hervey, Col. (Inniskillings), i., 50
Highland Borderers Militia, ii., 260
Highlanders, Royal, ii., 66
Highland Lt. Infantry, Vol. Batts., ii., 340
Highland Light Infantry Militia, ii., 259
Highland Rifle Militia, ii., 258
Hills, Johnes, Lt., R.A., i., 124
Hodson, Lt., 101st Regt., ii., 21, 23
Hollowell, Private, Seaforth Highlanders, ii., 87
Hope, Lt., Royal Fusiliers, ii., 65
Hopkins, Capt., Shropshire Regt., ii., 91
Hopkins, Sergt.-Major, 101st Regt., ii., 20
Home, Dr., 90th Regt., ii., 80
Horse Guards. i., 13
Houghton, Lieut., 11th Hussars, i., 85
House Carles of Canute, i., 6
Household Troops, i., 9—21, 140—166
Howard, Hon. E., 10th Hussars, i., 78
Howard, Private, 57th Regt., ii., 7
Hudson, Lieut., Carabineers, ii., 37
Hughes, Private, R. Fusiliers, ii., 65
Hundred and Eighth Regiment, i., 258
Hundred and Fifth Regiment, ii., 161
Hundred and Forty-fourth Regt., ii., 11
Hundred and Fourth Regt., The, ii., 26
Hundred and Ninth Regiment, i., 340
Hundred and Second Regiment, i., 215
Hundred and Seventh Regiment, ii., 119
Hundred and Sixth Regiment, i., 2 29

Hundred and Third Regiment, i., 215
Hundreth Regt., The, i., 340
Hunt, Cornet, 4th Hussars, i., 58—9
Huntingdon Militia, ii., 257
Hussar, Derivation of Name, i., 77
Hutton, Capt., 4th Hussars, i., 58, 60

Inveraity, Lieut., 16th Lanc., i., 88
Irish Militia, ii., 243
Irwin, Private, Shropshire Regt., ii., 92

James, Private, R. Fusiliers, ii., 66
Jee, Surgeon, Seaforth Highlanders, ii., 87
Jenyns, Capt., 13th Hussars, i., 90
Jervis, Lieut., 13th Hussars, i., 90
Johnson, Lieut., 17th Lanc., i., 99
Johnson, Trooper, Life Guards, i., 18
Joliffe, Lieut., 4th Hussars, i., 58, 59
Jones, Lieut., 9th Lanc., i., 74
Jones, Mitchell, Capt., R. Fusiliers, ii., 63

Keith, Private, Seaforth Highlanders, ii., 85
Kelly Militia, ii., 261
Kenny, Private, Shropshire Regt., ii., 92
Kent Artillery Militia, ii., 231
Kent, East, Militia, ii., 236
Kent, West, Militia, ii., 256
Kent, West, Royal (The Queen's), Vol. Batts., ii., 329
Kent, East (The Buffs), Vol. Battalions, ii., 296
Kildare Militia, ii., 261
King's County Militia, ii., 261
King, Cornet, 4th Hussars, i., 58
King's Own Royal Tower Hamlets Militia, ii., 261
Kinlock, Capt., Scots Guards, i., 165
Kirbekan, i., 106
Kirke, Col., Queen's Regt., ii., 113
Kitchener, Major, R.E., i., 139

Lambs, Kirke's, ii., 113
Lanarkshire (Queen's Own Royal Glasgow and Tower Ward of Lanarkshire), ii., 265
Lancashire Artillery Militia, R. ii., 232
Lancashire 5th Royal, Militia, ii., 248
Lancashire 4th Royal, Militia, ii., 251
Lancashire Hussars, ii., 265
Lancashire Royal, Militia, ii., 236
Lancashire 2nd Royal Militia, ii., 241
Lancashire 7th Royal Militia, ii., 243
Lancashire 3rd Royal, Militia, ii., 256
Lancashire, East, Regt., Vol. Batts., ii., 315
Lancashire Fusiliers, Vol. Batts., ii., 306—8
Lancashire, Loyal North, Regt., Vol. Batts., ii., 328
Lancashire Yeomanry, ii., 265
Lancaster, King's Own Royal, Vol. Batts., ii., 296
Lantry, Capt., 14th Hussars, i., 96
Leicestershire Hussars, ii., 266
Leicestershire Militia, ii., 243
Leicestershire Regt., Vol. Batts., ii., 305
Leith, Lieut., 14th Hussars, i., 92
Leinster Regt., Prince of Wales's, i., 340
Life Guards, The, i., 9
Limerick City Artillery, ii., 233
Limerick City Royal Militia, ii., 261
Lettler, Private, Grenadier Guards, i., 145
Levington, Lt., 12th Lanc., i., 86
"Lillywhite Seventh," Sobriquet of 7th Hussars, i., 65
Lincoln, North, Royal Militia, ii., 241
Lincolnshire Regt., The, i., 340
Lincolnshire Regt., Vol. Batts., ii., 301
Lindon, Lieut., R.I. Hussars, i., 69
Liverpool Regt., The King's, i., 345; Vol. Batts., ii., 300
London, City of, Regt., ii., 62
London, City of, Regt., Royal Fusiliers, Vol. Batts., ii., 299
London Royal Militia, ii., 241

Longford Militia, Royal, ii., 261
Lothians and Berwickshire Yeomanry, ii., 266
Louth Militia, ii., 259
Low, Capt., 4th Hussars, i., 58, 60
Lowe, Patrick, Private, 52nd Regt., ii., 50
Loyal Suffolk Hussars, ii., 267
Luard, Major, 16th Lanc., i., 97
Luck, Major, 15th Hussars, i., 96
Luke, Capt., Marines, ii., 198
Lutyens, Lieut., 11th Hussars, i., 82
Lysons, Lieut., 60th Regt., ii., 80

Mackenzie, Lieut., 9th Lanc., i., 75
Macgregor, Major, R.E., i., 137
M'Corrie, Private, 57th Regt., ii., 5
McGovern, Private, 101st Regt., ii., 24
McIntosh, Shropshire Regt., ii., 93
McLaren, Trumpeter, R.A., i., 122
McLean, Col., 24th Regt., ii., 120
McLean, Lieut., 93rd, i., 175
McMaster, Surgeon, Seaforth Highlanders, ii., 87
McMullens, Private, 17th Lanc., i., 99
Macleod, Col., Seaforth Highlanders, ii., 85
MacPherson, Major, 42nd Regt., ii., 71
McQuade, Sergt., 43rd Regt., ii., 46
Macrae, Sergt., Seaforth Highlanders, ii. 85
Malone, Cornet, 7th D.G., i., 39
Malone, Sergt., 13th Hussars, i., 91
Manchester Regt., The, i., 350
Manchester Regt., The, Vol. Batts., ii., 338
Manley, Dr., ii., 205
Manley, Surgeon, R.A., i., 126
Mansell, Genl., i., 30
Marine Artillery, Royal, ii., 190
Marines, Royal, The, ii., 180; at Acre, ii., 187; at Santa Maura, ii., 192; in Ashantee, ii., 195; in Egypt, ii., 197
Marlborough, Duke of, i., 55, 143, 145; Escape of, i., 46, 61
Marshall, Sergt., 19th Hussars, i., 105
Marter, Major, K.D.G., i., 25
Martin, Cornet, 4th Hussars, i., 58
Massachusetts, Ancient and Honorable Artillery Company of, ii., 223
Maude, Genl., i., 125
Maxwell, Lt.-Col., 19th Hussars, i., 106
Mayow, Major, i., 100, 101
Meath, Royal Militia, ii., 261
Medical Department, Army, The, ii., 203
Melville, Lieut., 24th Regt., ii., 123
Mercier, Lieut.-Col., R.A., i., 126
Meiklejohn, Lieut., R.E., i., 133
Middlemore, Major, 48th Regt., ii., 35
Middlesex, Duke of Cambridge's Huss., ii., 266
Middlesex Regt., Duke of Cambridge's Own, The, ii., 1
Middlesex Regt., The, Vol. Batts., ii., 330
Middlesex, 2nd Royal Militia, ii., 257
Middlesex, South Royal Militia, ii., 241
Middleton, Capt., R.A., i., 125
Milford, Major, 9th Lanc., i., 75
Miller, Col. Fiennes, Inniskillings, i., 51
Milne Home, Col., Blues, i., 20
Militia, The, ii., 224; Artillery, ii., 229; Engineers, ii., 235; Infantry, ii., 235; Submarine Miners, ii., 325
Molesworth, Lieut., R.I. Lanc., i., 61
Monaghan Militia, ii., 259
Money, Capt., i., 82, 83
Montanaro, Lieut., R.A., i., 127
Montgomery, Cornet, 13th Hussars, i., 90
Montgomery, Major, 80th Regt., ii., 103
Montgomeryshire Yeomanry, ii., 266
Morgan, Capt., 17th Lanc., i., 100
Morgan, Lieut., R.E., i., 136
Moriarty, Capt., 80th Regt., ii., 103
Morris, Lieut.-Col., 17th Lanc., i., 51, 100, 101
Mountain, Col., Cameronians, ii., 78
Mowat, Surgeon, i., 51
Much, Lieut., 24th Regt., ii., 121
Mullane, Sergt., R.A., i., 127
Mullen, Capt., Royals, i., 169

Munay, Major, 42nd Regt., ii., 67
Munster, Col., Inniskillings, i., 51
Munster Fusiliers, Royal, The, ii., 11
Murphy, Private, 24th Regt., ii., 122
Mussenden, Cornet, R.I. Hussars, i., 70
Myers, Col., 7th Regt., ii., 64

Napier, Genl., i., 24
Napier, Sir R., R.E., i., 135
Neale, Ensign, 43rd Regt., ii., 43
Need, Capt., 14th Hussars, i., 92
New Zealand, i., 126
Nineteenth (Prince of Wales's Own) Hussars, i., 104, 106
Nineteenth Regiment, ii., 168
Ninety-first Foot (Argyll and Sutherland High.) i., 171
Ninety-sixth Regt., The, i., 352
Ninety-ninth Regiment, ii., 146
Ninety-second Regiment, i., 240
Ninety-seventh Regiment, i., 280
Ninety-third Foot (Argyll and Sutherland High.), i., 174
Ninety-eighth Regt., ii., 100
Ninety-fifth Regt., ii., 53
Ninth Queen's Royal Hussars, i., 72, 76
Ninth Regt., The, ii., 27
Ninetieth Regt., ii., 79
Nolan, Capt., i., 101
Norcott, Major, Rifle Brigade, ii., 59
Norfolk Militia, ii., 241
Norfolk Regt., The, ii., 27
Norfolk Regiment, Vol. Batts., ii., 301
Northamptonshire Militia, ii., 256
Northamptonshire Regt., ii.,
Northampton Regt., Vol. Batts., ii., 329
North Cork Militia, ii., 257
North Devon Hussars, Royal, ii., 264
North Down, Royal Militia, ii., 259
North Somerset Yeomanry, ii., 267
Northumberland Fusiliers, ii., 38
Northumberland Hussars, ii., 266
Northumberland Militia, ii., 238
Northumberland Fusiliers, Vol. Batts., ii., 297
Nottinghamshire Sherwood Rangers Hussars, ii., 266
Nugent, Capt., R.E., i., 137

Officers, Lord Chelmsford on duty of, ii., 104
O'Hara, Capt., 95th Regt., ii., 56
O'Hara, Sergt., 17th Lanc., i., 100—1
O'Lavery, Corporal, 17th Lanc., i., 99
Oldham, Capt., 13th Hussars, i., 90
Ommaney, Capt., R.A., i., 125
Osborne, Lieut.-Col., 7th Hussars, i., 64
Oxford Militia, ii., 254
Oxfordshire Light Infantry, ii., 42
Oxfordshire Light Infantry, Vol. Batts., ii., 326

Paget, George, 4th Hussars, i., 58
Palmer, A., Grenadier Guards, i., 165
Palmer, Capt., R.A., i., 125
Palmer, Col., Carabineers, i., 37
Palmer, Lieut. R., 11th Hussars, i., 85
Parkes, Trooper, 4th Hussars, i., 60
Park, Sergt., 77th Regt., ii., 10
Parsons, Lieut., R.A., i., 127
Payne, Corporal, 14th Hussars, i., 92
Pembroke Artillery, Royal, ii., 234
Pembroke (Castlemartin) Hussars, ii.,266
Pennywick, Capt., 24th Regt., ii., 121
Pennycuick, Major, 17th Regt., i., 338
Pepper, Col., R.I. Hussars, i., 68
Perth Royal Militia, ii., 251
Perthshire Volunteers, ii., 79
Petits Grenadiers (Marines), ii., 185
Phillips, J., Trooper, K.D.G., i., 24
Phillips, Lieut., R.I. Hussars, i., 70
Pickard, Lieut., R.A., i., 126
Piggott, Capt., 21st Hussars, i., 107
Pitcairne, Major, Marines, ii., 185
Ponsonby, Col., 12th Lanc., i., 87
Ponsonby, Sir W., i., 35
Portal, Capt., 4th Hussars, i., 58

Prendergast Lieut., 14th Hussars, i., 92
Prettyjohn, Capt., 14th Hussars, i., 92
Prettyjohn, Corp., Marines, ii., 194
Price, Lieut., 11th Hussars, i., 83
Prince Imperial, The, i., 26, 102
Princess of Wales's Own Yorkshire Hussars, ii., 268
Pritchard, Major, R.E., i., 135
Purcell, Toby, Major, 23rd Regt., ii., 128
Pye, Sergt.-Major, Shropshire Regt., ii., 92

Queen's County Militia, ii., 261
Queen's Bays, see 2nd Dragoon Guards
Queen's Lancers, see 16th Lancers
Queen's Own Hussars, see 4th and 7th Hussars
Queen's Own Royal Tower Hamlets Militia, ii., 261
Queen's Own Oxfordshire Hussars, ii., 266
Queen's Own Worcestershire Hussars, ii., 267
Queen's Royal Lancers, see 9th Lancers

"Ragged Brigade," The, i., 89
Ramillies, i., 29, 37, 46, 144
Ramsay, Norman, R.H.A., i., 116, 7, 9
Reagan, Private, 101st Regt., ii., 21
Reilly, Private, 91st Foot, i., 172
Ricardo, Lieut., 9th Lanc., i., 75
Ridge, Col., 5th Regt., ii., 40
Ridout, Capt., 11th Hussars, i., 83
Rifle Brigade, The, ii., 52
Rifle Brigade, The, Vol. Batts., ii., 344
Rifle Corps, The King's Royal, Vol. Batts., ii., 334
Roberts, Major, 10th Hussars, i., 78
Roberts, Sir F., i., 125
Robinson, Major, Sussex Regt., at Maida, ii., 117
Rorke's Drift, i., 138; ii., 122
Rose, Capt., 16th Lanc., i., 97
Rosser, Sergt-Major, 13th Hussars, i., 88
Ross-shire Buffs, ii., 84
Royals, see 1st Dragoons and 1st Foot
Royal Scots, see 1st Foot
Royal East Kent Yeomanry, ii., 265
Royal Fusiliers, ii., 62
Royal Renfrew Militia, ii., 260
Royal Wiltshire Hussars, The Prince of Wales's Own Royal Regt., ii., 267
Royal Wiltshire Militia, ii., 258
Rowe, General, R. Scots Fusiliers, ii., 73
Rundle, Lieut., R.A., i., 127, 139
Russell, Sir Charles, Gren. Gds., i., 165
Rutland Militia, ii., 256

Sandford, Dr. (Royals), i., 170
Sandilli, i., 41
Sappers and Miners, i., 132
"Saucy Seventh," Sobriquet of 7th Huss., i., 65
Scarlett, Sir J. T., i., 35
Scots Guards, i., 162, 166; Colours of, i., 166
Scots, Royal, Vol. Batts., ii., 294
Scots, Royal, Fus., Vol. Batts., ii., 308
Scottish Borderers Militia, ii., 245
Scottish Borderers, King's Own, Vol. Batts., ii., 310
Seaforth Highlanders, ii., 81
Seaforth Highlands., Vol. Batts., ii., 342
Seager, Lieut., R.I. Hussars, i., 70-1
Seaton, Lieut.-Col., 6th D.G., i., 37
Second Dragoon Guards (Queen's Bays), i., 26, 29
Second Dragoons, "Scots Greys," i., 33, 45—9
Second Regt., ii., 112
Second and Third King's Own Stafford Militia, ii., 258
Sellars, Corporal, Seaforth Highlanders, ii., 83
Sergeants at Arms, i., 2
Service Corps, Army, ii., 206
Seventeenth (Duke of Cambridge's Own) Lanc., i., 98, 103

INDEX.

Seventeenth Regt. in Afghanistan, i., 339
Seventh (Princess Royal's) Dra. Gds., i., 37, 41
Seventh (Queen's Own) Hussars, i., 63, 66
Seventh Regt., ii., 62
Seventieth Regt., ii., 111
Seventy-eighth Regt., ii., 84
Seventy-first Regiment, i., 252
Seventy-fourth Regiment, i., 252
Seventy-ninth Regiment, i., 187
Seventy-second Regt., ii., 81
Seventy-seventh Regt., ii., 7
Seventy-sixth Regiment, i., 139
Seventy-third Regt., ii., 71
Seymour, Col., Scots Guards, i., 165
Shaw, Col., 12th Regt., ii., 107
Shaw, Life Guardsman, i., 18
Shepherd, Sergt., 4th Dragoons, i., 56
Sherlock, Capt., R.I. Hussars, i., 68
Sherlock, Lieut.-Col., 4th D.G., i., 32
Sherwood Foresters, ii., 328
Shewell, Col., R.I. Hussars, i., 70—71
Sherwood Foresters Royal Militia, ii., 254
Shropshire Light Infantry, The King's, Vol. Batts., ii., 330
Shropshire Militia, ii., 257
Shropshire Yeomanry, ii., 267
"Silver Stick," i., 12
"Six Hundred," Charge of the, i., 58
Sixth Dragoon Guards (Carabineers), i., 36, 38
Sixth Regt., ii., 124
Sixth Royal Lancashire Militia, ii., 258
Sixteenth (Queen's) Lancashire, i., 96-8
Sixth Inniskilling Dragoons, i., 49, 51
Sixtieth Regiment, i., 290
Sixty-eighth Regiment, i., 227
Sixty-fifth Regiment, ii., 155
Sixty-first Regiment, i., 236
Sixty-fourth Regt., ii., 97
Sixty-ninth Regiment, ii., 137
Sixty-second Regiment, ii., 146
Sixty-seventh Regiment, i., 248
Sixty-third Regt., The, i., 350
Slade, Col., 7th Hussars, i., 65
Slade, Lieut., R.A., i., 127
Sleigh, Capt., 11th Hussars, i., 82
Sligo Artillery, ii., 233
Smith, Gunner, R.A., i., 128
Smith, Lieut., 13th Lanc., i., 90
Smith, Major Piercy, i., 29
Snell, Hannah, Marines, ii., 184
Somerset Militia, ii., 242
Somersetshire Regt., Vol. Batts., ii., 303
South Cork Militia, ii., 261
South Down Royal Militia, ii., 259
South Nottinghamshire Hussars, ii., 266
South Wales Borderers, ii., 119
Southwell, Col., 6th Regt., i., 125
Sparks, Lieut., 4th Hussars, i., 58, 60
Spens, Capt., Seaforth Highlanders, ii., 83
Spottiswoode, Capt., 10th Hussars, i., 79
Stafford 1st King's Own Militia, ii., 251
Staffordshire, North, Regt., ii., 97
Staffordshire, South, Regt., ii., 100
Staffordshire Yeomanry (Queen's Own Royal Regt.), ii., 267
Staffordshire, South, Regt., Vol. Batts., ii., 322
Staffordshire, North, Regt., ii., 338
Stagpool, Drummer, 57th Regt., ii., 6
St. Cas, Disaster to Guards at, i., 147
Stephenson, Trooper, 7th D.G., i., 39
Sterling, Lieut.-Col., Cold. Gds., i., 161
Stewart, Private, 43rd Regt., ii., 45
Stistead, Capt., 7th Hussars, i., 66

Strangeways, Genl. Fox, i., 120, 122
Stuart, Major, 14th Hussars, i., 91—2
Suffolk Regt., ii., 105
Suffolk, West, Militia, ii., 242
Suffolk Regt., Vol. Batts., ii., 303
Sunderland, Major, Sussex Regt., ii., 119
"Supple Twelfth," Sobriquet of 12th Lancers, i., 86
Surrey, East, Regt., ii., 110 ; Vol. Batts., ii., 316
Surrey, 1st and 3rd Royal Militia, ii., 249
Surrey, Royal West, Regt., ii., 112 ; Vol. Batts., ii., 295
Surrey, Second Royal Militia, ii., 236
Sussex Royal Militia, ii., 250
Sussex Royal Regt., ii., 117
Sussex Regt., Royal, Vol. Batts., ii., 320
Swan, Major, 11th Hussars, i., 85
Swindley, Col., 15th Hussars, i., 96

Targett, Lieut., 57th Regt., ii., 5
Taylor, Gunner, i., 121
Temple, Surgeon, R.A., i., 126
Tenth Hussars, i., 76, 81
Tenth Regt., The, i., 340
Teviot, Earl of, i., 42
Third (King's Own) Hussars, i., 51, 55
Third (Prince of Wales's) Dragoon Guards, i., 29, 32
Third Regiment, i., 273
Third West York Militia, ii., 258
Thirteenth Hussars, i., 87, 90
Thirteenth Regiment, i., 94
Thirtieth Regiment, i., 305
Thirty-eighth Regt., ii., 100
Thirty-fifth Regt., ii., 117
Thirty-first Regt., ii., 110
Thirty-ninth Regiment, i., 211
Thirty-second Regiment, i., 222
Thirty-seventh Regiment, i., 248
Thirty-sixth Regiment, ii., 150
Thirty-third Regiment, ii., 139
Thomson, Lieut., 17th Lanc., i., 99
"Tichborne's Own," Sobriquet for Carabineers, i., 37
Tiddieman, Major, (3rd D.G.), i., 30
Tombs, Major, R.A., i., 124
Tomkinson, Capt., R.I. Hussars, i., 70
Topham, Capt., 7th Hussars, i., 66
Tremayne, Capt., 13th Hussars, i., 90
Trevelyan, Lieut., 11th Hussars, i., 85
Trevor, Lieut., R.E., i., 135
Tucker, Capt., R.M.A., ii., 197
Twelfth Lanc., i., 86, 87
Twelfth Regt., ii., 105
Twentieth Hussars, i., 106
Twenty-eighth Regiment, i., 236
Twenty-fifth Regiment, i., 285
Twenty-ninth Regiment, ii., 150
Twenty-first Hussars, i., 106, 107
Twenty-first Regt., ii., 73
Twenty-fourth Regt., ii., 119
Twenty-second Regiment, i., 190
Twenty-seventh Regiment, i., 258
Twenty-sixth Regt., ii., 77
Twenty-third Regt., ii., 127
Tyrone Royal Militia, ii., 245

Union Brigade at Waterloo, i., 44, 45, 51
Uxbridge, Lord, i., 18

Vandaleur, Col., R.I. Hussars, i., 68, 69
Vigoureux, Major, 13th Hussars, i., 88
Volunteer Force, ii., 268
Volunteer Force Summary
Volunteers., Prince of Wales's (South Lancashire). Vol. Batts., ii., 323

Wake, Col., R.A., i., 125
Wales, S. Borderers, Vol. Batts., ii., 310
Walker, Col., Scots Guards, i., 165
Walsham, Lieut., R.A., i., 121
Walsh, Private, 91st Foot, i., 172
Wardlaw, Capt., 6th D.G., i., 37
Ward, Lieut., 14th Hussars, i., 91
Warren, Capt., R.A., i., 125
Waterloo, i., 95, 103, 117, 119, 149, 160
Warwick Militia, ii., 240
Warwickshire Hussars, ii., 267
Warwickshire Royal Regt., ii., 124 ; Vol. Batts., ii., 298
Wassall, Private, 80th Regt., ii., 105
Webb, Capt., 11th Hussars, i., 101
Webb, Capt. 17th Lanc., i., 90, 100
Wellington, Duke of, i., 86
Welsh Fusiliers, Royal, ii., 127
Welsh Fusiliers, The, Vol. Batts., ii., 306
Welsh Regt., The, Vol. Batts., ii., 324
West Kent Hussars (The Queen's Own), ii., 265
Westmeath Militia, ii., 261
Westminster Royal Militia, ii., 239
Westmoreland and Cumberland Hussars, ii., 267
Westmoreland Royal Militia, ii., 249
West Riding Regt., Vol. Batts., ii., 318
West Somerset Hussars, ii., 267
White, Capt., 17th Lanc., i., 100
White, Trooper (Blues), i., 17
Wilkin, Lieut., 7th Hussars, i., 65
Wilkinson, Bombardier, R.M.A., ii., 194
Williams of Kars, i., 122, 123
Williams, Private, 24th Regt., ii., 123
Wilmer, Lieut., 17th Lanc., i., 98
Wilmot Eardley, Lieut., R.A., i., 126
Wilson, Capt., Marines, ii., 186
Wiltshire Regt., The, Vol. Batts., ii., 338
Winter, Capt., 17th Lanc., i., 100
Wiseman, Lieut., 17th Regt., i., 339
Witham, Capt., R.D., i., 42
Wood, Col., R.H.A., i., 125
Wooden, Sergt.-Major, 17th Lanc., i., 51
Wood, Lieut.-Col. (6th D.G.), i., 36
Wood, Major, 10th Hussars, i., 79
Woodthorpe, Capt., R.E., i., 136
Woolwich Academy, Early days of, i., 110, 111
Worcestershire Regt., The, Vol. Batts., ii., 314
Wright, Capt., 64th Regt., ii., 99
Wright, Private, 77th Regt., ii., 10
Wyndham, Capt., 10th Hussars, i., 78
Wyndham, Major, 21st Hussars, i., 107

Yeoman of the Guard, i., 2, 5, 8
Yeomanry, ii., 262, 264
Yorkshire Dragoons, ii., 268
Yorkshire, East, Militia, ii., 243
Yorkshire, 5th Militia, ii., 243
Yorkshire Light Infantry (King's Own), V. Batts., ii., 330
York and Lancaster Regiment, The, Vol. Batts., ii., 339
Yorkshire, East, Regt., Vol. Batts., ii., 304
Yorkshire, West, Regt., Vol. Batts., ii., 304
Yorkshire Regt., Vol. Batts., ii., 305
York, North, Militia, ii., 243
York, West, Militia, ii., 242
York, West, 1st Militia, ii., 257
York, West, 6th Militia, ii., 249
"Young Eyes," Sobriquet of 7th Hussars, i., 65

Zulu War, i., 173

www.ingramcontent.com/pod-product-compliance
Lightning Source LLC
Chambersburg PA
CBHW061934290426
44113CB00025B/2909